University Success

READING

ADVANCED

Laura Eickhoff, Laurie Frazier,
and Maggie Vosters

Series Editor: Lawrence Zwier
Authentic Content Contributor: Victoria Solomon

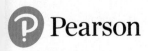 Pearson

University Success Reading, Advanced Level

Copyright © 2018 by Pearson Education, Inc.

All rights reserved.

No part of this publication may be reproduced, stored in a retrieval system, or transmitted in any form or by any means, electronic, mechanical, photocopying, recording, or otherwise, without the prior permission of the publisher.

Pearson Education, 221 River Street, Hoboken, NJ 07030

Staff credits: The people who made up the *University Success* team, representing content development, design, manufacturing, marketing, multimedia, project management, publishing, rights management, and testing, are Pietro Alongi, Stephanie Callahan, Kimberly Casey, Tracey Cataldo, Sara Davila, Dave Dickey, Gina DiLillo, Warren Fischbach, Nancy Flaggman, Lucy Hart, Sarah Henrich, Gosia Jaros-White, Niki Lee, Amy McCormick, Jennifer Raspiller, Robert Ruvo, Katarzyna Skiba, Kristina Skof, Katarzyna Starzynska-Kosciuszko, Joanna Szyszynska, John Thompson, Paula Van Ells, Joseph Vella, Rebecca Wicker, and Natalia Zaremba.

Project coordination: Lawrence Zwier

Project supervision: Debbie Sistino

Contributing editors: Lida Baker, Eleanor Barnes, Andrea Bryant, Barbara Lyons, Leigh Stolle, and Sarah Wales-McGrath

Cover image: Oleksandr Prykhodko / Alamy Stock Photo

Video research: Constance Rylance

Video production: Kristine Stolakis, assisted by Melissa Langer

Text composition and illustrations: EMC Design Ltd

Library of Congress Cataloging-in-Publication Data

A catalog record for the print edition is available from the Library of Congress.

Printed in the United States of America

ISBN-10: 0-13-465270-3

ISBN-13: 978-0-13-465270-2

1 18

Contents

PART 1: FUNDAMENTAL READING SKILLS

PART 2: CRITICAL THINKING SKILLS

PART 3: EXTENDED READING

Welcome to *University Success*

INTRODUCTION

University Success is a new academic skills series designed to equip intermediate- to transition-level English learners with the reading, writing, and oral communication skills necessary to succeed in courses in an English-speaking university setting. The blended instructional model provides students with an inspiring collection of extensive authentic content, expertly developed in cooperation with five subject matter experts, all "thought leaders" in their fields. By utilizing both online and in-class instructional materials, *University Success* models the type of "real life" learning expected of students studying for a degree. *University Success* recognizes the unique linguistic needs of English language learners and carefully scaffolds skill development to help students successfully work with challenging and engaging authentic content.

SERIES ORGANIZATION: *THREE STRANDS*

This three-strand series, **Reading**, **Writing**, and **Oral Communication**, includes five distinct content areas: the Human Experience, Money and Commerce, the Science of Nature, Arts and Letters, and Structural Science, all popular fields of study among English language learners. The three strands are fully aligned across content areas and skills, allowing teachers to utilize material from different strands to support learning. Teachers can delve deeply into skill development in a single area, or provide additional support materials from other areas for richer development across the four skills.

THE *UNIVERSITY SUCCESS* APPROACH: *AN AUTHENTIC EXPERIENCE*

This blended program combines the utility of an interactive student book, online learner lab, and print course to create a flexible approach that adjusts to the needs of teachers and learners. Its skill-based and step-by-step instruction enables students to master essential skills and become confident in their ability to perform successfully in academic degree courses taught in English. Students at this level need to engage with content that provides them with the same challenges native speakers face in a university setting. Many English language learners are not prepared for the quantity of reading and writing required in college-level courses, nor are they properly prepared to listen to full-length lectures that have not been scaffolded for them. These learners, away from the safety of an ESL classroom, must keep up with the rigors of a class led by a professor who may be unaware of the challenges a second-language learner faces. Strategies for academic success, delivered via online videos, help increase students' confidence and ability to cope with the challenges of academic student and college culture. *University Success* steps up to the podium to represent academic content realistically with the appropriate skill development and scaffolding essential for English language learners to be successful.

PUTTING STUDENTS ON THE PATH TO *UNIVERSITY SUCCESS*

Intensive skill development and extended application—tied to specific learning outcomes—provide the scaffolding English language learners need to become confident and successful in a university setting.

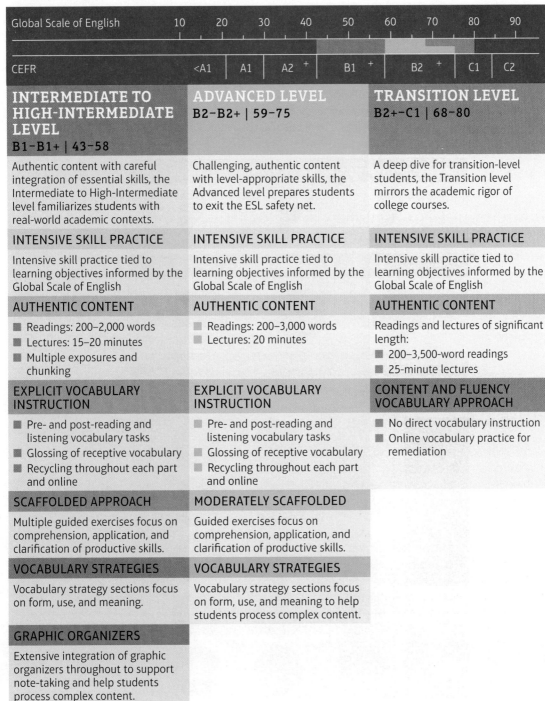

Global Scale of English	10	20	30	40	50	60	70	80	90
CEFR	<A1	A1	A2 +	B1 +	B2 +	C1	C2		

INTERMEDIATE TO HIGH-INTERMEDIATE LEVEL
B1–B1+ | 43–58

Authentic content with careful integration of essential skills, the Intermediate to High-Intermediate level familiarizes students with real-world academic contexts.

INTENSIVE SKILL PRACTICE

Intensive skill practice tied to learning objectives informed by the Global Scale of English

AUTHENTIC CONTENT

- Readings: 200–2,000 words
- Lectures: 15–20 minutes
- Multiple exposures and chunking

EXPLICIT VOCABULARY INSTRUCTION

- Pre- and post-reading and listening vocabulary tasks
- Glossing of receptive vocabulary
- Recycling throughout each part and online

SCAFFOLDED APPROACH

Multiple guided exercises focus on comprehension, application, and clarification of productive skills.

VOCABULARY STRATEGIES

Vocabulary strategy sections focus on form, use, and meaning.

GRAPHIC ORGANIZERS

Extensive integration of graphic organizers throughout to support note-taking and help students process complex content.

ADVANCED LEVEL
B2–B2+ | 59–75

Challenging, authentic content with level-appropriate skills, the Advanced level prepares students to exit the ESL safety net.

INTENSIVE SKILL PRACTICE

Intensive skill practice tied to learning objectives informed by the Global Scale of English

AUTHENTIC CONTENT

- Readings: 200–3,000 words
- Lectures: 20 minutes

EXPLICIT VOCABULARY INSTRUCTION

- Pre- and post-reading and listening vocabulary tasks
- Glossing of receptive vocabulary
- Recycling throughout each part and online

MODERATELY SCAFFOLDED

Guided exercises focus on comprehension, application, and clarification of productive skills.

VOCABULARY STRATEGIES

Vocabulary strategy sections focus on form, use, and meaning to help students process complex content.

TRANSITION LEVEL
B2+–C1 | 68–80

A deep dive for transition-level students, the Transition level mirrors the academic rigor of college courses.

INTENSIVE SKILL PRACTICE

Intensive skill practice tied to learning objectives informed by the Global Scale of English

AUTHENTIC CONTENT

Readings and lectures of significant length:
- 200–3,500-word readings
- 25-minute lectures

CONTENT AND FLUENCY VOCABULARY APPROACH

- No direct vocabulary instruction
- Online vocabulary practice for remediation

Key Features

UNIQUE PART STRUCTURE

University Success employs a unique three-part structure, providing maximum flexibility and multiple opportunities to customize the content. The series is "horizontally" aligned to teach across a specific content area and "vertically" aligned to allow a teacher to gradually build skills.

Each part is a self-contained module allowing teachers to customize a non-linear program that will best address the needs of students. Parts are aligned around science, technology, engineering, arts, and mathematics (STEAM) content relevant to mainstream academic areas of study.

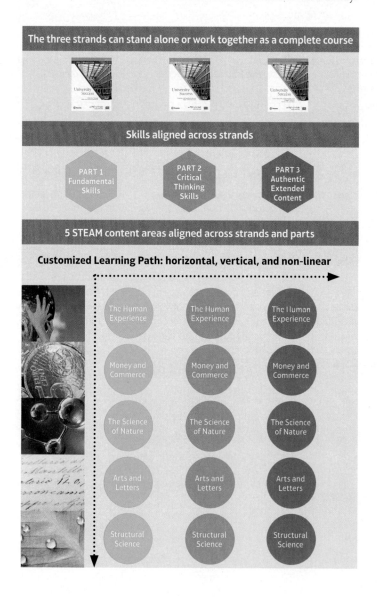

THE THREE PARTS AT A GLANCE

 Parts 1 and 2 focus on the fundamental reading skills and critical thinking skills most relevant for students preparing for university degrees. In Parts 1 and 2, students work with comprehensive skills that include:

- Recognizing organizational structures
- Reading fluently
- Understanding cause, effect, and correlation
- Determining an author's purpose and tone
- Understanding visuals

 Part 3 introduces students to extended practice with skills. Content created by top university professors provides students with a challenging experience that replicates the authentic experience of studying in a mainstream university class.

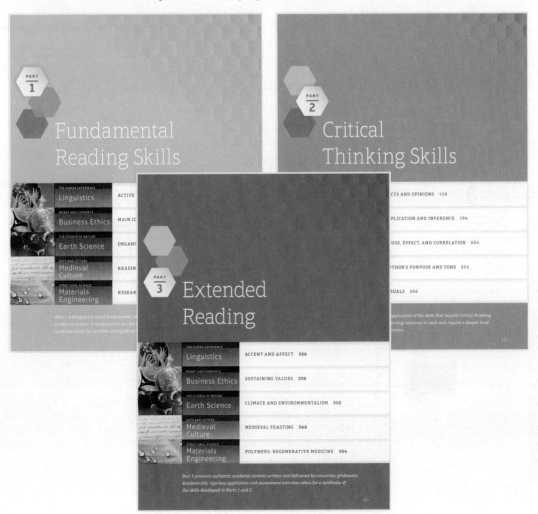

PART
1

Fundamental Reading Skills

THE HUMAN EXPERIENCE
Linguistics   ACTIVE

MONEY AND COMMERCE
Business Ethics   MAIN ID

THE SCIENCE OF NATURE
Earth Science   ORGANI

ARTS AND LETTERS
Medieval Culture   READIN

STRUCTURAL SCIENCE
Materials Engineering RESEAR

*Part 1 is designed to build fundamental r
academic content. Practice activities tied
understanding the function and applicati*

PART
2

Critical Thinking Skills

CTS AND OPINIONS 158

PLICATION AND INFERENCE 194

USE, EFFECT, AND CORRELATION 224

THOR'S PURPOSE AND TONE 254

SUALS 286

*application of the skills that require critical thinking.
arning outcomes in each unit require a deeper level
ontent.*

PART
3

Extended Reading

THE HUMAN EXPERIENCE
Linguistics   ACCENT AND AFFECT 326

MONEY AND COMMERCE
Business Ethics   SUSTAINING VALUES 338

THE SCIENCE OF NATURE
Earth Science   CLIMATE AND ENVIRONMENTALISM 352

ARTS AND LETTERS
Medieval Culture   MEDIEVAL FEASTING 368

STRUCTURAL SCIENCE
Materials Engineering POLYMERS: REGENERATIVE MEDICINE 384

*Part 3 presents authentic academic content written and delivered by university professors.
Academically rigorous application and assessment activities allow for a synthesis of
the skills developed in Parts 1 and 2.*

Student Book

MyEnglishLab

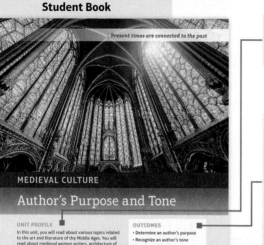

Present times are connected to the past

MEDIEVAL CULTURE

Author's Purpose and Tone

UNIT PROFILE

In this unit, you will read about various topics related to the art and literature of the Middle Ages. You will read about medieval women writers, architecture of the period, and examples of medieval art in various regions of the world.

Preview the reading "Appreciating Non-Western Art from the Middle Ages" on page 282. Quickly skim it to understand the main idea. Then try to answer the following set of questions: What is the author's attitude toward non-Western art from the Middle Ages? What is the author's purpose for writing this article? Who is the intended audience?

For more about MEDIEVAL CULTURE, see ① ①.
See also ⓦ and ⓞⓒ MEDIEVAL CULTURE ① ② ③.

254 MEDIEVAL CULTURE PART 2

OUTCOMES

• Determine an author's purpose
• Recognize an author's tone
• Use descriptive imagery
• Recognize figurative language
• Differentiate between denotation and connotation

A **unit profile** outlines the content.

Outcomes aligned with the Global Scale of English (GSE) are clearly stated to ensure student awareness of skills.

SUPPORTING SKILL 1

DETERMINING AN AUTHOR'S PURPOSE

WHY IT'S USEFUL By learning to recognize an author's purpose and intended audience, you can be a better judge of the importance or usefulness of a reading to your academic needs. This can help you to decide how quickly or slowly to read or whether to take notes, for example. Your comprehension of an author's purpose can then help you to understand the tone that an author uses.

The **purpose** of a reading is an author's primary reason behind writing a text. This is directly connected with the reaction the author hopes to elicit from readers. Does the author wish to convince readers of a certain point of view? Is the intention to advocate for a change? Or is the purpose merely to transmit information?

An author does not always have just one purpose in writing a given text. In fact, a text may have been composed with a number of objectives in mind, so purposes are often multiple and complex. For example, a writer may hope to first inform readers of something and then persuade them to take action related to the information they have just read. Or, an author may compare and contrast two options, then critique one and praise the other in hopes of persuading readers to adopt a certain point of view.

Regardless of the situation, strong writers consciously think about their intended goal before and while writing a piece, taking into consideration their readers' feelings, thoughts, background knowledge, and potential actions. Authors then work to develop a tone that best appeals to their particular audience(s) and aligns with the genre and publication type.

An author's purpose may be neutral, intended mainly to convey information, or biased—intended to persuade or convince. As previously stated, the three main purposes are to inform, to persuade, and to entertain. Some other common authorial purposes include:

Neutral Purpose	Biased Purpose
interpret	interpret
review	review
analyze	criticize / critique
classify	praise
compare	promote
contrast	

Self-assessments provide opportunities for students to identify skill areas for improvement and provide teachers with information that can inform lesson planning.

Professors provide a **preview** and a **summary** of the content.

Why It's Useful sections highlight the need for developing skills and support transfer of skills to mainstream class content.

A **detailed presentation** demonstrates the skills' value in academic study.

Periods of Medieval Architecture

1 In Europe, the Middle Ages refers to the roughly ten centuries between the fall of the Roman Empire and the cultural rebirth known as the Renaissance. A wide range of architectural styles developed over this lengthy period of time, but for the sake of convenience, medieval European architecture is divided into three main stages: early, middle, and late. Despite the variety of styles and designs found in these periods, medieval architecture overall does share some similarities. These include the building materials, which were primarily stone and wood, as well as the floor plans of cathedrals, which were often in the shape of the Latin cross with a long hall, or nave, and an area forming right angles to the nave called the transept. Castles of the Middle Ages, like cathedrals, also had similar design plans, which included battlements, or low walls around the top of a castle from which arrows could be shot to defend against intruders.

2 The earliest medieval architecture was characterized by structures much humbler in appearance than the grand and imposing cathedrals of the later Middle Ages. Anglo-Saxon architecture, which began in 5th-century England and endured well into the 11th, was usually produced with only wood and thatch—tightly packed, plant-based materials such as straw or reeds. Builders at the time were unskilled in masonry, and consequently, few Anglo-Saxon structures survive to this day. Those that remain served functional structures that were rather dull and small compared to the decorative cathedrals and heavily fortified castles of the later Middle Ages.

3 The Romanesque style asserted itself in Europe around the year 1000 as the Anglo-Saxon style declined. As the name implies, the Romanesque style imitates ancient Roman architecture, especially the rounded Roman arch. Many Romanesque designs have rounded arches, thick walls, and a low, stocky profile. Compared to early medieval architectural styles, however, Romanesque structures are usually quite large. Eventually, the Romanesque style evolved into the Gothic, which featured steeper, pointed arches, vaulted ceilings, spectacular stained-glass windows, and the famed flying buttresses, external arches that help support a building. One stunning example of Gothic architecture is the Chartres Cathedral, built between the late 12th and early 13th centuries on the ruins of a Romanesque church in Chartres, France. One of the finest examples of Gothic architecture, it is alive with magnificent sculptures and

Glossary

Anglo-Saxon architecture: English architecture during the Middle Ages from the 400s until the mid-1000s

Gothic: related to an architectural style common in western Europe between the 12th and 16th centuries

masonry: the skill of building with stone

vaulted: having curved arches that are joined together to form the roof of a structure such as a cathedral

House in recreated Anglo-Saxon village, West Stow, England

282 MEDIEVAL CULTURE PART 2

A **variety of reading types**, including magazine articles, journal passages, and textbook excerpts, represent "real-life" university experiences.

Visuals on the page support information in the readings.

Student Book

MyEnglishLab

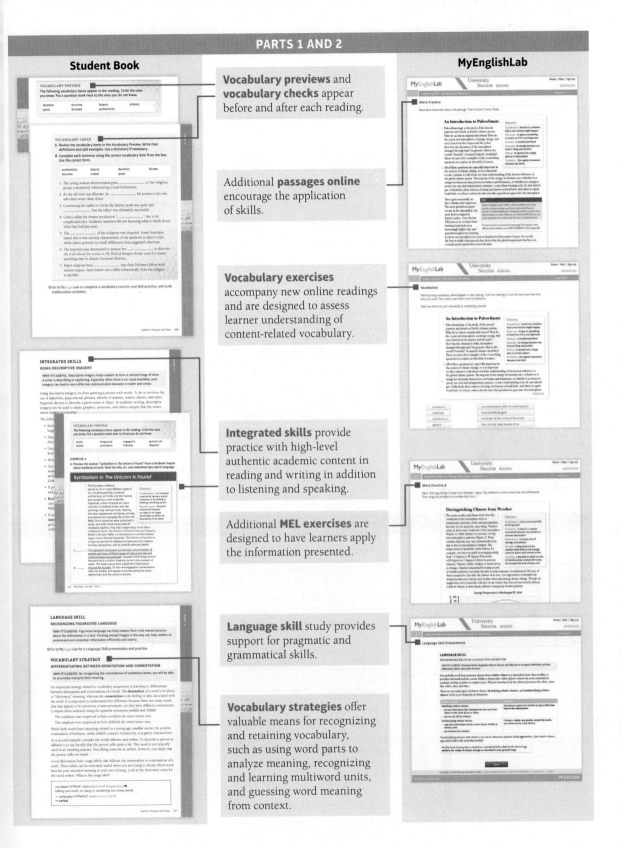

Vocabulary previews and **vocabulary checks** appear before and after each reading.

Additional **passages online** encourage the application of skills.

Vocabulary exercises accompany new online readings and are designed to assess learner understanding of content-related vocabulary.

Integrated skills provide practice with high-level authentic academic content in reading and writing in addition to listening and speaking.

Additional **MEL exercises** are designed to have learners apply the information presented.

Language skill study provides support for pragmatic and grammatical skills.

Vocabulary strategies offer valuable means for recognizing and retaining vocabulary, such as using word parts to analyze meaning, recognizing and learning multiword units, and guessing word meaning from context.

Student Book

MyEnglishLab

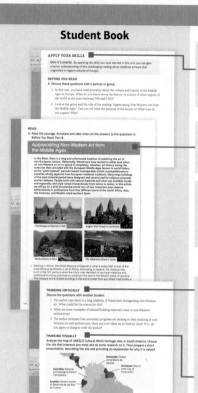

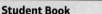

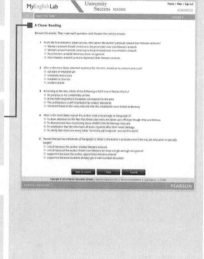

Parts 1 and 2 end with an extended **Apply Your Skills** section that functions as a diagnostic or formative assessment.

This longer **reading passage** allows students to apply skills practiced in the unit.

A closer reading gives students the opportunity to read the passage again and answer critical thinking questions.

Critical thinking activities ask learners to engage at a deep level with the content, using information from the reading to address specific real-world applications.

Visually thinking sections provide an opportunity for students to analyze and create or expand upon charts, maps, and other visuals.

Student Book

MyEnglishLab

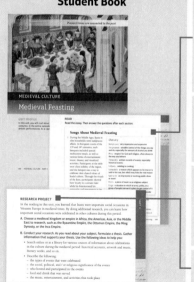

Students read an **authentic essay** written by a professor working in a specific STEAM field. The essays are presented in sections, to allow for clarifications and comprehension checks.

Students use **critical thinking** skills to consider a **situation** related to the essay and record their thoughts.

A **related extended reading**, written by the same professor, gives students another opportunity to practice their reading skills and check comprehension.

As a **final project**, students prepare and participate in a presentation and group discussion.

STRATEGIES FOR ACADEMIC SUCCESS AND SOFT SKILLS

Strategies for academic success and soft skills, delivered via online videos, help increase students' confidence and ability to cope with the challenges of academic study and college culture. Study skills include how to talk to professors during office hours and time management techniques.

TEACHER SUPPORT
Each of the three strands is supported with:

- Comprehensive **downloadable teaching notes** in MyEnglishLab that detail key points for all of the specialized, academic content in addition to tips and suggestions for how to teach skills and strategies.
- **An easy-to-use online learning management system** offering a flexible gradebook and tools for monitoring student progress.
- Essential tools, such as **audio and video scripts** and **course planners**, to help in lesson planning and follow-up.

ASSESSMENT

University Success provides a package of assessments that can be used as precourse diagnostics, midcourse assessments, and final summative assessments. The flexible nature of these assessments allows teachers to choose which assessments will be most appropriate at various stages of the program. These assessments are embedded in the student book and are available online in MyEnglishLab.

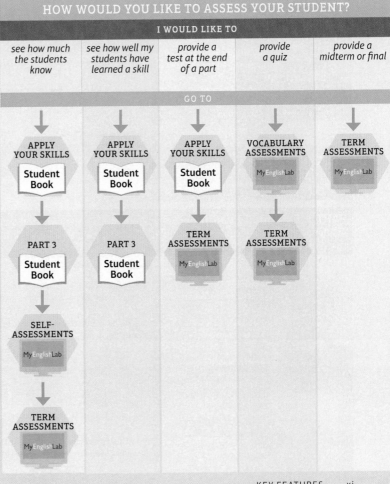

HOW WOULD YOU LIKE TO ASSESS YOUR STUDENT?

I WOULD LIKE TO

see how much the students know	see how well my students have learned a skill	provide a test at the end of a part	provide a quiz	provide a midterm or final

GO TO

APPLY YOUR SKILLS — Student Book	APPLY YOUR SKILLS — Student Book	APPLY YOUR SKILLS — Student Book	VOCABULARY ASSESSMENTS — MyEnglishLab	TERM ASSESSMENTS — MyEnglishLab
PART 3 — Student Book	PART 3 — Student Book	TERM ASSESSMENTS — MyEnglishLab	TERM ASSESSMENTS — MyEnglishLab	
SELF-ASSESSMENTS — MyEnglishLab				
TERM ASSESSMENTS — MyEnglishLab				

Scope and Sequence

Integrated Skills	Language Skills	Vocabulary Strategy	Apply Your Skills
Annotating	Understanding pro-forms	Choosing and writing vocabulary to learn	Read "The Ocracoke Brogue." Explain the need to preserve the Ocracoke dialect; analyze endangered languages in North and South America and create a map or chart about a different country or region.
Outlining a text	Simplifying complex sentences	Using word parts to analyze meaning	Read "The Role of Investment Banks in the Great Recession." Explore the ethics of investment bankers; analyze data about gross domestic product (GDP) in the United States and create a graph showing GDP in a different country.
Taking notes with graphic organizers	Recognizing relative clauses for definition	Understanding suffixes in scientific terms	Read "Climate Change on Mars and Earth." Explore how studying climate change on Mars can help us learn about Earth; evaluate conditions on Earth and Mars and present information about atmospheric conditions on a different planet.
Summarizing a text	Understanding language associated with chronology	Recognizing multiple meanings of words	Read "How the Spice Trade Drove Globalization." Evaluate why Venice was so successful in the spice trade; consider the history of the spice trade and create a timeline showing key events of the Middle Ages.
Summarizing a research article	Understanding modifiers	Recognizing and learning multiword units	Read "Polymer Applications in Soft Robotics." Explore the development and uses of soft robots; consider experiments related to soft robotics polymer applications and analyze characteristics of two specific soft robots.

Integrated Skills	Language Skills	Vocabulary Strategy	Apply Your Skills
Quoting material from a reading	Understanding structures used for hedging	Using a dictionary to strengthen vocabulary	Read "Grammar Goes to Hollywood: Linguists as Science Consultants." Explain how science consultants can contribute to movies; explore selected invented languages and complete a chart with this information.
Paraphrasing	Understanding noun clauses	Guessing word meanings from context	Read "High- Versus Low-Context Cultures." Explore international business communication; study countries considered low- and high-context cultures and create a graph about business communication in a different country.
Using flowcharts to note causes and effects	Understanding passive and active voice	Understanding collocations	Read "Critical Thresholds and Climate Tipping Points." Investigate global warming; analyze data about global carbon dioxide levels and create a graph showing changes in a different climate variable over time.
Using descriptive imagery	Recognizing figurative language	Differentiating between denotation and connotation	Read "Appreciating Non-Western Art from the Middle Ages." Consider historical attitudes toward non-Western art; analyze a map of UNESCO Cultural World Heritage sites in South America and prepare a presentation on one of the sites.
Explaining information in visuals	Understanding the use of passive voice in research writing	Recognizing Greek, Latin, and Germanic word roots	Read "How Nanotechnology Fights Cancer." Explore benefits and potential downsides of nanomedicines; determine major nanotechnology milestones and create a timeline of the five most important developments.

Research / Assignment

Choose and research a region within a country and research that region's accents. Explain how this accent can be distinguished from others as well as any changes or shifts that have occurred.

Choose and research a company that has experienced problems due to fraud or ethics violations. Determine the type of fraud, how using a framework of ethical decision making could help in such a situation, and changes that could be made to create a positive ethical environment.

Choose and research a region of interest when studying paleoclimate and climate change. Explore the types of research currently being conducted in that region, what type of proxies scientists are examining, and past and current climate change in this region.

Choose and research a medieval kingdom or empire. Explore historical accounts, artwork and music, literary works, and so on to find out about celebrations in that culture.

Choose and research a type of object that commonly uses materials made of polymers. Find specific examples of this type of object and learn more about the polymeric material, such as mechanical properties, conditions under which the material can be used, and its advantages and disadvantages.

A Note from Lawrence Zwier

Series Editor for *University Success Reading*

My advanced ESL reading students at Michigan State University have already accomplished a lot. For some of them, mine might be the last required ESL reading course before they begin their discipline-area studies. In any case, they have already been taught all the workhorse basics of English grammar, have heard a lot about text structure and cohesion, and have built vocabularies that are strong up to perhaps the 3.5K level (roughly, the 3,500 most common words in English). What they need is practice, exposure, and refinement.

It is important for them to work with serious, substantive reading material that is of a decent length and vocabulary level. Fluency is vital, for they won't be able to handle course reading loads unless they build it. Vocabulary development might be the most urgent of their needs. To compete in their freshman-level courses, they should ideally be strong up to about the 5K level, at a minimum. Unfortunately, they are still tentative in the 4K range, not to mention 5K. I push them relentlessly to stretch and work at these higher ranges. Much of my work involves, as the cliché goes, helping them help themselves. The development of both fluency and vocabulary must be up to them, because there is not enough class time in an entire year for me to put them through the necessary paces. All I can do is provide practice and explain things to the best of my ability.

The advanced level of *University Success Reading* is perfect for them. It offers serious, informative, expertly calibrated texts with which to practice. There is instruction in reading skills, but it serves more to remind than to reveal. The readings are of various lengths, including some long ones for practice with extended discourse. This volume has a personality—direct, mature, eager to explore difficult topic realms, high-level, and proud of it.

PART 1—FUNDAMENTAL READING SKILLS

In the first five units of *University Success Reading,* each of the five main subject areas (Linguistics, Business Ethics, Earth Science, Medieval Culture, and Materials Engineering) is introduced. The most fundamental aspects of structure and approach in academic texts—such as main ideas, cohesive patterns, fluency-building strategies, and the role of visuals—are featured and practiced in ways appropriate for advanced-level readers. The Stanford University professors who are the thought leaders for all three strands introduce themselves and their fields. This part of the text amps up the discourse in accessible yet challenging ways. It provides thematically related yet diverse reading passages that demonstrate fundamental text features and encourage advanced-level readers to tackle the passages with some scaffolding.

PART 2—CRITICAL THINKING SKILLS

In these units, each main subject area is explored in greater depth, with reading passages that demand more sophisticated processing and analysis. Critical thinking is more directly elicited so that advanced-level students engage in such processes as evaluating the quality of evidence, refining the inferences they draw, and appreciating the full depth of passages that are somewhat metaphorical. As in the Part 1 units, here the Stanford thought leaders have informed the content so that the reading passages are accessible and appealing yet rock-solid in their factuality and field-specific relevance.

PART 3—EXTENDED READING

University Success Reading opens up and brings the Stanford thought leaders front and center. Each of the readings in this part is long, serious, and substantive—penned by the professor and testing the frontiers of thought in his or her academic specialization. The Part 3 questions posed to our advanced-level students are not simple, but they are high-interest and meant to promote lively discussion among readers. In Part 3, *University Success* does something no other high-level ELT text does: It dives deep into the work of high-prestige professors and researchers and offers unique academic rigor as students step toward their life beyond ESL.

SUBJECT MATTER EXPERTS

Marisa Galvez specializes in the literature of the Middle Ages in France and Western Europe, especially literature written in Occitan and Old French. Her courses at Stanford focus on medieval and Renaissance French literature and the medieval imaginary in modern literature, film, and art. Her recent book, *Songbook: How Lyrics Became Poetry in Medieval Europe*, is the first comparative study of songbooks and was awarded the John Nicholas Brown Prize from the Medieval Academy of America.

Sarah Heilshorn is an Associate Professor in the Department of Materials Science and Engineering and, by courtesy, of Bioengineering and Chemical Engineering at Stanford University. She completed her PhD and MS degrees in Chemical Engineering at California Institute of Technology. She earned a BS in Chemical Engineering at Georgia Institute of Technology. She is an expert in the design of new materials that mimic those found in our own bodies.

Scotty McLennan is a Lecturer in Political Economy at the Stanford Graduate School of Business (GSB), where he teaches in the areas of business ethics and business and spirituality. He taught business ethics at the Harvard Business School from 1988 to 2000, and from 2000 to 2014 he was the Stanford University Dean for Religious Life as well as Lecturer at the GSB. He is the author of four books and a number of book chapters and articles.

Michael Osborne is a climate scientist turned multimedia producer for Worldview Stanford who teaches science communication classes at Stanford. He co-founded and produces the award-winning *Generation Anthropocene* podcast, a partnership between Stanford and Smithsonian.com featuring stories and conversations about planetary change. "Through the podcasts, we want to capture stories about the changing environmental and cultural landscapes from diverse perspectives … to help guide strategic, editorial, and partnership decisions that bolster Worldview's mission of creating unique learning experiences."

Robert Podesva is an Assistant Professor of Linguistics at Stanford University. He holds degrees from Stanford University (PhD, MA) and Cornell University (BA) and has been an Assistant Professor at Georgetown University. His research examines the social significance of phonetic variation and its role in the construction of identity, most notably gender, sexuality, and race. His most recent projects focus on the interrelation between linguistic variation and embodiment in the expression of affect. He has co-edited *Research Methods in Linguistics, Language and Sexuality*, and the forthcoming *Social Meaning and Linguistic Variation*.

SERIES EDITORS

Robyn Brinks Lockwood teaches courses in spoken and written English at Stanford University in the English for Foreign Students graduate program and is the program education coordinator of the American Language and Culture undergraduate summer program. She is an active member of the international TESOL organization, serves as Chairperson of the Publishing Professional Council, and is a past chair of the Materials Writers Interest Section. She is a frequent presenter at TESOL regional and international conferences. Robyn has edited and written numerous textbooks, online courses, and ancillary components for ESL courses and TOEFL preparation.

Maggie Sokolik holds a BA in Anthropology from Reed College, and an MA in Romance Linguistics and PhD in Applied Linguistics from UCLA. She is the author of over 20 ESL and composition textbooks. She has taught at MIT, Harvard, Texas A&M, and currently UC Berkeley, where she is Director of College Writing Programs. She has developed and taught several popular MOOC courses in English language writing and literature. She is the founding editor of *TESL-EJ*, a peer-reviewed journal for ESL / EFL professionals, one of the first online journals. Maggie travels frequently to speak about grammar, writing, and instructor education. She lives in the San Francisco Bay area, where she and her husband play bluegrass music.

Lawrence J. Zwier is an Associate Director of the English Language Center, Michigan State University. He holds a bachelor's degree in English Literature from Aquinas College, Grand Rapids, MI, and an MA in TESL from the University of Minnesota. He has taught ESL / EFL at universities in Saudi Arabia, Malaysia, Japan, Singapore, and the US. He is the author of numerous ELT textbooks, mostly about reading and vocabulary, and also writes nonfiction books about history and geography for middle school and high school students. He is married with two children and lives in Okemos, Michigan.

Acknowledgments

I would like to thank the entire team at Pearson for all of their roles in keeping the operation running. In particular, Debbie Sistino, Lida Baker, and John Thompson all provided keen insight, guidance, and feedback to facilitate the units coming together. Victoria Solomon was also an essential component of this book, and her creativity, intelligence, and large amount of work shine through in all of the articles. Lastly, I would like to thank my friends and family for their patience and support throughout the process. —*Laura Eickhoff*

I would like to thank Debbie Sistino, Amy McCormick, and all of those at Pearson who helped to make this book possible. I would also like to thank Shalle Leeming and Natasha Haugnes for their contributions to the content. Finally, thanks go to Lida Baker and Sarah Wales-McGrath for their valuable suggestions during development. —*Laurie Frazier*

I would like to thank Debbie Sistino for diligently managing the project timeline, keeping us all on track. Our developmental editor, Lida Baker, also deserves thanks for her close attention to detail and constructive feedback. Thanks are also due to John Thompson, who provided valuable comments in his edits to one unit. I would like to extend my sincere thanks to Victoria Solomon, who did an enormous amount of research on complex topics and distilled information into comprehensible content for non-specialists—not an easy task. It was a pleasure to work with her again. I wish to thank Larry Zwier, Series Editor for *University Success Reading*, for the invaluable insights and recommendations he provided. On a personal note, I would like to thank my family for everything they have done that has made it possible for me to get to the point of coauthoring my second textbook. I am deeply appreciative. Finally, I would like to express my gratitude to Eduardo Mello for his unwavering support, patience, and understanding from start to finish. Words cannot express how much this has meant to me. —*Maggie Vosters*

Reviewers

We would like to thank the following reviewers for their many helpful comments and suggestions:

Jamila Barton, North Seattle Community College, Seattle, WA; **Joan Chamberlin**, Iowa State University, Ames IA; **Lyam Christopher**, Palm Beach State College, Boynton Beach, FL; **Robin Corcos**, University of California, Santa Barbara, Goleta, CA; **Tanya Davis**, University of California, San Diego, CA; **Brendan DeCoster**, University of Oregon, Eugene, OR; **Thomas Dougherty**, University of St. Mary of the Lake, Mundelein, IL; **Bina Dugan**, Bergen County Community College, Hackensack, NJ; **Priscilla Faucette**, University of Hawaii at Manoa, Honolulu, HI; **Lisa Fischer**, St. Louis University, St. Louis, MO; **Kathleen Flynn**, Glendale Community College, Glendale, CA; **Mary Gawienowski**, William Rainey Harper College, Palatine, IL; **Sally Gearhart**, Santa Rosa Junior College, Santa Rosa, CA; **Carl Guerriere**, Capital Community College, Hartford, CT; **Vera Guillen**, Eastfield College, Mesquite, TX; **Angela Hakim**, St. Louis University, St. Louis, MO; **Pamela Hartmann**, Evans Community Adult School, Los Angeles Unified School District, Los Angeles, CA; **Shelly Hedstrom**, Palm Beach State University, Lake Worth, FL; **Sherie Henderson**, University of Oregon, Eugene, OR; **Lisse Hildebrandt**, English Language Program, Virginia Commonwealth University, Richmond, VA; **Barbara Inerfeld**, Rutgers University, Piscataway, NJ; **Zaimah Khan**, Northern Virginia Community College, Loudon Campus, Sterling, VA; **Tricia Kinman**, St. Louis University, St. Louis, MO; **Kathleen Klaiber**, Genesee Community College, Batavia, NY; **Kevin Lamkins**, Capital Community College, Hartford, CT; **Mayetta Lee**, Palm Beach State College, Lake Worth, FL; **Kirsten Lillegard**, English Language Institute, Divine Word College, Epworth, IA; **Craig Machado**, Norwalk Community College, Norwalk, CT; **Cheryl Madrid**, Spring International Language Center, Denver, CO; **Ann Meechai**, St. Louis University, St. Louis, MO; **Melissa Mendelson**, Department of Linguistics, University of Utah, Salt Lake City, UT; **Tamara Milbourn**, University of Colorado, Boulder, CO; **Debbie Ockey**, Fresno City College, Fresno, CA; **Diana Pascoe-Chavez**, St. Louis University, St. Louis, MO; **Kathleen Reynolds**, William Rainey Harper College, Palatine, IL; **Linda Roth**, Vanderbilt University ELC, Greensboro, NC; **Minati Roychoudhuri**, Capital Community College, Hartford, CT; **Bruce Rubin**, California State University, Fullerton, CA; **Margo Sampson**, Syracuse University, Syracuse, NY; **Sarah Saxer**, Howard Community College, Ellicott City, MD; **Anne-Marie Schlender**, Austin Community College, Austin, TX; **Susan Shields**, Santa Barbara Community College, Santa Barbara, CA; **Barbara Smith-Palinkas**, Hillsborough Community College, Dale Mabry Campus, Tampa, FL; **Sara Stapleton**, North Seattle Community College, Seattle, WA; **Lisa Stelle**, Northern Virginia Community College Loudon, Sterling, VA; **Jamie Tanzman**, Northern Kentucky University, Highland Heights, KY; **Jeffrey Welliver**, Soka University of America, Aliso Viejo, CA; **Mark Wolfersberger**, Brigham Young University, Hawaii, Laie, HI; **May Youn**, California State University, Fullerton, CA

Fundamental Reading Skills

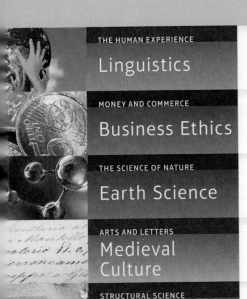

Part 1 is designed to build fundamental skills step by step through exploration of rigorous, academic content. Practice activities tied to specific learning outcomes in each unit focus on understanding the function and application of the skills.

Language communicates who we are

LINGUISTICS

Active Reading

UNIT PROFILE

In this unit, you will consider the subject of linguistics. Reading topics include background information about languages and linguistics, the phonetic alphabet, dialects, language change, and code-switching. You will also consider the extent to which language and thought interact.

Look at the reading "The Ocracoke Brogue" on page 26. Notice the title and map. What do you think the reading is about? Scan (read quickly) the first paragraph. What is the Ocracoke brogue?

OUTCOMES

- Preview a text
- Scan
- Annotate
- Understand pro-forms
- Choose and write new vocabulary to learn

For more about **LINGUISTICS**, see ❷❸. See also ⬜W and ⬜OC **LINGUISTICS** ❶❷❸.

GETTING STARTED

⊙ Go to MyEnglishLab to watch Professor Podesva's introductory video and to complete a self-assessment.

Discuss these questions with a partner or group.

1. How would you define language? Give examples of ways it helps or serves us.

2. What do you know about the difference between a language and a dialect?

3. According to Professor Podesva, what do linguists include in their description of a dialect? What do they exclude?

FUNDAMENTAL SKILL

READING ACTIVELY

WHY IT'S USEFUL Reading actively helps you to maintain concentration, understand a text on a deep level, and remember what you have read. Practicing active reading can also increase your overall confidence and fluency in reading.

Reading, especially in academic situations, should be an active, not a passive, process. Reading actively involves interacting with a text in order to understand it more deeply. The process begins even before reading: Active readers start by **previewing a text**—examining the title, looking at visuals, and noticing other prominent text features in order to begin considering the topic. Then, as they read, they interact with the text by asking themselves questions about it, and they

> **TIP**
>
> Consider how you read in different situations, whether in English or in your first language. For example, compare reading a website to find information and reading a newspaper article or a novel. How are the processes similar or different? Becoming more aware of the reading strategies you use and when, how, and why you use them can improve your active reading skills.

often annotate—mark the text—in some way. After they have finished reading, they might organize and reread notes and, depending on their purpose for reading, go back and **scan**—read quickly for specific information—all or part of the text to clarify or find answers to specific questions.

This unit breaks down reading actively into two supporting skills:

- previewing a text
- scanning

EXERCISE 1

A. Discuss the questions with a partner before you read.

1. What different kinds of human language can you think of? (Hint: Is language always spoken?)

2. Do you think some languages are simpler than others?

3. Look at the picture on page 5. What can you say about the man in the painting? For example, what is he doing? Why?

B. Preview the passage. Read the title and look quickly at the sidebar. Write three to four questions you think the passage might answer. Then read the passage quickly. Check (✓) any of your questions that were answered.

☐ ....

☐ ....

☐ ....

☐ ....

Language and Linguistics

1 Language may be defined broadly as the ability to communicate through spoken sounds, written symbols, and gestures. By these means, humans are able to convey information, emotion, creativity, personal opinions, and social and cultural values. Language serves different purposes: It facilitates social interaction, allows us to express identity, and functions as a mechanism of thought. The phenomenon of language is systematic, containing phonologic,

TERMS AND DEFINITIONS

Phonology: The study of the sound patterns in a particular language

Phonetics: The study of the production and description of speech sounds

Morphology: The branch of linguistics that studies and describes patterns of word formation

Syntax: The way in which words are put together to form phrases, clauses, and sentences

Semantics: The study of meaning in language

Pragmatics: The study of language as it is used by particular groups and in particular contexts

morphologic, syntactic, semantic, and pragmatic aspects. In every society, humans use the structures within the mouth—lips, tongue, palate, and so on—to pronounce the sounds of a particular language, or in some cases, multiple ones. For those unable to speak an oral language, sign language facilitates communication and contains the same structural rules as spoken language. These days, individuals who can neither speak nor sign are able to use digital communication technologies to communicate their thoughts, wants, and needs.

2   Throughout the ages, myths have persisted surrounding language, including the idea that certain languages are "simple" while others are "complex," or that some languages are "inferior" while others are "superior." The truth is that every language possesses rule-based complexity, and while a language may be simple in one aspect, such as syntax, it may well be complex in another aspect, such as morphology.

3   Many ancient cultures placed importance on language, especially as it relates to the mind and the soul, and the study of language was often closely connected with logic and religious philosophy. One of the first in-depth analytical works about language was the Indian scholar Panini's *Ashtadhyayi*, which is a grammar of the ancient Indian language Sanskrit composed between the 6th and 4th centuries BCE. More than a thousand years later, the study of language developed further when 19th-century Western scholars began to wonder about a "parent" Indo-European language from which Sanskrit, Latin, and many other languages were derived. This early comparative study focused mainly on historical aspects of language, and from this early linguistic tradition, the modern field of linguistics has grown. While some linguists today continue the study of ancient languages, others focus on different aspects of the structure, meaning, and use of language, including dialects and language variation, the connection between language and cognition, and the way languages are both learned and taught.

C. **Read the passage again. Then read the statements and write *T* (True) or *F* (False). If you need to check an answer, think about the key word(s) you will use to find the information in the text. Correct the false statements.**

....   1. Hand movements could be considered part of language.

....   2. Language is an organized system with multiple parts to it.

....   3. Sign language can be used for communication, but it is not as systematic as spoken language.

....   4. Some languages are less complex overall, and therefore inferior, to other languages.

.... 5. Panini, who was from India and analyzed Sanskrit, was one of the earliest linguists.

.... 6. Serious study of language began only when 19th-century scholars wondered about the origins of all languages.

.... 7. The foundation of modern linguistics comes from an early focus on comparing languages and studying their histories.

.... 8. Modern linguists are more interested in studying language variation than the history of ancient languages.

D. Answer the questions. Refer to the passage as needed. Then discuss answers with a partner.

1. How many purposes of language are listed in the passage? Underline or highlight them. Then discuss: What are some specific examples for each purpose? For example, how do we use language to express our identity?

2. The passage discusses the idea that languages may be more complex in one area, such as syntax, than in another area, such as morphology. Think of a language you know, and consider it in this way. Is one aspect more or less complex than another? If so, in what way?

3. Think about active reading. How did the Part A tasks influence your first reading of the passage? How did previewing the passage (Part B) affect your interaction with the text? Overall, what makes you feel that you have understood a text on a deep level?

VOCABULARY CHECK

A. Review the vocabulary items in the Vocabulary Preview. Write their definitions and add examples. Use a dictionary if necessary.

B. Complete each sentence using the correct vocabulary item from the box. Use the correct form.

cognition	comparative	facilitate	gesture (n)
inferior	means (n)	myth	systematic

1. When an important file went missing, the staff began a .... search of every location where it could have been misplaced.

2. This paper dictionary is .... to my online one because it doesn't give examples of how new words are used in sentences.

3. Drug companies must perform long-term .... studies on the effectiveness of new drugs versus older ones already in use.

4. When management and staff could not agree on the terms of a new contract, they hired a psychologist to .... the discussions.

5. Many people believe the .... that children learn to speak simply by imitating the adults around them.

6. Language students often use a variety of .... to record and learn new vocabulary.

7. The same .... that means "come here" in North America can mean "go away" in Japan.

8. A young child may be unable to speak yet have normal intelligence and ....

🔵 Go to MyEnglishLab to complete a vocabulary exercise and skill practice, and to join in collaborative activities.

SUPPORTING SKILL 1
PREVIEWING A TEXT

WHY IT'S USEFUL Previewing a text helps you to get a sense of the contents before you start to read. When you preview, you make predictions about the contents of a reading and consider what you already know about the topic. This helps you read faster and with better comprehension.

Active readers preview a text before they read it. **Previewing** means employing one or more of the following strategies:

- noticing the title of a passage
- looking at visuals or graphics that accompany the text
- considering what type or genre the text is
- reading the introduction, conclusion, and subheadings
- noticing the way the passage is organized
- forming questions you would like the text to answer

These strategies help you to make predictions about the information that might be presented in the passage. Then, as you read, you can check to see whether your predictions are confirmed in the text. This helps you to stay focused. Previewing also helps you to activate and draw on existing knowledge that you might have about the topic and develop or fine-tune your purpose for reading.

VOCABULARY PREVIEW

The following vocabulary items appear in the reading. Circle the ones you know. Put a question mark next to the ones you do not know.

distinction	quipped	implying	classification
evolve	blurred (v)	complexities	stem from

EXERCISE 2

A. Preview the reading using the strategies on page 7. Predict three things you believe will be discussed. Write two questions you have.

Predictions

1. ....

2. ....

3. ....

Questions

1. ....

2. ....

What Is a Dialect?

A dialect is a variety of a language that is spoken in a particular part of a country or region or by a particular group of people. Dialects contain some words, grammar, or pronunciations that are different from forms used in other areas or by other groups.

1 What is the difference between a language and a dialect? The dividing line is not always clear. Some linguists make a distinction based on the concept of *mutual intelligibility*, or understanding, between speakers of different varieties of a language. American English and South African English, for example, are mutually intelligible to people from both nations, but they differ enough in form that they are regarded as distinct dialects of the English language. Yet the concept of mutual intelligibility applies not just to dialects. The sociolinguist Max Weinreich once quipped that

"a language is a dialect with an army and a navy," implying that political factors often carry greater weight than linguistic ones in the classification of a speech variety as a language or a dialect. Swedish and Norwegian, for example, are mutually intelligible, yet they are called languages because of the historic and political separation between the two countries. The same may be said for Czech and Slovak, Tajik and Persian, and Irish and Scottish.

2 Dialects usually evolve as a consequence of geographic or sociocultural factors. Speech varieties associated with geographical locations are known as *regional dialects*. These can be local, such as the American English dialects of eastern New England and western New England, or broader, such as American English and South African English in general. *Social dialects*, on the other hand, are often determined by factors such as an individual's race, education, gender, and age though the distinctions between social divisions and regional divisions are sometimes blurred. A well-known example of a social dialect, also termed a *sociolect*, is the variety of upper-class English taught in British public schools. Nicknamed the "Queen's English" or "BBC English" after the speaking standard once required of announcers on the country's famous radio broadcasting service, this variety has traditionally been regarded as the only "correct" dialect of English. Every dialect, like every language, contains its own regularities, patterns, and complexities, yet judgments of correctness tend to stem from the social status of its speakers rather than right or wrong speech.

- New England Eastern
- New England Western
- Boston Urban
- Inland Northern
- New York City
- Eastern Pennsylvania

Dialect map of Northeastern United States

B. Read the passage. Then complete each statement with the correct information. Three items will not be used.

become more intelligible	dialects and languages	regional
broad	disappear	social
dialects	politics	spoken

1. The term *dialect* pertains mainly to .... language.

2. .... can be mutually intelligible.

3. The quotation by Max Weinreich illustrates the role of .... in designating a speech variety as a dialect or language.

4. The Portuguese of Portugal and the Portuguese of Brazil are examples of
.... dialects.

5. The passage implies that men and women may speak different
.... dialects.

6. It is probably true that as different social groups come into contact with one
another, social dialects are likely to ....

**C. Read the passage again. Check your answers to Part B. Then compare answers
with a partner.**

D. Work with a partner. Answer the questions about your use of the previewing skill.

1. Which preview strategies from page 7 did you use? Were any of the strategies new
for you? How did previewing affect your reading speed and comprehension?

2. Were your predictions in Part A correct?

3. Did the passage answer the questions you asked in Part A?

VOCABULARY CHECK

**A. Review the vocabulary items in the Vocabulary Preview. Write their
definitions and add examples. Use a dictionary if necessary.**

**B. Complete each sentence using the correct vocabulary item from the box.
Use the correct form.**

blur	classification	complexity	distinction
evolve	imply	quip	stem from

1. Harold's unusual accent in English .... the fact that his
mother was born in South Africa and his father in south Texas in the
United States.

2. I have trouble hearing the .... between an Australian and a
South African accent.

3. The Irish playwright George Bernard Shaw humorously ....
that England and America are two countries separated by the same language.

4. All languages .... There is no language that sounds the
same today as it did 1,000 or even 100 years ago.

5. Due to the .... of Turkish grammar, it can take a person
many years to learn the language well.

6. .... of languages into groups can be based on characteristics including word order or phonetic features.

7. In places, the border between the United States and Canada is .... because there is no fence.

8. The student's body language .... that she was uncomfortable being called upon to speak in class.

🔾 Go to MyEnglishLab to complete a vocabulary exercise and skill practice, and to join in collaborative activities.

SUPPORTING SKILL 2

SCANNING

WHY IT'S USEFUL Scanning is a technique that enables you to find specific information quickly, without wasting time on sentence-by-sentence reading. This is useful when you are previewing, reviewing, or looking for answers to questions on tests.

Part of active reading is scanning, or reading quickly, to find specific information. Scanning is closely associated with your purpose in reading. You might need to verify a fact to use in writing a paper, find the answer to a test question, fill in gaps in your notes, or check the meaning of a technical term. It is not necessary to read an entire passage in those situations. Rather, it is enough to run your eyes over the text quickly until you locate the specific information you are looking for. Once you find it, you can stop reading. You might want to annotate—circle or underline—the information if you think you might want to refer to it again in the future. (See more about annotating on page 16.)

Scanning Techniques		
To find ...	**Look for ...**	**Examples**
the name of a person, place, or organization	capital letters	Albert Einstein, Moscow, UN (United Nations)
the name of a book, movie, or song	capital letters and italics or quotation marks	*Gone with the Wind*, "The Star Spangled Banner," *Titanic*
a date or quantity	numbers	May 15; 4,000 kg
a definition	signal words and phrases such as *X means*, *X may be defined as*, etc.	Broadly, language *may be defined as* the ability to communicate ...

Scanning Techniques		
To find ...	**Look for ...**	**Examples**
information not signaled by unusual letters or numbers	key words likely to occur in the information you are seeking	Dialects change **as** people themselves change, reflecting **patterns of migration** and our **social interactions and divisions**. (The key word *as* signals reasons; the reasons are *patterns of migration* and *social interactions and divisions*.)

In formal text, numbers smaller than 11 (or 100 in some publications) may be written out: nine, fifty-two. Very large numbers may contain both numerals and words: 345 million.

VOCABULARY PREVIEW

The following vocabulary items appear in the reading. Circle the ones you know. Put a question mark next to the ones you do not know.

(a firm) grasp	alternate (v)	competence	convey
fit in	substandard	taboo	utterance

EXERCISE 3

A. Preview the reading. Notice the title and the illustration. What do you predict the reading will discuss? Discuss your answers with a partner.

B. Read each statement. Then set a timer on your device for 60 seconds. In that time, scan the reading to find the information needed. Check (✓) the correct answers.

1. Code-switching occurs when speakers alternate between ....

   ☐ a. languages only   ☐ b. languages or dialects

2. Maori is spoken in ....

   ☐ a. Kazakhstan   ☐ b. New Zealand

3. According to the passage, code-switching is a way for some speakers to ....

   ☐ a. appear superior   ☐ b. discuss taboo subjects in an acceptable way

4. The passage states that Kazakhstan is in ....

   ☐ a. Central Asia   ☐ b. Russia

5. Students in some former Soviet republics learn .... in school.

   ☐ a. Russian   ☐ b. English

6. By the 1980s, linguists had come to view code-switching as an indication of a speaker's ....

   ☐ a. confusion   ☐ b. communicative competence

Code-switching

1   The ability to switch back and forth between two languages is known as *code-switching*. Code-switching is common among bilingual and multilingual speakers, and it also occurs in distinct social groups when individuals alternate between dialects. Switching between languages or dialects occurs when a person is fluent in both speech patterns and has a deep understanding of the two cultures.

"No te olvides que tenemos una reunión a las tres de la tarde."

"Don't forget we have a meeting at 3 p.m."

2   Speakers of two languages or dialects may alternate the way they talk to fit in with their own social group or to be accepted in a larger group that includes speakers of a majority language or dialect. Research conducted in New Zealand, for example, shows that Maori New Zealanders often code-switch between the Maori language and English in the workplace. People may also choose a particular language to convey something in secret or simply because a phrase in one language or dialect is more suitable to the speaker for personal reasons. Research suggests that words considered taboo in some languages may be code-switched to more comfortably discuss a "forbidden" topic such as sex. Similarly, a person may switch into one language when discussing certain topics, such as family life, and another language when discussing

(Continued)

another topic, such as school. For example, in the former Soviet republics of Central Asia (Kazakhstan, Uzbekistan, and so on), many bilingual students study Russian in school and speak a different language at home. When speaking about school, these students often speak in Russian, but when a topic associated with family life is brought up, they often switch to their home language. Such alternation may occur smoothly within a single speaking utterance or conversation, with speakers being unaware of the switch unless it is pointed out to them.

3 In the 1940s and 1950s, code-switching was viewed negatively by some scholars, who viewed it as a substandard manner of speaking. Other myths over the years have included the idea that code-switching shows weaker skills in a language or that the speaker is confused or mixing up languages. By the 1980s, however, linguists had come to view code-switching as evidence of a speaker's communicative competence. Regular code-switching occurs only when individuals have a firm grasp of the structure of multiple speech patterns and of the contexts in which they should be spoken.

C. Read each statement. Then set a timer on your device for 60 seconds. Scan the passage to complete the reasons why speakers may choose to code-switch.

1. fit in with ....

2. be accepted in a ....

3. convey something in ....

4. discuss .... topics such as sex

D. Work with a partner. Answer the questions about previewing and scanning.

1. Was your prediction in Part A correct? If not, what information did you need in order to form a correct prediction?

2. How many questions did you answer correctly in Parts B and C?

3. Which scanning techniques from page 11 did you use?

4. Were you able to finish the exercises in the given time limit? If not, what can you do to improve your ability to scan quickly and accurately?

VOCABULARY CHECK

A. Review the vocabulary items in the Vocabulary Preview. Write their definitions and add examples. Use a dictionary if necessary.

B. Match the vocabulary items in bold with their meanings.

.... 1. In a normal conversation, people **alternate** between speaking and listening.

.... 2. People of all ages may use special words and phrases in order to **fit in** with their social group.

.... 3. Very young children become frustrated when they are unable to **convey** what they want using words.

.... 4. Almost every culture has **taboo** words. Often these are related to religion or family relationships.

.... 5. The speaker's **utterance** was so shocking that the room became instantly quiet.

.... 6. The report was written using **substandard** grammar and had to be rewritten.

.... 7. The multinational company is looking to hire people with **competence** in several languages.

.... 8. After I explained the problem, my boss had an immediate **grasp** of what needed to be done.

a. be accepted

b. switch

c. express or say

d. spoken word or phrase

e. less than average or acceptable

f. forbidden

g. ability to do something well

h. understanding

> Go to MyEnglishLab to complete a vocabulary exercise and skill practice, and to join in collaborative activities.

INTEGRATED SKILLS

ANNOTATING

WHY IT'S USEFUL Annotating a text can help you to identify and remember key points in a reading, make connections between course readings and lectures, and note information you may wish to reference in exams or writing assignments.

You will likely be asked to read a lot of texts for your classes. The amount—and often the density—of reading material can be challenging, and a crucial part of the academic experience is being able to understand and synthesize the information you read as efficiently as possible. Annotating is one way to help you do this.

Annotating means marking key information in a text. It is an active reading strategy that can help you to understand and recall reading content more deeply. It can also help you make connections between readings, classroom discussions, and writing assignments. Annotating can take two forms: in-text markings and margin notes. (If you are reading an e-book, try using reader software that includes an annotation function.)

- *In-text marking* is underlining, circling, highlighting, and inserting asterisks, numbers, arrows, or other marks to make important information stand out and to show connections between key points. It is useful to work out your own annotation system and use it as consistently as possible. For

> **TIP**
>
> Be careful about highlighting! Highlighting is a useful annotating strategy, but it loses its effectiveness if you overuse it. If you cover a page with a sea of yellow highlighting, you have no way of determining what is most important when you review your notes later. In general, try to reserve highlighting for only the most important words, ideas, and concepts. Do not highlight entire paragraphs or sections of a text.

  example, you might want to make a habit of highlighting main ideas, numbering supporting details such as reasons, and circling key concepts.

- *Margin notes* are a second method of annotating. You can use the margins—the white spaces on the sides of a page of text—to paraphrase, summarize, or outline key points in the text, write questions or reminders to yourself, or respond to the content. To save time and use less space, try to create your own system of abbreviations and symbols for annotating.

Now look at an annotated paragraph, excerpted from the upcoming reading "Language, Thought, and Identity." Observe how and what the student annotated. Think about these questions.

- What information did the student highlight, underline, and circle?
- What is the purpose of each annotation in the margins?
- What abbreviations and symbols does the student use?

3 Neo-Whorfian linguists continue to explore the intersection of language and cognition, but with a balanced approach. While accepting some aspects of Whorf's hypothesis, they concede it may be too extreme. They argue that language most likely has a (measurable) influence on worldview, and that this possibility is convincing enough to make linguistic relativity worthy of further consideration. Recent empirical neo-Whorfian studies have involved questioning speakers of different languages on notions such as time, color, and direction to uncover possible differences in perception. These studies reveal subtle distinctions among language groups. A classic example is color perception. Color is a gradation, and distinctions between colors vary from language to language. Russians, for instance, have different words for light blue and dark blue and were quicker on experimental perception tasks to distinguish between the shades of blue than English speakers, who have only one word for blue.

Margin notes:

neo-Whorfian linguists:
- Balanced approach
- Whorf too extreme
- Say lg. has infl. on wldview

(how much?)

Ex: color percep
Source? When done?
Ask Prof. Baker

Not true! Royal, aqua, navy, etc.

In the example above, the student annotated the text as follows:

- She highlighted the two main topics of the paragraph: *Neo-Whorfian linguists* and *neo-Whorfian studies*.

- She underlined key information concerning each of these topics.

- She circled the word *measurable* and wrote the question *how much?* in the margin, possibly as a reminder to ask about this later.

- In the right margin, she summarized the key points regarding neo-Whorfian linguists in her own words.

- She noted the example of the study on color perception as well as her questions about it—Who did it? When?—and wrote herself a reminder to ask her professor about it.

- Finally, she noted her disagreement with the author's statement that English has only one word for the color blue and gave examples to contradict this claim.

VOCABULARY PREVIEW

The following vocabulary items appear in the reading. Circle the ones you know. Put a question mark next to the ones you do not know.

concede	conduct (v)	diversity	empirical
intersection	measurable	perception	superiority

EXERCISE 4

A. Read the first paragraph of the passage and annotate it according to the instructions that follow. Then compare annotations with a partner.

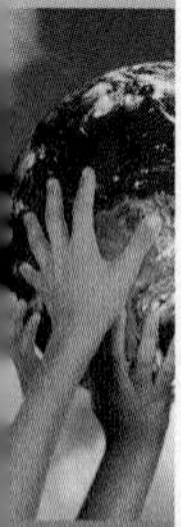

Language, Thought, and Identity

1   The question of how language relates to identity and cognition has long been the subject of study and speculation in many cultures. In Western scholarship, philosophers in the Golden Age of Greece in 500 BCE discussed the origin and function of language. Aristotle, the father of logic in philosophy, called language a representation of thought. The opposite of that theory—that thought is a representation of language—is a more recent idea about the way language works. This concept, known as *linguistic relativity*, holds that an individual's particular language shapes the way the person perceives the world, much like viewing the world through a pair of colored glasses. Linguistic relativity is also called the *Sapir-Whorf hypothesis* after scholars Edward Sapir and Benjamin Lee Whorf, who are credited with forming the theory in the early 20th century.

[margin annotations:]
500 BCE: Aristotle – thought > lang.

20th c.: _____ _____ _____

1. What main question does the passage address? Underline or highlight it, or use another technique you prefer.

2. The passage explains two views about the relationship between thought and language. Choose a way of annotating the key words of each view within the text. Use the same method for both views. This indicates that the ideas are related.

3. Circle or use another annotation to mark the key word in Sentence 4 that shows the relationship between the two views.

4. Fill in the summary of the key information from Sentences 2 and 3 in the right margin. Use your own words, abbreviations, and symbols.

5. Draw an arrow to connect *linguistic relativity* with another term that has the same meaning.

6. In the margin, place question marks next to words you don't understand or concepts you want to look up later.

7. Write one margin note in response to the content. For example, you can ask a question or express your opinion. Be sure to use abbreviations and symbols.

B. Read the rest of the essay. Make annotations to Paragraphs 2, 4, and 5, both in the text and in the margins. (Paragraph 3 is already annotated in the introduction to this section.)

Language, Thought, and Identity, *continued*

2 While the Sapir-Whorf hypothesis grew in the mid-20th century, the foundations were laid by much older European scholars, such as philosopher Johann von Herder, who in the 1700s speculated that language contributes to identity-shaping in individuals. Around the same time, philosopher Wilhelm von Humboldt wrote that different languages do not possess "a diversity of signs and sounds but a diversity of views of the world." Sapir, and later Whorf, expanded on these early theories about the shaping of thought by language. Sapir, who was a student of the famous anthropologist Franz Boas, wrote extensively on culture and language. Sapir argued that languages are a "guide" to culture and that they influence the social reality in which the speakers live. Whorf, inspired by Sapir, went a step further and argued that one's view of the world is largely, if not entirely, shaped by language.

3 Neo-Whorfian linguists continue to explore the intersection of language and cognition but with a balanced approach. While accepting some aspects of Whorf's hypothesis, they concede it may be too extreme. They argue that language most likely has a measurable influence on worldview, and that this possibility is convincing enough to make linguistic relativity worthy of further consideration. Recent empirical neo-Whorfian studies have involved questioning speakers of different languages on notions such as time, color, and direction to uncover possible differences in perception. These studies reveal subtle distinctions among language groups. A classic example is color perception. Color is a gradation, and distinctions between

(Continued)

Glossary

Gradation: a gradual progression from one color to another

colors vary from language to language. Russians, for instance, have different words for light blue and dark blue and were quicker on experimental perception tasks to distinguish between the shades of blue than English speakers, who have only one word for the color.

4   Other linguists reject linguistic relativity completely. These critics argue that distinctions in thought about word categories like color, direction, and shape are modest, and they are not enough to support the belief that speakers of different languages have different worldviews. Critics also argue that the belief that language shapes thought can be harmful if taken to an extreme. In the past, the Sapir-Whorf hypothesis was used to justify the superiority or inferiority of some languages and, by extension, of the people who spoke them. For example, it was assumed that people who lacked words for certain mathematical concepts were incapable of performing mathematical functions. Seeking out differences in languages and cultures can lead to inaccurate assumptions about people. Thus many linguists today regard the Sapir-Whorf hypothesis with caution.

5   Nevertheless, the question of whether the world looks different depending on the language a person speaks is one that will likely remain a matter of debate and speculation. The arguments of the early 20th century on linguistic relativity have come a long way since the days of Whorf. Modern linguists who explore the influence of language on thought conduct interdisciplinary language experiments that cut across the fields of linguistics, psychology, and anthropology, and the results continue to raise fascinating questions about the interaction between language and thought.

CULTURE NOTE

Benjamin Lee Whorf (1897–1941) was an American linguist best known for the Sapir-Whorf hypothesis and his ideas about linguistic relativity. However, Whorf did not start out as a linguist. Instead, he was educated as a chemical engineer and worked as a fire prevention engineer for most of his career. Whorf became interested in linguistics later on and eventually studied at Yale University with his mentor, Edwin Sapir. Whorf continued to work as a fire inspector even as he gained recognition as a linguist. He did field work on Native American languages in the United States and Mexico and published works on the findings from that research.

C. Use your notes from Parts A and B to match the thinkers with their views about language and thought. Some items have more than one correct answer.

Thinker	View
.... 1. Aristotle	a. Language helps shape identity.
	b. Language influences our social reality.
.... 2. von Herder	c. The view that language shapes thought may be harmful if used to justify the view that speakers of some languages are superior to others.
.... 3. von Humboldt	
.... 4. Sapir	d. Different languages possess a diversity of views of the world.
.... 5. Whorf	e. Language is a representation of thought.
.... 6. Neo-Whorfian linguists	f. Language has a measurable (not total) influence on our worldview.
.... 7. Critics of Whorfianism	g. One's view of the world is entirely shaped by language.

D. Work with a partner. Answer the questions about annotating.

1. Check your answers to Part C. Were you able to use your notes to answer the questions correctly? If not, what information was missing from your notes?

2. Did you write questions to yourself in the margins? If so, ask your partner to answer them.

3. Which did you use more—in-text notes or margin notes? Why?

VOCABULARY CHECK

A. Review the vocabulary items in the Vocabulary Preview. Write their definitions and add examples. Use a dictionary if necessary.

B. Complete each sentence using the correct vocabulary item from the box. Use the correct form.

concede	conduct (v)	diversity	empirical
intersection	measurable	perception	superiority

1. For generations scholars have been arguing about the .... of one language-teaching method over another.

2. The study concerned learners' .... of second-language sounds that did not exist in their first language.

3. There is a .... difference in the number of words that children at different ages can understand.

4. The professors have a .... of opinions regarding the relationship between speech and cognition.

5. There is now a large body of .... evidence about the most efficient ways to learn and remember new vocabulary.

6. The linguistics department will .... a survey about the number of languages spoken on campus.

7. The field of neurolinguistics is concerned with the .... between language and the structure and function of the brain.

8. Considering the students' poor performance on the latest exam, the instructor had to .... that his teaching method was not working and it was time to try something new.

⊙ Go to MyEnglishLab to complete skill practices.

LANGUAGE SKILL

UNDERSTANDING PRO-FORMS

WHY IT'S USEFUL Pro-forms, which include pronouns and other substitutions, are an essential part of cohesive writing. Writers use them to avoid repeating words and expressions. Understanding pro-forms will aid your reading comprehension and help you to read more quickly.

● Go to MyEnglishLab for the Language Skill presentation and practice.

VOCABULARY STRATEGY

CHOOSING AND WRITING VOCABULARY TO LEARN

WHY IT'S USEFUL In your English classes there is not enough time to study all the words you will need in order to read university texts fluently. By applying strategies for selecting and writing new vocabulary to learn on your own, you can expand your vocabulary more quickly and efficiently. A larger vocabulary will help you read with more speed and better comprehension.

It can take months or even years of study to learn enough English vocabulary items (words, phrases, idioms, and common collocations) to be able to read the texts that your university instructors assign. Two active learning strategies can speed up the process: Choosing "useful" items to learn and devising a system for recording the new items so that you can study and review them later.

> **TIP**
>
> According to vocabulary experts, readers of English need a vocabulary of 8,000–9,000 word families for near-perfect comprehension and a minimum of 4,000–5,000 words for successful university reading. Students at the B2 level typically have a vocabulary range of 3,250–3,750 word families.

Choosing "Useful" Items to Learn

Most vocabulary items are "useful" to some learners in some contexts. How can you decide which ones are most useful to you in your study of English? The following tips may help.

- In a text you are reading, choose items from the title, introduction, or topic sentences, or choose items that repeat throughout the text. These items are probably related to the main idea and are likely to be worth learning.

- Choose high-frequency items. A number of online tools exist to help you do this. One common tool, called a *vocabulary profiler*, sorts the words in a text into lists consisting of the most common

> **TIP**
>
> The Academic Word List (AWL) is a list of the 570 word families found most frequently in English academic texts. The list is divided into 10 sublists, organized in decreasing order of frequency. Sublist 1, for example, contains the 60 words used most frequently in academic writing.

1,000 words in English, the most common 2,000 words, words from the Academic Word List, and "off-list" words, that is, words that occur too rarely to appear on any list (and may therefore not be worth learning immediately).

- Use an online dictionary that includes word-frequency information. For example, some dictionaries indicate the frequency of an item using one, two, or three stars. A one-star (low-frequency) item may not be useful for you to learn at this time.

- Try skipping over an unfamiliar vocabulary item in a text. If you can understand the text without that item, it may not be useful to you at this time.

Writing New Vocabulary Items

There is no "right" or "wrong" way to record new vocabulary items. Some students enjoy making paper notecards or writing new words in a paper journal. Other students prefer a spreadsheet or other electronic recording system. Moreover, the information you include for each new item can differ from item to item and from student to student. For example, some students like to include a translation of the item into their first language.

A typical notecard or journal entry might look like this:

target word, part of speech	**evolution (n.)**
definition	process of change over a very long period of time
context	"Dialects, like languages, are in a constant state of **evolution**."
original sentence	The field of historical linguistics deals with the <u>evolution</u> of languages over time.

EXERCISE 5

A. Read the excerpt from "What Is a Dialect?" on page 8. Ten items are highlighted. Using the strategies for choosing "useful" vocabulary on page 23, choose the five words that would be the most useful to write and learn if you did not know them.

Dialects usually evolve as a consequence of geographic or sociocultural factors. Speech varieties associated with geographical locations are known as *regional dialects*. These can be local, such as the American English dialects of eastern New England and western New England, or broader, such as American English and South African English in general. *Social dialects*, on the other hand, are often determined by factors such as an individual's race, education, gender, and age though the distinctions between social divisions and regional divisions are sometimes blurred.

A well-known example of a social dialect, also termed a *sociolect*, is the variety of upper-class English taught in British public schools. Nicknamed the "Queen's English" or "BBC English" after the speaking standard once required of announcers on the country's famous radio broadcasting service, this variety has traditionally been regarded as the only "correct" dialect of English. Every dialect, like every language, contains its own regularities, patterns, and complexities, yet judgments of correctness tend to stem from the social status of its speakers rather than right or wrong speech.

....

B. Work with a partner. Share your answers from Part A. Explain why you chose the words you listed.

C. Write the five words you selected in Part A on notecards or in a journal, spreadsheet, etc. Include the definition, original context, example sentence, and a translation if you like.

APPLY YOUR SKILLS

WHY IT'S USEFUL By applying the skills you have learned in this unit, you can gain a better understanding of this challenging reading about a unique American dialect.

BEFORE YOU READ

A. Discuss these questions with a partner or group.

1. What is your experience talking to people who speak different dialects of English? Do you find some dialects easier to understand than others?

2. Do you think geography has an effect on the development of dialects? Consider geographic features such as mountain ranges or islands.

3. Are you aware of any disappearing languages or dialects? In your opinion, how significant is this loss? Who or what does it affect?

B. You will read a passage about a dialect known as the Ocracoke brogue. As you read, think about these questions.

1. What are examples of how the Ocracoke dialect is distinctive, compared to other dialects in the United States?

2. What is the dialect's relationship to Shakespearean, or Elizabethan, English?

3. How have economic changes on Ocracoke Island affected the dialect?

4. Why does sociolinguist Walt Wolfram say that the brogue is a "non-American" dialect?

5. What are researchers doing as the dialect is changing and possibly dying out?

C. Review the Unit Skills Summary. As you read the passage, apply the skills you learned in this unit.

UNIT SKILLS SUMMARY

Read actively

• Use active reading strategies to understand a text more deeply.

Preview a text

• Use strategies before you read to activate prior knowledge and prepare to read.

Scan

• Read quickly to find specific information.

Annotate

• Highlight key information in text and margins to make connections and deepen your understanding.

Understand pro-forms

• Recognize words that replace nouns, verbs, adjectives, adverbs, or whole sentences or paragraphs.

Choose and write new vocabulary to learn

• Choose high frequency words and record them for later study.

READ

A. Read the magazine article. Annotate and take notes on the answers to the questions in Before You Read, Part B.

The Ocracoke Brogue

1 It might be called "high tide" on most shores, but on Ocracoke Island in North Carolina's Outer Banks, it's "hoi toide." Ocracoke was largely isolated for centuries, making it a perfect incubator for distinctive speech patterns. The result is a dialect altogether different from mainland speech. Ocracoke's unique variety of English, known as "hoi toider speech," "the brogue," or "Banker speech," is sometimes mistaken for British English. According to folk legend, the dialect is a living form of the English spoken during Shakespeare's time. Linguists generally dismiss this notion, however. They stress that while Ocracoke has preserved some older features of English,

Glossary

Banker speech: a term derived from the location of Ocracoke in the Outer Banks, which are a chain of islands extending along the coast of North Carolina

Folk legend: stories or beliefs regarded as true and passed down from generation to generation

the language has changed considerably over the centuries. And the most dramatic changes are happening today, as the island is now easily accessible to outsiders—*dingbatters*, as locals call them. Contact with outsiders has led younger Ocracoke residents to speak a much "weaker" version of the dialect. Hoi toider speech is, like many endangered dialects and languages, drifting into the past.

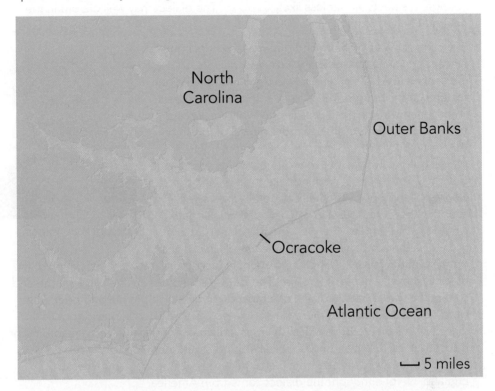

2 Many coastal-island communities like Ocracoke have formed distinct patterns of speech because of their remoteness. Historically, island residents almost never interacted with anyone beyond their own shores. Ocracoke Island, which was settled in the early 1700s, was relatively isolated for more than 200 years. Language change among islanders was inevitable, but it took a different path than might have occurred if outsiders had been involved. This unusual environment for language development—on Ocracoke and in similar isolated areas—appeals to linguists. Many are eager to study what happens in such special circumstances. But, in the brogue's case, they have to act fast if they hope to capture enough of the language to study it. The once-remote island, which boasts picturesque beaches, transformed into a tourist destination in the late 20th century. Cars, ferries, and tourists broke the hermetic seal on Ocracoke's one village decades ago, and the language pattern has changed as a result. The island's economy, which in the past relied almost entirely on fishing, is now fueled by income from tourists.

(Continued)

Outsiders speaking mainstream North American English have come to the island, and villagers have increasingly visited the mainland and picked up new language forms. Electronic media have also played a significant role in connecting Ocracoke with the outside. Although many older residents still speak the Ocracoke brogue, younger residents are far less likely to do so. The dialect may well die out in the next generation or two.

3   Sociolinguist Walt Wolfram and other researchers from North Carolina State University have interviewed Ocracoke's residents extensively to document the unique features of the brogue. The dialect is considered to be a "non-American" dialect, according to Wolfram, because the speech patterns are much more typical of British or Australian English. For example, a prominent hoi toide pronunciation involves the vowel in the words *caught* and *bought*. In the brogue, it sounds like the vowel in the words *put* and *book*. Another example is the vowel sound in the word *house*. Whereas most mainlanders would say the word as "hOWs," the traditional Ocracoke pronunciation is a combination of the vowels in *but* and

Linguist Walt Wolfram

boot, something like "hUH-OOs." And of course, there is the pronunciation of the dialect's informal name, *hoi toider*. The *i* vowel sound has an "ee" glide at the end so that the whole vowel is like a combination of the vowels in *but* and *beet*. The word *tide* actually sounds more like "tUH-eed." The most telling evidence of the dialect's similarity to British English emerged when a linguist played a recording of the brogue to 15 British-English speakers and asked them to identify the dialect's origin. The answers ranged from Derbyshire to East Anglia to southwestern England. No one thought the dialect came from America.

4   There is some evidence to support the notion that the Ocracoke dialect has its origins in Shakespearean (also called *Elizabethan*) English. The Ocracoke word *mommuck*, ("harassing") is thought to date back to Shakespeare, though in Shakespearian times it meant "to tear apart." The brogue word *quamish*, which means "queasy," is another fossil preserved in modern island speech. Wolfram's research shows that Elizabethan English may have been spoken by Ocracoke's original settlers, but the dialect has changed too much over time to be considered a modern-day variety of true Elizabethan English.

5　Endangered dialects typically do not have the same status as endangered languages. Not as many researchers are rushing to document dying dialects as dying languages. However, Wolfram argues that dialects reveal important distinctions that help us understand language variability. The Ocracoke dialect is unusual enough to deserve the same protections as an endangered language, he claims. Equally important, many of the island's significant cultural traditions are reflected in the Ocracoke dialect. If the dialect dies, a crucial window on the island's culture will close as well.

6　Hoi toide speech may be disappearing, but unlike other, less-fortunate dialects, it is attracting researchers who are documenting its features. Thanks to Wolfram and others like him, young Ocracoke residents and those of future generations will have the opportunity to hear their ancestors' speech in recordings and learn about their linguistic history. Some of the dialect's unusual features may even continue on in the speech of younger islanders. The isolation of the past cannot be regained, but some of the old ways may still be hinted at in the brogue of the future.

B. Work with a partner. Use your annotations to discuss the answers to the questions in Before You Read, Part B. Are there any questions you cannot answer? Which of the other reading skills you have learned in this unit could help you answer them?

◯ Go to MyEnglishLab to read the passage again and answer critical thinking questions.

THINKING CRITICALLY

Discuss the questions with another student.

1. How does the writer of the article feel about the need to preserve the Ocracoke dialect? How do you know?

2. How are folk legends different from scientific study?

3. Do you believe there will be any speakers of the Ocracoke dialect two generations from now? What evidence from the reading supports your point of view?

THINKING VISUALLY

A. Study the map. Then answer the questions with a partner.

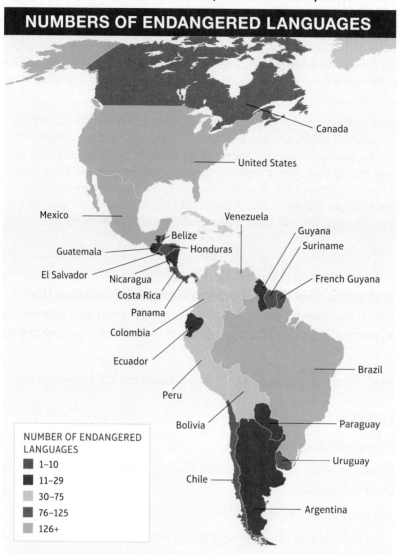

NUMBERS OF ENDANGERED LANGUAGES

NUMBER OF ENDANGERED LANGUAGES
- 1–10
- 11–29
- 30–75
- 76–125
- 126+

1. Fill in the chart with examples of countries in each column, based on the information in the map.

Number of Endangered Languages by Country				
1–10	11–29	30–75	76–125	126+

2. What might account for the different numbers of endangered languages in different countries? Consider the roles of geography, history, and population.

B. Choose a different country or geographic region. Do an Internet search on the number of endangered languages in that region. Create a map or chart like the ones above and give a report about your findings to your partner or group. If possible, include the following in your report:

- The number of endangered languages in your chosen country or area
- Examples of disappearing languages
- Possible reasons why the languages are disappearing

THINKING ABOUT LANGUAGE

Read the excerpts containing underlined pro-forms. Then write the word or words that the pro-forms replace.

1. It might be called "high tide" on most shores, but on Ocracoke Island in North Carolina's Outer Banks, it's "hoi toide." Ocracoke was largely isolated for centuries, making <u>it</u> a perfect incubator for distinctive speech patterns.

2. According to folk legend, the dialect is a living form of the English spoken during Shakespeare's time. Linguists generally dismiss <u>this notion</u>, however.

3. The most dramatic changes are happening today, as the island is now easily accessible to outsiders—*dingbatters*, as locals call <u>them</u>.

4. Ocracoke Island, which was settled in the early 1700s, was relatively isolated for more than 200 years. Language change among islanders was inevitable, but it took a different path than might have occurred if outsiders had been involved. <u>This unusual environment</u> for language development—on Ocracoke and in similar isolated areas—appeals to linguists.

5. <u>Many</u> are eager to study what happens in such special circumstances.

6. Although many older residents still speak the Ocracoke brogue, younger residents are far less likely to <u>do so</u>. The dialect may well die out in the next generation or two.

▶ **Go to** MyEnglishLab **to watch Professor Podesva's concluding video and to complete a self-assessment.**

How cultural and ethical values define a successful business

Main Ideas and Supporting Details

UNIT PROFILE

In this unit, you will consider the subject of ethics, specifically business ethics. Reading topics include an introduction to business ethics and the crime of fraud, the causes of fraudulent behavior, the benefits of building ethical companies, and ways to prevent fraud and promote ethics in the workplace. You will also read about the causes and effects of the economic decline known as the Great Recession of 2007–2009.

Preview the reading "The Role of Investment Banks in the Great Recession" on page 55.
Skim (read quickly) the reading. What are the main ideas? What are some details that support these main ideas?

For more about **BUSINESS ETHICS**, see ❷ ❸. See also Ⓦ and OC
BUSINESS ETHICS ❶ ❷ ❸.

OUTCOMES

• Identify main ideas
• Identify supporting details
• Outline a text
• Simplify complex sentences
• Use word parts to analyze meaning

GETTING STARTED

Go to MyEnglishLab to watch Dr. McLennan's introductory video and to complete a self-assessment.

Discuss these questions with a partner or group.

1. What do you know about the general subject of business ethics?

2. What is *fraud* and how can it be prevented?

3. In his introduction, Dr. McLennan talks about possible causes of the 2008 financial crisis. What causes does he mention? What does he mean when he says "in many ways we haven't gotten to the bottom of the total cause"?

FUNDAMENTAL SKILL

IDENTIFYING MAIN IDEAS AND SUPPORTING DETAILS

WHY IT'S USEFUL Identifying the topic, main ideas, and supporting details can help you to focus on the key points in a text and the evidence that supports those points. This can help you to comprehend better as you read, analyze the writer's ideas and arguments, and organize the information from a reading for taking notes and completing academic assignments.

Academic writing is usually organized around a single **topic**, or the main subject that the text is about. You can often locate the topic of a text by reading the title and the opening sentences and asking yourself the question "Who or what is the text about?" The **main idea** of a paragraph or passage is the writer's main comment or key message about the topic.

In addition, academic texts are organized into paragraphs, each of which contains a main idea and **supporting details**—specific pieces of information that the writer includes in order to describe, explain, prove, or support the main idea.

Identifying the topic, main ideas, and supporting details is essential for understanding the key content and relationships between ideas in a text. Recognizing these elements will help you to take well-organized notes that you can use for later study and review. It will also help you to prepare summaries, research papers, presentations, and other academic assignments that require you to report the key ideas found in texts.

> **TIP**
>
> Identifying the topic, main ideas, and supporting details begins with previewing a text. If you are reading a chapter in a textbook, it is useful to read the chapter title, introduction, and summary at the end of the chapter to predict the topic and main ideas and consider what you already know about the chapter contents. Headings, subheadings, and text in bold or italics can help you to identify main ideas and supporting details. These organizational features can also help you to organize your notes.

This unit breaks **identifying main ideas and supporting details** down into two supporting skills:

- identifying main ideas
- identifying supporting details

EXERCISE 1

A. Discuss the questions with a partner before you read.

1. How would you define *ethics*? What is an example of ethical behavior?

2. Why are ethics important in business?

B. Preview the excerpt from a business textbook. Predict the topic, main idea of the text, and main ideas of each paragraph. Then read the passage quickly. Underline one sentence in each paragraph that best expresses the main idea. (Note: The main idea may not be the first sentence of a paragraph.)

Introduction to Ethics

1 *In our daily lives, we are often faced with ethical choices. Imagine, for example, that you are a student and that you need a high grade on a test to pass a class. If you have the opportunity to copy someone else's work— which would guarantee a high grade—do you take it, or do you refuse it? Would cheating be fair to the other students who did their own work? Similarly, if you are in sales and you find a defect in a product, do you tell your manager or the public, or do you continue to sell the product even though it could harm those who use it? These are all questions that have to do with ethics, which is, at its core, about personal decisions. The study of ethics explores what is fair and unfair and what is morally acceptable and unacceptable.*

Business Ethics

2 The examination of ethical decisions in a business context is known as *business ethics*. Just as our personal ethics are determined by our everyday decisions, business ethics are determined by the decisions of the individuals who work in the business. Clearly, those at the top—business owners and executives—make the most important decisions that reflect a company's morals and values. In addition, through their decisions, business leaders determine the moral atmosphere of a company, which influences the ethical decision making of employees throughout an organization.

3 Business ethics are especially important because business decisions often affect not only a company and its employees but also customers, society, and the environment. If, for instance, a business manager decides to dispose of factory waste illegally in order to save money, that decision could have repercussions for many others. It could lead to legal problems for the manager and the company, and it could cause employees to lose their jobs, retirement savings, and health care. Customers may have problems buying the product. Investors could lose money, and the local economy and environment could be damaged. These are examples of local problems that can result from poor ethical choices. However, when large corporations make questionable decisions, the effects can be felt across the globe. The market collapse and financial crisis of 2007–2009, for example, which was brought about by ethics violations in some of the largest financial institutions in the United States, is an example of how poor ethical business choices have implications well beyond a business.

> **CULTURE NOTE**
>
> The financial crisis in the United States began with the collapse of the real estate market in mid-2007. The collapse was followed by the Great Recession, a period of economic decline that lasted until roughly 2011. The recession is considered by many economists to be the worst financial crisis since the Great Depression of the 1930s. It caused severe reductions in economic production and investment and high levels of unemployment in many countries across the globe.

C. Read the passage again. Then read the statements and write *T* (True) or *F* (False). Correct the false statements. Then compare answers with a partner.

.... 1. Deciding whether or not to cheat on an exam is an example of an ethical choice.

.... 2. The study of ethics focuses on teaching people to do what is right.

.... 3. Business ethics are determined by a company's rules and policies.

.... 4. The repercussions of business decisions usually stay within an organization.

.... 5. The decisions made at large corporations can have global effects.

.... 6. The financial crisis of 2007–2009 was caused by poor ethical decisions at large financial institutions.

D. Answer the questions. Refer to the passage as needed. Then discuss your answers with a partner.

1. Look again at your answers in Part A. Did your responses match what you learned in the reading?

2. How did you determine the topic of the text? The main idea in each paragraph? In other words, what approach or clues helped you to recognize the topic and main ideas?

3. Notice where the main idea appears in each paragraph. Why does it appear in different places in each paragraph? What is the purpose of the other sentences that lead up to or follow the main idea?

4. What types of supporting information—such as facts, reasons, or examples— support the main ideas? What language is used to signal supporting information?

VOCABULARY CHECK

A. Review the vocabulary items in the Vocabulary Preview. Write their definitions and add examples. Use a dictionary if necessary.

B. Complete each sentence using the correct vocabulary item from the box. Use the correct form.

bring about	collapse (n)	defect (n)	executive
implication	repercussion	retirement	violation

1. A CEO, or chief .... officer, holds the highest position in a company and is responsible for managing its overall operations.

2. A profit-sharing plan is a type of savings plan in which a company contributes some of its profits to help its employees save for .... After employees reach the age of 59½ and stop working, they can collect the money that was saved for them.

3. The stock market crash of 1929 contributed to an economic .... known as the Great Depression. By 1933, more than 20 percent of Americans were unemployed, and almost half of American banks had failed.

4. Although the company president spoke politely and did not raise his voice, the .... of his remarks was that he was not pleased with the company's performance in the previous year.

5. The car manufacturer had to recall thousands of cars after a .... was discovered in the air bags.

6. Workplace safety .... can cause serious problems. Not following established safety procedures can create a dangerous work environment and result in injury.

7. Employees should not face .... for reporting unethical behavior in the workplace, yet employees often fear they will be punished or lose their jobs if they speak up.

8. If company leaders want to .... positive change in the behavior of its employees, it needs to create ethical work environments and make decisions that encourage ethical behavior.

🔵 Go to MyEnglishLab to complete a vocabulary exercise and skill practice, and to join in collaborative activities.

SUPPORTING SKILL 1
IDENTIFYING MAIN IDEAS

WHY IT'S USEFUL Identifying the main ideas can help you to understand the most important points that a writer is making about a topic.

The **main idea** is the central or most important idea that a writer is expressing in a piece of writing. To determine the main idea of a text, first identify the topic (what the passage is about). Then ask yourself, "What is the writer's main point or main comment concerning the topic?" The answer will probably provide the main idea. In academic texts, the main idea is often found in the introduction and repeated in the conclusion. Titles, headings, and subheadings may also provide clues.

In addition, each paragraph within a text usually contains one main idea that expresses the writer's central point about the topic of the paragraph. Though main ideas often appear near the beginning of a paragraph, they can also appear in the middle or end. When looking for main ideas, it is helpful to look for key words that appear in the title or heading, or are in bold or italics. Main ideas can also be signaled by certain words such as *therefore*, *so*, *as a result*, *finally*, *essentially*, *basically*, or *mainly*.

The following vocabulary items appear in the reading. Circle the ones you know. Put a question mark next to the ones you do not know.

primary	promoted	single-minded	suppliers
substantial	initiatives	targeted	inclusive

EXERCISE 2

A. Preview the excerpt from a business textbook. Read the title and skim the introduction. Notice the words that appear in italics. With a partner, predict the topic and main idea of the text.

Theories of Corporate Governance

1 Corporate governance is the system of rules, policies, and processes that a corporation follows in order to meet its responsibilities. Since the 1980s, most corporations have followed a model of governance based on *shareholder theory*, or stockholder theory, which states that a company's primary responsibility is to increase earnings for its shareholders, the people who own shares of stock in a company. The economist Milton Friedman famously promoted this theory in the 1970s, when he argued that a corporation's only social responsibility is to increase profits. Though shareholder theory has been the dominant business model since the 1980s, its single-minded focus on profits has come under increasing criticism. As a result, other models of corporate governance that seek to consider the interests of those affected by a business have gained in popularity in recent years.

Hauptversammlu
01. Juni 2017

Shareholder meeting

2 One such model is *stakeholder theory*, which developed in the 1980s from the writings of business ethicist R. Edward Freeman. Stakeholder theory says that a business must consider the interests not just of shareholders but of all of a company's stakeholders. Stakeholders include anyone who affects or is affected by a company, including employees, suppliers, customers, members of the community, and even the natural environment. For example, imagine that a company has decided it could save a substantial amount of money by moving its manufacturing from its current location to another country. According to Friedman's shareholder theory, the company should move the factory, since that would allow it to increase profits. Stakeholder theory, on the other hand, would argue that the company has an obligation to its employees and the surrounding community. This may mean keeping the factory where it is, retraining the employees, or helping the community attract a new industry, even if doing so would reduce it profits.

3 A third model of corporate governance is known as *corporate social responsibility*, or CSR, which says a company should seek not only to make a profit but also to make a positive impact on the community and the environment. Google, Inc., for example, has a number of initiatives that are targeted to help the environment. Google is also trying to make a more inclusive workplace for women and minorities, and it releases statistics about its workplace diversity. Today, more consumers and investors demand such initiatives from businesses, and as a result, CSR is a trend that has increased considerably in the last decade.

B. Now read the passage and underline the sentence that expresses the main idea of the passage. Then underline one sentence in each paragraph that best expresses the main idea of each paragraph.

C. Read the passage again. Complete each statement. Use the words and phrases in the box. Then compare answers with a partner.

corporate governance	corporate social responsibility	inclusive
profits	shareholder theory	stakeholder theory

1. The system of rules, policies, and processes that a corporation follows in order to meet its responsibilities is called ....

2. .... is a theory of governance that states that a company's main responsibility is to increase profits.

3. A theory of governance that states that a company must consider the interests of anyone who affects or is affected by a company is called ....

4. According to stakeholder theory, a company has an obligation to its employees and the community, even if this reduces ....

5. A model of governance that states that a company should seek to make a positive impact on the community and the environment in addition to making a profit is called ....

6. One way that Google is trying to have a positive impact is by creating a more .... environment for women and minorities.

D. Work with a partner. Answer the questions about identifying main ideas.

1. Look again at your answers in Part A. Did your responses match what you learned in the reading?

2. How did you determine the topic, the main idea of the text, and the main idea of each paragraph? What clues helped you to identify them?

VOCABULARY CHECK

A. Review the vocabulary items in the Vocabulary Preview. Write their definitions and add examples. Use a dictionary if necessary.

B. Match the vocabulary items in bold with their meanings.

.... 1. The company Salesforce has hired an officer whose goal is to make the company more fair and **inclusive** of women and minorities.

.... 2. One environmental **initiative** at Google aims for the company to get all of its energy from renewable sources.

.... 3. The **primary** purpose of business ethics courses is to help future business leaders build responsible organizations.

.... 4. Many young business leaders **promote** corporate social responsibility as the best way to build ethical companies.

a. having one aim

b. make something have an effect on a limited group or area

c. large

d. open to everyone

e. a plan or program designed to improve a situation or address a problem

f. help something develop or become more popular

g. most important

h. a person or company that provides goods or services

5. Having a **single-minded** focus on increasing profits can often lead to ethics violations.

6. A **substantial** portion—more than half—of Internet searches are done on mobile devices.

7. Automobile manufacturers often rely on many **suppliers** to provide the parts needed to create their products.

8. One trend in product design and advertising is to **target** young people who are interested in buying "green" or environmentally friendly products

○ Go to MyEnglishLab to complete a vocabulary exercise and skill practice, and to join in collaborative activities.

SUPPORTING SKILL 2
IDENTIFYING SUPPORTING DETAILS

WHY IT'S USEFUL Identifying the supporting details will help you to better understand the main ideas of a text, analyze the evidence in support of the main ideas, and organize the information for taking notes and completing other academic assignments.

Supporting details are specific pieces of information that support main ideas. Writers provide different types of supporting details depending on the points they are making. They also use different words or phrases to signal statements of support.

Type of Supporting Detail	Purpose	Example Signals
Definition *"Internal fraud occurs when an employee commits fraud against his or her employer, such as by embezzling funds."*	Define new terms needed to understand ideas	This means … X is defined as … (See EARTH SCIENCE Part 1, page 66 for more information about recognizing definitions.)
Example *"For example, in 2005, former WorldCom CEO Bernie Ebbers was convicted of an $11 billion accounting fraud."*	Provide specific cases to clarify or illustrate an idea	For example, … For instance, … Take X … such as …

Type of Supporting Detail	Purpose	Example Signals
Fact *"Approximately 17,000 people lost jobs in what was, at the time, the largest bankruptcy in US history."*	Provide true, provable evidence to support an idea	According to … Studies show / indicate / find …
Reason *"According to shareholder theory, the company should move the factory, since it would allow it to increase profits."*	Provide reasons or causes to support ideas	because / since This is because … One reason is …
Quotation *"According to Brandon L. Garrett, a specialist in corporate crime at the University of Virginia Law School, 'More often than not, when the largest corporations are prosecuted federally, individuals aren't charged.'"*	Use the exact words of other writers or speakers to illustrate or support ideas	According to … , In the words of … As X says / suggests / explains, …

VOCABULARY PREVIEW

The following vocabulary items appear in the reading. Circle the ones you know. Put a question mark next to the ones you do not know.

commitment	consumption	dedicated	productivity
turnover	reputations	ultimately	staggering

EXERCISE 3

A. Preview the article about corporate social responsibility. Read the title, look at the photo, and skim the first paragraph. Then, with a partner, predict the main idea of the text.

Glossary

Absenteeism: the habit of being away from work or school

Through a lens (idiom): from a specific point of view

Social consciousness: awareness of important social issues

The Benefits of Corporate Social Responsibility

1 [1] Good or bad, corporations have an impact on society. [2] Today more corporations are creating business plans that demonstrate their commitment to making a positive impact on society or the environment through corporate social responsibility, or CSR, initiatives. [3] Socially responsible companies commit not only to the well-being of employees and other stakeholders, but also to the broader society, through such actions as donating to charities or community organizations, developing environmentally sustainable products, and reducing waste and energy consumption. [4] Critics argue that devoting a company's resources to social or environmental initiatives can take away from profits. [5] However, there are clear benefits for companies dedicated to making a positive social impact.

2 [6] To begin with, committing to CSR can help companies attract quality employees. [7] Surveys of young workers show that many are drawn to companies that are socially responsible. [8] A survey of 13- to 25-year-olds conducted by the Cone Millennial Cause group found that 80 percent want to work for a company that cares about how it impacts and contributes to society. [9] More than 50 percent said they would not work for a corporation that they felt was not socially responsible. [10] Moreover, engaging workers is essential to running a successful business. [11] A Gallup Organization study of 1.4 million employees found that companies with a high level of employee engagement, in which employees felt valued and connected to the organization, report higher productivity, as well as lower absenteeism, job turnover, and health and safety problems.

3 [12] There is also evidence that being socially responsible drives profitability. [13] Research shows that consumers are increasingly motivated to buy products from socially responsible companies. [14] In addition, companies who build ethical reputations attract investors, which ultimately leads to profits. [15] One example is Starbucks Corporation. [16] In 2008, Starbucks CEO Howard Schultz became determined to increase profits, but he recognized that "in order to do so and to do it well, we had to act through a lens of social consciousness." [17] As a result of continued ethical commitments to employees, suppliers, and the community, the company ranked #3 in *Fortune* magazine's 2017 list of World's Most Admired Companies, and it has been listed for ten years in a row as one of the world's most ethical companies by the Ethisphere Institute. [18] At the same time, stock shares jumped a staggering 1,200 percent from 2008 to 2015, demonstrating that social consciousness and increased profits can indeed go hand in hand.

B. Now read the passage. Then read the statements and write *T* (True) or *F* (False). Correct the false statements. Then compare answers with a partner.

.... 1. Corporate social responsibility means a company makes a commitment to having a positive impact on the lives of its shareholders.

.... 2. Reducing environmental waste and energy consumption is an example of a CSR initiative.

.... 3. According to one survey, more than half of young people would refuse to work for a company that is not profitable.

.... 4. Companies whose employees feel valued and connected see greater productivity.

.... 5. Investors are interested in companies with reputations for putting profits ahead of ethics.

.... 6. In 2008, Starbucks CEO Howard Schultz aimed to reduce spending while being socially responsible.

.... 7. In 2017, Starbucks was honored as one of the world's most profitable companies.

.... 8. From 2008 to 2015, Starbucks stock values increased by 1,200 percent.

C. Indicate the type(s) of supporting detail(s) found in the numbered sentences from the passage. Some sentences may include more than one type. Use these abbreviations: *D* (Definition), *E* (Example), *F* (Fact), *R* (Reason), or *Q* (Quote).

Sentence 2 ....   Sentence 15 ....

Sentence 3 ....   Sentence 16 ....

Sentence 8 ....   Sentence 17 ....

Sentence 13 ....

D. Work with a partner. Answer the questions about identifying supporting details.

1. Which signals from page 43 helped you to identify the supporting details?

2. Which type of supporting detail was most common in the passage? Why do you think the writer used these kinds of support in this text?

3. Where do the supporting details appear in each paragraph—the beginning, middle, or end? What types of sentences do they follow? How could recognizing main ideas help you to locate supporting details in a text?

VOCABULARY CHECK

A. Review the vocabulary items in the Vocabulary Preview. Write their definitions and add examples. Use a dictionary if necessary.

B. Complete each sentence using the correct vocabulary item from the box. Use the correct form.

commitment	consumption	dedicated	productivity
reputation	staggering	turnover	ultimately

1. In 2016, the banking industry had a .... rate of 18.1 percent, meaning about 18 percent of employees left their jobs and were replaced.

2. 3M Corporation has developed a .... as an ethical company because of the way it promotes ethical behavior and corporate responsibility.

3. B Corporations are for-profit companies that make a .... to ethical work practices in addition to social and environmental responsibility.

4. B Lab is the name of a nonprofit organization that is .... to building a community of companies that meet high ethical standards and make a positive social and environmental impact.

5. All of the employees in a company can affect a company's ethics, but its executives are .... responsible for creating an ethical work environment.

6. Patagonia is an American outdoor clothing company that has tried to limit unnecessary .... of resources and products through its "Don't Buy Our Jackets" advertising campaign.

7. Some studies show that having positive interactions with coworkers encourages .... Employees are likely to work harder when they feel connected to and valued by other employees in an organization.

8. CEO salaries have increased by over 900 percent since the 1970s. This .... increase has occurred over the same period that a typical worker's pay has risen by only about 10 percent.

◐ Go to MyEnglishLab to complete a vocabulary exercise and skill practice, and to join in collaborative activities.

INTEGRATED SKILLS

OUTLINING A TEXT

WHY IT'S USEFUL Outlining requires you to be an active reader and distinguish main ideas from details, helping you to better understand and remember what you have read. In addition, creating an outline provides you with a written study guide that you can use when completing assignments or studying for exams.

An **outline** is a type of graphic organizer that provides a framework for organizing and taking notes on the important content of a text. When you outline a text, you use indentation to show the relationship between ideas. Ideas that are more general are set further to the left. As information becomes more specific, it is indented to the right. A traditional outline uses a system of roman numerals (I, II, etc.), capital letters, and numbers to distinguish between the main ideas and supporting details in a text.

Read the excerpt from "What Is Fraud" and study the outline that follows. In this example, the main ideas of the text are indicated by roman numerals, the **major supporting details** are indicated by capital letters, and the **minor supporting details** are indicated by numbers. Major supporting details provide direct evidence for the main idea, while minor supporting details provide additional details, explanations, or examples that make an argument stronger or more vivid.

> In a business environment, intentionally lying or tricking someone for financial gain is a type of "white-collar crime" known as *fraud*. Internal fraud occurs when an employee commits fraud against his or her employer, such as by embezzling funds. External fraud is committed by those outside an organization, such as a vendor who bills a company for goods it didn't provide. Fraud against individuals includes crimes such as identity theft and Ponzi schemes—fraud in which criminals take money from new investors and use it to pay existing investors, rather than paying them from profits earned through actual investments.

What is fraud?

I. Fraud = type of "white-collar crime" = intentionally tricking or lying for financial gain

    A. Internal fraud = employee commits fraud against employer

        1. E.g., embezzling

    B. External Fraud = committed by someone outside an organization

        1. E.g., vendor bills for goods not provided

    C. Fraud against individuals

        1. identity theft

        2. Ponzi schemes = criminals take money from new investors to pay existing ones

When writing an outline, you can save space and reduce the amount of writing by following these tips for simplifying a text:

- Don't write complete sentences. Include only the key words.
- Use pronouns (*it, this, they, etc.*) to replace repeated words.
- Leave out transitions, expressions, and extra words (*a / an, one such, on the other hand*).
- Use abbreviations and symbols (*co., e.g., $*).

TIP

If you prefer a less formal outline, you can use graphic elements such as numbers, bullets, and hyphens to indicate main ideas and details. The key when outlining is to indent and to be consistent in the way you distinguish between main ideas, major supporting details, and minor supporting details.

VOCABULARY PREVIEW

The following vocabulary items appear in the reading. Circle the ones you know. Put a question mark next to the ones you do not know.

loyalties	principles	facilitating
prioritize	dilemma	be opposed to

EXERCISE 4

A. Skim the first part of a textbook chapter about ethical decision making. Notice the main ideas and supporting details. Then discuss the questions with a partner.

1. What are the four main topics in the reading? How would you indicate these in your outline?

2. What example is used throughout the reading to provide support? How will you indicate this example in each part your outline?

Potter's Box for Ethical Decision Making, Part 1

1 There are many questions that arise in the process of making an ethical decision. One useful guide for reasoning through this process is a theory known as "Potter's Box," named after ethicist Ralph Potter, who developed the theory in the 1960s when he was pondering his own ethical position on nuclear weapons. Potter organized his questions into four main categories: facts, loyalties, values, and principles of the issue. That is to say, solving an ethical problem using Potter's Box involves reasoning through the facts of the issue, considering the loyalties and values of the decision maker, and applying moral principles to the problem. All of the categories, or parts of the process, are equally important and interrelated. For this reason, the categories are often represented visually as a square—or a box—with each category in one quadrant of the box. Potter's Box is a useful tool for facilitating ethical decision making because it helps people to work through an issue and use clear reasoning.

FACTS	VALUES
PRINCIPLES	LOYALTIES

Figure 1: Potter's Box

2 The first category of Potter's Box involves looking at the *facts* of the situation. This is as simple as listing everything that is known about it. If, for example, a pharmaceutical company were selling a drug that might have negative side effects, the company would need to determine what actions to take, if any. In this case, the facts may include the cost of taking the drug off the market, the studies testing the safety of the drug, the potential good the drug would do if it stayed on the market, how much corporate officials know about the potential problem, and what steps have been taken along the way to deal with it.

Glossary

Pharmaceutical: relating to the selling of drugs and medicine

Side effects: unexpected or unwanted effects of a drug or treatment

Hypothetical: imagined; not real

Pacifist: someone who believes that violence and war are morally wrong

3 The next category in the Potter's Box framework requires the decision maker to prioritize *loyalties*. Determining loyalties is important because it gives a clear picture of what the repercussions might be for different parties who are affected by the situation. In the corporate world, loyalties often extend to more than just shareholders. In the case of the hypothetical pharmaceutical company, the company's loyalties may include shareholders, customers and their families, as well as the broader community. The company would need to think about which stakeholder is the most important, and which stakeholder has the most to lose.

4 Another significant item to consider in the Potter's Box framework of ethical decision making is personal *values*, or worldview. The things a person considers to be most important will determine how she or he looks at a situation. Ultimately, values can be the most important factor in a dilemma. For example, a pacifist might be morally opposed to working for a company that manufactures items used in war, and that worldview would likely take priority over the person's other values, such as earning a steady paycheck. In our hypothetical pharmaceutical case, the leaders of the company would need to determine what they value as they move forward in the decision-making process, whether it is the reputation of the company, the health of customers, or possibly the drive to make a profit.

B. Read Paragraphs 1 and 2 and complete the outline.

I. Potter's Box = useful guide for ....

   A. Dev. by ethicist Ralph Potter (1960s)

   B. Questions organized into 4 main categories — equal and ....

      1. Facts

      2. ....

      3. ....

      4. ....

II. Facts

   A. Listing ....

      1. Ex: .... co. sells drug w/negative side effects

      2. Facts, e.g.: cost of ....

         safety studies, benefits of keeping on the market, how much corp. knows, what has been done re: problem

C. Read Paragraphs 3 and 4 and outline them. Then compare outlines with a partner.

D. Work with a partner. Answer the questions about outlining.

1. Did outlining the text encourage you to be an active reader? Did it help you to distinguish between main ideas and supporting details? What did you find most challenging about outlining the text?

2. In what ways did you simplify the language in your outline? Are there any other ways you could have done this and still captured the important ideas?

3. How do you think you might use an outline for a school assignment, such as writing a summary or studying for an exam?

VOCABULARY CHECK

A. Review the vocabulary items in the Vocabulary Preview. Write their definitions and add examples. Use a dictionary if necessary.

B. Complete each sentence using the correct vocabulary item from the box. Use the correct form.

be opposed to	dilemma	facilitate
loyalty	principle	prioritize

1. According to shareholder theory, a company's primary .... is to those who hold stock in the company.

2. CEOs are often faced with .... , such as whether or not to fire workers. Being a good leader means being able to make difficult decisions.

3. When a company has a code of conduct, it can judge an employee's ethical performance according to a set of .... rather than the opinions of managers.

4. It is important that companies learn to .... their goals in order to develop plans for achieving them.

5. Developing a code of conduct .... the development of an ethical work environment.

6. Many young people .... working for companies that do not have corporate social responsibility initiatives.

> ● Go to MyEnglishLab to read part 2 of the reading and complete skill practices.

LANGUAGE SKILL

SIMPLIFYING COMPLEX SENTENCES

WHY IT'S USEFUL Simplifying complex sentences means identifying the essential information in long, complicated sentences. Learning to do this will enable you to read more quickly and improve your comprehension. Identifying the essential parts in a sentence is also necessary for writing summaries and the main ideas and supporting details in a text.

 Go to MyEnglishLab for the Language Skill presentation and practice.

VOCABULARY STRATEGY

USING WORD PARTS TO ANALYZE MEANING

WHY IT'S USEFUL Identifying word parts and their meanings can help you to learn the form and meaning of new words. This can help you to guess the meaning of new words as you read, increasing your fluency and comprehension. It can also help you to learn new words.

In the readings for your courses you will encounter many unfamiliar words, but it is almost certain that you will not have time to look all of them up. One strategy that can help you to understand new words more quickly is to learn the different parts that make up English words. The three basic parts of words are *roots*, *prefixes*, and *suffixes*. **Roots** are the basic forms or parts of a word; prefixes and suffixes modify or change the root.

Prefixes are a small group of letters added to the beginning of word. Adding a prefix to the word changes its meaning. For example,

im- means "not"	impossible = not possible	
re- means "again"	retrain = train again	

Common Prefixes		
Prefix	**Meaning**	**Example**
bene-	good, well	benefit
co-, com-, con-, col-	together with	commit
de-, dis-	opposite	depression
en-, em-	cause to	enforcement
ex-	out	extent
in-, im-	in	inclusive
inter-	between	interrelated

Common Prefixes

Prefix	Meaning	Example
mis-	bad, wrong	misleading
pre-	before	prevent
re-	again	repercussion
un-	not	unfair

Suffixes are also a small group of letters, but they are added to the end of the word. Suffixes usually change a word's part of speech. For example:

priority (-*y* is a common noun ending)   *prioritize* (-*ize* changes the noun to a verb)

Common Suffixes

Noun	Meaning	Example
-acy	state or quality	conspiracy
-ance, -ence	state or quality	experience
-ary	of or relating to	primary
-er, -ist, -ian	one who	ethicist
-ion, -sion, -tion	state of being; quality; act	decision
-ity, -ty	quality of	honesty
-ment	condition of	environment
-ness	state of being	business

Adjective	Meaning	Example
-able	able to be, worthy of	capable
-ful	full of	useful
-ic, -al, -ial, -al	relating to	ethical
-ious, -ous	having	conscious
-ive	having the nature of	positive
-y	characterized by	regulatory

Verb	Meaning	Example
-ate	to make or become	demonstrate
-ify	to make or become	qualify

EXERCISE 5

A. Read the excerpt. Circle all the prefixes and underline all the suffixes.

The final point of consideration in Potter's Box is personal principles. Applying moral principles, or a mode of reasoning, will help the decision maker come to a rational conclusion. Some examples of different modes of reasoning include end-based reasoning, virtue-based reasoning, and duty-based reasoning. *End-based* reasoning is the idea that doing what is good for the most number of people is the most ethical decision. End-based reasoning is also known as teleological ethics. *Virtue-based* reasoning states that moral decisions are made by pursuing certain beneficial virtues, such as prudence, fairness, courage, and respect. Finally, *duty-based* (or deontological) reasoning is the ethical argument that decisions must be considered in the context of a person's duty. If a company executive believed a decision was right because the duties of his position required it, he would, for example, be making an ethical decision using duty-based reasoning.

B. Use the prefixes and suffixes in these words to determine their part of speech and meaning.

	Part of Speech	Meaning
1. predictability		
2. cofacilitator		
3. beneficial		
4. unproductive		
5. consciousness		
6. implementation		
7. misstate		

C. Work with a partner. Brainstorm other words you have learned in this unit that have prefixes and suffixes. Analyze the word parts to explain the meanings of the words.

APPLY YOUR SKILLS

WHY IT'S USEFUL By applying the skills you have learned in this unit, you can gain a better understanding of a challenging reading about the role of investment bankers in the Great Recession of 2007–2009.

BEFORE YOU READ

A. Discuss these questions with a partner or group.

1. What are investment banks? Where are they traditionally located in the United States?

2. What caused the Great Recession of 2007–2009? What role did large banks play in causing it?

3. What challenges might large investment banks face in creating ethical work environments?

B. You will read a passage about the role of investment banks in the Great Recession of 2007–2009. As you read, think about these questions.

1. What do investment banks do? Why do they play such an important role in society?

2. What role did investment banks play in causing the Great Recession? Why are they mistrusted?

3. What consequences have investment banks faced as a result of their role in the financial crisis?

4. Who else was responsible for causing the financial crisis that led to the Great Recession?

5. Why is it challenging for investment banks to build a culture of ethics?

C. Review the Unit Skills Summary. As you read the passage, apply the skills you learned in this unit.

UNIT SKILLS SUMMARY

Identify main ideas

• Identify a writer's most important ideas in a text.

Identify supporting details

• Identify the types of information a writer uses to support the main ideas.

Outline a text

• Outline a text to improve comprehension and create written notes of a text.

Simplify complex sentences

• Use strategies for simplifying complex sentences in order to understand the main ideas.

Use word parts to analyze meaning

• Recognize common prefixes and suffixes to understand new words.

READ

A. Read and outline the passage. In your outline include answers to the questions in Before You Read, Part B.

Glossary

Bail out: to save a person or business from money problems

Embed: to plant; to put something deep into something else

Impose: to cause a fine or punishment to affect someone

Inherently: naturally; in a way that is a natural part of something

The Role of Investment Banks in the Great Recession

1   Investment banks are private companies that act as a bridge between buyers and sellers on a very large scale. Many people refer to investment banks simply as "Wall Street," which is the New York City location of their historic headquarters. Investment banks manage complex financial transactions worth billions of dollars, and their clients include wealthy individuals, large corporations, governments, and pension funds.

The largest investment banks include JPMorgan Chase, Goldman Sachs, Bank of America, Merrill Lynch, Morgan Stanley, and Citigroup. Investment banks play an important role in society because they advise companies in important financial transactions, buy and sell securities, and assist in the country's overall economic growth.   *(Continued)*

2 Like any company, investment banks aim to make a profit; however, because of their size and importance, their actions tend to have significant effects across the global economy. In the aftermath of the Great Recession of 2007–2009, many investment banks were accused of making deals that sacrificed ethics for profitability, leading to worldwide economic hardship. That was because some of the financial transactions that led to the financial crisis were, in fact, the responsibility of investment bankers. In the United States alone, millions of people lost their jobs, homes, and savings during the financial crisis. Moreover, the government paid billions of taxpayer dollars to bail out the very institutions that, in part, caused the problem, which further angered many Americans. Across the political spectrum, Americans today have a deep distrust of Wall Street. A Gallup poll revealed that less than 30 percent of Americans trust the banking industry.

3 The mistrust is not without reason. The US Financial Crisis Inquiry Commission, which explored what happened and what went wrong in the financial meltdown, pointed the finger at investment banks as a principal cause of the crisis. Investment bankers made questionable ethical decisions when they sold off risky subprime mortgage-backed securities to investors. These sales earned huge profits for investment banks while embedding risk throughout the entire economy. The commission report states, "Too many of these institutions acted recklessly, taking on too much risk, with too little capital, and with too much dependence on short-term funding. … They took on enormous exposures in acquiring and supporting subprime lenders and creating, packaging, repackaging, and selling trillions of dollars in mortgage-related securities … ."

4 Since the recession, the banking industry has paid the government about $110 billion in fines for the misconduct that led to the financial crisis. Goldman Sachs, for example, one of the largest investment banks, paid more than $5 billion in penalties associated with the sale of risky mortgage-backed securities. The banking industry has also been forced to deal with extensive new governmental regulations. Shortly after the financial crisis, the government enacted the Dodd-Frank Wall Street Reform and Consumer Protection Act, which imposes major regulations on the banking industry to improve transparency, accounting practices, and consumer protection.

5 Yet, despite their failings, investment banks are not inherently unethical. These institutions take care of important financial services in our economy, and individual bankers make plenty of ethical business decisions. Like all businesses, investment banks are made up of humans and are therefore subject to human error. Banks are also a product of government regulation and the wider business environment, so to some extent, unethical failures in the banking system may simply represent failings in the business community as a whole. It is important to note that while investment banks played a role in the crisis, the inquiry commission also accused other important institutions of major failings, including the US Federal Reserve, the Securities and Exchange Commission (SEC), and credit-rating agencies. Nevertheless, big banks are the ones that have faced the most public outrage over the financial meltdown.

6 Investment banks are very competitive in the business world, and the pressure to drive up profits in the short term makes it challenging for those in the industry to make ethical decisions. Yet improving ethics in trading would benefit investment banks because it would help to improve public opinion of their practices and avoid additional governmental regulations and financial penalties. In addition, it may well avert future financial disasters.

CULTURE NOTE

Wall Street is a street in the Financial District of Manhattan in New York City. Two of the world's largest stock exchanges are located there, and Wall Street is known as the leading financial center of the world.

B. Work with a partner. Use your outline to discuss the answers to the questions in Before You Read, Part B. Are there any questions you cannot answer? Which of the other reading skills you have learned in this unit could help you answer them?

⊙ Go to MyEnglishLab to read the passage again and answer critical thinking questions.

THINKING CRITICALLY

Discuss the questions with another student.

1. How does the writer of the article feel about the ethics of investment bankers in general? How do you know?

2. What makes the investment banking industry difficult to regulate? Why do you think ethics problems so often occur in investment banking?

3. Do you think it is possible to prevent economic crises like the Great Recession of 2007–2009 from happening again in the future? How?

THINKING VISUALLY

A. Study the graph showing changes in gross domestic product (GDP) growth rates for the United States from 2001 to 2016. (GDP represents the total value of the goods and services produced by a country and is used to determine the economic performance of a country.) Answer the questions with a partner.

1. Read the title. What does this graph show? What do the numbers on the side and across the middle represent?

2. What happened to US GDP growth between 2007 and 2009? How can you explain these changes? Think about what you have learned in this unit.

3. What happened after 2009? Do you know what might have caused these changes?

US GDP Growth Rate, 2001–2016

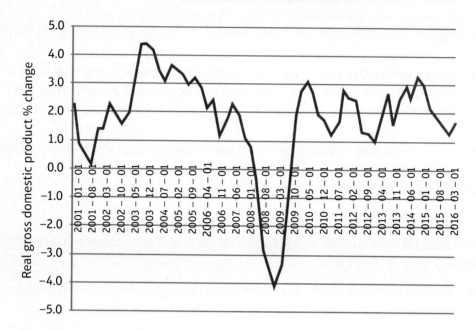

B. Choose a country. Do an Internet search for its GDP growth rates. Create a line or bar graph showing the GDP growth rates between 2007 and the most recent year, and give a report about your findings to your partner or group. If possible, include the following in your report:

1. What was the country's GDP growth rate in 2007? How does this compare with the rate in the United States?

2. What was the most recent GDP growth rate?

3. How can you explain the changes in GDP growth?

THINKING ABOUT LANGUAGE

Read the excerpts. Underline the subjects, verbs, and objects or complements in the sentences. Cross out unnecessary words. Place slashes between clauses. Then write the main idea.

1. The US Financial Crisis Inquiry Commission, which explored what happened and what went wrong in the financial meltdown, pointed the finger at investment banks as the principal cause of the crisis.

   ....

2. Goldman Sachs, for example, one of the largest investment banks, paid more than $5 billion in penalties associated with the sale of risky mortgage-backed securities.

   ....

3. In the aftermath of the Great Recession of 2007–2009, many investment banks were accused of making deals that sacrificed ethics for profitability, leading to worldwide economic hardship.

   ....

4. Moreover, the government paid billions of taxpayer dollars to bail out the very institutions that, in part, caused the problem, which further angered many Americans.

   ....

5. It is important to note that while investment banks played a role in the crisis, the inquiry commission also accused other important institutions of major failings, including the US Federal Reserve, the Securities and Exchange Commission (SEC), and credit-rating agencies.

   ....

6. Nevertheless, big banks are the ones that have faced the most public outrage over the financial meltdown.

   ....

🔊 Go to MyEnglishLab to watch Dr. McLennan's concluding video and to complete a self-assessment.

EARTH SCIENCE

Organizational Structures

UNIT PROFILE

In this unit, you will consider the subject of earth science. Reading topics include distinguishing weather from climate, describing the study of climate and climate change, and comparing and contrasting climates around the world and over time. You will also compare climate change on Earth to climate change on Mars.

Preview the reading "Climate Change on Mars and Earth" on page 86. Skim the reading. How is it organized? Do you notice any definitions of new terms? Do you notice any comparisons?

OUTCOMES

- Recognize definitions
- Identify comparison-and-contrast organization
- Take notes with graphic organizers
- Recognize relative clauses for definition
- Understand suffixes in scientific terms

For more about **EARTH SCIENCE**, see ②③. See also ⓌW and ⓄC **EARTH SCIENCE** ①②③.

GETTING STARTED

⊙ Go to MyEnglishLab to watch Dr. Osborne's introductory video and to complete a self-assessment.

Discuss these questions with a partner or group.

1. How would you define *climate* and *weather*? How are they similar to or different from one another?

2. What do you know about climates around the world and how they change?

3. What is the basic difference between the study of paleoclimate and global climate models, according to Dr. Osborne?

FUNDAMENTAL SKILL

RECOGNIZING ORGANIZATIONAL STRUCTURES

WHY IT'S USEFUL Recognizing organizational structures can help you to understand how the key ideas in a text are organized and how they relate to one another. This will help you to make predictions and improve your reading fluency and comprehension. Recognizing organizational structures also helps you to find key information, structure your notes, and recall the information later.

Organizational structures are patterns that writers use to communicate their ideas clearly, both within paragraphs and throughout a text. These patterns tend to be predictable in terms of both language and organization. Common organizational structures in academic English include:

Organizational Structure	Purpose	Example Signals
Cause / Effect	To describe the causes (reasons) and / or results (effects) of an event	an effect, as a result, because of, consequently, due to, for this reason
Chronology	To describe events in time order	first, secondly, later, next, finally, before, after
Classification	To describe different categories of things	one / another group, categories, class, one type / kind
Comparison / Contrast	To describe the similarities and / or differences between two or more things	like / unlike, similarly, compared to, although, but, different from, even though, however, on the other hand, nevertheless

Organizational Structure	Purpose	Example Signals
Definition	To define and explain a term	be, be defined / called / referred to, mean
Example	To provide examples to clarify a generalization or definition	for example, for instance, like, such as, to illustrate

Writers use different organizational structures depending on the type of information they want to communicate, and they may combine different structures within one text. For example, a writer may begin by defining a term and then provide examples or compare and contrast it with another term.

This unit breaks **recognizing organizational structures** down into two supporting skills:

- recognizing definitions
- identifying comparison-and-contrast organization

TIP

Textbook chapters are often designed with headings and subheadings that can provide clues to the organization as well as the content of the text. In addition, key terms will often appear in bold or italics, and key concepts may appear in charts that show how key information is related. Paying attention to these cues as well as previewing introductions and conclusions can help you to predict the organization of a text.

VOCABULARY PREVIEW

The following vocabulary items appear in the reading. Circle the ones you know. Put a question mark next to the ones you do not know.

atmosphere	dramatically	factors
anomaly	variability	cycle (n)

EXERCISE 1

A. Discuss the questions with a partner before you read.

1. Look at the graphs on the next two pages. How did the temperature change during 2016 in Washington, DC? What do you think causes changes in temperature like these over the course of a year? How did the average temperatures change between 1871 and 2010? What do you think caused these changes over time?

2. How would you describe the climate where you are from? Have you lived in or visited any places with a very different climate? Compare the climates in the two places.

3. Preview the excerpt from a reading about distinguishing climate from weather. What questions do you think the text might answer? Which organizational structures do you expect the writer to use?

B. Skim the passage and notice the organization. Underline words and phrases that signal definitions and examples of new terms. Circle words or phrases that signal comparisons (similarities) and contrasts (differences).

Distinguishing Climate from Weather

1 The terms *weather* and *climate* both describe conditions of the atmosphere such as temperature, pressure, wind, and precipitation, but they do not mean the same thing. Weather refers to short-term conditions of the atmosphere (Figure 1), while climate is a measure of long-term atmospheric patterns (Figure 2). Many weather elements may vary dramatically from day to day or even minute to minute. The temperature in Spearfish, South Dakota, for example, was once recorded as swinging wildly from –4 degrees to 45 degrees Fahrenheit (–20 degrees to 7 degrees Celsius) in just two minutes. Climate, unlike weather, is much slower to change. Climate is measured by using records of weather patterns over many decades or even centuries. A minimum of 30 years of data is required to describe the climate of an area. It is important to remember the distinction between climate and weather when discussing climate change. Though we might have a few unusually cold days in the winter, this does not necessarily indicate a shift in climate; it may simply indicate a temporary weather pattern.

Glossary

Precipitation: rain or snow that falls on the ground

Oscillation: in physics, a regular movement between one position or amount and another

Wreak havoc: to cause a lot of damage or problems

Drought: a long period of dry weather when there is not enough water for plants and animals to live

Flooding: a situation in which an area of land becomes covered with water, for example because of heavy rain

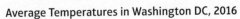

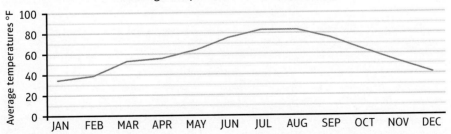

Average Temperatures in Washington DC, 2016

Figure 1: Example of change in weather

(Continued)

2   When factors such as clouds, wind, or air pressure in a given region change over a
    period of weeks or months, it can cause an anomaly in the climate patterns of the
    region. The El Niño Southern Oscillation, for instance, is considered a kind of climate
    variability. Also known simply as El Niño, it is a climate cycle that occurs every few
    years in the Pacific Ocean. This cycle is caused by changes in winds over the ocean,
    causing warm water in the western Pacific to shift eastward toward the coast of South
    America. This unusual ocean pattern can wreak havoc, causing droughts in some
    areas and flooding in others. Nevertheless, climate variations like El Niño are
    short-term compared to global climate change.

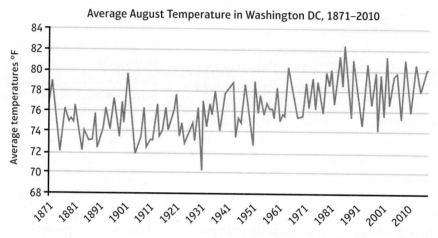

Figure 2: Example of change in climate

CULTURE NOTE

Fahrenheit is a temperature scale in which water freezes at 32 degrees and boils at 212 degrees.
It was developed in 1724 by the Dutch-German-Polish physicist Daniel Gabriel Fahrenheit.

By the end of the 20th century, Fahrenheit was used as the official temperature only in the
United States, the Bahamas, Belize, and the Cayman Islands. All other countries in the world
now use the *Celsius* scale, a metric scale that is named after the Swedish astronomer Anders
Celsius (1701–1744).

C. Read the passage again. Check (✓) the statements that are true for *weather*, *climate*, or *both*.

This condition ...	Weather	Climate	Both
1. describes conditions of the atmosphere.			
2. refers to short-term conditions.			
3. refers to long-term conditions.			
4. requires a minimum of 30 years of data to describe.			
5. can change.			
6. can vary dramatically from one minute to the next.			
7. can experience short-term anomalies such as El Niño.			

D. Read the following questions and refer back to the passage as needed to answer them. Then discuss your answers with a partner.

1. Look again at the predictions you made in Part A. Were they correct? How did making predictions help you to understand the passage?

2. Think about the organization of the passage. What is the purpose of each paragraph?

3. Which words or phrases helped you to identify definitions, examples, and comparisons? How did these phrases help you to understand the key ideas in the text?

4. How could you take notes in a way that would help you to study and recall the information later?

VOCABULARY CHECK

A. Review the vocabulary items in the Vocabulary Preview. Write their definitions and add examples. Use a dictionary if necessary.

B. Complete each sentence using the correct vocabulary item from the box. Use the correct form.

anomaly	atmosphere	cycle (n)
dramatically	factor	variability

1. Yesterday's rainstorm was a(n) .... It's usually dry this time of year.

2. La Niña is a weather pattern that occurs at the end of El Niño, when ocean temperatures in the eastern Pacific become cooler. The La Niña / El Niño .... repeats itself every three to seven years.

3. In Siberia, monthly average temperatures change .... throughout the year. In the city of Yakutsk, the average high temperature in July is 64°F, while January temperatures average an incredible −38°F.

4. Hawaii normally experiences little .... in temperature. It is rare for the temperature to drop below 65°F or rise above 90°F.

5. Earth's .... is composed of 78 percent nitrogen, 21 percent oxygen, and small amounts of other gases.

6. The distance between the Earth and the sun is an important .... that influences weather. When a region of the Earth is tilted toward the sun, that region experiences summer. When it is tilted away, it experiences winter.

🔊 Go to MyEnglishLab to complete a vocabulary exercise and skill practice, and to join in collaborative activities.

SUPPORTING SKILL 1

RECOGNIZING DEFINITIONS

WHY IT'S USEFUL In academic texts, you will often encounter new concepts and vocabulary as you read. Becoming familiar with the ways writers define new terms will enable you to identify meanings quickly so that you do not have to stop reading to use a dictionary. This will help you save time, understand more, and anticipate what comes next as you are reading.

Definitions of new terms can often be found in glossaries at the end of textbooks or sometimes at the bottom of a page, coded by an asterisk (*) or number that refers back to the word in the text. But sometimes definitions are embedded in the text itself. Writers use a variety of techniques for including definitions in a text.

Formal Definition

A writer may write a formal definition that consists of three main parts:

Term (Word or Phrase)	General Category That the Term Belongs To	Characteristics that Distinguish the Term from Others in Its Category
Climatology	is the scientific study of	long-term atmospheric patterns.

Definition Signals

Instead of writing formal definitions, authors often define terms using signals like the following:

	Definition Signals	
The scientific study of climate	is called is known as is referred to as	climatology.
Climatology	is defined as means	the scientific study of climate.

Punctuation

Various punctuation marks can also be used to set off definitions within a text.

Punctuation		Example
Dash	—	Climatology—the scientific study of climate—is a modern field of study.
Parentheses	( )	Climatology (the scientific study of climate) is a modern field of study.
Comma(s) with or without *or*	,	Climatology, (or) the scientific study of climate, is a modern field of study.
Quotation marks	" "	The scientific area of study that tries to reconstruct past climates is known as "paleoclimatology."
Italics	*italics*	The scientific area of study that tries to reconstruct past climates is known as *paleoclimatology.*

VOCABULARY PREVIEW

The following vocabulary items appear in the reading. Circle the ones you know. Put a question mark next to the ones you do not know.

shifts (n)	driving	retains	emitted
emissions	potential (n)	absorb	

EXERCISE 2

A. Preview the excerpt from an article about climate change. Notice the chart and the title. Then discuss the questions with a partner.

1. What are the major greenhouse gases? How do they contribute to climate change?

2. What terms will probably be defined in the text?

Glossary

Orbital pattern: the path followed by one object—for instance, a planet—around another

Climate Change and the Role of Greenhouse Gases

1 Many factors influence the climate of our planet. In the field of climatology, these are known as *forcings* because they literally force the climate system to change. Forcings can be natural; for instance, they include tiny shifts in Earth's orbital patterns, variations in the energy output of the sun, and volcanic activity. Since the Industrial Revolution, however, the dominant forcing driving climate change has been human production of greenhouse gases.

2 Greenhouse gases are defined as gases that trap heat in the atmosphere. These gases block and hold in the heat radiating from Earth toward space, much like a glass greenhouse retains warmth from the sun. Greenhouse gases are emitted when humans produce electricity, drive cars, power factories, and grow crops. The main greenhouse gases that contribute to global warming are carbon dioxide (CO_2), methane (CH^4), nitrous oxide (N_2O), and fluorinated gases—man-made gases that contain the chemical fluorine (F). Carbon dioxide makes up more than 80 percent of all greenhouse gas emissions in the United States. In contrast, fluorinated gases and nitrous oxide combined make up less than 10 percent of emissions.

3 To understand the impact of a particular greenhouse gas on the environment, we must know its *global warming potential*, or how much of a warming effect it can create. Often referred to as *GWP*, this potential is measured by examining the amount of energy the emissions of one ton of a gas will absorb over a given period of time as compared to one ton of CO_2. GWP was developed to compare the global warming effects of different gases. For example, fluorinated gases, which are found in air conditioners, are sometimes called high-GWP gases because they trap significantly more heat than CO_2. These types of gases are usually highly regulated because even small amounts can have a dramatic effect on global warming.

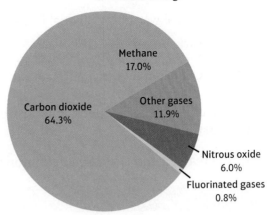

Major Greenhouse Gases Contributing to Climate Change

Source: Intergovernmental Panel on Climate Change (IPCC). 2014. Fifth assessment report: Climate change 2007. Cambridge, United Kingdom: Cambridge University Press. http://www.ipcc.ch/publications_and_data/publications_and_data_reports.shtml.

CULTURE NOTE

The Industrial Revolution started in the mid-1700s in Great Britain when machinery was invented and began to replace human labor. Before this era, most people lived in small, rural farming communities. However, by the mid-19th century, industrialization was established throughout western Europe and the American northeast as people moved to cities to work in factories. This period was a turning point in history, marked by major changes in agriculture, transportation, communication, and world trade. It also marked a shift from wood, windmills, and waterwheels to fossil fuels—coal, oil, and natural gas—as energy sources.

B. Read the passage. Then read the statements and write *T* (True) or *F* (False). Correct the false statements.

.... 1. Forcings are factors that affect the climate and cause it to change.

.... 2. Forcings refer only to man-made factors in climate change.

.... 3. Greenhouse gases heat the planet by increasing heat that radiates toward Earth from the sun.

.... 4. The main greenhouse gases are carbon dioxide, methane, nitrous oxide, and oxygen.

5. More than 80 percent of US greenhouse gas emissions come from carbon dioxide emissions.

6. Global warming potential is used to compare the global warming effects of various gases.

7. CO_2 has a higher GWP than fluorinated gases.

C. **Read the passage again. Check your answers to Part B. Then compare answers with a partner.**

D. **Scan the reading and circle five definition signals. Then complete the chart.**

Word / Concept	Signal	Meaning
1.		
2.		
3.		
4.		
5.		

E. **Work with a partner. Answer the questions about recognizing definitions.**

1. How many kinds of definition signals did the passage use? Did you have trouble recognizing any of them?

2. How did recognizing the definitions affect your ability to understand the passage?

VOCABULARY CHECK

A. Review the vocabulary items in the Vocabulary Preview. Write their definitions and add examples. Use a dictionary if necessary.

B. Complete each sentence using the correct vocabulary item from the box. Use the correct form.

absorb	drive	emission	emit
potential (n)	retain	shift (n)	

1. Wood does not transfer heat easily, which means it can .... heat longer than other materials such as metals.

2. In 2015, 29 percent of greenhouse gas .... were caused by the production of electricity. This represented the largest contributor of greenhouse gases that year.

3. When sunlight passes through the glass of the greenhouse, it is .... by the plants and the greenhouse floor, and the light converts to heat.

4. Airplanes .... heat and carbon dioxide as they fly through the air, and thus contribute to climate change.

5 .... energy is the energy that something has not used yet.

6. Man-made factors such as electricity production are .... the release of greenhouse gases into the atmosphere.

7. To reduce greenhouse gases in the atmosphere, industries will need to commit to a(n) .... from fossil fuels to renewable sources of energy, such as solar and wind.

◗ Go to MyEnglishLab to complete a vocabulary exercise and skill practice, and to join in collaborative activities.

SUPPORTING SKILL 2

IDENTIFYING COMPARISON-AND-CONTRAST ORGANIZATION

WHY IT'S USEFUL Identifying comparison-and-contrast organization can help you to distinguish the similarities and differences between key terms or ideas in a passage.

In academic texts, writers will often compare and contrast things, people, places, or ideas. When **comparing**, a writer explains the similarities between two or more items, and when **contrasting**, a writer explains the differences. Often both comparison and contrast are combined in one passage. A writer may focus on similarities and differences in separate paragraphs or "blocks." Alternately, writers may compare and contrast two or more things in the same paragraph, discussing first one of the items and then the next. You can often find clues to the organization at the beginning of a paragraph, as in this excerpt from "Distinguishing Weather from Climate":

> The terms *weather* and *climate* both describe conditions of the atmosphere such as temperature, pressure, wind, and precipitation, but they do not mean the same thing. Weather refers to short-term conditions of the atmosphere, while climate is a measure of long-term atmospheric patterns.

Within paragraphs, two or more items may be contrasted by using comparatives and superlatives, as in this example: *Climate, unlike weather, is much slower to change.*

In addition, certain signal words and phrases can help you to identify ways that two things are similar to or different from one another. These include:

Signal Words for Comparison	Example
also likewise similarly	**Similarly**, climate describes conditions of the atmosphere.
as / just as	**Just as** an orchestra is comprised of different musicians that play separately but in harmony with one another, climatology is informed by various scientists who collaborate to study the various aspects of Earth's systems.
both	The terms *weather* and *climate* **both** describe conditions of the atmosphere.
like	These gases block the heat radiating from Earth toward space, much **like** a glass greenhouse retains warmth from the sun.
the same as	Ocean sediment, which is a gathering of solid materials that have settled at the bottom of the sea floor, contains many of **the same** elements **as** ice cores.
similar to	*Climate*, **similar to** *weather*, describes conditions of the atmosphere.

Signal Words for Contrast	Example
although / though	**Though** we might have a few unusually cold days in the winter, this does not necessarily indicate a shift in climate.
but / yet	The terms *weather* and *climate* both describe conditions of the atmosphere, **but** they do not mean the same thing.
in contrast	**In contrast**, fluorinated gases and nitrous oxide combined make up less than 10 percent of emissions.
different	Each climate proxy contains **different** information.
however on the other hand	Since the Industrial Revolution, **however**, the dominant forcing driving climate change has been human production of greenhouse gases. An oceanographer, **on the other hand**, might research the effects of too much carbon dioxide in the oceans.
unlike	Climate, **unlike** weather, is much slower to change.
while / whereas	Weather refers to short-term conditions of the atmosphere, **while** climate is a measure of long-term atmospheric patterns.

VOCABULARY PREVIEW

The following vocabulary items appear in the reading. Circle the ones you know. Put a question mark next to the ones you do not know.

vary	humid	predictable
equator	reverse (v)	characterized

EXERCISE 3

A. Preview the excerpt from a textbook passage about climates around the world. Notice the title, headings, and map. Then discuss the questions with a partner.

1. What questions do you think the text might answer? What will probably be compared and contrasted?

2. Look at the map of the world's climate regions. What do you notice about the different regions? What factors do you think determine a region's climate?

Climates Around the World

1 Climates, which vary greatly around the world, are influenced by many factors. These include latitude, elevation, topography, wind, ocean currents, and distance from bodies of water. For example, the city of Esfahan in Iran is located at the same latitude as the city of Dallas in the United States, yet the two cities feel strikingly different on an average summer day. A July day in Esfahan is about 84°F (29°C) and extremely dry. In Dallas, the same summer day has a similar temperature, but the weather may feel warmer because the air is humid. This is because the climate of Dallas is influenced by warm air currents from the Gulf of Mexico, while Esfahan, located at a much higher elevation, is in a dry climate region.

Köppen Climate Classification System

2 The most widely used tool for distinguishing types of climate, the Köppen climate classification system, is based on the average monthly temperature and precipitation patterns of a region. The system separates climate into five main categories: tropical, dry, temperate, continental, and polar. Each category has its own special climatic features.

KÖPPEN CLIMATE CLASSIFICATION

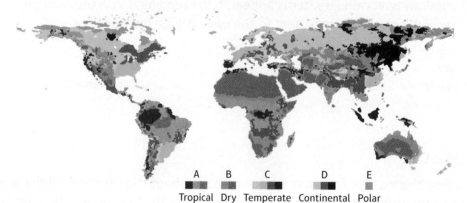

A   B   C   D   E
Tropical Dry Temperate Continental Polar

Tropical Climates

3 Tropical climates include tropical rainforest, tropical monsoon, and tropical savannah. Located near the equator, tropical regions are warm year-round, with an average temperature of at least 64°F (18°C) each month of the year. They also have significant precipitation though they vary in terms of rainfall and the presence or absence of a dry season.

4 The tropical rainforest is the most predictable climate region, with warm temperatures and regular rainfall throughout the year. Each month receives an average of at least 2.4 inches (6 cm) of precipitation. Tropical rainforests are found at latitudes within 25 degrees of the equator, most commonly in South America, central Africa, Indonesia, and Southeast Asia.

5 Like the tropical rainforest climate, the tropical monsoon climate is characterized by high temperatures all year; however, this climate features distinct wet and dry seasons created by monsoons—wind systems that reverse their direction, flowing from sea to land in the summer and from land to sea in the winter. During the hotter summer months, these winds bring a rainy season similar to that of the tropical rainforest climate: warm and humid, with frequent thunderstorms. Winter, on the other hand, is characterized by dry, desert-like conditions. The driest month sees less than 1.6 inches (6 cm) of precipitation, though the total annual precipitation is more than 4 inches (10 cm). Tropical monsoon climates are found in South and Central America, South Asia, western and central Africa, and the Caribbean.

B. Read the passage. Then write *T* (True) or *F* (False). Correct the false statements.

.... 1. Latitude is the main factor that determines a region's climate.

.... 2. Esfahan, Iran, and Dallas, Texas, have the same elevation but different climates.

.... 3. The Köppen climate classification system distinguishes climate types based on their annual temperature and precipitation patterns.

.... 4. According to the Köppen climate classification system, there are three types of tropical climate.

.... 5. Tropical climate regions are located near the equator.

.... 6. Tropical rainforests are warm and wet year-round.

.... 7. Monsoons are ocean currents that reverse direction.

.... 8. The tropical monsoon climate is rainier in summer than in winter.

C. Read the passage again. Check your answers to Part B. Then compare answers with a partner.

D. Scan Paragraphs 4 and 5 again and circle the signal words for comparison and contrast. Then complete the chart, noting the similarities and differences between the climate types.

Climates	Temperature	Precipitation	Location
Tropical rainforest			
Tropical monsoon			

E. Work with a partner. Answer the questions about understanding comparison-and-contrast organization.

1. How did the signals you identified in Part D help you to understand the relationships between the things being compared and contrasted?

2. Using the information in the Part D chart and the expressions on pages 72–73, take turns making sentences to compare and contrast the tropical rainforest and tropical monsoon climates.

3. Look at Paragraphs 1, 4, and 5. Do they discuss mainly similarities, mainly differences, or both equally? How are the similarities and differences organized?

VOCABULARY CHECK

A. Review the vocabulary items in the Vocabulary Preview. Write their definitions and add examples. Use a dictionary if necessary.

B. Complete each sentence using the correct vocabulary item from the box. Use the correct form.

characterized	equator	humid
predictable	reverse (v)	vary

The city of Macapa, Brazil, is known by locals as "the capital of the middle of the world" because the (1) .... runs through the center of the city. The climate of Macapa is tropical monsoon and does not (2) .... much. Daytime temperatures are (3) .... , averaging 88°F (31°C) year-round. Monsoon winds bring heavy rainfall from December through August, and then (4) .... direction to create a short dry season during the remaining three months of the year. Even the dry months are quite (5) .... however. Near Macapa is the Fazendinha Environmental Protection Area, which is (6) .... by its beautiful scenery and diverse plant and animal life.

⟐ Go to MyEnglishLab to complete a vocabulary exercise and skill practice, and to join in collaborative activities.

INTEGRATED SKILLS

TAKING NOTES WITH GRAPHIC ORGANIZERS

WHY IT'S USEFUL Taking notes with graphic organizers is an effective way to see the relationships between the key ideas in a reading. Using graphic organizers helps you to better comprehend a text and review it later.

Graphic organizers are visual representations of information. When you use them to organize information in your reading notes, you create a mental picture of the ideas. The process of creating a graphic forces you to analyze and see the relationships between the ideas in the text, and that process allows you to better understand and remember them. Because graphic organizers are a way of noting the key information in a reading, they are also useful as study aids.

Graphic Organizers for Formal Definitions

One way to note formal definitions is to create a graphic that shows the key information about a term in a logical pattern.

| Term (word or phrase) | + | General category that the term belongs to | + | Characteristics that distinguish the term from others in its category |

For example, read the textbook excerpt containing a definition of the term *paleoclimatology*. Then look at the graphic representation of the definition.

Paleoclimatology is the study of climate change over the entire history of Earth. In this field, scientists attempt to understand current climate patterns and predict future climate change by looking at evidence from the past that reveals how climate changed, what caused the changes, and how the changes affected the planet.

| Paleoclimatology | is | the study of historical climate change over the entire history of Earth | that | • attempts to understand current climate patterns and predict future climate change.
• looks at evidence from the past.
• reveals how climate changed, what caused the changes, and how the changes affected the planet. |

Graphic Organizers for Comparison and Contrast

A **chart** is one way of organizing information from a reading in order to be able to compare and contrast the key ideas easily. For example, this chart compares and contrasts various characteristics of two tropical climates.

Climate	Temperature	Precipitation	Location
Tropical rainforest	Avg. temp ≥ 64°F (18°C) / month	- Regular rainfall year-round - Avg. ≥ 2.4 inches (6 cm) / month	Within 25 degrees of equator (South America, central Africa, Southeast Asia)
Tropical monsoon	Same as above	- Distinct wet and dry seasons: rainy summer, dry winter - < 1.6 inches / driest month; > 4 inches annually	South and Central America, South Asia, western / central Africa, Caribbean

A **Venn diagram** is yet another way to create a picture of the similarities and differences between two or three things. Similarities are noted in the overlapping section in the middle, while differences are noted in the outer area of each circle.

TROPICAL RAINFOREST

Regular rainfall year round

Avg. ≥ 2.4 inches of rain (6 cm) / month

Within 25 degrees of equator (South America, central Africa, Southeast Asia)

BOTH

Avg. temp ≥ 64°F (18°C) / month

TROPICAL MONSOON

Distinct wet and dry seasons: rainy summer, dry winter

< 1.6 inches of rain / driest month; > 4 inches annually

South and Central America, South Asia, western / central Africa, Caribbean

---

TIP

In addition to using charts to structure ideas from the text in your reading notes, you can also use a chart to structure your reflections before, during, and after reading with a KWL chart.

K	W	L
What do you already KNOW?	What do you WANT to know?	What did you LEARN?

VOCABULARY PREVIEW

The following vocabulary items appear in the reading. Circle the ones you know. Put a question mark next to the ones you do not know.

excess (n)	abundant	decay (n)
account for	trap (v)	potency

EXERCISE 4

A. Skim the magazine article about carbon dioxide and methane. Then discuss the questions with a partner.

1. Which words are defined? Circle them.

2. In what ways are carbon dioxide and methane compared and contrasted?

3. Notice the organization of the article. Which paragraph discusses only carbon dioxide? Which paragraph discusses the similarities between carbon dioxide and methane? Which paragraphs discuss the differences?

4. Which type(s) of graphic organizer(s) would probably be useful for taking notes on this article?

B. Create graphic organizers for the definitions you circled in the article. Then compare graphic organizers with a partner.

Carbon Dioxide Versus Methane: Which Is Worse for the Environment?

1 Were it not for the existence of greenhouse gases, the planet's average temperature would be a freezing −0.4°F (−18°C). Yet, while both plant and animal species on Earth need the warming effect of greenhouse gases to survive, the excess of human-created greenhouse gases in the atmosphere today is more than the planet's forests and oceans can absorb, and it is resulting in global warming. The most significant greenhouse gases in the discussion of global warming are carbon dioxide (CO_2) and methane (CH_4). These two gases, which are emitted when humans burn fossil fuels, are the most abundant human-created greenhouse gases in the atmosphere.

2 Carbon dioxide and methane are emitted as a product of both natural processes and human activities. Carbon dioxide is emitted naturally by plant decay and volcanic eruptions. It is also produced when humans burn coal, oil, and natural gas. Likewise, methane is emitted naturally from wetland areas, melting permafrost, and other microbial sources. Methane emissions from human activities come from cattle farming, landfills, and the production of natural gas and other fossil fuels.

Glossary

Permafrost: a layer of soil that is always frozen

Microbial: relating to microbes, very tiny and often harmful living things

3 Carbon dioxide accounts for about 80 percent of all human-created greenhouse gas emissions in the United States. Worldwide, the carbon dioxide level in the atmosphere is more than 400 parts per million, the highest it has been in hundreds of thousands of years. Until the Industrial Revolution, the amount remained at approximately 280 parts per million. Once emitted into the

atmosphere, carbon dioxide enters what is known as the *carbon cycle*, which is a process that distributes it between the atmosphere, ocean, and land. The result is that although 65 to 85 percent of carbon dioxide emissions are absorbed by the oceans within 200 years, some stay in the atmosphere for thousands of years.

4 Methane, the second most abundant, human-created greenhouse gas in the atmosphere, accounts for only about 11 percent of all emissions in the United States. Methane also has a shorter lifetime than carbon dioxide. It lasts only about a decade, so efforts to limit methane emissions would have an impact in a single generation. While methane is less abundant and lasts for a shorter time in the atmosphere compared to carbon dioxide, it is a much more powerful greenhouse gas. All greenhouse gases have a *global warming potential*, a number determined by how much energy the gas is able to absorb from the sun and by how long the gas lasts in the atmosphere over a specific time period, typically 20, 100, or 500 years. Methane's global warming potential is approximately 30 percent greater than that of carbon dioxide, meaning it is more effective at trapping heat in the atmosphere.

5 Methane's higher global warming potential relative to carbon dioxide is important because methane emissions have risen by 30 percent in the past decade. Carbon dioxide emissions worldwide, meanwhile, have not risen significantly in recent years. This is due to a number of reasons, including reduction in coal use and more alternative energy options. As for methane, scientists are not certain why the emission rate has risen so dramatically. Causes may include melting permafrost, cattle farming, and natural gas production, among others. While the amount of carbon dioxide emissions is the major concern in the discussion about global warming today, methane's potency and its increase in the atmosphere in recent years mean that it cannot be ignored as a powerful contributor to the planet's climate change.

C. **Read the article again. Create a Venn diagram to compare and contrast carbon dioxide and methane. Then compare graphic organizers with a partner.**

D. **Work with a partner. Answer the questions about using graphic organizers.**

1. Do you think a Venn diagram is the best graphic organizer for taking notes on the similarities and differences in the article? Why or why not?

2. How did taking notes with graphic organizers help you to understand the article?

3. How could you use graphic organizers to complete assignments or study for exams?

VOCABULARY CHECK

A. Review the vocabulary items in the Vocabulary Preview. Write their definitions and add examples. Use a dictionary if necessary.

B. Read the sentences. Then write the vocabulary items in bold next to their definitions.

1. Carbon dioxide is more **abundant** than methane in the atmosphere. It makes up 80 percent of US greenhouse gas emissions, while methane makes up only 11 percent.

2. Nitrous oxide (NO_2) **accounts for** about 6 percent of all US greenhouse gas emissions.

3. Destruction of forests contributes to global warming because plant **decay** causes carbon dioxide to be released into the atmosphere.

4. Global warming is not the only effect of rising carbon dioxide emissions. Scientists have observed that an **excess** of carbon dioxide may also be changing the chemistry and biology of the oceans.

5. The global warming potential (GWP) of a greenhouse gas is used to describe its **potency** compared to other gases. A gas with a high GWP, such as methane, is able to absorb a large amount of energy.

6. Greenhouses **trap** heat in the same way that Earth's atmosphere does. Because heat is unable to escape, the greenhouse stays warm.

a. .... (n)
   larger amount of something than is suitable

b. .... (v)
   to make up a particular amount or part of something

c. .... (n)
   the natural chemical change that causes the slow destruction of something

d. .... (v)
   to prevent from escaping

e. .... (adj)
   existing in large quantities

f. .... (n)
   the strength of something

⬥ Go to MyEnglishLab to complete skill practices.

LANGUAGE SKILL

RECOGNIZING RELATIVE CLAUSES FOR DEFINITION

WHY IT'S USEFUL Knowing how to recognize relative clauses can help you to recognize definitions and key information about new terms in texts.

⊙ Go to MyEnglishLab for the Language Skill presentation and practice.

VOCABULARY STRATEGY

UNDERSTANDING SUFFIXES IN SCIENTIFIC TERMS

WHY IT'S USEFUL Understanding certain suffixes can help you to determine both the grammar and the meaning of many science-related words.

Most scientific words are made up of word stems (the main part of the word) plus prefixes and suffixes. If you know the meaning of all of the individual pieces, you can often figure out the meaning of a word. For example, if you know that the word stem *climate* means "weather patterns," and that *-ology* means "a subject of study," then you can figure out that climatology is the study of weather patterns.

Below are some suffixes that are commonly attached to science-related stems.

	Suffix	Meaning and Notes	Examples
Nouns: Field of Study	-ology	Meaning: the study of, the science of Note: Many medical fields use this suffix.	climatology, cardiology
	-(o)graphy	Meaning: the descriptive science of	geography
	-ics	Meaning: a body of facts, knowledge, or principles	mathematics
Nouns: People Who Work in Fields of Study	-ist -er	Meaning: someone who works or studies Notes: *-ist* is used for fields that end in *-ology*. *-er* is used for fields that end in *-graphy*.	climatologist, biologist geographer
Adjectives	-ic -ical	Meaning: adjective Note: *-ic* is the more common form.	organic biological

EXERCISE 5

A. Underline the science-related suffixes in the following sentences.

1. The study of climate encompasses many different scientific fields, including atmospheric science, geology, mathematics, solar physics, oceanography, and historical climatology.

2. Some geologists conduct radiometric dating of rocks to reveal how recurring volcanic eruptions influenced climate at particular points in history.

3. Paleoclimatology relies on many areas of scientific study. For example, dendrochronology, the study of climate change as recorded in tree growth rings, provides another kind of proxy data.

B. Use the information in each sentence to guess the meaning of the boldfaced word. Discuss your answers with a partner.

1. A cardio workout is an exercise routine that raises your heart rate. A cardiogram measures your heartbeats. A **cardiologist** is probably

....

2. You can buy medicines at a pharmacy. A pharmacist sells and mixes drugs and medicines. **Pharmacology** is probably ....

3. An aquarium is a large tank filled with water and fish. Aquamarine is a color that is blue like the ocean. People who study **aquatic sciences** probably study

....

4. Physical anthropology is the study of human biology and evolution. Anthropomorphism is the assigning of human characteristics to animals. A **cultural anthropologist** probably studies ....

5. Poisonous substances are toxic. A toxicology report reveals drugs and poisons in a person's body. A **toxicologist** probably studies ....

6. A therm is a unit of heat. Thermal insulation is a material used to prevent the transfer of heat. The study of **thermodynamics** is the physical science that examines the relationships between .... and other forms of energy.

C. Read the passage. Add the correct endings to the word stems. Some stems may need two suffixes. Make spelling changes as needed.

Two fields of earth science sometimes get confused. Both *geography* and *geology* come from the word stem *geo-*, which means "earth," but one describes the visible earth and land, while the other concerns what is beneath the surface and how the earth formed over time.

Geo_____ (1) is the study of the Earth and its land, features, and inhabitants. Geo_____ (2) are interested in what the land looks like. Some people think that they make maps, but people who make maps are actually called cart_____ (3).

Geo_____ (4) is the scientific study of the earth and its formation. Many people think that geo_____ (5) only study rocks, but in fact they are also interested in aquat_____ (6) and atmospher_____ (7) sciences. Some geo_____ (8) specialize in paleont_____ (9) or volcan_____ (10).

APPLY YOUR SKILLS

WHY IT'S USEFUL By applying the skills you have learned in this unit, you can gain a better understanding of this challenging reading that compares climate change on Mars and on Earth.

BEFORE YOU READ

A. Discuss these questions with a partner or group.

1. What do you know about space missions to Mars? What kinds of information have scientists learned from recent missions?

2. People have searched for and fantasized about finding life on Mars for hundreds of years. What similarities between Earth and Mars have contributed to this fascination?

B. You will read a passage comparing climate change on Mars and on Earth. As you read, think about these questions.

1. In general, how are Mars and Earth similar to each other? How are they different?

2. What are interglacial periods?

3. What are Milankovitch cycles? What is the connection between these cycles and climate change on Earth and on Mars?

C. Review the Unit Skills Summary. As you read the passage, apply the skills you learned in this unit.

UNIT SKILLS SUMMARY

Recognize definitions
- Look for punctuation and language clues to help you identify definitions in a text.

Identify comparison-and-contrast organization
- Notice compare-and-contrast language and organizational patterns to help you understand and remember information in a text.

Take notes with graphic organizers
- Use graphic organizers for definitions, charts, and Venn diagrams as tools to show relationships between ideas.

Recognize relative clauses for definition
- Recognize identifying and nonidentifying relative clauses that define and explain terms.

Understand suffixes in scientific terms
- Recognize common suffixes to determine the meaning of scientific terms.

READ

A. Read the magazine article. Use graphic organizers to take notes on the answers to the questions in Before You Read, Part B.

Climate Change on Mars and Earth

1   Mars and Earth, neighbors in our solar system, share many similarities. For example, the planets are similar in composition, with a substantial amount of iron on the surface and in the core. The amount of rock and the planets' chemical makeup also make them more similar to each other than to other planets, many of which consist predominantly of gases. Mars, like Earth, also has water. NASA's Mars Reconnaissance Orbiter, a spacecraft that examines the planet by using cameras, radar, and other tools, has provided evidence that Mars, like Earth, has experienced ice ages, spans of time when a planet becomes cooler. These ice ages are followed by warmer periods, which are known as *interglacial periods*. On Earth, ice ages occur about every 100,000 years, with the most recent ice age ending about 12,000 years ago. Radar images of ice caps reveal that Mars, also known as "the red planet," experienced its most recent ice age about 370,000 years ago.

> **Glossary**
>
> Tilt: a movement or position in which one side of something is higher than the other
>
> Wobble: movement in an unsteady way from side to side

2 In the past, these changes in temperature on Mars and Earth were due largely to variations in orbital patterns known as *Milankovitch cycles*, which affect the amount of solar energy that reaches a planet. There are three types of Milankovitch cycles: *eccentricity*, the changing shape of the planet's orbit around

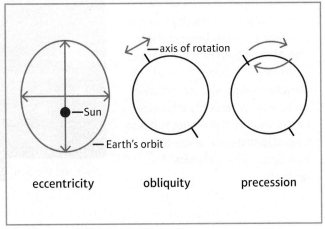

the sun; *obliquity*, or the tilt toward the sun; and *precession*, a planet's wobble along its axis. The Milankovitch cycle that most contributes to climate change is obliquity. The change of the angle, or tilt, of Earth varies only slightly—a few degrees—whereas Mars's tilt varies dramatically over time, up to 60 degrees. This results in ice ages on Mars that look very different from those on Earth.

Figure 1: Milankovitch cycles

3 When Earth experiences an ice age, the polar regions freeze first. Then, as the weather remains cooler, the polar ice and high-latitude glaciers spread outward toward the equator. These ice ages result in major changes in climate, sea level, and topography. In the most recent ice age, for instance, global temperatures and sea levels dropped, and the ice grew to more than 12,000 feet thick. Sheets of ice spread across Canada, Scandinavia, Russia, and South America. When our current interglacial period began about 12,000 years ago, the climate began to warm and glaciers began to melt, creating lakes and rising sea levels.

4 On Mars, in contrast, climate change and ice formation occur over time at a variety of latitudes. The planet's extreme tilt causes the polar regions to be exposed to more sun, making them warmer. As the polar regions warm up, the mid-latitude regions of the planet become cooler. Ice from the polar regions retreats and moves closer to the center of the planet. After many thousands of years, when Mars's axial tilt straightens again, the climate becomes interglacial: the polar regions become colder again, and ice deposits in the mid-latitude regions evaporate. These transitions between cooler and warmer periods create erosion paths in the ice. Evidence of past ice ages on Mars can be seen in glacier ice covered by rock and dust as well as buried ground ice at latitudes where ice can't exist at the surface.

(Continued)

5 Both computer climate models that simulate climate change and research on radar images show that Mars is currently in a warmer interglacial period. The study of climate change and ice behavior on Mars may not only influence exploration of the planet but also help scientists understand the way cycles affect climate on Earth.

Mars and the Sun

B. Work with a partner. Use your graphic organizers to discuss the answers to the questions in Before You Read, Part B. Are there any questions you cannot answer? Which of the other reading skills you have learned in this unit could help you answer them?

🔊 Go to MyEnglishLab to read the passage again and answer critical thinking questions.

THINKING CRITICALLY

Discuss the questions with another student. Use evidence from the reading to support your answers.

1. What can we learn about Earth by studying climate change on Mars?

2. Do you think that life may exist on Mars now or may have existed in the past? What evidence supports your position?

3. The United States is planning to send a manned mission to Mars in the 2030s. Do you think this is a good idea? Why or why not? What are some benefits of such a mission compared to earlier unmanned missions?

THINKING VISUALLY

A. Study the chart. Then answer the questions with a partner.

Conditions on Earth and Mars

Planet	Atmospheric Composition	Surface Temperature
Mars	Carbon dioxide: 95.32% Nitrogen: 2.70% Argon: 1.60% Oxygen: 0.13%	−76°F (−60°C)

Planet	Atmospheric Composition	Surface Temperature
Earth	Nitrogen: 75.52% Oxygen: 23.13% Argon: 1.29% Carbon dioxide: 0.05%	59°F (15°C)

1. How are the atmospheres of Mars and Earth similar? How are they different?

2. Based on the information from the reading and the chart, how likely is it that humans would be able to live on Mars? Explain your answer.

B. **Choose a different planet. Do an Internet search on the atmospheric conditions there. Create a chart like the one above and give a report about your findings to your partner or group. If possible, include the following in your report:**

- Atmospheric composition
- Surface temperature(s)
- Geologic conditions and absence or presence of water

THINKING ABOUT LANGUAGE

Read the items containing embedded definitions with relative clauses and appositives. Then write formal definitions of the underlined terms.

1. Mars, like Earth, has experienced <u>ice ages</u>, spans of time when a planet becomes cooler.

   ....

2. These ice ages are followed by warmer periods, which are known as <u>interglacial periods</u>.

   ....

3. Historic climate changes on both Mars and Earth have been most influenced by cyclical variations in orbital patterns known as <u>Milankovitch cycles</u>, which produce variations in the amount of solar energy that reaches a planet.

   ....

4. The Milankovitch cycle that most contributes to climate change is <u>obliquity</u>.

   ....

○ Go to MyEnglishLab to watch Dr. Osborne's concluding video and to complete a self-assessment.

Present times are connected to the past

MEDIEVAL CULTURE

Reading Fluency

UNIT PROFILE

In this unit, you will be exploring subjects related to medieval culture including food, art, literature, religion, and architecture. You will also be reading about how medieval European culture was related to other world cultures at that time and how the various cultures influenced each other.

Preview the reading "How the Spice Trade Drove Globalization" on page 120. Quickly skim through the reading to understand the main idea. What are some of the main reasons the author states for the popularity of spices in the Middle Ages?

OUTCOMES

- Increase reading fluency
- Manage ambiguity
- Summarize a text
- Understand language associated with chronology
- Recognize multiple meanings of words

For more about MEDIEVAL CULTURE, see ❷ ❸.
See also Ⓦ and [OC] MEDIEVAL CULTURE ❶ ❷ ❸.

GETTING STARTED

Go to MyEnglishLab to watch Professor Galvez's introductory video and to complete a self-assessment.

Discuss these questions with a partner or group.

1. The European medieval period, or Middle Ages, lasted from around 500 to 1500 CE. What do you already know about medieval culture or history?

2. Think about the time period in the previous question. What major events or cultural changes were occurring in your own country during this period?

3. In her introduction, Professor Galvez describes the food and events at a medieval feast. Describe a feast in your culture. When and why is it held? Who attends? What typical foods are served? What other activities take place before, during, or after the meal?

FUNDAMENTAL SKILL

READING FLUENTLY

WHY IT'S USEFUL Reading fluently is important in academic contexts because university students are required to read and understand large quantities of text. Therefore, they must learn to read both quickly and efficiently.

In academic contexts, students are expected to read and remember many pages of text for each class. Doing this quickly and effectively requires good reading fluency.

Reading fluently means progressing through a reading at a steady pace with very little stopping or going back. Yet fluency is more than just reading fast. It involves reading quickly enough to track and remember what you are reading yet slowly enough not to miss important information. Fluent readers are also good at managing ambiguity; that is, they are good at deciding when to stop and use a strategy to clarify content versus skipping over words or details that do not contribute to their understanding of the important ideas of a reading passage.

This unit breaks down reading fluently into two supporting skills:

- increasing reading fluency
- managing ambiguity

VOCABULARY PREVIEW

The following vocabulary items appear in the reading. Circle the ones you know. Put a question mark next to those you do not know.

lavish	hierarchical	mobility	virtually
nutritious	roasted (adj)	staple (n)	noble

EXERCISE 1

A. You will read a text called "Differences in Diet Between the Rich and Poor in the Late Medieval Period." What do you think some of those differences might have been? Write three predictions in the spaces.

☐ ....

☐ ....

☐ ....

B. Read the passage at a smooth, steady pace. Do not stop to look up unknown words or to reread difficult passages. After reading, look again at your predictions in Part A. Put a check (✓) next to the topics you predicted correctly.

Differences in Diet Between the Rich and Poor in the Late Medieval Period

1 Many paintings of medieval society portray people eating and drinking at lavish feasts, but in reality, very few people in the Middle Ages were wealthy enough to dine in such a way. Western Europe in the medieval period was feudalistic, meaning that societies were hierarchical, and mobility between the upper and lower classes was  virtually nonexistent. Social class divisions were evident in multiple ways, including how people dressed, where they lived, and what kind of work they did. Daily meals of the poor and the wealthy also differed greatly, and poor people, unlike members of the upper classes, had limited access to nutritious food.

2 Meats, such as mutton and pork, were costlier than grains and beans, and the preparation of roasted meats used more firewood, which was also expensive. While meat was a common food for wealthier people, soups and stews were the staple of poorer ones. The stew pot was the most common cooking tool in a typical lower-class, one-room home. Wealthier people, in contrast, had a cooking staff working in a large kitchen equipped with an oven and different kinds of pots, grills, and spits for roasting.

3 In addition to roasted meats, a common meal for men and women of the noble classes would have included meat pies, sauces, an assortment of vegetables, fruits, and even small candies to close the meal. All these would have been flavored with expensive spices, such as pepper, cinnamon, and saffron. A common meal for a poor person, on the other hand, was much simpler. One record from 1493 of a daily meal plan for farm workers in Bavaria, now a province of Germany, lists foods that were common for the lower class. To start the day, breakfast was a thin soup with pork fat. The midday meal, the largest of the day, was a loaf of barley bread, cooked cabbage, and milk. Supper was a milk soup with cabbage.

C. Read the passage again. Then put a check (✓) next to the reasons given in the passage for the differences in diet between social classes in the medieval period.

.... 1. Beans and grains were less expensive than meat.

.... 2. Firewood for cooking meat was costly.

.... 3. Lower-class people had less sophisticated tastes than members of the upper classes.

.... 4. Wealthier people had a cooking staff to prepare their food.

.... 5. Poor people preferred to eat soups and stews.

.... 6. Members of the lower classes did not have time to cook elaborate meals.

D. Work with a partner. Discuss the questions. Refer to the passage as needed.

1. Besides eating habits, what were some other differences between social classes in the Middle Ages, according to the passage?

2. The passage explains that medieval societies offered little opportunity for social mobility. Do you think this is a problem in your own country today? Why or why not?

3. Think about reading fluently. Were you able to read without stopping or looking back? How did previewing the task help you to read more smoothly? What other strategies could contribute to reading a text more fluently?

VOCABULARY CHECK

A. Review the vocabulary items in the Vocabulary Preview. Write their definitions and add examples. Use a dictionary if necessary.

B. Complete each sentence using the correct vocabulary item from the box. Use the correct form.

hierarchical	lavish	mobility	noble
nutritious	roasted (adj)	staple (n)	virtually

1. The clothes worn by men and women of the .... class were often made of costly materials such as silk, feathers, and fur.

2. .... meat, which is cooked directly over a fire, has been a popular dish in the cuisine of many cultures for thousands of years,

3. Rice and beans are a(n) .... of the diets of many countries, particularly in Central and South America.

4. In nearly every country on Earth, education is the key to social .... and financial stability.

5. In most cultures, weddings are .... affairs in which the parents of the bride and groom spend large amounts of money to feed and entertain their guests.

6. Bread, pasta, and sweet foods are not as .... as meat, fish, fruit, and vegetables and should make up only one part of a healthy diet.

7. As recently as one hundred years ago, Great Britain was a(n) .... society in which people born into the lower classes had little chance of getting an education or marrying a person "above" them.

8. Some medieval languages, notably Latin, have .... disappeared as spoken languages and survive only in written form.

🔊 Go to MyEnglishLab to complete a vocabulary exercise and skill practice, and to join in collaborative activities.

SUPPORTING SKILL 1

INCREASING READING FLUENCY

WHY IT'S USEFUL Increasing your ability to read fluently, without becoming overly concerned with small details or unknown words, will not only enable you to read faster but also improve your reading comprehension.

Among the factors necessary for fluent reading, three are most important: pace, automaticity, and accuracy. All three of these affect your ability to read fast without sacrificing comprehension.

Pace

Reading *pace* simply refers to how fast you can read, measured in *words per minute* (wpm). Calculating your pace is fairly simple:

CULTURE NOTE

Although reports vary, it is estimated that the average reading speed for native-speaker adults is about 300 wpm, while many college students read faster than this, at about 450 wpm. Many English language learners read at a slow speed of about 150 words per minute.

> Pace (wpm) = (# of words in a text ÷ # of seconds) × 60

The obvious importance of pace is that the faster you can read, the less time it takes you to complete reading assignments or research. But maintaining a certain speed is also important because it actually helps improve reading comprehension. Reading too slowly may reduce your comprehension because it causes you to process meaning on a sentence level instead of focusing on global understanding. Reading too slowly can also result in losing track of the main idea and forgetting the information at the beginning of a passage before you get to the end.

Of course, reading pace is affected by a number of factors, including:

- your familiarity with the content
- your previous experience with the text, if any
- the number of unknown words and concepts
- your purpose for reading
- the genre of the text

Reread the passage "Differences in Diet Between the Rich and Poor in the Late Medieval Period" on page 92 and calculate your speed using the formula above. The reading has 318 words. Because you have already read the passage and understand the main ideas and vocabulary, your reading pace will no doubt be faster than it was the first time you encountered the passage.

Write your reading speed in the blank: .... wpm

Automaticity

Reading *automaticity* refers to how naturally or smoothly you read and is very much related to pace. It means having the language skills necessary to read a text so fluently that you are not consciously aware of reading. The following are just a few of the strategies that can help you to develop greater automaticity:

TIP

Prereading strategies such as looking for main ideas, examining visuals, and activating prior knowledge are very useful for improving both pace and automaticity. Try to use these strategies whenever possible. The more you know about a topic before reading, the more smoothly you will be able to read through a text.

- **Pay special attention to content words**. Focusing on content words—words that convey meaning, especially nouns and verbs—and not stopping for function words like articles or prepositions can help you to develop greater automaticity.

- **Think in English** as much as possible. Try to avoid translating word for word.

- **Read in chunks.** That is, try to read word groups such as collocations, idioms, phrasal verbs, and other multiword units as one unit of meaning. This will become easier as your vocabulary grows.

- **Don't backtrack.** In other words, push yourself to keep moving forward and try to skip over unfamiliar or confusing bits of text.

- **Use your finger, a pencil, or a pen to help guide you forward**. This can help to keep you moving at a smooth speed.

- **Don't read aloud or move your mouth when reading.** *Subvocalizing*, as this is called, can cause you to read more slowly, and it decreases your ability to read in chunks. This is because most people can actually read faster than they can speak.

Accuracy

The reality is that there is no point in improving your reading speed and automaticity if you do not understand or remember what you have read. Reading *accuracy* refers to being able to understand the main ideas of a text the first time you read through it. When testing your reading speed, it is also important to check your reading accuracy. Did you understand the majority of what you read? To check your comprehension as you are reading, stop periodically and try to restate or take notes on the main ideas in the previous passage. (You can do this orally or in writing.) If you find you cannot recall the main ideas when you are reading, slow down.

TIP

All of the tips in this section can help you to improve your reading speed and automaticity, but the reality is that increasing one's reading fluency is a gradual process that takes time. Research shows that the best way to improve your general reading skills is simply by reading more. The more text of any kind you are exposed to, the easier it will be to start using strategies like reading in chunks, spotting key information to focus on, and not backtracking. Reading every day, whether the material is academic or not, is the best way to increase your reading fluency.

VOCABULARY PREVIEW

The following vocabulary items appear in the reading. Circle the ones you know. Put a question mark next to those you do not know.

spectacles	went to great lengths	on a regular basis	sustenance
mythical	appeal (n)	cuisine	ornate

EXERCISE 2

A. Preview the passage. Read the title and look at the picture. What do you think the article will be about? Write down words or phrases you know that are related to this topic.

☐ ....

☐ ....

☐ ....

☐ ....

☐ ....

B. Read the passage and calculate your wpm. There are 371 words in the reading. Write your reading speed.

.... wpm

Elaborate Feasts of the Middle Ages

1 Medieval European feasts were elaborate, showy spectacles intended to honor guests and celebrate holidays. The lead-up to a feast involved decorating the great hall of a wealthy manor or castle and choosing clothing with care—hosts and servants alike. Entertainers, minstrels in particular, usually performed, and cooks went to great lengths to serve meals that were not only delicious but also visually impressive. The meals featured many of the same foods that noblemen and noblewomen ate on a regular basis, but they differed dramatically in their presentation.

> **Glossary**
>
> **Minstrel:** an entertainer in the Middle Ages, primarily a musician or singer
>
> **Pièce de résistance:** (French) the most significant or important part of something
>
> **Carcass:** the dead body of an animal
>
> **Stag:** a male deer
>
> **Gut (v):** to remove the insides of an animal
>
> **Crenellations:** the top part of a castle's walls

Typical foods enjoyed at a medieval feast

2 Special dishes at feasts were known in England as *subtleties* and in France as *entremets*. Providing more than simple sustenance, such dishes became the pièce de résistance of the meal over the course of time. To please diners, cooks would sometimes make a roasted animal dish look alive. A chef, for example, would carefully remove the insides of a peacock, leaving the skin and feathers intact, and would then stuff a cooked goose inside the peacock carcass. The "live" peacock was carefully arranged on a large platter with its tail feathers spread out, after which it was carried out to the hall and presented to diners. Cooks employed this particular food-preparation technique with all manner of animals, even those as large as stags. Dishes in the form of imaginary and mythical animals were created this way as well. *The Forme of Cury*, a 14th-century English cookbook, includes one recipe that describes how to sew a rooster's head onto the hindquarters of a pig after the animals have been gutted and cooked.

3 While the appeal of such medieval animal creations is mostly lost on contemporary audiences, other fancy presentation techniques from medieval cuisine are still in use today. One of these is coloring foods with dyes made from natural sources. Parsley and egg yolk, for example, produce a bright green. Violet flowers make a purple hue, saffron colors foods yellow, and cooked purple carrot peel creates a blue shade. These dyes can be added to clear jellies, sauces, rice, and almond meal for visual appeal. Medieval cooks also created ornate pastries that were sculpted to resemble cathedrals, complete with banners, crenellations, and gold glaze. Such creations were not unlike fancy wedding cakes today.

C. It should take you about 75 seconds (300 wpm = (371 ÷ 75) x 60) to read at the speed of an average native speaker (300 wpm). Set a timer on your device for 75 seconds, and try to read the entire text again in that time.

Record your reading speed: .... **wpm**

TIP

If your reading pace is much slower than 300 wpm, set a more realistic goal for the second reading and work your way up to a faster pace. A pace of 250 wpm should take about 1 minute and 35 seconds; 200 wpm should take about 2 minutes; and 150 wpm should take roughly 2 minutes and 35 seconds.

D. Without referring back to the passage, read each statement and write *T* (True) or *F* (False). Then compare answers with a partner.

.... 1. Dishes served at feasts differed from everyday dishes in their presentation.

.... 2. Roasted peacock was a main dish at medieval feasts.

.... 3. A large variety of animals was used for the elaborate feast displays.

.... 4. Elaborate animal-imitation dishes are still popular today.

.... 5. Medieval chefs colored their dishes with dyes made from plants and flowers.

.... 6. Fancy pastries such as today's wedding cakes had their origins in medieval feasts.

E. Work with a partner. Answer the questions about your ability to read fluently.

1. Did previewing the text help you to read more fluently? How?

2. Did your reading speed improve from the first reading to the second?

3. How many questions did you answer correctly in Part D? Considering both your reading speed (Part C) and accuracy (Part D), how fluently were you able to read the passage? Did you miss any main ideas from the text because you were reading too quickly or too slowly?

VOCABULARY CHECK

A. Review the vocabulary items in the Vocabulary Preview. Write their definitions and add examples. Use a dictionary if necessary.

B. Complete each sentence using the correct vocabulary item from the box. Use the correct form.

appeal (n)	cuisine	go to great lengths	mythical
on a regular basis	ornate	spectacle	sustenance

1. The painting was so .... that I discovered new details every time I looked at it.

2. With waiters in costume and a live band, the party was a(n) .... that the guests would not soon forget.

3. Rare and expensive foods, such as meat dishes, are not served .... in many countries.

4. Plants such as soy, which are the basis of vegetarian diets, can provide as much .... as meat.

5. Children are often fascinated by stories involving .... creatures such as unicorns, mermaids, and werewolves.

6. Modern art does not hold much .... for me. I prefer paintings from much earlier periods, such as the Middle Ages or the Renaissance.

7. The restaurant is known for its "fusion" dishes that combine the .... of very different cultures, for example Japanese and Italian.

8. In honor of the king's birthday, the royal cooks .... to prepare a feast that the guests would never forget.

⬆ Go to MyEnglishLab to complete a vocabulary exercise and skill practices, and to join in collaborative activities.

SUPPORTING SKILL 2

MANAGING AMBIGUITY

WHY IT'S USEFUL A passage that is ambiguous is difficult to understand, is unclear in some way, or may have more than one meaning. Ambiguity can interfere with reading speed and fluency. By learning ways to manage ambiguous portions of a text, you will be able to maximize the amount of meaning that you can get from the text and increase your reading fluency.

In an ideal world, you would understand every word, every historical reference, and every bit of technical, idiomatic, or figurative language that you read. However, this is unrealistic. Even native speakers frequently encounter parts of a text that are unknown or confusing. This is especially true in academic courses, where reading material becomes more and more complex—and very often more ambiguous—as students advance.

Possible Causes of Ambiguity

- Unfamiliar, technical, or discipline-specific language or terminology
- Unknown cultural and historical references
- Complex syntax or grammar
- Figurative, poetic, or idiomatic language
- Words from other languages
- Words with multiple meanings
- Unfamiliar text structure or writing genre
- Unfamiliar abbreviations and acronyms
- Implied information

Managing Ambiguity

When you encounter ambiguous information you have two choices: to keep reading, or to stop reading and figure out a way to clear up the ambiguity. Which should you choose? It depends. In reality, there will be many occasions when time, resources, or circumstances (such as a test) prevent you from being able to stop and look up ambiguous information. In these cases, you must accept some level of ambiguity and focus your energy on getting the most out of the content that you *do* understand. The following strategies may be helpful:

- Continue reading even when you come across unfamiliar grammatical structures.
- Accept that discipline-specific readings will have challenging vocabulary and terminology.
- Learn to tolerate the discomfort that comes from reading texts with figurative or metaphorical language.

- Acknowledge that you may have little or no background information on a topic, and work with what you do know.
- Make inferences about the possible meaning of a text even if you do not understand much of it.

On the other hand, if you are *not* limited by time or other circumstances, the following strategies can help you to clarify ambiguous content:

TIP

If you reach the end of the text or section of text and can summarize it, that means you have successfully managed ambiguity—accepted what you do not understand in a text and / or used strategies to get as much meaning as possible from it.

- Use a website like *Wikipedia* to do some quick background reading on your topic. This is especially useful for obtaining context about readings that contain unfamiliar cultural or historical references.

- Consider your purpose for reading. Will you be expected to memorize and recall minor details or just demonstrate that you understood the gist? If it is the latter, then it is likely that you will be able to pull out the main ideas of a reading even if you do not understand some of the technical, figurative, or otherwise confusing language.

- Make use of techniques for rewording or simplifying text containing complex or unfamiliar syntax or grammar. (See BUSINESS ETHICS, Part 1, page 51.)

- Use strategies for dealing with unfamiliar vocabulary items. Try to determine which items are essential for getting the gist of a text and look up only those words. For example, terms that repeat many times throughout a reading are probably more important than items that only appear once or twice. (See BUSINESS ETHICS, Part 2, page 216, for strategies for guessing meaning from context.)

VOCABULARY PREVIEW

The following vocabulary items appear in the reading. Circle the ones you know. Put a question mark next to those you do not know.

flourished	conquest	reverence	prominent
penned (v)	genres	mystical	lyricism

EXERCISE 3

A. Scan the passage. Note any unfamiliar language and content. Think about strategies you could use to manage this ambiguity.

Persian Poetry in the Middle Ages

1 Persian poetry flourished in the Middle Ages and influenced literature not only in Persia but also in other parts of the world including India, Central Asia, and Turkey. The golden age of Persian poetry began two centuries after the Arab conquest of Iran in the 7th century, and it extended well into the late medieval period. Famous Persian poets including Sanai, Rumi, Hafiz, and Jami produced works that are still celebrated today. Since many Persian poets served at court, they produced panegyric poems overflowing with reverence for their masters. Persian poetry in the Middle Ages fell into three

Masnavi illuminated manuscript, India, 1663

main categories: The first, the Khorasani style, was native to Khorasan, a region in eastern Iran ruled by the Samanids. The second, *Irāq-i 'Ajam*, or the Persian-Iraqi style, became prominent throughout Iran, particularly in the southern city of Shiraz. The third style, *sabk-i Hindi*, or Indian style, developed in northern India, where Persian was the language of the ruling classes in the late Middle Ages.

2 Khorasani poets penned their verse from about the 10th to the 12th centuries. The major genres of Khorasani poetry include the epigram, which is a short poem, the *quasideh*, a midlength poem intended to praise something or someone, the lyric *ghazal* (perhaps the most famous genre of Persian poetry), and the long narrative poetic form. However, most of the Persian poetry that is famous in the West today is in the Persian-Iraqi style, such as the poetry of Rumi, who authored the *Masnavi*. Persian-Iraqi poetry is often mystical, with rich lyricism and complex themes. Finally, the Indian style of Persian poetry was modeled after the Persian literary genres but was also uniquely Indian in its expression of bold ideas and use of unique metaphors about unusual topics. One famous Indian poet who wrote in Persian was Amir Khusrau, whose 14th-century work introduced Persian poetic forms into Indian music.

B. Read the passage at a smooth, steady pace. Do not stop to look up unknown words or reread difficult passages. Use the strategies you have learned for managing ambiguity. Then read each statement and write *T* (True) or *F* (False).

.... 1. Persian poetry was influenced by Turkish literature.

.... 2. The golden age of Persian poetry lasted until the end of the Middle Ages.

.... 3. Persian poetry became widespread both in Iran and in northern India.

.... 4. Medieval Persian poetry is not well known today.

.... 5. Rumi was a genre of Persian poetry.

.... 6. Indian-Persian poetry included bold ideas and unusual metaphors.

C. Read the passage again. Check your answers to Part B. With a partner, correct the false statements.

D. Work with a partner. Discuss the questions about managing ambiguity.

1. How did you feel when you encountered ambiguous parts of the passage? Was it easy or difficult for you to continue reading?

2. The passage contains words from other languages. What was your reaction upon encountering them? What strategy or strategies did you use to manage the ambiguity?

3. Some words in the passage have more than one meaning (*native, rich, work, pen*). Were you confused by this? Were you able to keep reading, or did the ambiguity slow you down?

4. Which additional strategies to manage ambiguity did you use before, during, or after reading the passage? Which ones do you think will be most useful for you when you encounter ambiguous texts in the future? Why?

VOCABULARY CHECK

A. Review the vocabulary items in the Vocabulary Preview. Write their definitions and add examples. Use a dictionary if necessary.

B. Complete each sentence using the correct vocabulary item from the box. Use the correct form.

conquest	flourish	genre	lyricism
mystical	pen (v)	prominent	reverence

1. The Roman .... of Greece took place in 146 BCE following the Battle of Corinth.

2. The Persian poet Sanai .... his masterwork, *The Walled Garden of Truth*, in the early 12th century.

3. The woman felt an almost .... connection to the poem she had just read, which brought back memories of the religious teachings of her childhood.

4. The *ghazal* style of Persian poetry became .... in the 12th century, and it continues to be important today in many Indian languages.

5. The practice of extravagantly presenting food .... for many years during the Middle Ages and continues to this day in the form of wedding cakes and other fancy pastries.

6. The book is considered to belong to the spiritual ...., for it goes into depth about the main character's belief that the soul plays a central role in a person's well-being.

7. The artist was treated with utmost .... by his contemporaries, who regarded him as the most talented sculptor of their time.

8. The .... of Maya Angelou's song-like writing is enough to bring many readers to tears.

🔊 Go to MyEnglishLab to complete a vocabulary exercise and skill practices, and to join in collaborative activities.

INTEGRATED SKILLS

SUMMARIZING A TEXT

WHY IT'S USEFUL In academic classes, you will encounter a significant amount of information in written and spoken form. In order to effectively demonstrate your comprehension of information and complete class assignments, it is important that you refine your ability to summarize accurately and efficiently.

Paraphrasing, as you may have learned (see BUSINESS ETHICS, Part 2, page 211), is putting a piece of writing into your own words, resulting in a text that is about the same length as the original but that uses different vocabulary, grammar, and syntax. **Summarizing** is similar to paraphrasing in that it involves capturing the meaning of a text using your own words. However, unlike paraphrasing, summarizing requires you to restate *only the main points of the original text*. This means that your resulting summary is significantly shorter than the original text.

In academic courses, you may be asked to summarize in a variety of situations. A professor may ask you to read and summarize a text to demonstrate your comprehension. Or, after watching a film for a class, you might participate in a discussion in which you are asked to summarize and explain your understanding of the principal events. A specialized use of summarizing is found in the abstract portion of a research paper (see MATERIALS ENGINEERING, Part 1, page 142).

CULTURE NOTE

While some may associate summarizing only with academics, the skill is actually used frequently in daily life. Examples include telling a friend what a movie was about or what happened in a missed class. In both cases, you are extracting and then restating the main ideas, points, or events of a text or situation. When you think about summarizing this way, it becomes much less of a foreign idea.

Written summaries tend to be formal, with a number of distinguishing features. Reread the following paragraph, excerpted from the reading "Persian Poetry in the Middle Ages" on page 103. Think about the main idea as you read.

Persian poetry flourished in the Middle Ages and influenced literature not only in Persia but also in other parts of the world including India, Central Asia, and Turkey. The golden age of Persian poetry began two centuries after the Arab conquest of Iran in the 7th century, and it extended well into the late medieval period. Famous Persian poets including Sanai, Rumi, Hafiz, and Jami produced works that are still celebrated today. Since many Persian poets served at court, they produced panegyric poems overflowing with reverence for their masters. Persian poetry in the Middle Ages fell into three main categories

The first, the Khorasani style, was native to Khorasan, a region in eastern Iran ruled by the Samanids. The second, *Irāq-i 'Ajam*, or the Persian-Iraqi style, became prominent throughout Iran, particularly in the southern city of Shiraz. The third style, *sabk-i Hindi*, or Indian style, developed in northern India, where Persian was the language of the ruling classes in the late Middle Ages.

Now read this one-paragraph summary of the excerpt:

In "Persian Poetry in the Middle Ages," Castillo (2017) writes about the impact of Persian poetry on literary works in Persia as well as in other regions of the world. He goes on to mention some medieval Persian poets who are still admired in the present. Finally, he briefly describes the three types of medieval Persian poetry.

Note these characteristics of a strong summary:

- Only main ideas are included.
- The writer paraphrases language from the original text, with the exception of items that do not have synonyms, such as proper nouns.
- The writer does not provide his or her opinion. Summaries should contain only ideas from the original text and not your evaluation of them.
- It is significantly shorter than the original text.
- It includes a summary introduction, including the title of the reading, the author's last name, and the year of publication.
- It includes summary reminder language to refer back to the author (*He goes on to mention …*).
- It is written in the present tense.

Summaries can be of various lengths, from one sentence to several pages. Professors may specify the required length of written or spoken summaries when they give instructions for assignments.

TIP

Use your previewing skills to identify the main ideas that should be included in a summary. Note elements such as the title, visuals, and the genre of the text. In addition, remember what you have learned about annotating (see LINGUISTICS, Part 1, page 16). Making in-text markings and margin notes is a way for you to indicate what you think is a main idea and what is a supporting detail. Visual learners may consider writing this information in a grid instead.

EXERCISE 4

A. Read the title and first paragraph of the essay "Symbolism in Chaucer's *The Canterbury Tales.*" Underline or annotate the main ideas.

B. Read the three summaries of the first paragraph. Then discuss the questions with a partner.

1. Which summary is the best? Why do you think so?

2. What problems did the other summaries have? Refer to the characteristics of a good summary on page 107.

Summary 1

Hewitt (2014) writes about one of the most recognized medieval works—*The Canterbury Tales* by Geoffrey Chaucer. The story is about a group of fictional pilgrims traveling to the shrine of Saint Thomas Becket in Canterbury, England. In the collection, Chaucer criticizes society in 14th-century England, especially the Catholic Church. He does this by discussing clothing and other symbols to demonstrate how moral and immoral the characters and the Church are. These tales are similar to Dante's *Divine Comedy* and the troubadour poems, as they are written in the language of the people to make them more appealing to less-educated readers.

Summary 2

In "Symbolism in Chaucer's *The Canterbury Tales,*" Hewitt (2014) discusses *The Canterbury Tales*, a group of poems written in English by the 14th-century author Geoffrey Chaucer. Hewitt says the story is about 20 people traveling to see the shrine of Saint Thomas Becket in Canterbury, England. He goes on to briefly describe the symbols that Chaucer employs in order to reveal the virtues and failings of the Catholic Church in England in the 1300s.

Summary 3

Hewitt (2014) applauded the creativity of Chaucer's *The Canterbury Tales* in "Symbolism in Chaucer's *The Canterbury Tales*." In his discussion of the pilgrims' 14th-century journey to the shrine of Saint Thomas Becket in Canterbury, England, he praised Chaucer's ingenuity and wit in condemning the Church in an indirect manner. He emphasized Chaucer's talent in using symbols like clothing to highlight the Church's immorality, doing so using everyday language in order to attract readers from the unfortunate lower classes.

C. Read the rest of the article. Underline, make in-text markings, or write margin notes to mark the main ideas. Then work with a partner and compare annotations.

Symbolism in Chaucer's *The Canterbury Tales*

Pilgrims on their journey in *The Canterbury Tales* by Geoffrey Chaucer

Journal of Medieval Studies
Volume 6, Number 1: May 2014

1   One of the most recognized medieval works in Western literature is *The Canterbury Tales*, a 14th-century collection of narrative poems by English writer Geoffrey Chaucer. The tales, written in Middle English, are about a group of fictional pilgrims traveling to the shrine of Saint Thomas Becket in Canterbury, England. Much of the story is a critique of 14th-century English society, particularly the Catholic Church. Chaucer uses clothing and other symbols to illustrate the morality and immorality of his characters, and, by extension, of the Church itself.

> **Glossary**
>
> **Shrine:** a place connected with a religion, holy event, or holy person that people visit to pray
>
> **Commission (v):** to pay someone to make a specific product, such as a building or a work of art
>
> **Satirize:** make someone or something seem funny so that readers will see their faults
>
> **Adorned:** decorated
>
> **Brooch:** a piece of jewelry that a woman attaches to her clothes
>
> **Rosary:** a string of beads used by Catholics for counting prayers

(Continued)

Like Dante's *Divine Comedy* and the poems of the troubadours, *The Canterbury Tales* were composed in the language of the people rather than in Latin or French—languages known only to the educated classes—in order to increase their appeal to the common reader.

2 Many writers have described the medieval Catholic Church in 14th-century England as severely corrupt. This point of view is supported by historical fact. Some church officials lived like princes, and the Church used money taken forcefully from laypeople to commission extravagant building projects and works of art. In the eyes of many, the Church had strayed far from its religious duty to guide men and women to live holy lives, and many of Chaucer's characters satirize this slide in moral leadership. *The Canterbury Tales* has six main religious characters, and all except one are revealed to be corrupt in some way. One immoral character, the Monk, is described as wearing expensive, fur-lined clothing and golden jewelry—Chaucer's method of revealing to a reader the Monk's wealth and desire for worldly accessories. The narrator of the story portrays the Monk as follows:

> I saw his sleeves lined at the hand
> With squirrel fur, the finest of the land;
> And fastening his hood under his chin,
> He had a golden, skillfully made pin;
> A love-knot in the larger end there was.

This depiction is revealing because laws at the time actually forbade monks from wearing fur-trimmed clothing, as it was a fashion of the noble class. Monks were meant to live simple, prayer-filled lives in monasteries. The Monk in Chaucer's story, however, reveals a stronger desire for material goods than for a life of prayer.

3 Chaucer also paints the Prioress in *The Canterbury Tales* as a somewhat hypocritical character. A prioress, or head nun, would normally be conservative and humble. However, as the narrator in the story observes, the Prioress takes great care with her appearance in a way that signals to the reader that she is rather the opposite of humble:

> Her cloak was very elegant, as I was aware.
> A small coral about her arm she bore
> A pair of beads, adorned all with green,
> And thereon hung a brooch of golden sheen,
> On which there was first written a crowned A,
> And after *"Amor vincit omnia."*

4 By describing the fineness of her beaded coral rosary, Chaucer makes a mockery of her position as a holy woman. The Prioress is also described as having pet dogs that she weeps over, so the Latin words on her brooch, *Amor vincit omnia*, which translate to "Love conquers all," may be a jab at her focus on superficial matters rather than on the divine.

5 Clothing is not the only symbol used to call attention to the religious characters' hypocrisy. Chaucer also uses physiognomy—a pseudoscience in which outward appearance was considered to be a reflection of the person's true inner nature—to symbolically point out the foul traits of other characters. The Pardoner and the Summoner, members of the clergy in the story, are described in a manner that immediately arouses suspicion in the reader. The Pardoner, for example, has greasy, long hair and feminine characteristics, considered shameful in a man during Chaucer's time. The Summoner is described as stinking of onions and garlic and having a "fire-red" face covered in blisters that cannot be healed.

6 The Church is not the only object of Chaucer's biting social commentary in *The Canterbury Tales*. In fact, Chaucer represents society as a whole with his characters, who are taken from the upper, lower, and emerging middle class of the time. In addition to his pointed critique of the Church, Chaucer concurrently examines popular themes of the medieval period throughout the *Tales*, including courtly love, nobility, and gender roles.

D. Rewrite the main ideas you marked in Part C. Use your own words. Then use your paraphrases to write a one- or two-paragraph summary of the article.

E. Work with a partner. Answer the questions about summarizing a text.

1. How long is your summary? After comparing your summary with your partner's, is there any information that you would add or remove? If so, what?

2. Put a check (✓) next to the statements that are true regarding your summary. Which of these features were easy for you to implement? Which were more difficult?

.... I included only main ideas.

.... I used my own words as much as possible.

.... I did not include my opinion.

.... I included a summary introduction consisting of the name of the author, the title of the article, and the year of publication.

.... I included summary reminder language.

.... I used present tense.

VOCABULARY CHECK

A. Review the vocabulary items in the Vocabulary Preview. Write their definitions and add examples. Use a dictionary if necessary.

B. Complete each sentence using the correct vocabulary item from the box. Use the correct form.

clergy	critique (n)	depiction	extravagant
immoral	laypeople	monastery	severely

1. The feast was ....—there were huge tables loaded with meat, pies, and baskets of fruits and vegetables.

2. Many religious communities depend on donations from .... to help pay for building maintenance, social events, and staff salaries.

3. The newspaper published a strong .... of the way kitchen workers in some expensive restaurants were treated.

4. Members of the .... were invited to participate in a lecture series addressing modern-day problems facing their congregations.

5. The heroic .... of the male character in the story is misleading, as further into the tale, the reader comes to realize that the "hero" falsely takes credit for another man's actions.

6. The diet of the lower classes was .... limited in comparison to the wide variety of foods available to medieval noblemen and women.

7. Different religions have varying ideas about behavior that is considered .... and should be either forbidden or punished.

8. We visited the Alcobaça .... in Portugal (built in 1153) and learned about the day-to-day lives of the religious men who lived there.

◐ Go to MyEnglishLab to complete skill practices.

LANGUAGE SKILL

UNDERSTANDING LANGUAGE ASSOCIATED WITH CHRONOLOGY

WHY IT'S USEFUL Language associated with chronology is found across all academic writing genres. By becoming familiar with it, you will be better able to both understand and use such language.

Go to MyEnglishLab for a Language Skill presentation and practice.

VOCABULARY STRATEGY

RECOGNIZING MULTIPLE MEANINGS OF WORDS

WHY IT'S USEFUL Many words in English have more than one meaning. (The technical name for this is *polysemy*.) An essential dictionary skill is being able to choose the meaning that fits the context in which you encounter a word you don't know.

When you see an unknown vocabulary item in a text, you probably look at the context surrounding the item to try to understand its definition. If that strategy is ineffective, your next step may be to consult a dictionary. But what should you do if the dictionary provides more than one definition of an item? How do you choose the correct one? The following steps can help guide your choice:

1. Note that the first definition listed in the dictionary is usually the most common one. But that does not mean it is the definition you are looking for. If several definitions are listed for the same part of speech, read through all of them and see which one makes the most sense in the context where the item appears.

2. If a vocabulary item has more than one part of speech, it can be easier to select the correct definition. Go back to the original sentence and determine the part of speech in which the target word is used. Then consult the dictionary for meanings matching that part of speech.

3. After choosing the definition that seems to fit your context the best, go back to the text and double-check that it makes sense.

TIP

Some words are more commonly used than others, and it makes sense to learn them before less-common words. For example, *thin* is used more often than *lean* to describe a person. A dictionary may show common words using symbols, such as dots, or a different color.

Consider the word *standard*, which can be used as an adjective or a noun.

---

standard¹ /ˈstændərd/ ••• [S2] [W2] *noun* ◀))
[ETYMOLOGY] [COLLOCATIONS]

1 [LEVEL OF QUALITY] [countable, uncountable] a level of quality, skill ability, or achievement that is considered to be necessary or acceptable in a particular situation, and by which someone or something is judged:
◀)) *Air quality standards vary from state to state.*

2 [JUDGING/COMPARING] [countable, usually plural] the ideas of what is good or normal that people use to compare one thing with another:
◀)) *Shakespeare is the standard against which other playwrights are measured.*

3 [MORAL PRINCIPLES] **standards** [plural] moral principles about what kind of behavior or attitudes are acceptable:
◀)) *There is a concern about the **moral standards** of today's youth.*

standard² [S2] [W2] *adjective* ◀))

1 accepted as normal or usual:
◀)) *A work week of 40 hours is standard in the U.S.*

As you can see, there are three different noun definitions for the item *standard* and one adjective definition. Examine how *standard* is used in the following sentences. Which part of speech and definition matches each usage?

The company maintains the highest ethical **standards** for its employees.

The car rental company required us to sign a **standard** contract and show proof of insurance.

The trade organization has established **standards** that all participating companies must follow.

EXERCISE 5

A. Study the dictionary entries for the word *demand* used as a verb and the word *roast* used as a noun. Then read the sentences. Write the number of the definition that matches the meaning of the word in each sentence.

---

demand² ••○ [W3] *verb* [transitive] ◀))
[ETYMOLOGY] [VERB TABLE] [COLLOCATIONS] [THESAURUS]

1 to ask strongly for something, especially because you feel you have a right to do this:
◀)) *The president demanded the release of the hostages.*

---

demand (that)

🔊 *Rainey demanded that his lawyer be called.*

🔊 *I demand to know what's going on here!*

2 to ask a question or order something to be done very firmly:

🔊 *"Did you do this?" Kathryn demanded angrily.*

3 **demand something of somebody** to expect someone whom you have authority over to do something, especially something difficult [SYN] **expect:**

🔊 *Some parents demand too much of their children* (= they ask them to do things they cannot yet do).

4 if something demands your time, skill, attention, etc. it makes you use a lot of your time, skill, etc. [SYN] **require:**

🔊 *The job demands most of Cindy's time.*

1. The workers complained that their boss **demanded** too much of them while simultaneously doing too little work herself. ....

2. These days, studying for the law school entrance exam **demands** nearly all of Richard's time. ....

3. When the children laughed at the new student's unusual name, the teacher **demanded** that they apologize to him. ....

4. "Where were you at ten o'clock last night?" the judge **demanded**. ....

roast² ●●○ *noun* [countable] 🔊

1 a large piece of roasted meat → see also POT ROAST

2 an occasion at which people celebrate a special event in someone's life by telling funny stories or giving speeches:

🔊 *We're going to have a roast for Jack when he retires.*

3 an outdoor party at which food is cooked on an open fire [SYN] **cookout:**

🔊 *an oyster roast*

5. Joshua's friends had a **roast** for him at a restaurant the night before his marriage. ....

6. When my family gets together for special occasions, my mother usually cooks a **roast**. ....

7. To celebrate Thanksgiving, the families on my street get together for a turkey **roast**. ....

B. Read the sentences with vocabulary items in bold. Use the context to determine the word's part of speech. Then study the dictionary entry for each boldfaced word. Copy the definition that matches the way the word is used in each sentence.

1. I printed out the report and **stapled** the pages together.

   Part of speech: ....

   Definition: ....

2. Rice is a **staple** food in many parts of southern and eastern Asia.

   Part of speech: ....

   Definition: ....

---

staple¹ /ˈsteɪpəl/ ●●○ *noun* [countable] ◀))
[ETYMOLOGY]

1 a small piece of thin wire that is used to hold pieces of paper together, by using a special tool to push the ends through the paper and bend them over

2 a small U-shaped piece of metal with pointed ends, used to hold something in place

staple² *verb* [transitive] ◀))
[VERB TABLE] [THESAURUS]

to fasten two or more things together with a staple

staple³ *adjective* [only before noun] ◀))

1 forming the greatest or most important part of something:
◀)) *Oil is Nigeria's staple export.*

2 **staple diet/food** the food that you normally eat:
◀)) *Potatoes are part of the staple diet in Russia.*

---

3. After months of lifting weights daily, Shinji was **leaner** than he'd ever been in his life.

   Definition: ....

4. Unaware that the room had just been painted, Maria **leaned** against the wall.

   Definition: ....

lean¹ /lin/ ••• [S3] [W2] *verb* ◀))

[ETYMOLOGY] [VERB TABLE] [THESAURUS]

1 [intransitive always + adv./prep.] to move or bend your body in a particular direction:
lean forward/back/over etc.

◀)) *Celia leaned forward.*

◀)) *Then he leaned over and kissed his wife.*

2 [intransitive always + adv./prep.] to sit or stand in a position that is not upright and use another surface for support:
lean on/against

◀)) *She leaned on her cane as she walked.*

◀)) *The bicycle was leaning against a tree.*

lean² •○○ *adjective* ◀))

[ETYMOLOGY] [COLLOCATIONS] [THESAURUS]

1 thin in a healthy and attractive way:

◀)) *He is a lean and athletic man.*

2 lean meat does not have much fat on it:

◀)) *Try to choose lean cuts of meat.*

5. In Mexican-style cooking, chefs often use leafy plants such as parsley or cilantro as a **garnish**.

Part of speech: ....

Definition: ....

6. The state has the right to **garnish** the pay of a person who does not provide money to support his or her children.

Part of speech: ....

Definition: ....

gar·nish¹ /ˈɡɑrnɪʃ/ *verb* [transitive] ◀))

VERB TABLE | COLLOCATIONS

1 to add something to food in order to decorate it:

garnish something with something

◀)) *Roasted turkey garnished with fresh orange and lemon slices.*

2 (*also* **garnishee**) *technical* to take money from someone's salary because he or she has not paid a debt:

◀)) *The state **garnished my wages** to pay for the parking tickets.*

garnish² *noun* [countable] ◀))

ETYMOLOGY

something that you add to food to decorate it

TIP

It is important to keep your vocabulary study system updated to include new definitions of familiar items. You may wish to mark the most common definition of a word by highlighting or starring it.

C. **Using your preferred dictionary, copy the definition of each numbered vocabulary item as it is used in the sentences. Then compare answers with a partner.**

1. **fuel**

   a. We need to stop for fuel, or we won't be able to make it to our destination.

   ....

   b. The rising cost of gasoline fueled a demand for hybrid cars.

   ....

2. **value**

   a. The value of the dollar goes up and down daily in the international currency market.

   ....

   b. Most employers value hard work and dedication from their employees.

   ....

3. **direct**

   a. Helena has direct control over her sick mother's financial affairs.

   ....

   b. The professor directed the students' attention to the photograph.

   ....

4. **mask**

a. The man's outward confidence masked his inner feelings of fear and shame.

....

b. At the conclusion of the long surgery, the doctors and nurses took off their masks.

....

APPLY YOUR SKILLS

WHY IT'S USEFUL By applying the skills you have learned in this unit, you can gain a better understanding of this challenging reading about the impact of the spice trade on globalization beginning in the late 15th century.

BEFORE YOU READ

A. Discuss these questions with one or more students.

1. Spices are an essential part of the cuisine of nearly every culture around the world. Which spices would it be difficult for you to live without? Which part of the world do you think they come from?

2. What food products, if any, is your native country known for exporting? Which ones does it import? Do you know which other countries trade with yours?

3. Sometimes, as a food, product, or technology that was once considered "exclusive" gains popularity and becomes more accessible to the general public, it becomes less desired. What are some foods, products, or technologies for which this is true?

B. You will read a passage about how the medieval spice trade led to globalization. As you read, think about these questions.

1. What countries (or regions) of the world benefited most from the spice trade? Why?

2. What spices were the most desired in the spice trade?

3. What were some effects of the global spice trade on the availability, price, and use of spices? What other effects did the spice trade have?

C. Review the Unit Skills Summary on the next page. As you read the passage, apply the skills you learned in this unit.

READ

A. Read the passage. Annotate and take notes on the answers to the questions in Before You Read, Part B.

How the Spice Trade Drove Globalization

1 The international trade in spices has been documented by merchants since ancient times, and spices, similar to gold and silver, fueled many wars and conquests during the Middle Ages. The spice trade was the driver of early globalization, particularly during the medieval era, when spices were a highly sought-after commodity and one of the most expensive items in the kitchen of a wealthy manor. By the close of the 15th century in western Europe, nations were embarking on exploratory journeys to find more affordable ways to get spices, which in turn led to more extensive knowledge of world geography. A dash of pepper hardly seems like a consequential item today, but over the course of time, pepper and other spices influenced the geopolitical future of many countries.

2   Western Europe—particularly England—was at the far reaches of the globe in terms of access to spices. Some spices, of course, were native to England, such as mustard, sage, basil, and rosemary. The most coveted spices of the time, however, included nutmeg, cinnamon, pepper, ginger, and mace. These were all native to warmer regions and so, by necessity, had to be traded to cold-climate European countries. Trading routes had become well established in the era before the Middle Ages, when the Romans ruled much of western Europe and traded spices from India through the port city of Alexandria in Egypt. After the fall of the Roman Empire (476 CE), the spice trade dwindled. That changed in the Middle Ages, however; from about 1000 to 1500 CE, spices became very popular in Europe, and there was a high demand for these precious commodities.

3   No one knows exactly why spices became so popular. One old theory that has been debunked by modern scholars is that medieval cooks used spices to mask the taste of spoiled meat—food that obviously has a short shelf life without refrigeration. The notion that medieval people regularly ate spoiled meat is slightly ridiculous, to start with. More significant to the debate is the fact that spices were much too valuable to be wasted in such a way. Sugar, which was used as a spice and was tremendously popular in Europe, was nearly as expensive as silver. A more plausible reason for the demand for spices in the medieval period is that spiced food made a good impression. This was no small matter at a time when entertaining was strongly linked to fancy presentation of food. A dish spiced with pepper, cinnamon, mace, and cloves would impress diners simultaneously with its color, flavor, and costly, exotic ingredients. The closest parallel today might be the artfully plated haute cuisine of a famous restaurant, where dinners cost $300 a person.

4   The impression that spices made, however, was likely not enough to explain why people paid such exorbitant rates for them. The other probable reason for the increase in the demand for spices is that they were widely believed to have medicinal properties. Cinnamon and pepper, for example, were thought to be hot and dry foods, which balanced out cold and wet foods such as fish or sauce. Eating the correct food was believed to keep a person in good health—not unlike the practice of herbal medicine today, in which someone might take a plant-based supplement to treat a dizzy spell, for example. In addition, spices were occasionally given by themselves to treat specific health problems. Buying and using spices was, therefore, akin to taking contemporary prescription medication.

5   As the spice trade grew in Europe, the city that profited the most was the port city of Venice, which held a monopoly on trade with spice-rich cities, including Constantinople and Alexandria. As Venice grew richer, other European nations grew resentful. Portugal, Spain, and other countries began to search for a way to circumvent the Venetian ports. In the 1490s, ships sailed west and south in hopes of discovering spices elsewhere. Christopher Columbus, for instance,

(Continued)

sailed west and landed in the Caribbean, which opened up an enormous new territory—the Americas—that was later exploited for resources. Vasco da Gama, a Portuguese nobleman, sailed to Asia around the Cape of Good Hope on the southern tip of Africa, establishing a new trade route for getting spices to Europe.

6　The discovery of new lands rich in spices led to a race among European nations eager to colonize other territories. Once European nations colonized India and other warm-climate countries, spices—among other goods—were introduced into their economies. This led inevitably to a drop in the price of spices, making them accessible to everyone, even the poor. Ironically, after the mid-1600s, Europeans stopped spicing their food so heavily. This may have been due to a change in beliefs about the medicinal quality of spices, or it may have been the result of a change in attitudes about food. Spiced food, once the exclusive domain of the wealthy, was now available to all, so it was not quite so desirable. As subtler flavors began to take the place of stronger ones, merchants began trading in new commodities instead of spices.

B. Work with a partner. Use your annotations to discuss the answers to the questions in Before You Read, Part B. Are there any questions you cannot answer? Which of the other reading skills that you have learned in this unit could help you to answer them?

◐ Go to MyEnglishLab to read the passage again and answer critical thinking questions.

THINKING CRITICALLY

Discuss the questions with another student.

1. In Paragraph 5, the author states that Venice became the most successful spice-trading city in the Middle Ages. Think about what you know about Venice or look it up on a map. What are some reasons that Venice may have held such a monopoly?

2. The author mentions that many wars in the past were fought over spices. Why do you think this might be?

3. Which commodities are as precious today as spices were in the past? Do you foresee a time when wars will be fought over these commodities, just as wars were once fought over spices?

THINKING VISUALLY

A. The key events below are discussed in the unit. Scan the readings to find the date, dates, or time period when each event occurred. Write this information in the blanks. Note the order in which the events occurred.

1 .... Spanish and Portuguese explorers sail west and south in search of new sources of spices.

2 .... The fall of the Roman Empire marks the beginning of the Middle Ages.

3 .... Spices start to become popular in European cuisine.

4 .... Rumi lives and composes poetry.

5 .... The European spice trade declines.

6 .... Arabs conquer Iran.

7 .... Geoffrey Chaucer writes *The Canterbury Tales*.

8 .... Hafiz lives and composes poetry.

B. Write the events from Part A in the correct places on the timeline. Write notes; for example, you can reduce "Spices start to become popular in European cuisine" to "Spices become popular in Euro."

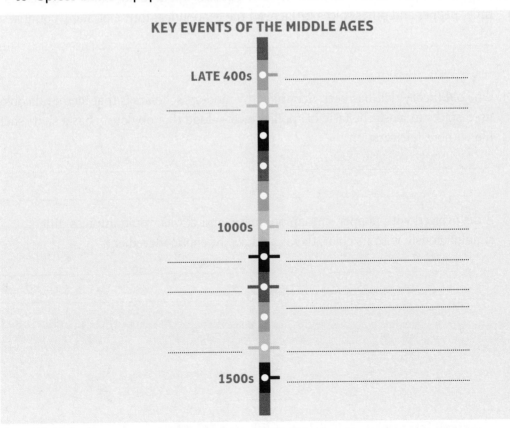

KEY EVENTS OF THE MIDDLE AGES

LATE 400s

1000s

1500s

THINKING ABOUT LANGUAGE

Read these excerpts from "How the Spice Trade Drove Globalization." Underline the language associated with chronology. Then go online and find authentic uses of this language. Copy the sentences in which the language is used and note the sources. Compare sentences with a classmate.

1. The spice trade was the driver of early globalization, particularly during the medieval era, when spices were a highly sought-after commodity and one of the most expensive items in the kitchen of a wealthy manor.

   ....

   ....

2. By the close of the 15th century in western Europe, nations were embarking on exploratory journeys to find more affordable ways to get spices, which in turn led to more extensive knowledge of world geography. (*Note*: You may use any century in your Internet search.)

   ....

   ....

3. A dash of pepper hardly seems like a consequential item today, but over the course of time, pepper and other spices influenced the geopolitical future of many countries.

   ....

   ....

4. One old theory that has been debunked by modern scholars is that medieval cooks used spices to mask the taste of spoiled meat—food that obviously has a short shelf life without refrigeration.

   ....

   ....

5. A dish spiced with pepper, cinnamon, mace, and cloves would impress diners simultaneously with its color, flavor, and costly, exotic ingredients.

   ....

   ....

6. Eating the correct food was believed to keep a person in good health—not unlike the practice of herbal medicine today, in which someone might take a plant-based supplement to treat a dizzy spell, for example.

    ....

    ....

7. Buying and using spices was, therefore, akin to taking contemporary prescription medication.

    ....

    ....

8. At the turn of the 16th century, ships sailed west and south in hopes of discovering spices elsewhere. (*Note*: You may use any century in your Internet search.)

    ....

    ....

▶ Go to MyEnglishLab to watch Professor Galvez's concluding video and to complete a self-assessment.

How the study of molecules relates to the real world

MATERIALS ENGINEERING

Research Articles

UNIT PROFILE

In this unit, you will consider the subject of materials engineering. You will read about polymers (certain chemical compounds) and their use in vehicles, home construction, and NASA technology. You will also learn about polymers used in recycling and for cosmetic and medical purposes.

Preview the reading "Polymer Applications in Soft Robotics" on page 152. Read the title and look at the art. What is the article about? Scan through the different sections of the article. Identify the Introduction (including literature review), Methodology, Results, and Discussion.

OUTCOMES

- Understand the introduction
- Understand the discussion
- Summarize a research article
- Understand modifiers
- Recognize and learn multiword units

For more about **MATERIALS ENGINEERING**, see **2** **3**.
See also [W] and [OC] **MATERIALS ENGINEERING** **1** **2** **3**.

GETTING STARTED

Go to MyEnglishLab to watch Professor Heilshorn's introductory video and to complete a self-assessment.

Discuss these questions with a partner or group.

1. What kinds of manufactured materials (e.g., plastic, glass, paper) are used to make the objects you use every day? What do you know about the production of these materials?

2. Scientists often use designs inspired by nature to create new inventions. This is called *biomimicry*. Can you think of any examples of this?

3. In her introduction, Professor Heilshorn introduces chewing gum as an example of a polymer. What are some unique physical properties of chewing gum? Can you think of any other natural or manufactured materials that behave this way?

FUNDAMENTAL SKILL

UNDERSTANDING RESEARCH ARTICLES

WHY IT'S USEFUL As a university student in almost any field, you will be expected to read a great many research articles. Familiarizing yourself with the content and format of this kind of text will help you to understand the contents more effectively and enable you to use the information for other purposes.

Researchers write research articles to share information they discover with the rest of their relevant academic community. An original research article is one in which the researchers pose a specific research question, collect original data or perform an original study, and publish the results. Such a publication, usually in an academic or scientific journal, is considered a primary source of information, unlike sources that may quote or refer to the original study, which are regarded as secondary sources.

Although the style and contents of research articles vary among academic disciplines, the genre has some features that are generalizable across different fields of study. Most basically, these are the introduction, methodology, results, and discussion sections (often abbreviated as IMRD):

Introduction	This section introduces the topic of the article in a general sense and begins to narrow the focus, leading to the methodology section that follows.
	It includes a **literature review**, which summarizes previous research on the topic to justify why there is a need for the present study. It also contains the researchers' **hypothesis**, or prediction about what they expect to find as a result of their research.
Methodology	This section gives step-by-step information about how the researchers conducted their study. Typically, it includes a description of participants (if relevant), types of data collected, and other important parts of the research process.
Results	This section covers what the researchers learned and why that information is important. It can also include implications of these findings for the academic community or general public, limitations of the study, and ideas for further research.
Discussion	This section concludes the article and leaves the reader with the most important information to remember about the study.

Research studies published in academic journals usually begin with an **abstract**, a short summary paragraph introducing the focus, justification, and basic results of the study. The abstract follows the same basic organization as the rest of the research article. It explains why the researcher(s) believe there needs to be a new study on their topic and what specific goals they had in doing the research.

CULTURE NOTE

The abstract is the first thing most readers look at when doing research on a specific topic and trying to find articles about it. At academic conferences, abstracts are similarly used to summarize the information that will be presented in various sessions. The purpose of an abstract is to provide enough information in one short paragraph to enable readers to decide whether or not a topic interests them or is relevant to their purposes.

This unit breaks down **understanding research articles** into two supporting skills:

- understanding the introduction
- understanding the discussion

VOCABULARY PREVIEW

The following vocabulary items appear in the reading. Circle the ones you know. Put a question mark next to the ones you do not know.

fluctuations	fracture (v)	durability
longevity	simulate	concur

EXERCISE 1

A. Discuss the questions with a partner before you read.

1. What are polymers?

2. Why is it important for scientists to study how different building materials react at different temperatures? How might scientists be able to test this?

3. Why must scientists be careful when considering materials to use in inventions related to medical devices and cars?

B. Preview the abstract from a research article about polymers. Read the title and look at the image. Note two topics that might be covered in the reading. Then read the passage quickly. Were your predictions correct?

....

....

Mathematical Models to Describe Polymers at Different Temperatures

ABSTRACT ─────────────────────────────────

[1] Polymers are substances composed of long chains of molecules, and they are used in many everyday objects, including cars, phones, and clothing. [2] They can be man-made or occur naturally. [3] Polymers respond to fluctuations in temperature, becoming hard and brittle in colder temperatures, stretchy and ductile in warmer ones. [4] Polymeric materials may experience thermal shock, or fracture, when they undergo temperature changes. [5] Since polymers are common in building materials, medical implants, aerospace materials, and other applications that concern human safety, knowing the durability and longevity of a polymeric material is important. [6] The objective of this study was to observe in the short term how our company's product would meet these performance requirements. [7] In this study, polymers were heated in calibrated ovens to break down the material and simulate the aging process that occurs in the material in real life. [8] When exposed to heat, the polymers in the chosen material experienced different levels of degradation (worsening condition). [9] Our findings concur with other published results of polymeric materials testing. [10] The results of these tests demonstrate which polymeric materials are appropriate for specific applications. [11] The results also predict how well the material will function years later in their applications when other temperature-changing factors come into play.

Glossary

Brittle: hard and rigid but can be easily broken into many small pieces

Ductile: can be pressed or pulled into shape without breaking

Calibrated: adjusted very carefully and precisely to a specific standard

Scientists heat-testing polymeric materials

C. Read the passage. Then read the statements and write *T* (True) or *F* (False). Correct the false statements.

.... 1. There are many molecules in each polymer.

.... 2. Polymers are not affected by changes in temperature.

.... 3. Medical devices are unaffected by brittle polymers.

.... 4. Polymeric material that is not durable may cause injuries.

.... 5. In addition to knowing the durability of polymers, scientists also need to know how long they can last without breaking down.

.... 6. Putting polymeric materials into the oven can be a way to test their aging process.

.... 7. This study will help predict if certain polymeric materials will be useful in the long term.

.... 8. The results of this study are different from the results of other studies.

D. An abstract follows the same basic organization as a full-length research article. Identify the range of sentences from the abstract that represent each part (e.g., Sentences 1–5).

Parts of a Research Article	Sentence Range
Introduction	
Methodology	
Results	
Discussion	

VOCABULARY CHECK

A. Review the vocabulary items in the Vocabulary Preview. Write their definitions and add examples. Use a dictionary if necessary.

B. Complete each sentence using the correct vocabulary item from the box. Use the correct form.

concur	durable	fluctuate
fracture (v)	longevity	simulate

1. The .... of a computer depends on the brand and the care it is given.

2. The researchers .... a crash to see how well the car's seat belts would work in an accident.

3. Because of the intense amount of heat put on the polymeric material in the study, the material .... and broke into pieces.

4. The company researchers are attempting to create a polymer-based hiking boot that is .... enough to withstand water, heat, and rough terrain.

5. The committee presented a new version of the product, and the executive board .... with them that it was superior to the original.

6. The new heart implant was designed to accommodate .... in levels of physical activity so that it could work for people with different lifestyles.

⊙ Go to MyEnglishLab to complete a vocabulary exercise and skill practice, and to join in collaborative activities.

SUPPORTING SKILL 1

UNDERSTANDING THE INTRODUCTION

WHY IT'S USEFUL Understanding the introduction of a research article is useful because it helps orient you to the topic of the article and familiarize you with related research that has already been conducted.

No good research project exists in isolation. For every new study, there is a foundation of earlier research that has influenced the researchers' decisions in some way. Whether the research is being done to prove or disprove a theory, to understand a concept better, or to test a related idea, researchers demonstrate their awareness of what studies already exist and how the present study relates to them.

To acknowledge this background in a research article, researchers include an introduction section, which includes, among other things, a **literature review**—a summary of important research findings related to the current study. Overall, the introduction has three main purposes:

To show awareness of previous research: Authors establish their credibility by demonstrating their awareness of research that has already been conducted on the topic. This indicates that the new research is not random or redundant.

To critically evaluate sources and draw relationships between them: Authors should also select sources (that is, the other research they have read before conducting a study) carefully. Sources should be reliable and significant to the context. Making connections between different sources enables authors to illustrate trends in the research or to outline contrasting theories and viewpoints.

To justify the need for the new research study: After thoroughly describing important prior research on a topic, authors explain why their research is necessary and how the results contribute to the field. This shows that the research is new and unique but not detached from what currently exists.

Being aware of what to look for in a literature review can help you to critically evaluate the reliability of the study you are reading and be more aware of major trends in the field.

TIP

Every research article ends with a list of sources that the researchers consulted. If a source mentioned in the literature review section seems particularly interesting or relevant to you or to your topic of research, you can find the full citation, or reference, at the end of the article and use it to locate the piece.

VOCABULARY PREVIEW

The following vocabulary items appear in the reading. Circle the ones you know. Put a question mark next to the ones you do not know.

nonrenewable	emissions	legislated	reduction
advantageous	novel (adj)	components	comprehensive

EXERCISE 2

A. You will read the introduction to a research article. Look at the image and read the title of the passage. Write two questions you predict the reading will answer.

1. ....

2. ....

B. Now read the passage. Review your questions from Part A. Were they answered in the passage?

Polymers Saving Energy

1 Oil is a nonrenewable resource, and using it produces fossil fuel emissions that are harmful to the environment. Approximately 14 percent of all emissions worldwide are caused by the burning of fuel used in transportation. In the past decade, public awareness of global warming has pushed various industries to offer more environmentally-friendly product options. In some cases, the development of such products has been legislated. In the automotive industry, both legislation and demand for fuel-efficient cars have driven companies to find ways to make cars use less gasoline. Weight reduction, or "lightweighting," has become increasingly popular as a method to improve fuel efficiency. Some studies point to a 7 percent improvement in fuel economy with only a 10 percent reduction in weight of vehicles. Cars were once constructed mostly of steel, but today they are being built with aluminum and plastic composite materials. Polymer-based materials in vehicles weigh an estimated 50 percent less than other materials, which makes them advantageous for use in vehicle design. Building vehicles with polymer-based materials, therefore, has double benefits for the automotive industry because it is both economically and environmentally beneficial.

2 Today, approximately 15 to 20 percent of vehicles are made with polymer products. Polymer materials are commonly located in vehicle bumpers, instrument panels, fenders, the front ends of the car, and other areas within the car. Novel ways of including weight-reducing polymer material are also being researched. For example, glass panes in car windows can be replaced with polycarbonate plastic, and even joints within the vehicle can be made with more lightweight polymer materials. The US Department of Energy estimates that putting these types of components in just one

Car made of polymer-based materials

quarter of the cars in the United States would save more than 5 billion gallons of fuel annually by the year 2030. These advancements are promising in the effort to improve fuel efficiency.

(Continued)

3 To gain a comprehensive look at what types of polymer materials are the most promising in vehicle engineering today, we have investigated some high-performance polymer products on the market. This paper describes eight plastics that are commonly found in vehicles today: polypropylene (PP), polyamide (PA), acrylonitrile butadiene styrene (ABS), polybutylene terephthalate (PET), polyoxymethylene (POM), polyvinylchloride (PVC) polyurethane (PU), and polyethylene (PE). We list each polymer product, how it is used, and how it improves fuel efficiency in cars. In addition, we have noted the use of "bioplastics," or polymers produced from renewable resources, and how they may be incorporated into automotive design in the future.

4 **References:**

1. US Environmental Protection Agency, accessed July 2017. https://www.epa.gov/ghgemissions/global-greenhouse-gas-emissions-data
2. Lyu, Min-Young and Choi, Tae Gyun. 2015. Research Trends in Polymer Materials for Use in Lightweight Vehicles. *Journal of Engineering and Manufacturing*. Vol. 16, Issue 1, p. 213–220.
3. The American Chemistry Council, accessed July 2017. https://plastics.americanchemistry.com/Automotive/ Plastics—Major Markets: Automotive.
4. *Wall Street Journal*. Detroit Sheds Pounds for Gas-Mileage Gains. Jan. 14, 2013. https://www.wsj.com/articles/SB10001424127887324595704578239812708897212
5. Braganca, I.M.F., et al. 2017. Lightweight Joining of Polymer and Polymer-Metal Sheets by Sheet-Bulk Forming. *Journal of Cleaner Production*. Vol. 145, p. 98–104. DOI: https://doi.org/10.1016/j.jclepro.2017.01.049
6. US Department of Energy, accessed July 2017. https://energy.gov/eere/vehicles/lightweight-materials-cars-and-trucks

C. Read the passage a second time. Then choose the best answer to each question according to the reading.

1. Which of the following is true about the design of cars before the adaptations described in the passage?

   a. They did not use a lot of heavy metals.
   b. They had worse fuel efficiency than modern cars.
   c. They were lightweight.
   d. They were less harmful to the environment than modern cars.

2. Which of the following car parts are not mentioned in the article as being made of polymers?

   a. fenders
   b. bumpers
   c. windows
   d. seats

3. According to the passage, what is the main advantage of using polymers in car manufacturing?

   a. Polymers create a more visually attractive car.
   b. The majority of cars today are already made primarily of polymer-based materials.
   c. Fuel efficiency is better in polymer-based cars.
   d. Polymer-based cars are more comfortable to drive.

4. Which statistic is true, based on the passage?

   a. Today, vehicles are made of about 15–20 percent polymeric materials.
   b. By 2030, 5 billion gallons of gas could be saved every year by replacing components with polymeric material in 25 percent of US cars.
   c. Fuel used in transportation is responsible for 7 percent of worldwide fuel emissions.
   d. Fuel economy can be improved by 10 percent if vehicle weight is reduced by 7 percent.

5. Which of the following is NOT a source referenced in the introduction?

   a. the *Wall Street Journal*
   b. the *New York Times*
   c. the US Department of Energy
   d. the *Journal of Engineering and Manufacturing*

6. How does the study plan to investigate the efficacy of polymer-based materials in vehicles?

   a. The researchers have weighed several types of vehicles on the market today.
   b. The researchers have measured the effects of vehicles on global warming over the past 30 years.
   c. The researchers have invented new polymer-based products to test in vehicles.
   d. The researchers have tested several common types of polymer plastics used in car manufacturing.

D. Write the number of the paragraph that matches each component of the literature review. Then compare answers with a partner.

.... 1. Referencing sources

.... 2. Justifying the need for the new research

.... 3. Showing awareness of previous research

.... 4. Description of the current research

VOCABULARY CHECK

A. Review the vocabulary items in the Vocabulary Preview. Write their definitions and add examples. Use a dictionary if necessary.

B. Complete each sentence using the correct vocabulary item from the box. Use the correct form.

advantageous	component	comprehensive	emission
legislate	nonrenewable	novel (adj)	reduction

1. .... standards exist for vehicles in order to help reduce the negative environmental effects of burning fossil fuels.

2. It can be .... for consumers to buy vehicles made with polymer-based plastics, as such cars require less gasoline and are cheaper to run.

3. A worldwide .... in fossil fuel usage can be a positive step toward slowing down the rate of global warming.

4. Water is a(n) .... resource because there is a fixed amount of it on the planet, and it cannot be replaced.

5. An ideal scenario for car manufacturers wishing to cut costs would be to build vehicles made of .... that are both lightweight and inexpensive.

6. Safety standards for airbags and seat belts are .... by governments to ensure the well-being of drivers and passengers.

7. When making decisions about the effectiveness of polymers in their products, developers must take a(n) .... look at several factors, including cost, safety, and weight.

8. Using polymeric materials in technology is not .... because these types of products have existed for decades.

 Go to MyEnglishLab to complete a vocabulary exercise and skill practice, and to join in collaborative activities.

SUPPORTING SKILL 2

UNDERSTANDING THE DISCUSSION

> **WHY IT'S USEFUL** Understanding the types of information found in the discussion section will help you identify key ideas when reading a research article.

The final section of a typical research article is the discussion. Here authors interpret the previously-reported results based on their own knowledge of the topic as well as the review of related research in the introduction. It is in the discussion that authors provide possible explanations of the results and sometimes speculate on factors that may have led to them. The interpretation of results generally appears in the same order in which each result was presented in the results section. This organization lends continuity to the article and makes it easier for readers to locate a particular result should they care to refer back to it.

In addition, the discussion section generally

- connects back to the introduction. Authors remind readers of the objective and hypotheses of the study and may demonstrate how the results provide additional related information.

- analyzes and interprets any patterns, relationships, or trends that surfaced in the results, and may indicate conclusions that can be drawn from them.

- refers to relevant studies done by other researchers and discusses whether the current results are compatible with those of such studies, using in-text citations to refer to them. The discussion may also state how the results of other studies assisted in interpreting the results of the current study.

- mentions any unexpected findings and provides possible explanations for them.

- addresses flaws in the study or any factor the study did not take into account and how future studies might be designed differently to address these issues.

- discusses theoretical and practical implications and applications of the results.

VOCABULARY PREVIEW

The following vocabulary items appear in the reading. Circle the ones you know. Put a question mark next to the ones you don't know.

carry a risk	contamination	viable	outlets
filters (n)	promising (adj)	nourishes	noteworthy

EXERCISE 3

A. Preview the discussion section of a research article titled "Microalgae Collection Systems." Note the title, image, and subhead. Predict what an *algae collection system* might be and what it could be used for. Write two questions you have.

Prediction

....

Questions

1. ....

2. ....

B. Now read the passage. Review your predictions and questions from Part A. Were your predictions correct? Were your questions answered?

Microalgae Collection Systems

Discussion

1 [1] The first result of this study on the strengths and weaknesses of different types of algae collection systems shows that open-pond systems are more affordable than closed-collection systems, but that open-pond systems carry a significantly higher risk of algae contamination than closed systems. [2] An "open-pond system," as previously noted, is a system in which algae is cultivated without any type of cover in a contained body of water like a lake or a pond. [3] The aforementioned findings regarding system affordability are significant because cost is a major issue in determining the type of system for using algae to produce biofuels. [4] Accordingly, Hannon (2010) stated that the cost competitiveness of open-pond systems may be the only viable way to support large-scale algae cultivation systems. [5] The implication of our results is that closed-collection algae systems must be designed in a way that makes them cost competitive with open-pond systems.

2 [6] Another key finding is that the location of closed-collection algae-growing systems is central to their ability to produce algae in a sustainable, productive manner. [7] Systems that are placed near wastewater outlets, in particular, have the potential to be successful because these systems act as natural filters for the water. [8] Closed-collection systems, which are known as photobioreactors (PBRs), are often made with flexible polymeric material. [9] As stated earlier, algae grow inside PBRs, where the species can be more carefully regulated than in open-pond systems.

> ### Glossary
>
> Algae: plants without roots, stems, or leaves that grow in or near water
>
> Aforementioned: mentioned before in an earlier part of a document, article, book, etc.
>
> Biofuel: an energy source made from plant and animal waste, such as cow manure

Photobioreactor algae collection system

(Continued)

^{10} One promising PBR is NASA's OMEGA (Offshore Membrane Enclosures for Growing Algae) system. OMEGA uses clear, flexible polyethylene tubes that float offshore in a protected bay area (Trent et al. 2012). ^{11} The OMEGA project's location alongside city wastewater is ideal, as the algae work to sanitize the wastewater while the wastewater nourishes the algae. ^{12} The implication of our finding about location is that a system located near wastewater may be ideal for growing algae on a large scale. ^{13} In this study, no information was gathered regarding whether floating PBRs were tested against high waves and storms. ^{14} This should be investigated in future research. ^{15} The decay of the plastic itself is also a noteworthy concern that requires further investigation, as pointed out by other researchers (Zittelli et al. 2013). ^{16} While still in the early stages of research and development, the cultivation of microalgae through improved PBRs is an exciting step toward converting it into a mass-produced biofuel source.

C. **Read the passage again. Then read the statements and write _T_ (True) or _F_ (False). Correct the false statements.**

.... 1. The algae in open-pond systems are more likely to be contaminated than the algae in closed-collection systems.

.... 2. Results demonstrate that closed-collection systems must have low enough costs for them to be able to compete with open-pond systems.

.... 3. Location of closed-collection algae-growing systems is of little importance when considering a system's capacity for effectively growing algae.

.... 4. Photobioreactors (PBRs) are open-pond systems for hosting algae.

.... 5. A major strength of the OMEGA system is that it is positioned next to city wastewater, which provides the algae with a ready source of nutrients.

.... 6. Growing microalgae with enhanced photobioreactors indicates that we are closer to making wider use of this species for the production of biofuel.

D. Work with a partner. Answer the questions about understanding the discussion section.

1. In which sentence does the author of this study refer back to the objective of the study? What language is used to do this?

2. Paraphrase the author's interpretation of the finding related to costs of algae collection systems (Sentence 3). Then explain how that finding is supported by Hannon's (2010) research.

3. What is the stated implication about the findings about cost of algae collection systems? Does it make sense based on the aforementioned finding and interpretation of it? Explain why or why not.

4. What is the reason that the in-text citation (Trent et al. 2012) is included?

5. For what reason is the location of NASA's OMEGA system next to city wastewater mentioned?

6. Which aspects of micro algae collection systems require further research, according to the author? How is this information supported?

VOCABULARY CHECK

A. Review the vocabulary items in the Vocabulary Preview. Write their definitions and add examples. Use a dictionary if necessary.

B. Complete each sentence using the correct vocabulary item from the box. Use the correct form.

carry a risk	contamination	filter (n)	noteworthy
nourish	outlet	promising (adj)	viable

1. Groundwater .... resulted from the draining of strong chemicals from the nearby car wash.

2. Scientists are studying foods that not only .... the body but also appear to have the ability to prevent disease.

3. The scientists presented several .... results of their study on biofuel production that got their audience's attention.

4. The solution to the problem would be extremely costly, but as it was the only .... one, the researchers decided to seek additional government funding to pay for it.

5. The apartment building's water .... began to have problems, which were noticed when residents saw discolored water coming out of their taps.

6. After reviewing the materials-engineering student's outstanding thesis, her professor told her that she had a(n) .... career ahead of her.

7. Conducting the experiment online .... that participants would not provide as much information as they would in person.

8. The wastewater treatment plan is right on the water, near the river's .... to the ocean.

⬥ Go to MyEnglishLab to complete a vocabulary exercise and skill practice, and to join in collaborative activities.

INTEGRATED SKILLS

SUMMARIZING A RESEARCH ARTICLE

WHY IT'S USEFUL In order to write or present effective reports of research articles, it is essential to further develop your ability to summarize accurately and efficiently.

A significant part of your time as a university student will be spent reading articles from academic publications. To demonstrate your understanding of what you read— or to share your understanding with classmates—it is likely that you will be asked to write or present oral summaries of such articles. To do so, you will draw on the same principles of summarizing that you learned previously (see MEDIEVAL CULTURE, Part 1, page 107):

- Include only main ideas, but not your opinion of them.
- Paraphrase language from the original text.
- Write in the present tense.
- Cite sources consulted.
- Ensure that the summary is significantly shorter than the original text.

As research articles typically follow the IMRD format (see FUNDAMENTAL SKILL, page 127), it is important for you not only to read each section of an article carefully but also to summarize the content of each part succinctly. Your resulting summary (or report—depending on the terminology your professor uses) should contain a summary of the introduction, methodology, results, and discussion sections of the article.

With that said, it is important to realize that every assignment is different. For example, your professor may ask you to focus your summary on the results or the discussion section of an article. This would mean that those sections of your summary would be a bit longer than the others. The length of your summary may also depend on the length of the research article you are asked to summarize. Finally, summary formats may vary. Some professors may instruct you to divide your summary into the sections of a research paper, while others may leave the formatting up to you. A follow-up to writing a summary may be an in-class presentation, which will likely affect the formatting and content of your summary. The important message here is that while there are some guiding principles for how to effectively summarize a research article, there is no one-size-fits-all approach. It is extremely important that you follow the guidelines given to you by your professor.

TIP

The abstract of a research article is a good place for you to start to get ideas for information to include in your summary. That does not mean, however, that you can skip reading the rest of the article and simply paraphrase the abstract as your summary. While the abstract does contain the main points of a research article, additional important information may not be found in this section. You will need to read the entire article carefully to identify or fully understand those points.

VOCABULARY PREVIEW

The following vocabulary items appear in the reading. Circle the ones you know. Put a question mark next to the ones you do not know.

composed of	denture	deterioration	orthopedic
fillings (n)	position	aesthetic	versatility

TIP

A **review article**, unlike a research article, provides a summary of the research that has been conducted on one given topic. Authors of review articles read through many studies related to the topic and compile the important information into a review article. Review articles differ from research articles in that they do not report new results from original studies.

A. You will read a review article called "Use of the Polymer PEEK in Dentistry."
Skim the article. Write three things you predict will be discussed. Then read the
passage quickly. Were your predictions correct?

1. ....

2. ....

3. ....

Use of the Polymer PEEK in Dentistry

July 2017

Introduction

1 For thousands of years, humans have used
natural materials in dentistry. Teeth have
been replaced with gold, horns, hooves, and
beeswax. In one of the oldest recorded cases,
researchers found that humans in the Ice Age
used bitumen, a tar-like substance, for tooth-
filling material (Oxilia et al. 2017). It was not
until the early 1800s that modern materials
came into use. One of these is amalgam,

> **Glossary**
>
> **Alloy:** a metal that is a mixture of two
> or more metals, or of a metal and a
> substance that is not metal
>
> **Vulcanize:** to make rubber stronger
> using a special chemical treatment
>
> **Thermoplastic:** a plastic that is soft
> and bendable when heated but hard
> when cold

a metal alloy composed of silver, copper, tin, and mercury. Amalgam became widely
used for tooth replacement in the mid-1800s (Bharti et al. 2010). Now, more than
150 years later, amalgam is still a commonly used material in dentistry. Other metals
include gold and titanium, a strong, light metal. In the late 1800s, after the invention
of vulcanized rubber, polymer materials were introduced into dentistry. Rubber was
used as a denture base (Sideridou 2010). In the 1900s, porcelain, which is a kind of
ceramic, became popular for use in veneers—a coating fixed to an imperfect tooth—
due to its natural appearance. After the 1950s, composite materials—made from a
plastic that is chemically combined with other hard materials, such as glass—became
widely used in many applications in dentistry (Bhola 2009). Composite materials are
very hard and resistant to scratching and deterioration.

2 One polymer material known as PEEK (polyetheretherketone) is used in composites
and has great potential in dentistry. Polyetheretherketone, an engineered
high-performance polymer substance (HPP), is a semicrystalline thermoplastic
polymer with very high temperature resistance (260°C). The stiffness of this material
is comparable to that of bone, and in the medical industry it is used in spinal surgeries
and other orthopedic applications. In recent years, dentists have been using PEEK as
an alternative to metal. One of the concerns with metal fillings raised in recent years
is that the mercury in amalgam is harmful to humans (Bharti 2010).

However, the American Dental Association's position on amalgam is that the alloy is "a valuable, viable, and safe choice" for patients. Regardless of the safety reports though, there has been a public push for nonamalgam fillings, both out of health concerns and for aesthetic reasons. In addition, in a small percentage of patients, metals cause allergic reactions or an unpleasant metallic taste. In this study, PEEK will be reviewed as a material in dentistry, and applications for this material will be discussed.

Methodology

3 A search of journal articles in the online database of the US National Library of Medicine through the National Institutes of Health (PubMed.gov) about PEEK and dentistry was conducted, and all articles in the past decade were reviewed. A total of 74 articles were reviewed. More weight was given to research on material published in the past several years. Information in the articles was summarized and key findings are presented.

Results

4 PEEK is already used successfully as a framework for dentures and partial dentures. It has also been tested as a filler in dentures, bridges, crowns, and abutments. An abutment is a fixture underneath a tooth replacement that attaches the tooth to the jaw. Studies are limited on the use of PEEK as an implant material. Implants are screws that are drilled into the jawbone to anchor tooth replacements, and they are made primarily of titanium. PEEK showed high biocompatibility in all the reports, indicating that it safely interacts with human tissue. Multiple studies reviewed demonstrate that PEEK is not thought to cause allergies, nor is it carcinogenic—cancer causing—or toxic in other ways (Panayotov et al. 2016; Wiesli 2015). In addition, PEEK's versatility as a composite material may be expanded with the technology of 3D printers. This is because 3D printers make it possible to efficiently print very complex shapes, expanding the possible applications and uses of the material. One downside to PEEK is that its appearance, which is slightly beige-tinted, is not a natural match for teeth. Though it is not as different in color as amalgam, PEEK still is not as close in appearance to the natural white of teeth, porcelain, or acrylic polymer.

Discussion

5 PEEK should be viewed as a promising material for a number of different applications in dentistry, particularly for denture or partial-denture frameworks. One of the benefits of the material is that it could be a suitable alternative to metal for patients with metal allergies or concerns about amalgam. Based on the findings of this study, if PEEK is used in any forward-facing location in the mouth, it is recommended that it be covered with a composite material to conceal the beige tone. Clinical studies of PEEK are still somewhat limited at this point in the use of the material as an alternative to titanium in implants, and further research is needed to determine its efficacy in this particular application.

B. Read the journal article. Put a checkmark (✓) next to seven main ideas.

.... 1. Throughout history, individuals have used materials such as horns, beeswax, and bitumen for dental purposes.

.... 2. Amalgam has been used in dentistry since the 1800s and is still used in this field today.

.... 3. PEEK is used for many different purposes in dentistry.

.... 4. One of PEEK's strong points is that it is approximately as stiff as bone.

.... 5. Dentists have recently been using PEEK instead of metal because some believe that mercury in amalgam is unsafe for human use.

.... 6. The American Dental Association believes that amalgam is "a valuable, viable, and safe choice."

.... 7. This review article summarized findings from all journal articles related to PEEK and dentistry that were published in the online database of the US National Library of Medicine through the National Institute of Health (PubMed.gov) in the last decade.

.... 8. It was determined that PEEK is effectively used in dentures. Tests have also been done on its use in other dental applications.

.... 9. A number of studies indicated that PEEK is safe for humans to use.

.... 10. PEEK should be regarded as an ideal material for many different dental purposes.

C. Use the main ideas you identified in Part B to summarize the article. Ensure that you discuss each section equally. Your summary should be no longer than two paragraphs.

D. Work with a partner. Compare your summaries. Answer the questions about summarizing.

1. Did you follow the assignment instructions? Is each section of the article given a relatively equal amount of discussion in your summary? Is it two paragraphs or less?

2. Is the content of your summary similar to that of your partner? What information does yours contain that your partner's does not, and vice versa?

3. Did you consciously use techniques to paraphrase ideas from the original text? If so, which ones?

VOCABULARY CHECK

A. Review the vocabulary items in the Vocabulary Preview. Write their definitions and add examples. Use a dictionary if necessary.

B. Complete each sentence using the correct vocabulary item from the box. Use the correct form.

aesthetic	composed of	denture	deterioration
filling (n)	orthopedic	position	versatility

1. The .... the medical device organization took on its products was that they were of higher quality than all of its competitors.

2. The nursing professor worked on the .... floor of the hospital, where she taught students how to care for patients who suffered from bone and muscular conditions.

3. Metal crowns may be stronger, but dentists generally use ceramic crowns on visible teeth for .... reasons. Dentists want the color to match that of patients' natural teeth.

4. The patient was informed that he needed a(n) .... because he had a large cavity in one of his teeth.

5. The dental association was .... dentists from only the southern region of the state.

6. The patient was informed that she would have to get .... since her natural teeth were diseased following years of smoking and poor dental care.

7. Doctors are concerned about rapid .... in the patient's health. She is no longer able to walk without help.

8. Polymers are a preferred material in many kinds of medical and dental applications due to their ....

◔ Go to MyEnglishLab to complete a skill practice.

LANGUAGE SKILL

UNDERSTANDING MODIFIERS

> **WHY IT'S USEFUL** Recognizing modifiers and their correct placement will allow you to better understand what an author is explaining, stressing, or describing.

🔊 Go to MyEnglishLab for a Language Skill presentation and practice.

VOCABULARY STRATEGY

RECOGNIZING AND LEARNING MULTIWORD UNITS

> **WHY IT'S USEFUL** Being able to recognize and use multiword units—chunks of language that frequently occur together—will quickly expand your vocabulary and make you a more fluent, natural-sounding speaker and writer.

Multiword units are groups of words that frequently combine to form meaningful phrases (see LINGUISTICS, Part 2, page 185). The words are tightly bound into an inseparable unit that should be learned as a single vocabulary item. For example:

Type of Multiword Unit	Examples
Adjective + preposition combination	(be) interested in, depending on (the results)
Collocation	strong tea
Compound noun	gas station, main event
Connector (linker)	as mentioned in Part A
Idiom	sink or swim
Phrasal verb	give (it) up, stare at
Prepositional phrase	by the door, around the corner

Good dictionaries provide lists of multiword units in which a given term regularly appears. For example, the entry for the word *run* also includes definitions of the multiword units *run down, run on,* and *run someone off the road.* However, you also need to learn how to recognize multiword units in natural written or spoken contexts. The problem is that they can sometimes be difficult to notice, especially if you tend to read one word at a time.

Here are some strategies for recognizing and understanding multiword units:

- Read in chunks (see MEDIEVAL CULTURE, Part 1, page 96).
- Write multiword units as part of your regular vocabulary learning.
- Look out for other examples of the multiword unit in other readings.
- Try to use new multiword units in your own speaking and writing.

EXERCISE 5

A. Read the sentences that are excerpted or adapted from readings in this unit. Identify the category or categories of the underlined multiword units and write the letter(s) in the space following each sentence. Compare answers with a partner.

1. There is a <u>direct correlation</u> between changes in viscosity and the amount of shear stress applied in non-Newtonian fluids. ....

2. Another <u>key finding</u> is that the location of closed-collection algae-growing systems is central to their ability to produce algae in a sustainable, productive manner. ....

3. <u>In some cases</u>, the development of such products has been legislated. ....

4. <u>As previously noted</u> in this study reviewing the recycling of polymer waste, plastic usage is increasing substantially each year. ....

5. Polymers are substances <u>composed of</u> long chains of molecules, and they are used in many everyday objects, including cars, phones, and clothing. ....

Type of Multiword Unit

a. Adjective + preposition combination
b. Collocation
c. Compound noun
d. Connector (linker)
e. Idiom
f. Phrasal verb
g. Prepositional phrase

B. Work alone or in a group. Do an Internet search for sentences that use the following multiword units. Use the context to write a definition for each one. Check your answers in a dictionary.

1. come into play: ....

2. direct correlation: ....

3. key findings: ....

4. in some cases: ....

5. as previously noted: ....

6. in basic terms: ....

7. composed of: ....

8. based on the results: ....

APPLY YOUR SKILLS

WHY IT'S USEFUL By applying the skills you have learned in this unit, you can gain a better understanding of this challenging reading about how polymers are used in the field of soft robotics.

BEFORE YOU READ

A. Discuss these questions with a partner or group.

1. What do you know about robots? For example, what are they capable of doing? What applications do they have? What fields are they often used in?

2. Both polymers and animals play a role in the field of robotics. What role do you think that might be?

3. Have you ever heard the term *soft robotics*? If so, what do you know about it? If not, what do you think it might mean?

B. You will read a research article about polymers that are used to create soft robots. As you read, think about these questions.

1. What are soft robots modeled after?

2. What are some applications of soft robotics?

3. How was this study on soft robotics conducted?

4. What are the results of this study?

5. What are some aspects of soft robotics that require further research?

C. Review the Unit Skills Summary. As you read the passage, apply the skills you learned in this unit.

UNIT SKILLS SUMMARY

Understand the introduction

- Understand the purpose of the introduction and statement of objectives in a research article.

Understand the discussion

- Identify key types of information in the discussion section of a research article.

Summarize a research article

- Develop your ability to summarize research articles.

Understand modifiers

- Understand the types and correct placement of words, phrases, and clauses that modify sentences or sentence parts.

Recognize and learn multiword units

- Recognize and use chunks of language that frequently occur together.

A. Read the review article. Annotate and take notes on the answers to the questions in Before You Read, Part B.

Polymer Applications in Soft Robotics

May 2017

Introduction

1   Robots are typically built with hard materials, particularly metal. Such rigid robots are easily programmed to complete specific tasks, but the range of tasks is narrow, and the robots' adaptability and movability is limited (Rus and Tolley 2015). With new types of soft polymeric material and advanced computing and electronic technology, a new era of soft robots has begun. Many developments in soft-robot technology are inspired by creatures in nature, many of which have soft tissue that gives them flexibility and mobility. Biological species move quite differently than rigid robots, changing the shapes of their bodies by rolling, flipping, crawling, and twisting. This type of movement allows animals to burrow—make a hole or passage in the ground—and access areas that would be impossible to reach otherwise. Recently created soft robots mimic the movement patterns of animals, including octopuses, snakes, fish, and even larvae (the early form of some animals like frogs or insects) (Bartlett et al. 2015). The applications for soft-bodied robots able to move in this way are far-reaching. Soft robots have already been introduced in the manufacturing industry, and their use is likely to become more widespread. Such robots could be used in disaster-rescue operations, or they could be adapted for use in the military. In addition, soft robotics could be incorporated into medicine in the future. For example,

> ### Glossary
>
> **Silicone:** one of a group of chemicals that are not changed by heat or cold, do not let water pass through them, and are used in making artificial rubber, body parts, and many other products
>
> **Elastomer:** a material similar to rubber
>
> **Mallet:** a wooden hammer with a large end

if soft-bodied robots were made with dissolvable materials, they could be used in tissue-engineering applications as a drug-delivery method (Kim et al. 2017). Multiple researchers have also noted that soft-bodied robots with living cells implanted in them may be particularly useful in minimally invasive surgery (Rus 2015; Sangbae 2013; Kim 2017). In this article, soft-bodied robots and their various features are introduced. Information is provided to support the proposal that polyethylene (PET) and soft silicone elastomers are ideal polymer materials for building soft robots.

Methodology

2 This study reviewed existing literature on soft robotics and examined the polymeric materials that have been most effective in the construction of soft robots. The subjects of this study were three soft robots that mimic the motion of animals. The first example reviewed is the Meshworm, a robot created by researchers to simulate the movement of a worm (Seok et al. 2010). This motion is called *peristalsis*. The research team that created the Meshworm used polyester polymeric fibers shaped into a tubelike— wormlike—structure. The researchers then inserted a metal rod made from a thin nickel-titanium alloy into the tube. The alloy is sensitive to temperature, so when parts of it are heated with an electric pulse, the wire contracts and the Meshworm moves. The second soft-bodied robot examined is the GoQBot, created by a team of researchers from Tufts University (Lin et al. 2011). This robot mimics the shape and movement of caterpillars. Researchers used a soft silicone polymer material to build the caterpillar-like robot. Like the worm robot, the caterpillar robot moves via the contraction of a metal alloy that is wound into the robot's silicone body. The third soft-bodied robot that was investigated was developed by researchers to mimic cephalopods, which are ocean creatures such as squid or octopus (Whitesides et al. 2012). The cephalopod robot moves as though it is floating, and, like an octopus, it can camouflage itself. The robot creature is built with layers of soft silicone and tiny tubes that can be filled with different colors of fluid. Not only can the robot camouflage itself with different colors, but it can also glow in the dark. The cephalopod robot is powered by pneumatic inflation, or air pressure, inside tiny tubes woven throughout the body of the robot.

(Continued)

Results

3　This review of research demonstrates that soft silicone and PET are optimal materials for use in soft robotics. Silicone is durable and soft, which allows for movement that mimics that of biological creatures. It also functions well when combined with the circuitry of electronics in the robots. The silicone in the soft-bodied caterpillar robot withstands temperature changes of the metal alloy. In addition, the tubes of silicone with which the octopus robot was built allowed it to be filled with different colors of liquid for camouflage. In the Meshworm, the strong PET polymeric mesh was flexible and durable enough to withstand being hit with a mallet. The only drawback of PET is that it is sensitive to temperature.

Discussion

4　Based on the aforementioned results, soft silicone elastomers and PET are ideal for the construction of soft robots. The soft robots in this study mimicked the movement of biological creatures, and this is a promising first step in the development of soft robotics. However, it should also be pointed out that more research and development is needed with respect to how soft robots are actuated, or moved. The results of this study align with Kim's conclusion that actuation remains one of the major challenges in the field (Kim et al. 2017). In the case of the worm robot, temperatures must be very carefully controlled. If this is not done, the metal in the robot can become excessively hot. One other issue that remains to be addressed is how soft robotics will be implemented in certain industries, such as the medical industry. To date, the applications of soft robotics in that field are limited. Further research and development is necessary in the field of soft robotics. It is predicted that soft robotics will advance many kinds of machines in the coming years.

B. Work with a partner. Use your annotations to discuss the answers to the questions in Before You Read, Part B. Are there any questions you cannot answer? Which of the reading skills you have learned in this unit could help you answer them?

🔊 Go to MyEnglishLab to read the passage again and answer critical thinking questions.

THINKING CRITICALLY

Discuss the questions with another student.

1. The introduction of the article describes possible uses of soft robots. What other possible uses can you think of, and what would the benefits of these be?

2. The methodology section describes three experiments in which soft robots were modeled after the movement of animals—worms, caterpillars, squids, and octopuses. Based on the description in the text, your prior knowledge, or any research you have done, why do you think these animals were chosen as models?

3. In the discussion section, the writer explains that further research must be conducted on soft robots, including how they move. In your opinion, what other important considerations should scientists pay attention to when studying soft robots?

THINKING VISUALLY

A. Complete the chart using information from the article "Polymer Applications in Soft Robotics" to identify key characteristics of the three experiments described in the study. Then compare answers with a partner.

Polymer Applications in Soft Robotics

Soft Robot	Animal Mimicked	Materials Used	Description of Movements	Results
Meshworm				
GoQBot				
Cephalopod robot				

B. Work with a partner. Look at the pictures of robots. Discuss: Do they share any of the features of the soft robots described in the chart? If not, what animal or human-like features do they possess? Imagine the movements and consider how they may be more natural or lifelike than the movements of traditional robots.

THINKING ABOUT LANGUAGE

Underline the modifiers in the excerpts from "Polymer Applications in Soft Robotics." There may be more than one modifier in each excerpt.

1. Such rigid robots are easily programmed to complete specific tasks, but the range of tasks is narrow, and the robots' adaptability and movability is limited (Rus and Tolley 2015).

2. The subjects of this study were three soft robots that mimic the motion of animals.

3. The first example reviewed is the Meshworm, a robot created by researchers to simulate the movement of a worm (Seok et al. 2010).

4. The research team that created the Meshworm used polyester polymeric fibers shaped into a tubelike—wormlike—structure.

5. The cephalopod robot moves as though it is floating, and, like an octopus, it can camouflage itself.

6. It also functions well when combined with the circuitry of electronics in the robots.

7. The silicone in the soft-bodied caterpillar robot withstands temperature changes of the metal alloy.

8. In the case of the worm robot, temperatures must be very carefully controlled. If this is not done, the metal in the robot would become excessively hot.

⬤ Go to MyEnglishLab watch Professor Heilshorn's concluding video and complete a self-assessment.

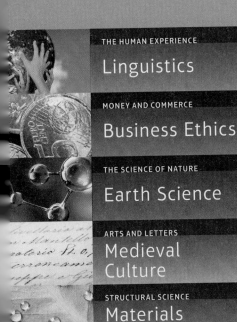

Critical Thinking Skills

Part 2 moves from skill building to application of the skills that require critical thinking. Practice activities tied to specific learning outcomes in each unit require a deeper level of understanding of the academic content.

LINGUISTICS

Facts and Opinions

UNIT PROFILE

In this unit, you will consider the subject of linguistics. Some topics you will read about are researching speech emotions, sound symbolism, phonemes and phonetics, and the role of linguists as consultants to TV shows and movies. You will also consider whether certain theories about language are mainstream—accepted by most people—or on the fringes of the discipline.

Look at the reading "Grammar Goes to Hollywood: Linguists as Science Consultants" on page 189. Read the full title and look at the art. What is the article about? Scan the first two paragraphs. Find examples of factual statements, opinion statements, and statements that include both fact and opinion.

OUTCOMES

- Identify and understand statements of fact
- Identify and understand statements of opinion
- Quote material from a reading
- Understand structures used for hedging
- Use a dictionary to strengthen vocabulary

For more about **LINGUISTICS**, see ① ③. See also Ⓦ and ⓞⒸ **LINGUISTICS** ① ② ③.

GETTING STARTED

🔾 Go to MyEnglishLab to watch Professor Podesva's introductory video and to complete a self-assessment.

Discuss these questions with a partner or group.

1. What aspects of language do you find most interesting? If you were a linguist, what would you specialize in?

2. Besides helping people translate from one language to another, what are some practical uses for the work of linguists?

3. Why are vowel sounds difficult to describe, according to Professor Podesva? Can you guess how many vowel sounds there are in American English? Say as many of them as you can.

CRITICAL THINKING SKILL

IDENTIFYING AND UNDERSTANDING FACTS AND OPINIONS

WHY IT'S USEFUL To fully understand a passage, you have to recognize which parts are statements of fact and which are not. You also have to recognize that some statements are partly factual and partly nonfactual.

Most academic reading passages are presented mainly as fact. However, it is not unusual for a presentation that is mostly factual to include some statements of opinion and some statements that are part fact and part opinion.

Your job as a critical reader is to try to recognize the author's intentions—whether the author presents a statement as fact or not. Sometimes authors are wrong; a statement presented as a fact may be untrue or incorrect. If information presented as a fact seems wrong, you may want to fact-check it when you have time—do some research to find out if it is accurate.

> **CULTURE NOTE**
>
> Do facts really exist? Is there a difference between facts and truth? Philosophers have struggled for thousands of years with these questions. Some philosophers have argued that statements we consider factual, like "Coal is black," are just opinion because there is no agreement about what *black* means. If you are interested in finding out more about the philosophy of factuality, search online for *philosophy* plus a word like *being, essence, ontology,* or *epistemology.*

For the sake of convenience, we often contrast **facts** with **opinions**. This is not always accurate. To be exact, we need to judge between factual and nonfactual statements. Some nonfactual statements do express opinions. However, other nonfactual statements express neither a fact nor an opinion. Examples include rhetorical questions, exclamations, and transitions. For example, *Let us move now to the second key aspect of the issue.*

This unit breaks down recognizing and understanding facts and opinions into two supporting skills:

- identifying and understanding statements of fact
- identifying and understanding statements of opinion

VOCABULARY PREVIEW

The following vocabulary items appear in the reading. Circle the ones you know. Put a question mark next to the ones you do not know.

enable	input	subtle	prior to
ensure	nonsense	cues	

EXERCISE 1

A. Discuss the questions with a partner before you read.

1. What are some ways that speakers can convey emotion without using words?

2. Do speakers of different languages express emotion in the same ways?

3. How could researchers study the way speakers express emotions? Why would it be useful to study this?

B. Preview the passage. Read the title and note two topics that might be covered in the reading. Then read the passage quickly. Were your predictions correct?

....

Researching the Emotional Power of Speech

1 Consider the question "Really?" Spoken with different intonations, it can convey a speaker's sense of disbelief, surprise, disapproval, or amusement. As illustrated by this simple example, spoken language often communicates emotion beyond the meaning of a speaker's words. The emotional power of speech is a complex issue, and researching it is not easy.

Glossary

Intonation: the way a speaker's voice rises and falls to express meaning

Vocal cue: a characteristic of the voice, such as speaking speed or intonation, that expresses something

Replicate: repeat part of the scientific research process to ensure that the results of the first study were true or correct

2 Until the middle of the 20th century, recording technology was too poor to enable reliable research into speech and emotion. Philosophers since before the time of Cicero (106–43 BCE) have recognized that vocal quality can communicate emotion even without words, but real research had to wait for tape recorders. Recorded voices, not live speech, are necessary for an effective study. Such recordings are the only practical tool for presenting the same input to a large number of listeners in different places at different times. Also, the recordings have to be high-quality. Many vocal cues to emotion are subtle, easily lost in the scratchy recordings in use prior to the 1950s. In a related concern, researchers have to identify which voice features convey emotion; any experimental recordings must contain them. Scientists still disagree about exactly what those features are, but Baider and L'Anse (1996) have identified a good basic list. In simplified terms, they are: (1) basic pitch (high or low "notes"); (2) amplitude (loudness); (3) voice quality or *timbre*; and (4) speed and pauses.

TIP

Readings about research have several features in common, giving them a recognizable "academic" style. Look for the following in such readings:

- the family names of researchers
- the years in which the research was published
- summaries of the research findings
- references to research methods

3 Researchers must also ensure that recognition of emotion in vocal features is based on the sound of the voice rather than on the meaning of words. Researchers have to achieve this with actual speech, in some real language. As it turns out—and no one really knows why this is—speech-like nonsense sounds are not good carriers of emotional cues, so they are not good research tools. Some experiments have investigated whether listeners can identify vocal signs of emotion in a foreign language they do not know. Interestingly, there might be some evidence that listeners can. However, even the scientists who report such findings (e.g., Erdling, 2013) urge us to be cautious. The recognition rate in the unknown language is much lower than in one's native language, and no such experiment has ever been successfully replicated.

The names of researchers in this article are fictional, for instructional purposes only.

C. **Read the passage again. Then read the statements and write _T_ (True) or _F_ (False). Compare answers with a partner. Correct the false statements.**

.... 1. The main idea of the reading is that words do not have emotional meanings.

.... 2. Philosophers have recognized the existence of vocal cues to emotion for more than 2,000 years.

.... 3. After about the 1950s, the quality of voice recordings became good enough to capture emotional cues in speech.

.... 4. Baider and L'Anse drew up a list of vocal cues that all researchers now use.

.... 5. The term _pitch_ refers to whether a voice is at a high or low "note."

.... 6. The author says that timbre and voice quality are the same thing.

.... 7. Erdling reported some evidence that listeners can understand emotion in an unknown language.

.... 8. Most listeners can understand emotion in a foreign language as well as in their native language.

D. **Work with a partner. Consider the reading again in terms of facts and opinions. Follow the instructions.**

1. Underline three statements that you think express facts.

2. Circle three statements that you think express opinion.

3. Put brackets [ ] around two statements that you think mix fact and opinion.

VOCABULARY CHECK

A. Review the vocabulary items in the Vocabulary Preview. Write their definitions and add examples. Use a dictionary if necessary.

B. Complete each sentence using the correct vocabulary item from the box. Use the correct form.

cue	enable	ensure	input
nonsense	prior to	subtle	

1. Consulting a dictionary as you write will .... that you are spelling words correctly.

2. In the experiment, all participants heard the same .... —a high, loud sound. Then they were asked to identify it. Some people thought it was some kind of animal, and others thought it was some kind of machine.

3. In many languages, a rising intonation at the end of a sentence is a(n) .... that the speaker is asking a question.

4. Visitors and outsiders may not be able to hear the .... differences in the way English is spoken in different sections of New York City.

5. .... the Roman conquest of what is now France, the people of the region spoke a Celtic language called "Gaulish," which is unrelated to modern French.

6. Some private language lessons might .... you to learn strategies for reading faster in English.

7. "Jabberwocky" is a poem by Lewis Carroll that includes real-sounding .... phrases like "slithy toves," "jub-jub bird," and "beamish boy."

⬆ Go to MyEnglishLab to complete a vocabulary exercise and skill practice, and to join in collaborative activities.

SUPPORTING SKILL 1

IDENTIFYING AND UNDERSTANDING STATEMENTS OF FACT

WHY IT'S USEFUL Statements of fact communicate most of the information in many academic readings. You cannot read to learn without them. With them, you can build a foundation of knowledge in a given academic content area.

Statements of fact are about real situations, possibilities, or events. Authors usually state facts as direct statements with neutral language. Explicit signals like *it's a fact that* or *the fact is* may be used but are not frequent. To recognize statements of fact, look for the following language features:

Objective Language

The most common clue that an author intends a statement to be factual is the absence of subjective language. *Subjective* means that something is based on personal thoughts, beliefs, aesthetic judgements, preferences, and so on. The opposite of subjective is *objective*. Contrast these two statements:

Factual (objective): The Kryts language of Azerbaijan is not widely spoken.

Nonfactual (subjective): The Kryts language of Azerbaijan is strange
and mysterious.

The objective vocabulary in the factual statement (*not widely spoken*) creates a different tone from the subjective vocabulary of the nonfactual one (*strange and mysterious*).

Neutral Verbs

"Neutral" verbs—meaning, in this case, verbs without accompanying modals or hedging phrases, are another feature of objective writing. For example, *English is descended from an ancient language called Proto-Indo-European* is meant as a factual statement. However, if the verb were changed to *might be descended* or *could possibly have been descended*, the author's intent is less factual.

Declarative Sentences

Declarative sentences, in contrast to questions, commands, or exclamations, are a third characteristic of factual statements. Contrast these sentences:

Factual (declarative): Of the estimated 7,000 languages spoken in the world today,
linguists say nearly half are in danger of extinction.

Nonfactual (question): Of the world's 7,000 languages, how many are in danger
of extinction?

Does a statement of fact have to be supported by evidence? No. You may guess that a factual claim *could* be supported by evidence, but the author may not actually offer any. Conversely, many nonfactual statements are followed by evidence. For example:

> Nonfactual statement: James Buchanan was the worst president in American history.

> Evidence: His failure to get tough with rebellious supporters of slavery showed not just weakness but laziness.

Despite the evidence, this is a nonfactual passage, clearly an expression of the author's opinion.

Finally, many statements are hybrids, that is, a mix of factual and nonfactual material. Consider this sentence:

> To no one's surprise, most listeners feel more threatened by loud voices than by soft ones.

The sentence includes a fact about perception of loud voices, plus the author's opinion that this is not a surprise.

TIP

Remember that a fact or opinion is not necessarily one complete sentence—it may be a part of a sentence or even a group of two or more sentences.

VOCABULARY PREVIEW

The following vocabulary items appear in the reading. Circle the ones you know. Put a question mark next to the ones you do not know.

universal	mainstream	arbitrary	took it from there
draw	adherents	sweeping (adj)	innate

EXERCISE 2

A. Look at the shape below. Imagine that it is a newly discovered kind of animal. You have to make up a name for this kind of animal; it's not a duck or a cat, it's a ....

Why did you choose that name for this kind of animal? Discuss your choice with a partner.

B. Preview the passage. Notice the title and art. Predict three topics you believe will be discussed.

....

....

....

C. Now read the passage. Which of your predictions from Part B are discussed?

The Relationship of Sound and Meaning

1   [1]A few linguists are attracted to a rather odd concept called *sound symbolism*. [2]This is the arguable idea that a natural, universal connection exists between certain sounds in words and particular meanings. [3]For example, supporters of this idea might call the [t] sound in the words *tiny* and *tip* a "smallness" sound. [4]Opponents—most linguists—say that no such natural association exists.

2   [5]Anyone who speaks a language (other than soundless languages like American Sign Language) is familiar with the idea of using sounds to convey meaning. [6]After all, that is what spoken words do. [7]However, the mainstream view among linguists is that the relationship between a word's sound and its meaning is completely arbitrary. [8]Why is a chair called *chair*? [9]Not because of any special relationship between the sounds written phonetically as [tʃ], [eɪ], and [r], and the idea "thing to sit on." [10]Instead, long ago, some word that is the oldest ancestor of *chair* was arbitrarily constructed. [11]Historical processes took it from there, until we arrived at our present-day English word.

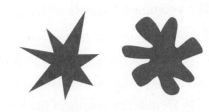

Which shape would you call a kiki?
Which would you call a bouba?

3 [12] However, sound symbolism continues to draw some adherents. [13] They are occasionally encouraged by bits of evidence from research. [14] Let us look at one. [15] The so-called "kiki / bouba" experiment (Ramachandran and Hubbard 2001) has become somewhat famous. [16] In this study, neuroscientists presented subjects with two shapes, one spiky and the other rounded. [17] The subjects were American college students whose main language was English and speakers of Tamil, a South Indian language. [18] The researchers asked study participants to decide which shape should be called *kiki* and which *bouba*. [19] About 95 percent of individuals—an astonishingly high percentage—associated the sounds in *kiki* with the sharp object and those in *bouba* with the round one. [20] These researchers concluded that the human brain automatically associates certain sounds with certain shapes. [21] If it were correct, this conclusion could mean that language sounds are not as arbitrary as once believed.

> **CULTURE NOTE**
>
> Some words—like *beep, crunch,* or *meow*—are meant to resemble the sounds of the things they refer to. Different cultures try to replicate real-world sounds in different ways. But sometimes similarities among them are striking. Cats from Japan to East Africa to Norway to Chicago all say something like "meow"—with a nasal [m] or [n] followed by some vowel combination like [au].

4 [22] Much more evidence, however, would have to be gathered before such a sweeping conclusion could be made. [23] The kiki / bouba study, and others like it, are limited by a number of factors. [24] The sound-symbolism hypothesis is not the only possible explanation for the results. [25] Perhaps the study participants, though from different cultures, had mostly grown up watching cartoons or hearing stories where rounder characters had names like *bouba* and spikier characters had names like *kiki*. [26] In English, certainly, the name *bouba* is a lot like the word *blob,* and the word *spiky* is a lot like *kiki*. [27] In other words, learned associations, not natural or innate ones, could have influenced the results.

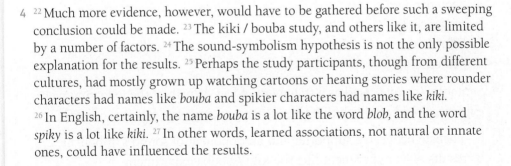

D. Circle the letter(s) of the best answer(s) to each of the following questions. Then compare answers with a partner.

1. Which statement best expresses the author's point of view regarding the relationship of sound and meaning?

   a. It has received substantial support from research.
   b. Despite the results of the Ramachandran and Hubbard study, the relationship between sound and meaning is probably arbitrary.
   c. Any association between sound and meaning is likely to be universal, not culture-specific.
   d. The "kiki / bouba" experiment proves that language sounds are not as arbitrary as once believed.

2. Which of the following phrases illustrates the writer's opinion about the sound-meaning relationship?

   a. rather odd
   b. mainstream view
   c. historical processes
   d. sweeping conclusion

3. Which sentence in Paragraph 1 is written entirely as a statement of fact, without any nonfactual elements?

   a. Sentence 1
   b. Sentence 2
   c. Sentence 3
   d. Sentence 4

4. Sentence 7 is presented as a statement of fact. Which of the following pieces of evidence could establish that the author's statement of fact is accurate?

   a. a debate between a supporter and an opponent of sound symbolism
   b. results of an experiment like the kiki / bouba experiment
   c. an analysis of a soundless language, such as American Sign Language
   d. results of a survey that show what most linguists believe

5. Which of the following is a nonfactual statement but is NOT an opinion statement?

   a. Sentence 12
   b. Sentence 13
   c. Sentence 14
   d. Sentence 15

6. In the description of the kiki / bouba experiment, which of the following is NOT a statement of fact?

   a. Sentence 16

   b. Sentence 17

   c. Sentence 18

   d. Sentence 19

E. Work with a partner. Answer the questions about identifying and understanding statements of fact.

1. What is the main idea of Paragraph 1? Does the author use mostly factual or mostly nonfactual language in this paragraph? Why?

2. In Sentences 16–18, does the writer use mainly factual or nonfactual language to describe the kiki / bouba experiment? How do you know?

3. If you are not sure a "fact" is true, where can you go to check the information?

4. What is your field of academic study? Is the balance of factual and nonfactual information in this passage typical of texts in your field? Why or why not?

VOCABULARY CHECK

A. Review the vocabulary items in the Vocabulary Preview. Write their definitions and add examples. Use a dictionary if necessary.

B. Complete each sentence using the correct vocabulary item from the box. Use the correct form.

adherent	arbitrary	draw	innate
mainstream	sweeping (adj)	take it from there	universal

1. The linguist Noam Chomsky claims that all human children have a natural, ... ability to learn language.

2. Many elementary-level teachers are .... of the view that it is best for children to learn to read in their first language.

3. My psycholinguistics professor is teaching us about some interesting new ideas that are not widely accepted. However, I am glad that my other professors concentrate on .... ideas and theories so that I can get a good education in the basics of the field.

4. You can really only learn new vocabulary items by reading and practicing. Your teacher can give you strategies for learning, but then you have to ....

5. The main speaker at the conference was a well-known linguist whose online lectures about language .... many thousands of viewers every year.

6. If you do not believe in the concept of sound symbolism, then you will agree that the English word *dog*, the French word *chien*, and the Arabic word pronounced *kalb* are entirely ....

7. Some anthropologists argue that certain practices, such as using fire, are .... among human cultures. Other anthropologists say that nothing is common to every culture—that somewhere, at some time in history, a group must have existed that didn't fit the pattern.

8. The new director made .... changes at the language school, redoing the curriculum and choosing new textbooks for every course.

Go to MyEnglishLab to complete a vocabulary exercise and skill practice, and to join in collaborative activities.

SUPPORTING SKILL 2

IDENTIFYING AND UNDERSTANDING STATEMENTS OF OPINION

WHY IT'S USEFUL Identifying and understanding statements of opinion can help you to get the full meaning of a reading. Statements that convey details of an author's opinion help you to interpret the author's general attitude toward a topic or general position on controversial issues.

Sometimes authors use obvious signals like *in my opinion* or *I think* to mark statements of opinion. More often, smaller, less-obvious vocabulary choices indicate that a statement conveys opinion (or is otherwise nonfactual). Consider this sentence: *Harding's findings about the perception of loud voices have totally reshaped the field of linguistics.* How can you tell that this is a statement of opinion? The phrase *have totally reshaped* is subjective language indicating the author's opinion of Harding's work—that it has been exceptionally influential.

It would be difficult to learn all the expressions that can indicate a nonfactual statement. If there are no obvious opinion signals, some strategies are:

Strategy	Examples
Look for subjective (qualitative) adjectives and adverbs.	Adjectives: good, brilliant, important, weak Adverbs: disturbingly, helpfully, cleanly, well
Look for verbs that indicate subjective relationships.	The *New York Yankees crushed the Detroit Tigers* is a statement of opinion. The verb *crushed* communicates a subjective viewpoint. A different, more neutral verb like *beat* or *defeated* would have created a statement of fact.
Consider the context.	Some terms, like *enough* (or *visible, dark, adequate*, etc.), can have a factual or nonfactual meaning depending on the context. They are often used in stating opinions, as in *His voice was not loud enough.* However, they are often factual in scientific, technical, legal, or medical writing, where there are objective standards for what is enough, what is visible, etc. For example: **Statement of fact:** Amounts of lead (Pb) as small as 6 micrograms **are enough** to cause brain damage. **Statement of opinion**: Government regulations **are not enough** to protect us from lead (Pb) poisoning.

VOCABULARY PREVIEW

Read the vocabulary items below. Circle the ones you know. Put a question mark next to the ones you don't know.

empirical	iffy	cognitive	constraints
in isolation	boundary	presumed (v)	complementary

EXERCISE 3

A. Preview the passage. Read the title and study the map. Predict three things you believe will be discussed.

1. ....

2. ....

3. ....

B. Now read the passage. Review your predictions from Part A. Were they correct?

Doing Linguistics Despite Constraints

1   Linguistics is a science. It values empirical research—experiments that have clearly defined independent variables, control groups, large sample sizes, and so on. Linguists distrust unsupported claims about language just as fiercely as astrophysicists distrust iffy ideas about outer space. But linguists labor in the shadow of certain special disadvantages.

2   Linguistics is a cognitive science because language is a product of human thought processes. Like other sciences that have cognitive components, such as psychology or neuroscience, linguistics has to be satisfied with indirect evidence for many of its hypotheses. The parts of the brain on which much attention still focuses, such as Broca's area, were discovered (though certainly not mapped or explored) in the 19th century. Yet despite recent advances in brain-imaging technology, to this day we cannot actually observe language being generated or decoded in the brain. We can only observe electrical activity in some brain locations at certain times and then make inferences about what the electrical activity means. We can say that this advance is tiny without implying any criticism of cognitive linguists. They do great work on a daily basis. But the difficulty of exploring much more of the brain highlights the constraints on the field.

3   No discipline operates in isolation. There are not even any firm boundaries between one field and another, which is why hybrid—combined— fields like biochemistry and astrophysics have come into being. They exist at the borderlands where biology and chemistry, or astronomy and physics, blend into one another. Linguistics has borders with an especially large number of other fields—history, biology, computer science, philosophy, anthropology, and dozens more. Linguists have an especially hard time defining their field and keeping less-than-informed observers at bay. Physicists from Sir Isaac Newton to Niels Bohr have presumed to blame language

CULTURE NOTE

In a movie called *The Martian*, a man finds himself left alone on the planet Mars. As he looks around at his equipment, he determines how he might be able to survive. "I'm going to have to science the [expletive] out of this," he says.

What he means is that he has to apply his knowledge of physics, chemistry, and so on to survive. This quotation from the movie reflects a general respect for science in American culture. Linguistics enjoys greater respect than some other academic fields because it uses scientific methods.

itself (not just English) for being inadequate to convey the realities of physics. Not many readers have challenged either Newton's or Bohr's right to speak about linguistics even though it was neither person's specialty. After all, they spoke languages, didn't they? Linguists are rather used to having nonspecialist visitors criticizing the drapes and the furniture.

4 As intrusive as these relationships among fields might sometimes be, a broad relevance is part of what makes linguistics exciting. Consider the map in Figure 1, a concise demonstration of why historical linguistics— one of those hybrid borderland fields—is not only interesting but vitally current. History

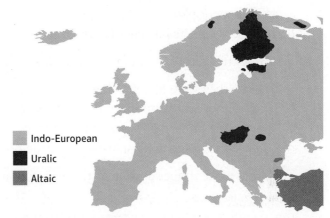

Indo-European

Uralic

Altaic

Figure 1: Historical linguistics is vitally important today

and linguistics are truly complementary disciplines. There is a reason, or rather a whole encyclopedia full of reasons, why Indo-European languages are represented on every continent and why there is an island of Uralic (that is, non-Indo-European) speakers in Central Europe. Historians have a valid claim to speaking about at least some aspects of linguistics. Similarly, many linguists have learned enough about history to have their own views of how the fields interrelate.

C. Read the passage again. Then read each sentence and choose the best answer.

1. Why does the author mention "independent variables, control groups," and "large sample sizes"?

   a. They are important linguistic theories.
   b. They are characteristics of scientific experiments.
   c. They are kinds of disadvantages for linguists.
   d. They are unsupported claims.

2. What is the author's view of modern brain-imaging technology?

   a. Its weaknesses show that cognitive linguistics is not a real science.
   b. It has allowed us to see how language is really generated in the brain.
   c. It gives us some evidence, but it can't tell us exactly how language is generated.
   d. It has transformed linguistics from an art to a science.

3. According to the author, why have fields like biochemistry and astrophysics come into being?

    a. because there are not strict divisions between certain branches of science
    b. because all the basic questions in simpler fields, like biology or chemistry, have been answered
    c. because it is impractical for universities to teach individual fields like astronomy or physics
    d. because scientists have not been acting in a disciplined way

4. Why does the author mention Sir Isaac Newton and Niels Bohr?

    a. because they were famous linguists of earlier times
    b. because they were important theorists in physics
    c. because their observations about linguistics are often challenged
    d. because they were nonlinguists who made observations about linguistics

5. The phrase "the drapes and the furniture" is an indirect reference to _____ .

    a. the work of physicists
    b. laboratories where linguists work
    c. linguistic research methods
    d. the author's office

6. Which of the following is a statement that is at least partially nonfactual?

    a. Linguistics is a science.
    b. Linguistics is a cognitive science.
    c. Broca's area was discovered in the 19ᵗʰ century.
    d. Historians have a valid claim about linguistics.

7. An example of a subjective verb in the text is _____ .

    a. labor
    b. were discovered
    c. observe
    d. exist

8. In the last sentence, the word *enough* conveys _____ .

    a. an objective fact about the interrelationship between history and linguistics
    b. the author's subjective view about linguists' knowledge of history
    c. a criticism of the work of historians
    d. the author's disapproval of the interrelationship between linguistics and history

D. In the following statements from the reading, underline one or more words or phrases that make the statement nonfactual.

1. Linguists distrust unsupported claims about language just as fiercely as astrophysicists distrust iffy ideas about outer space.

2. We can say that this advance is tiny without implying any criticism of cognitive linguists.

3. Linguists have an especially hard time defining their field and keeping less-than-informed observers at bay.

4. Linguists are rather used to having nonspecialist visitors criticizing the drapes and the furniture.

5. As intrusive as these relationships can sometimes be, a broad relevance is part of what makes linguistics exciting.

6. Consider the map in Figure 1, a concise demonstration of why historical linguistics—one of those hybrid borderland fields—is not only interesting but vitally current.

E. Work with a partner. Answer the questions about recognizing and understanding statements of opinion.

1. Compare your answers to Part D. Several possibilities are correct. Which words or phrases did you underline? Why?

2. Choose three items from Part D. Make the statements factual by deleting or replacing subjective words and phrases with neutral language.

3. What is the author's overall opinion about the field of linguistics and the work that linguists do? How do you know?

VOCABULARY CHECK

A. Review the vocabulary items in the Vocabulary Preview. Write their definitions and add examples. Use a dictionary if necessary.

B. Complete each sentence using the correct vocabulary item from the box. Use the correct form.

boundary	cognitive	complementary	constraint
empirical	iffy	in isolation	presume (v)

1. It is difficult to learn a new word .... To understand how a word is actually used, you have to look at it in context.

2. A characteristic of the professor's writing is that the .... between fact and opinion is always clear.

3. Since language is the product of .... processes, it's very difficult to research. Experimenters cannot really get inside anyone's brain and trace the formation of thoughts.

4. I .... that Dr. Ladd will agree to speak at the linguistics conference just as she does every year, but I haven't received a confirmation from her yet.

5. The two colleagues had a(n) .... relationship. One of them was great at research but not good at public relations. The other dealt well with the public but was weak at research.

6. I think I'll be attending the linguistics conference next week, but maybe not. My plans are .... because I don't know whether I can get the time off or whether I can book a last-minute flight.

7. We should do some .... studies to investigate whether the lesson works. We could build some controlled experiments involving a few classes to try it out.

8. I would like to sell our app in Canada and Mexico, but we operate under several .... The biggest one is our small marketing budget.

⬆ Go to MyEnglishLab to complete a vocabulary exercise and skill practice, and to join in collaborative activities.

INTEGRATED SKILLS
QUOTING MATERIAL FROM A READING

WHY IT'S USEFUL In your university courses you will probably get many assignments that require you to report on material you have read. To succeed in these assignments, you have to be able to quote—both directly and indirectly—from the reading material.

When you report information from a reading, you will probably use a mix of direct and indirect quotations.

Direct quotations use the original author's own words. This is indicated by a set of quotation marks (" ").

An indirect quotation communicates the original author's meaning, but in different words and without quotation marks. A "hybrid" quotation includes both direct and indirect segments.

Direct Quotation	Reigle says, "Like most rules, grammar rules are broken or bent every day."
Indirect Quotation	Reigle says that, like most rules, grammar rules are broken or bent every day.
Hybrid Quotation	Reigle says that, like most rules, grammar rules are broken or "bent" every day.

Both direct and indirect quotations include a reporting verb like one of the following. (You can do an Internet search to find longer lists of reporting verbs.)

agree	mention	say
argue	note	state
claim	observe	suggest
explain	point out	warn

Normally the reporting verb is in the present (or sometimes the present perfect), as in *Reigle says … .* This verb form is called the *reportorial present.* The reportorial present communicates that the source is relevant to the present. Especially for written sources, the present form implies that the source is still available and could be consulted by anyone who might care to.

Sometimes you may want to leave out part of a direct quotation, especially if it is quite long. If you remove a piece from the middle of a quote, indicate the removal with three periods—[…], a punctuation mark known as *ellipsis points*. For example:

> Leiden and Smith note, "In terms of language-family relationships, … the closest cousin to English is Frisian."

If you leave out a part at the beginning or end of a passage, it is usually not necessary to use ellipsis points. Simply start or end the quotation wherever you wish.

When should you quote directly or indirectly? Direct quotations are useful if the author's words are especially interesting or if they must be conveyed precisely. Indirect quotations might be better if the author's original statement is not unique or especially interesting. Use a hybrid quotation if only part of the author's original material uses an interesting expression or choice of words—as with the word *bent* in the hybrid example above.

In actuality, writers tend to use both direct and indirect speech sparingly. Hybrid quotations are more common. Most common of all in academic writing is the use of *summary* and *paraphrase*, that is, shortening and restating the key information from a text in your own words. (See BUSINESS ETHICS, Part 2, page 211, and MEDIEVAL LITERATURE, Part 1, page 106.)

VOCABULARY PREVIEW

The following vocabulary items appear in the reading. Circle the ones you know. Put a question mark next to the ones you do not know.

strung together	vibrating	restriction	cavity
physiological	constricts	manner	click

EXERCISE 4

A. Scan the passage. Notice the many quotations from various sources. Write the names of three sources the author quotes. Then read the passage.

1. ....

2. ....

3. ....

Segmentals and Articulatory Features

1 ¹ You probably know that most phonemes in a language fall into one of two categories: consonant or vowel. ² The consonant-vowel distinction is important to professional linguists as well—although for specialists the situation is a bit more complicated. ³ Consonants and vowels are called *segmentals* because they are important segments—small parts that can be strung together into longer items, such as words. ⁴ *Articulatory features* are the even-smaller characteristics of these small parts, such as voicing or the puff of air that accompanies the [p] sound at the beginnings of words.

2 ⁵ The description of consonants and vowels makes reference to the vocal tract and the various ways in which the tongue, lips, and other structures shape it. ⁶ The *vocal tract* is a long passageway from the throat to the openings of the mouth and nose (see Figure 1), involving not just the open areas of the throat, mouth (oral cavity), and nose (nasal cavity) but also a number of structures and surfaces along the way. ⁷ Parini (2007)¹ suggests becoming aware of your vocal tract by opening your mouth and throat as much as possible and forcing air from your lungs through the passages. ⁸ You will get "a breathy sound somewhat like an [h]." If you keep your mouth in the same open position but, as she says, "bring your vocal folds (also called vocal cords) into play," you'll get a low, open vowel that sounds somewhat like [a] as in *pa*.

Figure 1: The human vocal tract

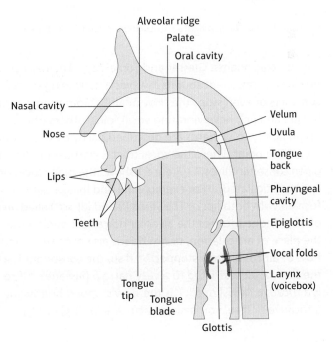

Labels: Alveolar ridge, Palate, Oral cavity, Nasal cavity, Nose, Lips, Teeth, Tongue tip, Tongue blade, Glottis, Velum, Uvula, Tongue back, Pharyngeal cavity, Epiglottis, Vocal folds, Larynx (voicebox)

(Continued)

3 [9]Glesser and Tomei (2016) define a vowel as "a sound produced with the vocal folds vibrating and an open vocal tract above the vocal folds." [10]Vowels do not involve any stopping or tight restriction of the flow of air. [11]Instead, one shapes the oral cavity in different ways by moving the jaw, tongue, and lips. [12]The nasal cavity can also be opened up to further influence vowel quality. [13]Figure 2 (Walski 2002) details the various mouth shapes used in producing American English vowels. [14]The left edge of the chart indicates tongue positions. [15]By *close*, Walski means "high; close to the top of the mouth." [16]The top of the chart indicates how far forward the oral cavity has been shifted by moving the tongue. [17]The tongue can be, as Walski says, "high for a vowel like [i] as in *beat*, mid-height for a vowel like the [ɛ] in *bet*, or open for a vowel like the [æ] in *bat*."

Figure 2: Vowel phonemes in American English

General American Vowel Phonemes						
	Front		Central		Back	
	long	short	long	short	long	short
Close	iː	ɪ			uː	ʊ
Mid		ɛ	ɜː	ə	ɔː	
Open		æ		ʌ	ɑː	
Diphthongs		eɪ aɪ ɔɪ aʊ oʊ				
		ɪə eə				

Source: J. Walski. (2002). American Articulation. Boston: Deventer Press.

4 [18]As for consonants, Glesser and Tomei say, "The basic physiological mechanism for producing consonant sounds involves a narrowing of the vocal tract, which tightly constricts or even stops the flow of air." [19]Some consonants (the voiced ones like [b], [d], and [m]) have vibrating vocal folds; others (the unvoiced ones, like [p] and [t]) do not. [20]Consonants are described partly by their *point of articulation*. [21]Walski says, "The point where the vocal tract is closed—or almost closed—is where any given consonant lives." [22]Figure 1 shows the many locations where consonants can be articulated. [23]For example, [b] and [p] are called *bilabials* because they are formed with both lips. [24]The stops [t] and [d] are called *alveolars* because the tip of the tongue touches the alveolar ridge, just behind the top front teeth. [25]Besides the place of articulation, phoneticians also note the *manner of articulation*. [26]Is the flow of air completely stopped? [27]If so, the consonant is a *stop* like [b] or [d]. [28]Is the flow of air restricted to a very narrow passage? [29]If so, the resulting consonant is a *fricative* like [s] or [f]. [30]Is the flow stopped briefly and then released to form a fricative? [31]If so, you have an *affricate* like [tʒ] or [dʒ].

Figure 3: Consonant phonemes in American English

			Labial	Dental	Alveolar	Post-alveolar	Palatal	Velar	Glottal
Nasal			m		n			ŋ	
Stop, Affricate		unvoiced	p		t	t͡ʃ		k	
		voiced	b		d	d͡ʒ		g	
Fricative	**sibilant**	unvoiced			s	ʃ			
		voiced			z	ʒ			
	non-sibilant	unvoiced	f	θ				x	h
		voiced	v	ð					
Approximant					l	r	j	w	

Source: J. Walski. (2002). *American Articulation*. Boston: Deventer Press.

5 ³²We mentioned earlier that not all spoken sounds fall neatly into vowel or consonant categories. ³³Among these are several English sounds—[l], [r], [j], and [w]—that are called variously *glides*, *approximants*, *semi-vowels*, or *liquids*. They appear in Figure 3 as approximants. ³⁴As Walski puts it, "Are they vowels? ³⁵They certainly sound like vowels, but then again they do the same work as consonants in creating syllable boundaries."

6 ³⁶It may seem that American English is difficult, but its system of phonemic sounds is actually quite tidy. ³⁷Matabole (2013) notes that English is far less complicated than the southern African Khoisan languages—often called the "click" languages because some of their consonants are made by clicking the tongue at various points of articulation. ³⁸Some click languages have more than 85 phonemic consonants.

The names of researchers in this article are fictional, for instructional purposes only.

B. In the following excerpts from the reading, circle every reporting verb. Underline the name of the source for each quotation. In the blanks, write *D* if the excerpt is a direct quotation, *I* if it is indirect, or *H* if it is hybrid.

.... 1. Parini (2007) suggests becoming aware of your vocal tract by opening your mouth and throat as much as possible and forcing air from your lungs through the passages.

.... 2. Glesser and Tomei (2016) define a vowel as "a sound produced with the vocal folds vibrating and an open vocal tract above the vocal folds."

.... 3. The tongue can be, as Walski says, "high for a vowel like [i] as in *beat*, mid-height for a vowel like the [ɛ] in *bet*, or low for a vowel like the [æ] in *bat*."

.... 4. Glesser and Tomei say, "The basic physiological mechanism for producing consonant sounds involves a narrowing of the vocal tract, which tightly constricts or even stops the flow of air."

.... 5. Walski says, "The point where the vocal tract is closed—or almost closed—is where any given consonant lives."

.... 6. Matabole notes that English is far less complicated than many languages, such as the southern African Khoisan languages.

C. Follow the directions to write quotations based on "Segmentals and Articulatory Features." Punctuate as needed.

1. Complete the direct quotation based on the first part of Sentence 2.

The author says, ...

2. Complete the shortened, direct quotation based on Sentence 6. Note the use of ellipsis points to replace unnecessary information.

The author defines the vocal tract as " ....

involving .... ,

and nose . . . . "

3. Complete the hybrid quotation based on Sentence 10. Note the use of ellipsis points.

The author points out that vowels do not involve " . . . . "

4. Complete the indirect quotation based on Sentence 15.

By *close*, Walski means .... or ....

5. Complete the hybrid quotation based on Sentence 21. It will be a "quotation within a quotation" because you will quote the author remarking about what Walski said. The part that is quoted directly should contain the most interesting phrasing from the original.

The author quotes Walski as noting that the point where the vocal tract is closed is

" .... "

6. Complete the hybrid quotation of Sentence 36.

The author observes that American English may seem difficult, but " ....

.... "

D. Work with a partner. Compare your answers to Part C. Then discuss the questions.

1. Notice the reporting verbs. Which other reporting verbs could you use in each item?

2. Look back at "Segmentals and Articulatory Features" on page 179. Which type of quotation appears most often: direct, indirect, or hybrid? Is this balance similar to what you have seen in other academic passages?

3. Is the ability to quote material from a reading important in your academic area? Explain your answer.

VOCABULARY CHECK

A. Review the vocabulary items in the Vocabulary Preview. Write their definitions and add examples. Use a dictionary if necessary.

B. Complete each sentence using the correct vocabulary item from the box. Use the correct form.

cavity	click	constrict	manner
physiological	restriction	string together	vibrate

1. I am confused about how to pronounce words written with several vowels .... , such as *bureaucracy*.

2. When you are giving a presentation in a university class, you should speak in a(n) .... that is formal but not *too* formal.

3. Bats and and some other animals make .... sounds as a way to find their way in the dark. Technically this is called *echolocation*.

4. Put your fingers on the front of your neck. Now talk. Do you feel the movement? Those are your vocal cords .... as air passes over them.

5. A cold or an infection in one's sinus .... can cause a person to pronounce nasal sounds like dental ones. For example, the word *mean* might sound like *bead*.

6. Most languages have .... about where certain consonants can appear. In English, for example, there cannot be an /s/ after affricates. That is why we say "watch*es*," not "watchs."

7. The course covers every aspect of singing, from the .... process of sound production to proper artistic expression.

8. When Robert is nervous, his throat .... , making it difficult for him to speak.

🔵 Go to MyEnglishLab to complete two skill practices.

LANGUAGE SKILL
UNDERSTANDING STRUCTURES USED FOR HEDGING

WHY IT'S USEFUL Academic authors commonly soften or limit their remarks, especially when speaking or writing about controversial matters. This is called *hedging*. If you can recognize and understand hedging, you will be able to appreciate an author's approach to a topic more precisely.

◐ Go to MyEnglishLab for the Language Skill presentation and practice.

VOCABULARY STRATEGY
USING A DICTIONARY TO STRENGTHEN VOCABULARY

WHY IT'S USEFUL By becoming familiar with three features of dictionary entries, you can further develop and strengthen your vocabulary.

Your dictionary can be a valuable tool for improving your vocabulary. Three features of many dictionaries are especially important—**multiple definitions** for most entries, **collocation notes** for many entries, and the inclusion of **multiword units** as entries.

Multiple Definitions

It is common for an English word to have many definitions. Even if a word is familiar to you, its meaning in a given context may be unclear. To find the meaning you need, quickly scan the term's dictionary entry. Check each meaning, plus any example phrases or sentences. If your scanning does not reveal the correct definition, slow down and read each definition (and any examples) more carefully. Then look back at the context in the reading where you found the word. Decide which definition best fits that context. For example:

Original context: The orientation of the lines on the map was from southwest to northeast.

Possible definitions:

o·ri·en·ta·tion /ˌɔːriənˈteɪʃən/ **noun**
1. the type of activity or subject that a person or organization seems most interested in and gives most attention to
2. the political opinions or religious beliefs that someone has
3. a period of time during which people are trained and prepared for a new job or course of study
4. the angle or position of an object, or the direction in which it is facing

The fourth definition best fits the original context, which is about directions ("southwest to northeast"). Being able to choose the best definition in this manner will help expand your knowledge even of words you already know partially.

Collocation Notes

Collocation is the process by which certain words frequently occur together. For example, *do* and *homework* often appear together (but not *make* and *homework*). So do *heavy* and *traffic*—but not *weighty* and *traffic*. Common collocations may be indicated in a dictionary entry by bold type, italics, or capitals—or by appearing in example sentences. Some dictionaries even highlight collocations in special boxes. Recognizing collocations can increase your reading fluency because it helps you to deal with words in groups instead of word-by-word. Command of collocations can also make your writing and speech sound smoother and more sophisticated.

Multiword Units

A multiword unit is a vocabulary item made of two or more words very tightly bound to each other. This binding is so tight that the words form a single unit, which you should learn, remember, and use as one vocabulary item. You already know many of these units. They include phrasal / prepositional verbs (e.g., *put up with* ["tolerate"], *use up*), compound nouns (e.g., *gas station, cell phone*), and complex prepositions (e.g., *next to, in terms of*).

EXERCISE 5

A. Work alone or in a group. Read each sentence. Look at the dictionary entry to find the definition that best fits the meaning of the underlined word in the context of the item. Write the number of the definition in the blank.

---

dead¹ /ded/ **adjective**

1 no longer alive
◀)) *Both of her parents were **dead***

2 not working due to a lack of power
◀)) *The batteries in the remote are **dead**.*

3 (of a place) not interesting or exciting
◀)) *The place was **dead**, so we moved on to somewhere with more atmosphere.*

4 very tired
◀)) *I was **dead** on my feet by the end of the shift.*

5 completely or precisely (used for emphasis)
◀)) *He pointed **dead** ahead.*

6 (of the ball in some games) no longer in play or on playing area
◀)) *The attacking player gave chase but gave up when the ball went **dead**.*

.... 1. When the runner saw a snake on the path, he came to a <u>dead</u> stop.

.... 2. The campus is <u>dead</u>, and everything's quiet because the students are on spring break.

.... 3. By the time the emergency medical technicians arrived, the driver of the car was <u>dead</u>.

.... 4. I haven't slept much, so I'm really <u>dead</u> now. Go bowling without me this time.

.... 5. My watch went <u>dead</u> at 12:45. What time is it now?

.... 6. Don't visit France in August. Everyone's on vacation then, and the place is really <u>dead</u>.

B. Work alone or in a group. Use the dictionary collocation box to decide which collocation best fits each sentence. Write it in the blank. There may be more than one acceptable answer. You will not use all the collocations.

---

help /help/ noun

COLLOCATIONS

be a big help

◄)) *When I had to move to a new apartment, my brother **was a big help**.*

call for help

◄)) *A man fell down the stairs. I think his leg is broken. Can you please **call for help**?*

give [someone] help

◄)) *I can't twist the top off this jar. Maybe you can **give me some help**.*

need help

◄)) *These homework problems are difficult. Let me know if you **need any help**.*

offer help

◄)) *My dad likes to do things by himself. Sometimes he gets upset if anyone **offers help**.*

outside help

◄)) *Our police department doesn't have enough officers. When they get busy, they have to call for **outside help**.*

professional help

◄)) *You've been sick for a long time. It's time to see a doctor. You need **professional help**.*

---

1. We'll never get the car out of this snow. Do you have a phone? Can you
   .... ?

2. My grandfather .... walking up stairs.

3. There's a difference between simple sadness and real depression. You'll get over
   sadness yourself, in time. To deal with depression, you need ....

4. The young woman was having trouble opening the door while holding her baby.
   My mother .... , and the woman was very grateful.

5. We don't have anyone on our staff who can set up the computer database.
   I think we'll have to get some .... with this project.

6. I can't lift this table by myself. Can you .... ?

C. **Each item is excerpted or adapted from readings in this unit. Underline the
   multiword unit(s) in each item. With a partner, discuss the meanings of the items
   you underlined.**

1. Many vocal cues to emotion are subtle, easily lost in the scratchy recordings in
   use prior to the 1950s.

2. First, your friend's vocal shakiness conveyed, all by itself, some kind of
   emotional distress.

3. Linguists have an especially hard time defining their field and keeping less-than-
   informed observers at bay. (2 multiword items)

4. Long ago, some word that is the oldest ancestor of *chair* was arbitrarily constructed.

5. The notes Jessica Coon took as she tried to make sense of the puzzle actually
   appear in the movie as notes taken by one of the characters.

6. For the most part, subjects would come first, objects would come second, verbs
   would come last.

APPLY YOUR SKILLS

> **WHY IT'S USEFUL** By applying the skills you have learned in this unit, you can gain a better understanding of this challenging reading about a linguist who worked as a consultant for a science-fiction film.

BEFORE YOU READ

A. Discuss these questions with a partner or group.

1. Think about the term *science fiction* (often shortened to *sci-fi*). What is science fiction? Why is it called that?

2. If two people who come from different cultures and who speak different languages meet, how can they begin to establish communication? If you were in that situation, what would you do?

3. Many animals communicate with other members of their species. Bees, ants, whales, and chimpanzees are just a few examples. Is their communication an example of language use?

B. You will read a passage about linguists who are called in as consultants to movies. As you read, think about these questions.

1. What "real linguistics" does the character Louise Banks perform in the film *Arrival*?

2. According to linguist Jessica Coon, what sorts of "different cognitive realities" might be reflected in the language of an alien species?

3. How does linguist Scott Kubiak explain the Sapir-Whorf hypothesis?

4. What kinds of tasks have other linguists been asked to perform when serving as expert consultants to the movies?

C. Review the Unit Skills Summary. As you read the passage, apply the skills you learned in this unit.

UNIT SKILLS SUMMARY

Identify and understand statements of fact

- Recognize and interpret statements that the author presents as fact.

Identify and understand statements of opinion

- Recognize and interpret statements that the author presents as opinion.

Quote material from a reading

- Recognize and compose direct, indirect, and hybrid quotations.

Understand structures used for hedging

• Understand how certain language can be used to hedge or "soften" statements.

Use a dictionary to strengthen vocabulary

• Use a dictionary to select definitions and to learn collocations and multiword units.

READ

A. Read the article. Annotate and take notes on the answers to the questions in Before You Read, Part B.

Grammar Goes to Hollywood: Linguists as Science Consultants

1 In the 2016 movie *Arrival*, alien ships appear at 12 locations around Earth and silently hover over the ground. One of them is in the US state of Montana, and the US government and military struggle to understand its purpose and assess whether it poses a threat. The problem is that, although the aliens seem willing to contact humans (the ships open to accept human visitors every 18 hours), no one on Earth has the slightest idea how to communicate with them. Enter the hero of the movie, Dr. Louise Banks, a professor of linguistics whose talent for language analysis saves the world.

> **Glossary**
>
> Lionize: to present or praise as something great
>
> Nerd: a person who becomes excessively interested in the details of a field, usually involving science, science fiction, or digital technology

2 Linguists may be used to being ignored in the movies, as opposed to doctors, engineers, and other professionals. Thus most were probably delighted to see their field not only portrayed but lionized in a hit film. Bjarni Gunarsson a linguist at Scotus University in Chicago, writes, "Linguists in movies are usually portrayed only as translators. Finally, this character does real linguistics. She doesn't just translate. She analyzes, synthesizes, reconceptualizes." Gunarsson hints at a common misconception concerning the work of linguists—that their job is to know a lot of languages. Although it is not unusual for linguists to speak more than one language (Louise Banks can apparently speak English, Mandarin, and Farsi), multilingualism is not at the heart of their profession. They are specialists not so much at using other languages as at analyzing them, applying principles of their science to discern patterns. *Arrival* is a movie, and some linguistic concepts may be warped somewhat for cinematic effect, but Louise Banks is broadly believable as a linguist.

(Continued)

Much of the credit for this belongs to a Canadian linguist from McGill University named Jessica Coon, who served as a consultant to the director (also a Canadian), Denis Villeneuve.

3   Part of Coon's job was to interpret for Villeneuve certain linguistics concepts that appear in the movie's source, a short story by Ted Chiang called "The Story of Your Life." She brought a sense to this task that, while all human languages share certain very basic features, the language of an alien species could reflect entirely different cognitive realities. Coon writes, "When it comes to the language of the Heptapods [the aliens], even the most skilled linguist has to admit that all bets are off. Will aliens have nouns and verbs as we do, or understand the difference between a statement and a question, as we do?" Eventually, the Heptapods in the movie produce statements, circular patterns that look like inkblots and contain entire constellations of thoughts within a single pattern of inky bumps along the circle. To get an idea of how a linguist might handle such a form of communication, Villeneuve gave some to Coon, with no hint of any meaning. The notes she took as she tried to make sense of the puzzle actually appear in the movie as notes taken by Louise Banks.

4   Coon most crucially helped Villeneuve—and Amy Adams, who plays Louise Banks—understand a linguistic concept that drives the movie's plot but is not well received by most modern linguists. This is the Sapir-Whorf hypothesis. As Scott Kubiak, a linguist at Warburton College, describes it, Sapir-Whorf says that the concepts built into one's language affect one's ability to think in certain ways. According to Kubiak, "a true believer in Sapir-Whorf would say it determines your thinking. If your language's words for relatives included only your parents and your siblings, you would not consider yourself related to your uncles, aunts, and cousins." Coon herself—like most other linguists—has reservations about Sapir-Whorf. Chiang, in his short story, may have given too much credence to Sapir-Whorf, but there is no point in trying to remove it. The plot of the story (and the movie) depends on the hypothesis being plausible.

5   On several notable occasions, linguistics consultants have faced different challenges. Whereas Coon consulted about linguistic principles, others have actually created languages. Linguist Marc Okrand (following up on earlier work by actor James Doohan) is legendary for creating most of the Klingon language for the *Star Trek* films and the entire Atlantean language for a Disney animated feature, *Atlantis: The Lost Empire* (2001). Klingon has become a nerd-culture phenomenon. Certain fans claim to speak it to each other (although many of them just put Klingon words into English grammar). Even earlier, linguist Victoria Fromkin had invented a language called Pakuni for a 1970s TV show called *Land of the Lost*. Both Fromkin and Okrand earned great respect for building their artificial languages on plausible principles of grammar and word formation.

6   Linguist Blair Rudes from the University of North Carolina didn't so much create a language as resurrect one. For his 2006 film *The New World*, about the early English colony of Jamestown in Virginia (and the relationship of Pocahontas and John Smith), director Terrence Malick wanted the Powhatan people to speak in their own language, Virginia Algonquian (VA). However, the language had been dead for about 200 years, and the only records of it were sparse word lists from Smith and another colonist, William Strachey. Rudes used these, plus evidence from a few still-spoken relatives of VA, to construct a language that is plausible in terms of its grammar and vocabulary. He readily admits that the reconstruction is a guess. "I jokingly refer to the language in the film as the Blair Rudes dialect of Virginia Algonquian," he says.

7   Unlike Coon, Rudes had a task rooted in human cognition and the principles behind human language. He was also able to refer to real-life languages, especially three languages spoken in Maine and eastern Canada. "I would turn to three other Algonquian languages and say, 'How would you say this word in those languages?'," he says. If at least two of the three had a similar word, he assumed the VA word would probably be similar as well. For the grammar, there were clear patterns in the relatives of VA. Rudes notes, "For the most part, subjects would come first, objects would come second, verbs would come last. But sometimes objects would come after verbs. Adverbs would frequently come at the very beginning of a sentence. So if they're saying, 'I love you always,' it would be, 'Always I love you.'" Like Coon, Rudes was an analyst and synthesist, not a translator. And just by chance, the linguists share something else. One of the languages that aided Rudes is Miq'maq, an Eastern Algonquian language in Canada that is one of Coon's special areas of expertise.

The names of most researchers and universities in this reading are fictional, presented for instructional purposes only. Jessica Coon, Victoria Fromkin, Marc Okrand, and Blair Rudes are actual linguists, and their accomplishments as detailed in this reading are real.

B. **Work with a partner. Discuss the answers to the questions in Before You Read, Part B. Are there any questions you cannot answer? Which of the reading skills you have learned in this unit could help you answer them?**

🔼 Go to MyEnglishLab to read the passage again and answer critical thinking questions.

THINKING CRITICALLY

Consider how other movies might have benefited from the services of a science consultant. Choose one movie—a science-oriented or science fiction film would be best, but historical, war, or crime movies may work as well. Create a three-column chart and fill it in as follows:

1. In the left column, make a list of three or four events, scenes, pieces of equipment, or other aspects of the movie that have a technical aspect.

2. In the middle column, write down the kind of scientist or other expert (doctor, lawyer, military general, etc.) who would be able to help the moviemaker with the events in column 1.

3. In the right column, write one or two things you think the scientist or expert would be likely to tell the movie director about the event, scene, and so on.

Event	Specialist	Information
Example from *Arrival*		
Louise Banks ...	Hazardous materials ...	What kind of ... ?

THINKING VISUALLY

Use information from the timeline at the top of page 193 and do Internet research to discover any additional information you need to complete the chart.

Selected Invented Languages

Language	Year	Creator	Purpose	Sample Word or Phrase (in the Roman Alphabet)*
Dothraki			For use in the HBO television series *Game of Thrones*	sekke verven ("very violent")
Elvish			For the book *The Lord of the Rings*	
	1887		To promote international cooperation	
The first phrases of Klingon		James Doohan		
The main body of the Klingon language	1984			jaghpu' ("enemies")
	December 2009		For the James Cameron film *Avatar*	
Pakuni			For the TV show *Land of the Lost*	
	1827		To promote multimodal communication (via spoken sounds, musical notes, and colors)	fala ("tasty"), remiresi ("brother")

Samples found in Wikipedia entries for the various languages

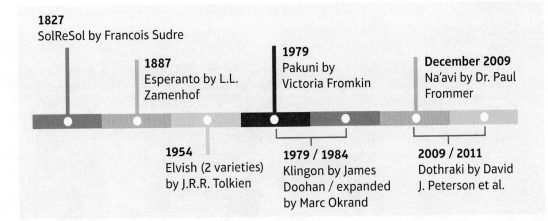

1827
SolReSol by Francois Sudre

1887
Esperanto by L.L.
Zamenhof

1979
Pakuni by
Victoria Fromkin

December 2009
Na'avi by Dr. Paul
Frommer

1954
Elvish (2 varieties)
by J.R.R. Tolkien

1979 / 1984
Klingon by James
Doohan / expanded
by Marc Okrand

2009 / 2011
Dothraki by David
J. Peterson et al.

THINKING ABOUT LANGUAGE

Underline the hedging word or phrase in the excerpts from "Grammar: Goes to Hollywood: Linguists as Science Consultants."

1. Linguists may be used to being ignored in the movies, as opposed to doctors, engineers, and other professionals.

2. Gunarsson hints at a common misconception concerning the work of linguists—that their job is to know a lot of languages.

3. To get an idea of how a linguist might handle such a form of communication, Villeneuve gave some [logograms] to Coon, with no hint of any meaning.

4. *Arrival* is a movie, and some linguistic concepts may be warped somewhat for cinematic effect, but Louise Banks is broadly believable as a linguist.

5. Chiang, in his short story, may have given too much credence to Sapir-Whorf, but there is no point in trying to remove it.

6. If at least two of the three had a similar word, he assumed the VA word would probably be similar as well.

▶ Go to MyEnglishLab to watch Professor Podesva's concluding video and to complete a self-assessment.

How cultural and ethical values define a successful business

BUSINESS ETHICS

Implication and Inference

UNIT PROFILE

In this unit, you will consider the influence of culture on how people do business. Reading topics include an introduction to cultural ethos, cultural dimensions theory, and six main areas of cultural difference that affect the way people do business. You will also read about the effects of directness and indirectness on business practices.

Preview the reading "High- Versus Low-Context Cultures" on page 219. Skim the reading. What is the author's opinion about doing business internationally?

OUTCOMES

- Make predictive inferences
- Identify strong and weak inferences
- Paraphrase
- Understand noun clauses
- Guess word meanings from context

For more about **BUSINESS ETHICS**, see ① ③.

See also W and OC **BUSINESS ETHICS** ① ② ③.

GETTING STARTED

🔊 Go to MyEnglishLab to watch Dr. McLennan's introductory video and to complete a self-assessment.

Discuss these questions with a partner or group.

1. How would you define "culture"?

2. How can culture affect the way people do business? Give an example.

3. What is the difference between communitarian and individual values, according to Dr. McLennan?

CRITICAL THINKING SKILL

UNDERSTANDING IMPLICATION AND INFERENCE

WHY IT'S USEFUL Understanding implication and inference can help you to more fully comprehend an author's intentions, purpose, and point of view. It can also help you to think critically about what you have read.

A written text may have ideas that are implied, meaning they are not stated directly by the author. As a reader, you can understand the implied meanings, or **implications**, in a text by making **inferences**. An inference is a logical conclusion that you reach based on your background knowledge and evidence that is presented in the text.

To make inferences, you should consider what you already know, have experienced, or believe about a topic, as these will influence how you perceive the ideas presented in a text. If you already know something about a topic, this knowledge can help you to comprehend a text more easily. However, your background knowledge and opinions about a topic can also mislead you, causing you to make false conclusions about an author's intended meaning. By being aware of your own biases, or tendency to favor or believe certain ideas, you can engage more deeply with the ideas presented in a text and focus on what the author intends to communicate.

By considering your background knowledge and by looking for evidence in the text—clues that indicate the author's intended meaning—you can use your reasoning skills to make strong, well-supported inferences. The stronger the evidence you gather, and the more carefully you reason, the more likely you are to make logical inferences that reflect the author's intent.

This unit breaks **understanding implication and inference** down into two supporting skills:

- making predictive inferences
- identifying strong and weak inferences

VOCABULARY PREVIEW

The following vocabulary items appear in the reading. Circle the ones you know. Put a question mark next to the ones you do not know.

expectations	invisible	apparent	punctuality
dimensions	perspective	underlying	

EXERCISE 1

A. Discuss the questions with a partner before you read.

1. What are some ways in which cultures differ from one another? In other words, what are some ways you might be different from someone from another culture?

2. Look at the photo of the iceberg. Why do you think the author chose to show this photo? What do you think the connection is between an iceberg and culture?

3. The passage you will read is an excerpt from an introductory textbook on business ethics. What can you infer about the style of writing or type of information you expect to encounter in the passage?

B. Preview the passage. Read the title and skim the first paragraph. Then discuss these questions with a partner.

1. Based on your background knowledge, predict the meaning of *cultural ethos*. Underline the definition in the first paragraph and compare it with your prediction. How are they similar or different?

2. Based on what you read in the first paragraph, what do you expect the rest of the text to discuss?

Introduction to Cultural Ethos

1 When we think of culture, we might define it as the observable characteristics of a group of people, such as their dress, food, art, and customs. Culture, in fact, includes all of these, but it is also much more. *Cultural ethos* is a broad set of beliefs, moral values, and *norms*—the expectations and rules of behavior—that belong to a group of people. To better understand these hidden aspects of culture, social psychologists often compare culture to an iceberg. What you see on the surface of an iceberg is only a small part of what is really there because most of the ice actually lies under the surface of the water. Similarly, what you see on the surface when you visit a culture is only part of a culture's whole identity, so to speak. A much larger, invisible part of a culture, its *ethos*, lies under the surface. When people connect across cultures, such as in a business environment, our attitude is influenced by our cultural values and can affect our behavior. These cultural differences in thinking may not always be apparent, but they can cause misunderstanding. An American businesswoman's attitude about punctuality, for example, might cause her to be offended if a person arrives late to a meeting. An Indian businesswoman, on the other hand, might not think twice about a late arrival.

2 Three main dimensions of cultural ethos are *worldview*, *mindset*, and *ideology*. Worldview is the overall way that members of a culture view life and the world. In other words, it is the shared perspective of the members of a culture. Cultural mindset, on the other hand, is the set of attitudes that individuals develop based on their worldview but filtered through their own personal experiences. Mindset, unlike worldview, is unique to each individual. For example, two people may share an American worldview, yet they may have very different mindsets if one is wealthy and the other poor. It is from this individual perspective that each understands and judges the world. Finally, an ideology, or a system of beliefs and ideas, is also often part of culture and influences a person's way of thinking. Ideologies are often religious, political, or economic. A capitalist ideology, for example, is common in the United States. That is to say, many people in America have the underlying belief in a capitalist approach to managing the economy.

C. Read the passage again. Then match each term with its meaning.

.... 1. cultural ethos

.... 2. cultural norms

.... 3. attitude

.... 4. worldview

.... 5. mindset

.... 6. ideology

a. the overall way that members of a culture view life and the world

b. a system of beliefs and ideas that is often religious, political, or economic

c. the way a person feels about something

d. a set of beliefs, moral values, and norms held by a group of people

e. the set of attitudes that a person develops that is informed by his or her worldview and personal experiences

f. the expectations and rules that guide behavior in a culture

D. Answer the questions. Refer to the passage as needed. Then discuss your answers with a partner.

1. Look again at your predictions in Part A. How do you think your own experience or background knowledge may have influenced your responses? Did your responses match what you learned in the reading? If not, how did the information in the text change your perspective?

2. What does the author imply about American and Indian attitudes toward punctuality? What evidence is presented in the text to support your inference?

3. What does the author imply about the personal experiences of rich people compared to poor people in America? What evidence is presented in the text to support your inference?

VOCABULARY CHECK

A. Review the vocabulary items in the Vocabulary Preview. Write their definitions and add examples. Use a dictionary if necessary.

B. Complete each sentence using the correct vocabulary item from the box. Use the correct form.

apparent	dimension	expectation	invisible
perspective	punctuality	underlying	

1. A business environment includes economic, political, social, legal, and technological .... Each part of the overall business environment should be considered when making business decisions.

2. In business negotiations, it is important for each side to consider the .... of the other in order to reach a fair solution.

3. Facial expressions are one indication of a person's attitude, but an individual's true feelings may be .... to the eye.

4. Good business leaders will examine a situation carefully to determine the .... cause of a problem, which may be hidden beneath other, more obvious explanations.

5. .... is important in Canadian business culture. Most Canadians expect to start meetings on time.

6. Some cultural characteristics are obvious, such as dress and language, but other features, such as beliefs and attitudes, are often not immediately .... to those new to a culture.

7. Visitors to a new culture are often confused when their .... about "normal" behavior are not met.

○ Go to MyEnglishLab to complete a vocabulary exercise and skill practice, and to join in collaborative activities.

SUPPORTING SKILL 1

MAKING PREDICTIVE INFERENCES

WHY IT'S USEFUL Making inferences about upcoming content before and during reading helps you to engage actively with a text, assess your background knowledge, and check your expectations against the information presented and implied in the text. This can help you to gain a deeper understanding as you read.

In LINGUISTICS, Part 1, page 7, you learned that previewing a text can help you to get a sense of the contents before you read, predict the topics that might be covered, and activate your background knowledge. Making **predictive inferences**, or educated guesses about what you will read, will help you to engage actively with a text and use your background knowledge to help you to improve your comprehension. This can be done both before and while you read a text.

Before Reading

When previewing a text, you can make predictions by asking yourself questions such as these:

- What type or genre of text is this? How will this affect the style of writing or kind of information in the text?

- What is the purpose of the text? Is it meant to inform or teach the topic? Persuade? Entertain?

- Who is the author? What is the author's background? How might this influence the ideas in the text?

- What do the title and visuals tell me about the topic? How can this help me to predict the content?

- What do I already know about this topic? What new information can I expect to learn? Is there anything I expect to find confusing?

- How do I feel about this topic? Do I expect to agree or disagree with the author's opinions about anything?

While Reading

As you read you can check your predictions and make new ones by asking questions such as:

- Were the predictions I made before reading correct? If not, what is different? What evidence in the text supports or discounts my predictions?
- According to the text, is my background knowledge about this topic accurate?
- Do I agree with the ideas or opinions of the author? If not, why might my perspective be different?
- Based on what I have read so far, what information do I expect will come next?

VOCABULARY PREVIEW

The following vocabulary items appear in the reading. Circle the ones you know. Put a question mark next to the ones you do not know.

feminine	masculine	traits	tough
sexist	tendencies	stereotypes (n)	derive

EXERCISE 2

A. Preview the article. Look at the photo and title. Then discuss the questions with a partner.

1. What is the genre of this text? In other words, what type of reading is it? Who is the intended audience? How do you think this will affect the style of writing or information included in the text?

2. Based on the photo and title of the article, what do you predict this article will focus on? What do you know about this topic? Do you have any opinions about it?

Now skim Paragraph 1 of the text. Then discuss the questions with a partner.

3. Were your predictions in 1 and 2 correct? If not, how were they different from what you read in the text? What evidence can you find in the text to explain any differences? How did your background knowledge affect your understanding?

4. Based on what you read in Paragraph 1, what do you predict will be discussed in the rest of the text?

CULTURE NOTE

Geert Hofstede is a Dutch social psychologist who is Professor Emeritus of Organizational Anthropology and International Management at Maastricht University in the Netherlands. He is a former employee of IBM who has done research in the areas of organizational culture, economics, and management.

B. Read the entire article. Stop at the numbered points and write predictive inferences in the margin about what you will read next. Then continue reading and check your predictions.

Global Business Culture: Getting in Touch with Your Feminine Side

1 It goes without saying that global business leaders need to be aware of cultural differences when doing business abroad, but one difference that many of us may not be aware of is the distinction between "masculine" and "feminine" cultures. The cultural domain of "masculinity-femininity" is part of social psychologist Geert Hofstede's cultural dimensions theory and is based on what are considered to be traditional male and female traits. **[1]** It is meant to describe the focus on competition and achievement in some cultures in contrast to the emphasis on cooperation in others. Assertiveness and ambition are considered masculine characteristics in the theory, while modesty and caring are designated as feminine ones. Hofstede also refers to this contrast as the "tough-tender" cultural dimension. These traditional distinctions between "masculine" and "feminine" traits may seem old-fashioned and sexist in today's workplace, but keep in mind Hofstede originally developed this theory more than 40 years ago! At the time, his goal was to describe general cultural tendencies, not to create gender stereotypes. Despite its name, the masculinity-femininity category has nothing to do with the expectations people place on either men or women in the workplace.

[1] ....
....
....

Glossary

Assertiveness: the quality of being confident

Modesty: the quality of not being too proud or confident

Tender: showing concern and gentleness

Arrogant: thinking and acting as if you are better, smarter, or more important than others

2 Most nations fall somewhere in the middle on the tough-tender dimension. A few nations, however, have strong tendencies one way or the other. **[2]** Italy, Mexico, and China are nations in which many people are competitive and may aim to be number one at any given task. On the other hand, Hofstede would point to the Scandinavian countries—Norway, Denmark, and Sweden—as well as, for instance, Guatemala, Costa Rica, and Chile—as ranking low on the masculinity-femininity scale. In these nations, a high quality of life is generally valued more than individual achievement or financial rewards. In "feminine" Sweden, for example, people may measure success according to how much happiness they derive from doing their work. A good Swedish manager would not try to promote competition between employees. By contrast, **[3]** Italian workers might judge their success based on how well they perform relative to others around them. Further, Italian employees may be offended if their individual efforts are not acknowledged. If you are an American, **[4]** you would be wise to consider these differences when doing business abroad. The United States leans toward the masculine side due to our emphasis on financial success, power, and dominance, especially on Wall Street. As a result, we may come across as too aggressive or arrogant when operating in more feminine cultures.

[2] ....
....
....

[3] ....
....
....

[4] ....
....
....

C. Read the passage again. Complete each statement. Use the words and phrases in the box. Three items will not be used. Then compare answers with a partner.

competitive	Scandinavian
dominance	stereotypes
modesty	tough-tender
quality of life	traits

1. The masculinity-femininity cultural domain is based on traditional male and female .... , according to the article.

2. Masculine cultures are more .... than feminine cultures, which focus on cooperation.

3. According to the cultural dimensions theory, ... and caring are characteristics of feminine cultures.

4. Another name for the masculinity-femininity category is the .... dimension.

5. The goal of the cultural dimensions theory is not to create gender ....

6. Feminine cultures measure success based on .... rather than individual achievement.

7. Italy, Mexico, and China are examples of masculine countries, whereas .... countries are considered to be more feminine.

8. US culture is more masculine due to its emphasis on financial success, power, and ....

D. Work with a partner. Answer the questions about making predictive inferences.

1. How did making predictions help you to comprehend the text? Were any of your predictions incorrect? If so, what do you think led you to these incorrect predictions? What evidence in the text helped you to correct them?

2. Did your background knowledge help you to comprehend the content of the text? If so, how?

3. Were you surprised by any of the information in the text? Do you agree or disagree with any of the ideas? How might your background knowledge or experiences affect your opinions?

VOCABULARY CHECK

A. Review the vocabulary items in the Vocabulary Preview. Write their definitions and add examples. Use a dictionary if necessary.

B. Match each vocabulary item in bold with its meaning.

.... 1. My managers **derive** a lot of satisfaction from meeting their production goals.

.... 2. In my workplace, most of the women wear traditionally **feminine** clothing, such as skirts and dresses.

.... 3. The man who answered the phone had a deep **masculine** voice.

a. an often untrue and overly general belief about all members of a group

b. very strict or determined

c. unfair or unequal treatment of people based on their being male or female

d. to get something from something else

e. characteristics or qualities of a person

4. **Sexist** behavior is not tolerated in our workplace. Hiring or favoring some employees over others based on their sex violates the code of conduct.

5. It is a **stereotype** to say that all men are competitive.

6. My coworker has the **tendency** to blame others for problems. He usually claims his mistakes are my fault.

7. My new boss is **tough** on us. He expects us all to work really hard to meet our goals.

8. Other **traits** of his that I admire are his intelligence and sound judgment. He has several qualities of a good leader.

f. the chance that something will happen or that a person will behave in certain way

g. relating to women or girls

h. relating to men or boys

⬡ Go to MyEnglishLab to complete a vocabulary exercise and skill practice, and to join in collaborative activities.

SUPPORTING SKILL 2
IDENTIFYING STRONG AND WEAK INFERENCES

WHY IT'S USEFUL By making strong inferences you can infer a writer's intended meaning more accurately and avoid misunderstandings.

We all make inferences as we read, but our goal should be to make strong inferences rather than weak ones. A **strong inference** is a logical conclusion that is well supported by evidence in a text. In other words, it is a likely interpretation of the author's intended meaning. A **weak inference**, on the other hand, is a conclusion that may not be well reasoned or supported by the text. It may be influenced by your own ideas or assumptions but lack textual support. Read the following excerpt and the strong and weak inferences that follow:

By contrast, Italian workers might judge their success based on how well they perform relative to others around them. Further, Italian employees may be offended if their individual efforts are not acknowledged. If you are an American, you would be wise to consider these differences when doing business abroad. The United States leans toward the masculine side due to our emphasis on financial success, power, and dominance, especially on Wall Street. As a result, we may come across as too aggressive or arrogant when operating in more feminine cultures.

Inference		Explanation
Strong	The author of the article is from the United States, and the audience is likely to be other Americans who may do business abroad.	This inference is supported by the fact that the author directly addresses "Americans" when giving advice for doing business in other cultures and mentions "*our emphasis on financial success, power, and dominance,*" indicating that he or she is also from the United States.
Weak	The author has done business in Italy.	This inference is not supported by the text. The author mentions Italy as an example to illustrate the concept but never mentions working there.
Weak	Americans are too aggressive and arrogant.	This inference is weak because it is also unsupported by the text. By mentioning that Americans "may come across as too aggressive or arrogant" in other cultures, the author implies that it is possible that Americans will appear this way to others, but never indicates that it is his or her opinion.

To make sure an inference you draw while reading is strong, you can ask yourself the following questions:

- What evidence is there in the text to support my inference?
- Does the author's language support the inference I am making?
- What does the author say explicitly, and what does he or she intend for me to understand by "reading between the lines"?

VOCABULARY PREVIEW

The following vocabulary items appear in the reading. Circle the ones you know. Put a question mark next to the ones you do not know.

uncertainty	aversion	ambiguity
stability	innovative	bureaucracy

EXERCISE 3

A. Preview the article from a business journal. Notice the title and graph. Then discuss the questions with a partner.

1. Who do you think is the intended audience of the article?

2. What do you think the title means? What do you predict the article will be about? What do you know about this topic?

3. Look at the graph. What is being compared? Do you notice any patterns? How are uncertainty avoidance and innovation related, according to the graph?

Uncertainty Avoidance: The Dangers of Playing It Safe

1   In the aftermath of the Greek debt crisis, one thing has become certain: Greeks need to become more economically competitive. To do this, we need to embrace innovation. But with innovation comes risk, and risk is not something most Greeks seek out. This avoidance of risk and uncertainty may have a lot to do with our cultural values. Social psychologist Geert Hofstede calls this risk-aversion tendency the "uncertainty-avoidance" dimension of culture. According to Hofstede, citizens of nations that rank low on the uncertainty-avoidance scale, such as Denmark, Sweden, and the UK, are more willing to calmly accept the possibility of a certain degree of unpredictability and ambiguity in the future. Conversely, people from countries that rank higher on the continuum, including Greece and Portugal, for example, are less comfortable with uncertainty. In these countries, where people feel threatened by the unknown, there is often a higher tolerance for laws and regulations because they give citizens a sense of order and stability even though rules can get in the way of progress. In Greece, completing the necessary paperwork and procedures to establish and run a business can be a time-consuming and frustrating experience.

Glossary

Entrepreneurial ventures: new business activities that involve taking risks

Risk-averse: afraid of risk and, as a result, tending to avoid it

CULTURE NOTE

The Greek debt crisis began in 2009 when the country's economy developed a trade and budget deficit, meaning it was consuming more than it was producing and was unable to pay its debts. Many blame the crisis in part on the fact that Greece had slow economic growth.

(Continued)

2 There are other clear downsides to this discomfort with uncertainty. A Greek businessman in search of a product to sell would be more likely to choose one that appears familiar over one that is innovative. Similarly, new entrepreneurial ventures and business models are less likely to originate in places like Greece, which ranks at the top of Hofstede's uncertainty-avoidance continuum, than in less risk-averse countries. In those countries that rank low on the scale, there is more innovation and less bureaucracy because workers are not afraid to take risks. Such nations also seem to be able to recover from financial crises better than those displaying a greater fear of uncertainty. For example, investors in low uncertainty-avoidance countries may not be as worried about entering the market again, despite future uncertainties. The lesson to be learned is that if we Greeks wish to innovate, grow our economy, and stay competitive in the world, we will need to become more tolerant of risk and uncertainty.

UNCERTAINTY AVOIDANCE AND INNOVATION IN EUROPEAN COUNTRIES

	Uncertainty Avoidance *The Hofstede Centre Index*	Innovation *European Commission Index*
Greece	100	38
Portugal	99	41
Belgium	94	63
Slovenia	88	51
Spain	86	41
France	86	57
Italy	75	44
Czech Rep.	74	42
Austria	70	60
Germany	65	71
Estonia	60	50
Finland	59	68
Netherlands	53	63
Ireland	35	61
UK	35	61
Sweden	29	75
Denmark	23	73

B. Now read the passage. Check (✓) the statements that are true for countries that are high or low on the uncertainty-avoidance dimension.

Countries in This Category ...	High Uncertainty Avoidance	Low Uncertainty Avoidance
1. are more averse to risk.		
2. will accept more ambiguity.		
3. are likely to have more laws and regulations.		
4. include countries such as Greece and Portugal.		

Countries in This Category ...	High Uncertainty Avoidance	Low Uncertainty Avoidance
5. include countries such as Denmark, Sweden, and the UK.		
6. tend to be more innovative.		
7. are less likely to start new entrepreneurial ventures.		
8. may be able to recover from financial crises better.		

C. Read the passage again. Check your answers to Part B. Then compare answers with a partner.

D. With a partner, discuss the following inferences about the article and check (✓) *strong* or *weak*. Explain your choices with evidence (or lack of evidence) in the passage.

Inference	Strong	Weak
1. The writer of the article is Greek.		
2. Rules and regulations may discourage new business in Greece.		
3. Although paperwork can be time-consuming, Greek citizens don't mind doing it because it gives them a sense of stability.		
4. Greeks feel threatened by those from risk-taking countries.		
5. Citizens of Denmark, Sweden, and the UK are calmer than Greeks.		
6. Compared to countries like Sweden, Greece probably does not have a large number of entrepreneurs.		
7. Greece's culture is to blame for its current economic troubles.		
8. Becoming less fearful of risk would probably help the Greeks to recover from financial crises.		

E. Work with a partner. Answer the questions about strong and weak inferences.

1. What is the essential difference between strong and weak inferences?

2. Were you able to identify the strong inferences in Part D? If not, what was the source of your error?

3. How will understanding the difference between strong and weak inferences change the way you read in the future?

VOCABULARY CHECK

A. Review the vocabulary items in the Vocabulary Preview. Write their definitions and add examples. Use a dictionary if necessary.

B. Complete each sentence using the correct vocabulary item from the box. Use the correct form.

ambiguity	aversion	bureaucracy
innovative	stability	uncertainty

1. Silicon Valley in California is known for companies that create .... technology and products.

2. There are plenty of .... when you take on a new business venture. Many things can go wrong, and it is common for new businesses to fail.

3. When living or working in a different culture, it is important to be tolerant of .... You will encounter attitudes and behaviors that may be confusing to you.

4. When choosing a career, you should consider if you prefer to work for yourself or if you prefer the .... of a job that provides a regular paycheck.

5. Government jobs are not a good choice for people who want to avoid the rules and paperwork that are required in a(n) ....

6. If you have a(n) .... to working in an office, you would be better off finding a career that allows you to be outdoors.

🔊 **Go to MyEnglishLab to complete a vocabulary exercise and skill practice, and to join in collaborative activities**

INTEGRATED SKILLS

PARAPHRASING

WHY IT'S USEFUL Paraphrasing—restating information you read in your own words—helps you to assess whether you have understood a text. It is also a crucial skill for avoiding plagiarism, or copying another writer's original words or ideas.

In academic writing assignments, you will often be asked to incorporate the ideas of other authors into your own writing. To do so, you need to be able to **paraphrase**. Paraphrasing—restating an original text in your own words without changing the meaning—is an aid to both reading and writing. Paraphrasing while reading is a useful technique for determining whether you understand what you have read. Furthermore, in academic writing you are expected to demonstrate your understanding by using your own words rather than copying from the original text, a practice that is called *plagiarism*. Plagiarism is considered a form of academic dishonesty in many cultures, and committing plagiarism can have serious negative consequences both academically and professionally.

A good paraphrase should

- use different words, phrases, sentence structure, and word order from the original text.
- contain the key ideas from the original text.
- communicate the same relationship between ideas as in the original text.
- NOT contain any additional information that is not in the original text.

Read the following text excerpt:

> It goes without saying that global business leaders need to be aware of cultural differences when doing business abroad, but one difference that many of us may not be aware of is the distinction between "masculine" and "feminine" cultures.

The excerpt contains two key ideas:

1. It goes without saying that global business leaders need to be aware of cultural differences when doing business abroad.
2. One difference that many of us may not be aware of is the distinction between "masculine" and "feminine" cultures.

Now read two paraphrases of the excerpt. Which one is stronger? Why?

Paraphrase 1

It is clear that those who conduct business overseas must be conscious of the ways in which cultures vary; however, the cultural dimension of "masculinity-femininity" is often not considered.

Paraphrase 2

> It goes without saying that business leaders who work abroad need to think about cultural differences, but most don't understand the difference between "masculine" and "feminine" cultures.

The first paraphrase is stronger because it retains the two key ideas from the original while using different words and sentence structures. In contrast, the second paraphrase contains many of the same words and sentence structures as the original. It also differs in meaning.

The following techniques can help you to write successful paraphrases. The ones you use may vary depending on the text you are paraphrasing.

- Use synonyms for words and phrases in the original text, except for technical or unique words and concepts that have no synonyms.
- Change active sentences to passive sentences or vice versa.
- Change the order of clauses in complex sentences.
- Change the location of transitions, time expressions, and prepositional phrases.
- Reduce adjective or adverb clauses to participial phrases.
- Use quotation marks around any phrases that you keep from the original text.

TIP

Even when paraphrasing, it is important to give credit to the original author of a text. You can attribute the ideas to the author with phrases such as *According to (author)*, and / or by providing citations. Check with your instructors to find out the style that they prefer for citing sources.

For more on quotations, see LINGUISTICS, Part 2, page 177.

VOCABULARY PREVIEW

The following vocabulary items appear in the reading. Circle the ones you know. Put a question mark next to the ones you do not know.

strict	optimism	spectrum
destiny	pessimistic	pursuing

EXERCISE 4

A. Read the first paragraph of the passage "Indulgence Versus Restraint." Identify the key ideas as you read. Then read the paraphrase and discuss the questions with a partner.

1. Does the paraphrase use synonyms and different sentence structures? If not, how could it be changed?

2. Does the paraphrase contain the same key ideas as the original?

3. Does the paraphrase show the same relationship between the key ideas?

4. Are there any ideas in the paraphrase that are not present in the original text?

5. Is the paraphrase a reasonably accurate restatement of the original?

Indulgence Versus Restraint

1 **Original:** Geert Hofstede's cultural dimensions theory identifies and explains various cultural values. One of these values is the extent to which a cultural group is willing to be more indulgent or restrained, which means how interested a culture is in enjoying life versus following strict social norms. In Hofstede's theory, this value is called the "indulgence-versus-restraint" cultural dimension.

Paraphrase: The cultural dimensions theory describes several different cultural values. One of them, the "indulgence-versus-restraint" dimension, explains the degree to which a culture seeks personal enjoyment as opposed to following rigid rules of conduct.

B. Read additional excerpts from the passage. Use the suggested techniques to paraphrase the underlined sentences.

2 <u>More-indulgent societies are comfortable with the idea of people pursuing pleasures and having fun, and they place great importance on individual leisure time.</u> More-restrained societies, on the other hand, have a tendency to suppress, or put aside, personal desires. Restrained cultures often have strict moral values and carefully regulated social norms. <u>The degree to which a society is indulgent versus restrained is important for managers and employees to keep in mind when working abroad because it helps them to determine how to behave in certain situations.</u>

Paraphrase 1: ....

....

....

Paraphrase 2: ....

....

....

Glossary

Leisure: time when you can relax and do things you enjoy

Introverted: quiet and shy

Extroverted: confident and enjoying being with other people

3 Nations that rank high on the indulgence scale include Mexico, Nigeria, South Africa, the United States, Canada, and Australia. In fact, most of North America and South America are composed of indulgent countries. In Europe, Great Britain, Sweden, and the Netherlands, also rank high on the scale. <u>Some of the cultural values of these societies include a strong interest in happiness, a perception of control over one's</u>

Sweden ranks high on the indulgence scale.

<u>own life, optimism, extroverted attitudes toward strangers, and a firm belief in freedom of speech</u>. In addition, these societies tend to be more flexible when it comes to social rules about sex. They also tend to have higher crime rates but smaller police forces. It is important to note that not all of these characteristics apply to every country that ranks high on the indulgence scale, and of course, these characteristics represent just a range of behaviors and attitudes that might be present.

Paraphrase 3: ....

....

4 According to Hofstede's theory, nations that are on the opposite end of the spectrum are more restrained. In these countries, generally speaking, there is a weaker sense of overall happiness and a belief that one is not in control of one's own destiny. <u>Many of these societies do not place a great deal of importance on leisure time, and compared to indulgent societies, restrained societies are more pessimistic.</u> In addition, Hofstede's research found that many people in restrained cultures are introverted—or at least not overtly friendly—toward strangers. So, for example, people may not be as likely to smile at or greet strangers. The countries that fall into this category include some Asian nations, as well as many countries in the Middle East. In Europe, those countries in eastern Europe tend to be more restrained than those in western Europe.

Paraphrase 4: ....

....

5 <u>In addition, cultures in restrained societies place more importance on national stability than on free speech, and because of this, many of these nations have lower crime rates but larger police forces than those found in indulgent societies.</u> Of course, restrained countries are also very different from one another in many ways, and the characteristics mentioned here, like those of indulgent countries, vary from place to place.

Paraphrase 5: ....

....

D. **Work with a partner. Answer the questions about paraphrasing.**

1. Did paraphrasing help you to clarify your understanding of the ideas in the text? How?

2. How did you change words and phrases or sentence structure while you were paraphrasing? Which techniques did you use the most?

3. What was the most challenging aspect of paraphrasing?

4. How do you think you might use paraphrasing for school assignments, such as research papers?

VOCABULARY CHECK

A. **Review the vocabulary items in the Vocabulary Preview. Write their definitions and add examples. Use a dictionary if necessary.**

B. **Match each vocabulary item in bold with its meaning.**

.... 1. In most cultures there is a broad **spectrum** of opinions and behaviors.

.... 2. Despite the company's financial problems, the president expressed **optimism** that business would improve.

.... 3. He believes that a higher power is in control of his **destiny** and will determine his future.

.... 4. Our business is not doing well. I am **pessimistic** about its long-term success.

.... 5. With profits falling, company managers are interested in **pursuing** new customers and new sources of income.

.... 6. My school has a **strict** dress code. We need to wear uniforms every day.

a. used to describe a rule that must be followed

b. expecting that bad things will happen in the future or that a situation will have a bad result

c. a complete range of something, going from one extreme to the opposite

d. a belief that good things will happen

e. the things that will happen to someone in the future, especially those that cannot be changed or controlled

f. going or chasing after something that someone wants

● Go to MyEnglishLab to complete a skill practice.

LANGUAGE SKILL

UNDERSTANDING NOUN CLAUSES

WHY IT'S USEFUL Recognizing noun clauses can help to improve your comprehension of complex sentences as you read.

◔ Go to MyEnglishLab for the Language Skill presentation and practice.

VOCABULARY STRATEGY

GUESSING WORD MEANINGS FROM CONTEXT

WHY IT'S USEFUL Using context clues to guess the meaning of unfamiliar vocabulary can help you to read more quickly and to learn the meanings of new words.

In reading academic texts, you will encounter many unfamiliar words. Sometimes new words will be defined in the text (see EARTH SCIENCE, Part 1, page 66), and sometimes you will need to consult a dictionary, but often you can guess the meaning of new words from **context clues** in the surrounding words and phrases.

The following strategies can help you guess the meaning of unfamiliar words.

1. Look for a **synonym**, or a word that has the same or a similar meaning, before or after the unknown word. For example:

   Social psychologist Geert Hofstede calls the risk-aversion tendency the "uncertainty-avoidance" dimension of culture.

   Although you may not know the word *aversion*, the synonym *avoidance* gives a clue to its meaning later in the sentence. The same is true with the unknown word *uncertainty*; you can guess its meaning from the word *risk*, which appears earlier in the sentence.

2. Look for an **antonym**, a word or phrase that has an opposite or contrasting meaning, before or after the unknown word. For example:

   If someone in Greece or Portugal wanted to sell a product, for example, he would be more likely to choose a product that is safe over one that is innovative.

   In this sentence, you may not know the word *innovative*, but you can guess from the context that it contrasts with the word *safe* and has an opposite or contrasting meaning.

3. Try to guess the meaning of the word through **inference**, that is, by using logic along with context clues to guess the meaning of a word. In the following example, you can infer that *leisure time* is related to *pursuing pleasure and having fun*.

   More indulgent societies are comfortable with the idea of pursuing pleasures and having fun, and they place great importance on individual leisure time.

EXERCISE 5

A. Read the sentences. Underline the words or phrases that help you to guess the meaning of the boldfaced word.

1. Worldview is the overall way that members of a culture view life and the world. In other words, it is the shared **perspective** of the members of a culture.

2. In addition, culture can be a **fluid** structure, changing in response to any number of influences such as globalization and technology, as well as changes in attitude from generation to generation.

3. The cultural domain of **"masculinity-femininity"** is part of social psychologist Geert Hofstede's cultural dimensions theory and is based on what are considered to be traditional male and female traits.

4. The United States leans toward the masculine side due to our emphasis on financial success, power, and dominance, especially on Wall Street. Americans may come across as too aggressive or **arrogant** when operating in more feminine cultures.

5. According to Hofstede's cultural dimensions theory, people in nations that rank low on the uncertainty-avoidance scale are more willing to calmly accept a certain degree of unpredictability and **ambiguity** in the future.

6. When a nation ranks high in the power-distance category, it means that the people of the country expect organizations to be organized in **hierarchies**, with power concentrated at the top.

B. Read the sentences. Underline the context clues that help you to guess the meaning of the boldfaced word. Write a synonym or meaning on the line.

1. Many people in restrained cultures are **introverted**—or at least not overtly friendly—toward strangers. ....

2. Likewise, long-term-oriented cultures have more interest in **thrift** and saving— be it in money or other resources. ....

3. Restrained cultures often have **strict** moral values and carefully regulated social norms. ....

4. A much larger, **invisible** part of a culture, its ethos, lies under the surface.

....

5. Hofstede conducted his initial research between 1967 and 1973. **Subsequent** studies confirmed the earlier results. ....

6. Hofstede's research was one of the most **comprehensive** studies of culture, as it involved questioning a wide range of workers in over 70 countries.

....

C. **Work with a partner. Read the excerpt. Circle the vocabulary items you don't know. Use context clues to guess the meanings of the items. Then discuss the strategies that you used to guess.**

> High-context cultures, on the other hand, exchange information in a more reserved and indirect manner, with implied meanings behind messages. In other words, people rely on the context, situation, or even knowledge of the culture to help communicate and interpret messages. For example, in high-context cultures, criticizing or disagreeing with others or being negative—particularly to a boss—can be seen as extremely rude and offensive. As a result, people from these cultures may send indirect verbal or nonverbal hints of their disapproval that may not be easy for direct communicators to interpret, especially those who are unaware of the nuances and social norms of the culture.

APPLY YOUR SKILLS

WHY IT'S USEFUL By applying the skills you have learned in this unit, you can gain a better understanding of this challenging reading about different communication styles.

BEFORE YOU READ

A. **Discuss these questions with a partner or group.**

1. The reading discusses "high-context" and "low-context" cultures. What do you think these terms might mean?

2. How do you think a "direct" communication style might be different from an "indirect" communication style?

3. How might a direct or indirect communication style affect the way people do business?

B. **You will read a passage about high-context and low-context cultures. As you read, think about these questions.**

1. According to the author, how can international business travelers benefit from understanding the high-context and low-context theory of communication styles?

2. How do people from high-context versus low-context cultures communicate?

3. How do high- and low-context cultures differ in their online marketing techniques?

4. How do high- and low-context cultures differ in their management styles?

C. Review the Unit Skills Summary. As you read the passage, apply the skills you learned in this unit.

UNIT SKILLS SUMMARY

Make predictive inferences

- Understand how to make predictions before and during reading.

Identify strong and weak inferences

- Understand how to identify inferences that reflect the author's intentions.

Paraphrase

- Use strategies to paraphrase texts.

Understand noun clauses

- Understand noun clauses to improve reading fluency and comprehension.

Guess word meanings from context

- Use strategies for guessing the meaning of new words from context.

READ

A. Read the article from a business magazine and take notes on the questions in Before You Read, Part B.

High- Versus Low-Context Cultures

1 In my position as vice president of global marketing for Joldosh, Inc., I have extensive experience traveling and doing business around the world, and I've seen both the positive and the more challenging aspects of working abroad. Unfortunately, what I consider to be the benefits of cross-cultural interactions are often portrayed negatively in international business literature. The key to unlocking all the benefits of doing business in another country is being prepared and knowledgeable about different cultural values before stepping onto a plane. These benefits include an improvement in one's negotiating skills, the professional enrichment of exposure to international business approaches, and of course the personal growth that develops as a result of learning to operate in cultures that may be very different from your own.

(Continued)

2 One key cultural difference was described by the American anthropologist Edward Hall in his so-called high-context versus low-context theory of cross-cultural communication. This theory is useful for anyone who plans to work abroad because it can help the international business person to understand cultural differences in communication styles, and, in turn, avoid misunderstandings and communication breakdowns.

3 According to Hall, people from low-context cultures like the United States communicate in a very direct way. We speak frankly. We voice our opinions, even if—and sometimes especially if—we disagree with others. Other cultures that are considered low-context include Canada, the Netherlands, and Germany. High-context cultures, on the other hand, exchange information in a more reserved and indirect manner, with implied meanings behind messages. In other words, people rely on the context, situation, or even knowledge of the culture to help communicate and interpret messages. For example, in high-context cultures, criticizing or disagreeing with others or being negative—particularly to a boss—can be seen as extremely rude and offensive. As a result, people from these cultures may send indirect verbal or nonverbal hints of their disapproval that may not be easy for direct communicators to interpret, especially those who are unaware of the nuances and social norms of the culture. Some examples of high-context cultures include Saudi Arabia and other Middle Eastern nations. Many Asian nations are also high-context cultures, including China, Japan, and South Korea. The contrasting approaches to communication in these various cultures have a distinct effect on the way business is done around the world.

4 One way that high- and low-context cultures vary is in the way they approach online marketing. Websites in low-context cultures may feature direct messages with logical, clear information. Navigation is simple. Websites from high-context countries, on the other hand, are more interactive and have more "contextual interplay," according to one market study. This means the websites often encourage users to interact with the content to discover the key messages, rather than just stating them directly. Some sites are bursting with graphics, while others may have nuanced content that invites the viewer to explore.

5 Another important difference between high- and low-context cultures lies in the approach to collaborative projects and management. In an American and other low-context workplaces, employees are generally expected to report to a manager about setbacks or even failures. In a high-context culture, on the other hand, employees may be expected to solve problems without discussing issues with managers. If you are from a high-context culture and you are working in a low-context culture, it might be shocking to see the way your employees speak so openly and candidly about what you would see as sensitive information.

Conversely, as a manager from a low-context culture who is working in a high-context culture, you might not get information from employees about setbacks, which could make you assume that they are being secretive or even irresponsible. Before making this kind of value judgment, however, you need to realize that this is simply the way business is done in other parts of the world, where saving face often matters more than communicating an error. Similarly, understand that hearing "yes" from your high-context business partners may not actually mean "yes," and "maybe" might really mean "no." This is because those in high-context cultures prefer to avoid offending someone with a direct answer.

6 Despite the challenges of adapting to different communication styles, the learning experiences from cross-cultural interactions add depth to any management experience, and the opportunity to look beyond one's worldview and "zoom out" of your own culture can provide immense personal rewards.

B. Work with a partner. Use your notes to discuss the answers to the questions in Before You Read, Part B. Are there any questions you cannot answer? Which of the other reading skills you have learned in this unit could help you answer them?

◑ Go to MyEnglishLab to read the passage again and answer critical thinking questions.

THINKING CRITICALLY

Discuss the questions with another student.

1. How does the writer of the article feel about doing business internationally? How can you tell?

2. What are some potential misunderstandings that can occur between direct and indirect communicators?

3. What do you think is a more effective communication style? Use examples and evidence from the text to support your answer.

THINKING VISUALLY

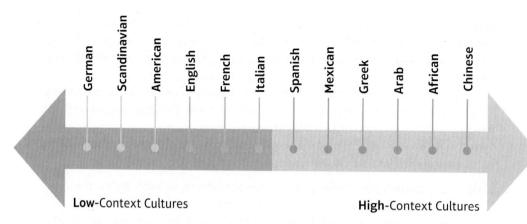

German | Scandinavian | American | English | French | Italian | Spanish | Mexican | Greek | Arab | African | Chinese

Low-Context Cultures   **High**-Context Cultures

A. Study the graph. Answer the questions with a partner.

1. Which cultures tend to be low-context? Which are high-context?

2. Where does your culture fall on this continuum?

3. What cultural differences do you think might cause these countries to vary in their communication styles?

B. Choose a country. Do an Internet search on typical business communication practices there. Create a visual like the one above that shows the country in relation to other countries, regions, or cultures on the continuum, and give a report about your findings to your partner or group. If possible, include the following in your report:

1. Is this a low- or high-context culture?

2. What are some examples of how business is conducted in this country?

3. How does the communication style of this country compare to that of other cultures on the continuum?

4. What advice would you give to travelers doing business in this country?

THINKING ABOUT LANGUAGE

Complete the sentences with noun clauses. Use information from the unit or your own ideas. Then compare answers with a partner.

1. Before you make a value judgment about the communication style of people from other cultures, you should remember that ....

2. One way that people from high- and low-context cultures differ is in how ....

3. People in low-context cultures tend to communicate directly about what .... even if they disagree with you.

4. What .... can cause us to misinterpret the behavior of people from other cultures.

5. Managers from high-context cultures may expect that ....

6. How .... can vary quite a bit by culture. Japanese websites, for example, tend to have a lot of "contextual interplay."

○ **Go to MyEnglishLab to watch Dr. McLennan's concluding video and to complete a self-assessment.**

Decisions we make today will shape our future

EARTH SCIENCE

Cause, Effect, and Correlation

UNIT PROFILE

In this unit, you will consider the subject of earth science. Reading topics include causes of climate change, the effects of climate change on human and animal populations, and the contribution of fossil fuels to global warming, pollution, and extreme weather. You will also read about critical thresholds and "tipping points" in climate change.

Preview the reading "Critical Thresholds and Climate Tipping Points" on page 250. Skim the reading. What processes are described? What cause-and-effect relationships are described?

OUTCOMES

- Understand cause-and-effect relationships
- Understand causation and correlation
- Use flowcharts to note causes and effects
- Understand passive and active voice
- Understand collocations

For more about **EARTH SCIENCE**, see ❶❸. See also Ⓦ and ⓄⒸ **EARTH SCIENCE** ❶❷❸.

GETTING STARTED

⬆ Go to MyEnglishLab to watch Dr. Osborne's introductory video and to complete a self-assessment.

Discuss these questions with a partner or group.

1. What has caused climate on Earth to change in the past? What were the results?

2. What is the main cause of climate change today?

3. According to Dr. Osborne, what is the most profound consequence of climate change? What other impacts can you think of?

CRITICAL THINKING SKILL

UNDERSTANDING CAUSE, EFFECT, AND CORRELATION

WHY IT'S USEFUL Understanding cause, effect, and correlation can help you to see how certain events or actions are connected to one another.

Cause, effect, and correlation are common in academic writing. **Causation** occurs when one event results directly in another. **Correlation** occurs when an event occurs together with another, but it cannot be proved that one causes the other. Descriptions of natural and human-made processes, as well as research and experimental findings, often contain language for causation and correlation to explain the relationships between events or actions.

This unit breaks down understanding cause, effect, and correlation into two supporting skills:

- understanding cause-and-effect relationships
- understanding causation and correlation

VOCABULARY PREVIEW

The following vocabulary items appear in the reading. Circle the ones you know. Put a question mark next to the ones you do not know.

fluctuated	output	block (v)	massive
tissues	concentration	models (n)	

EXERCISE 1

A. Discuss the questions with a partner before you read.

1. Look at the graph. How did temperatures change between 1900 and 2000?

2. What are natural factors in climate change? What are human factors?

3. Preview the article about the causes of climate change. Notice the title and introduction. What cause-effect or correlation relationships do you think will be discussed?

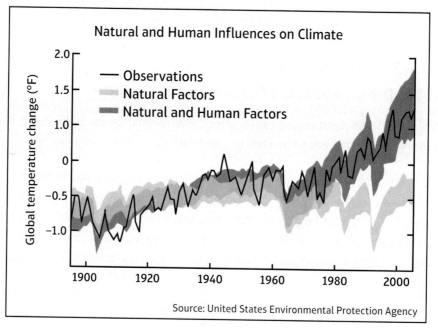

Natural and Human Influences on Climate

Source: United States Environmental Protection Agency

B. Skim the passage and underline the words and phrases that signal cause-effect or correlation.

What Causes Climate Change?

1 Climate on Earth has fluctuated over time between hotter and cooler periods. In the past, natural factors have caused climate change. In modern times, however, the main driver behind climate change on our planet is *anthropogenic*, or human-made, factors.

2 For most of Earth's existence climate change has been driven by natural factors. The first of these is variations in Earth's orbital patterns,

Glossary

Ash: the soft gray powder that remains after something has been burned

Aerosol: a substance, e.g. hair spray, that is kept in a container under pressure and is released as a spray when a button is pushed

Deforestation: clearing or burning trees and other vegetation to make land available for other uses

which influence temperature as the planet moves closer to or farther away from the sun. Second is the sun's solar output, which fluctuates in an 11-year cycle. There is evidence that these changes in solar activity cause Earth to become warmer or cooler. Another natural cause of climate change is volcanic activity. Volcanoes release clouds of dust and ash that block the sun, resulting in a temporary cooling effect. In addition, volcanoes often emit sulfur dioxide (SO_2) into the atmosphere, and this combines with water to form sulfuric acid aerosols. These aerosols in turn reflect solar radiation and cause the planet to cool. Volcanoes also release greenhouse gases such as water vapor and carbon dioxide (CO_2). At times in the past, massive volcanic activity has caused enormous amounts of greenhouse gases to be released into the atmosphere. This has led to periods of global warming due to the well-known *greenhouse effect*. In this process, greenhouse gases in the atmosphere absorb the sun's energy, preventing heat from escaping back into space. As a result, global temperatures increase.

3 Today, climate change is mainly the consequence of anthropogenic production of greenhouse gases. The most abundant of these gases is carbon dioxide, which is produced by burning fossil fuels. When carbon burns, it changes from a liquid, as in oil, or a solid, as in coal, to a gas, which is then released into the atmosphere. CO_2 is also produced by deforestation. Trees and vegetation normally absorb CO_2 from the atmosphere and store carbon in their plant tissues. But when plants are burned or cut down and left to decay, they release CO_2 back into the atmosphere.

4 Since humans began burning fossil fuels in the 18th century, the concentration of CO_2 in the atmosphere has been increasing, and it is higher now than at any time in the past 400,000 years. As atmospheric levels of CO_2 have increased, average global temperatures have also risen, most significantly in recent years. Scientific models of Earth's temperatures show that due to greenhouse gas emissions, Earth is warming up three times faster now than in 1950.

C. **Read the passage again. Then read the statements and write *T* (True) or *F* (False). Correct the false statements. Compare answers with a partner.**

.... 1. In the past, the main cause of climate change was anthropogenic, or natural factors.

.... 2. The sun's solar output fluctuates over hundreds of years.

.... 3. Temperatures fluctuate with Earth's orbital patterns.

.... 4. Dust, ash, and sulfur dioxide released from volcanoes can cause the planet to warm.

.... 5. Volcanic eruptions emit greenhouse gases into the atmosphere.

.... 6. Massive volcanic activity has led to periods of global warming in the past.

.... 7. The concentration of CO_2 in the atmosphere has remained steady since the 18th century.

.... 8. Scientific models show that recent increases in temperature are due to greenhouse gas emissions.

D. Work with a partner. List seven causal or correlational relationships that are mentioned in the passage. Check (✓) if the factors are natural or anthropogenic.

Causal / Correlational Relationship	Natural	Anthropogenic
1. Earth's orbital patterns influence temperature.	✓	
2.		
3.		
4.		
5.		
6.		
7.		

E. Answer the questions. Refer to the passage as needed. Then discuss your answers with a partner.

1. Look at your predictions in Part A. Were they correct? How did they help you to understand the passage?

2. What language of causation or correlation did you identify? How did this language help you to understand the passage?

VOCABULARY CHECK

A. Review the vocabulary items in the Vocabulary Preview. Write their definitions and add examples. Use a dictionary if necessary.

B. Complete each sentence using the correct vocabulary item from the box. Use the correct form.

block (v)	concentration	fluctuate	massive
model (n)	output	tissue	

1. Jupiter, which has 318 times the mass of Earth, is the most .... planet in the solar system.

2. Changes in solar .... can lead to temperature changes on Earth.

3. CO_2 levels and temperatures .... over time, but in the last 100 years, there has been a steady increase in both.

4. In 2013, the .... of CO_2 in the atmosphere passed 400 parts per million, the highest level in recorded history.

5. Plants consist of three main types of .... that together make up their roots, stems, leaves, and flowers.

6. Climate .... help scientists to understand and predict climate change.

7. When the Tambora volcano in Indonesia erupted in 1815, it killed about 90,000 people and .... sunlight, turning summer into winter across the Northern Hemisphere.

⬆ Go to MyEnglishLab to complete a vocabulary exercise and skill practice, and to join in collaborative activities.

SUPPORTING SKILL 1

UNDERSTANDING CAUSE-AND-EFFECT RELATIONSHIPS

WHY IT'S USEFUL Understanding the language used to signal cause-and-effect relationships can help you to understand the reasons behind events, actions, and processes, to make predictions as you read, to organize your notes, and to increase comprehension.

A **cause-and-effect** relationship occurs when one event makes another event happen. Discussions of causes and effects are common in academic writing, especially in science writing, when a writer's purpose is to describe processes such as climate change.

Causes and effects are signalled in a variety of ways. Notice the grammar, sentence structure, and punctuation in the examples.

Language That Signals Causes	Example
After / Once / When	**When** CO_2 enters the atmosphere, it absorbs heat.
As	**As** atmospheric CO_2 levels increase, temperatures rise.
As a result of / Because of / Due to	**As a result of** increased CO_2 emissions, global temperatures have increased.
the consequence of / result of	Increased CO_2 levels are mainly **the consequence of** anthropogenic factors.

Language That Signals Effects	Example
As a result / Consequently / For this reason	In this process, CO_2 in our atmosphere absorbs the sun's energy, preventing heat from escaping back into space. **As a result,** global temperatures increase.
causes	CO_2 in the atmosphere **causes** the planet to warm in a process called *the greenhouse effect*.
creates / produces	The burning of fossil fuels **creates** CO_2.
leads to / results in	The burning of fossil fuels **leads to** global warming.
The reason for / driver behind	The main **reason for** climate change today is greenhouse gas emissions.

Causes and effects can also be indicated by comparatives:

The higher the CO_2 levels, **the greater the** warming effect on the planet.

As you have learned see LINGUISTICS, Part 2, page 184, writers often limit controversial statements through the use of hedging. Hedging is a common tool used to limit the certainty of a cause-and-effect relationship. For example:

> **Areas where ancient Mesopotamian civilization once thrived have faced severe drought in recent years, which may have contributed to regional conflict.**

In this example, the writer used hedging to indicate that the drought was *a possible* cause of conflict in the region.

VOCABULARY PREVIEW

The following vocabulary items appear in the reading. Circle the ones you know. Put a question mark next to the ones you do not know.

volume	thermal	expands	accelerate
thawing	relocating	displacement	

EXERCISE 2

A. Preview the reading. Notice the title and photo. Working with a partner, predict two or three cause-and-effect relationships you think will be discussed. Write two questions you have.

Predictions

1. ....

2. ....

3. ....

Questions

1. ....

2. ....

Global Warming, Rising Sea Levels, and Climate Refugees

1 **Global temperatures have been steadily increasing for the last century, with negative effects including a rise in sea levels around the world. Many coastal areas have begun experiencing flooding that is both more frequent and more severe than anything in the recent past. In addition, many island nations are in danger of becoming entirely submerged, leading to a possible refugee crisis as island residents search for new nations to take them in.**

Glossary

Shrink: become smaller

Salinity: the concentration of salt in water

2 Global warming is mainly *caused by* the burning of fossil fuels, which emit greenhouse gases into the atmosphere. Once they enter the atmosphere, these gases trap heat, causing the planet to become warmer. At least 80 percent of this excess heat is absorbed by the oceans. When temperature rises, water increases in volume in a process known as *thermal expansion*. Warmer temperatures from increased greenhouse gases also cause polar ice and high-latitude glaciers to melt. When water expands and ice melts, sea levels rise. In the last century, sea level has risen by only about 6–8 inches (15–20 centimeters), but the rate of the rise in sea level has increased over time and will continue to accelerate in the years to come. Scientists predict sea levels may rise by several feet by 2100. According to one analysis, levels could rise by as much as 49 feet (15 meters) by 2500.

3 While predictions about rising sea levels are still being debated in some places, other communities have begun to experience the reality of rising seas and shrinking coastlines. In Alaska, for example, where temperatures have warmed at a much higher rate than in the lower 48 states, thawing permafrost and rising sea levels are beginning to leave parts of coastal towns underwater. In January 2017, residents in the city of Newtok, Alaska, asked the US government for financial help to support their efforts in relocating to higher ground. More than 180 other coastal Alaskan villages are also in danger of becoming submerged. In other low-lying areas of the world, such as the Nile delta in Egypt and Bangladesh, residents face displacement because *of* rising sea level and soil salinity. Perhaps the most dramatic loss related to rising sea level, however, may be for the citizens of tiny island nations like Kiribati, located in the Pacific Ocean about halfway between Hawaii and Australia. As a *result of* rising sea levels, the entire island country may become submerged within a few decades, leaving residents country-less. The UN Refugee Agency and other human rights groups estimate that this may be just the first sign of what will surely become a growing climate-refugee crisis worldwide.

Kivalina, Alaska, is threatened by rising sea levels.

CULTURE NOTE

Alaska is a US state located in the extreme northwest of North America. It is the largest state by area at 663,268 square miles (1,717,856 km²). Alaska has more than 2,600 islands and 34,000 miles (54,720 km) of coastline. Much of Alaska is made of wetlands and permafrost, in addition to over 100,000 glaciers, more than half in all the world. Snow and ice reflect much of the sun's energy back into the atmosphere; however, as global temperatures rise, this snow and ice are melting, creating more dark areas of land and water. These dark areas absorb more of the sun's heat, which further increases temperatures. As a result, Alaska is warming about twice as quickly as the rest of the United States.

B. Read the passage. Then read the statements and write *T* (True) or *F* (False). Correct the false statements.

.... 1. The oceans absorb most of the excess heat in the atmosphere.

.... 2. Thermal expansion occurs when water is heated.

.... 3. Sea levels are rising at a steady rate.

.... 4. Sea levels may rise by several inches by 2100.

.... 5. Temperatures are increasing more in the lower 48 states than in Alaska.

.... 6. Parts of Alaska are beginning to become submerged.

.... 7. Residents of the Nile delta may lose their homes due to rising sea levels and destruction of the soil.

.... 8. The island nation of Kiribati may disappear within a few years.

C. Read the passage again. Check your answers to Part B. Then compare answers with a partner.

D. Complete the causal chain with the sentences from the box.

Sea levels rise.   Residents are displaced.
Global temperatures increase.   Coastal and low-lying areas become submerged.
Polar ice and glaciers melt.   Ocean waters expand.

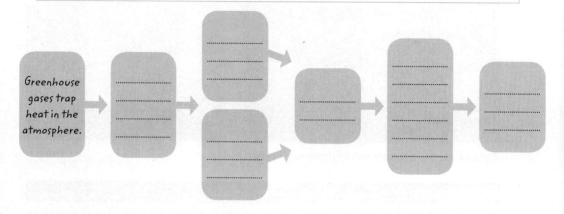

E. Work with a partner. Answer the questions about understanding cause-and-effect relationships.

1. Which signals of cause and effect did you notice? Underline them.

2. Did you face any challenges using cause-and-effect signals to understand the relationship between events?

3. Which sentence in the reading includes hedging to signal possible causation? Which hedging signal is used?

VOCABULARY CHECK

A. Review the vocabulary items in the Vocabulary Preview. Write their definitions and add examples. Use a dictionary if necessary.

B. Complete each sentence using the correct vocabulary item from the box. Use the correct form.

accelerate	displacement	expand	relocate
thaw	thermal	volume	

1. Scientists predict that the warming of the planet will continue and is likely to .... in years to come.

2. As global temperatures are increasing, our oceans are ....

3. The United Nations (UN) estimates that since 2008, climate or weather-related events have caused the .... of more than 20 million people.

4. As temperatures rise, causing permafrost to .... , carbon dioxide and methane from animal and plant decay are released into the atmosphere.

5. Many small Alaskan villages need to .... to higher ground but don't have the money or resources to do so.

6. Heat is the transfer of .... energy from one object to another, for example, from a stove to a pot of water.

7. About 97 percent of Earth's water is in the oceans. The oceans contain a total .... of more than 300 million cubic miles (1.3 billion cubic kilometers) of water.

⬤ Go to MyEnglishLab to complete a vocabulary exercise and skill practice, and to join in collaborative activities.

SUPPORTING SKILL 2

UNDERSTANDING CAUSATION AND CORRELATION

WHY IT'S USEFUL Understanding the difference between causation and correlation will help you to analyze how events or actions are connected to one another. This is especially useful when analyzing the results of research or experiments and drawing conclusions from what you have read.

It is important to understand the difference between causation and correlation, but it is easy to confuse them. **Causation** occurs when an event or action results in another. For example, we know that heating water *causes* it to expand. Repeated controlled experiments in which water is heated will achieve the same result—an increase in the water's volume.

Events or actions that are **correlated** occur *together*. Correlations are often used to predict outcomes, but a correlation does not mean that one event necessarily causes the other. Other factors may cause or contribute to the outcome. For example, breathing polluted air *correlates* to the occurrence of asthma, meaning the two events often occur together; however, that does not mean that breathing polluted air will necessarily cause someone to develop asthma. Other factors, such as genetics and allergies, may play a role.

Many verbs commonly signal correlation. These include:

Verbs That Signal Correlation	Example
X { affects, coincides with, contributes to, influences, is a factor in, is associated with, is connected to, is correlated with, is related to, is tied / linked to } Y	These patterns **influence** temperature as the planet moves closer to or farther away from the sun.

VOCABULARY PREVIEW

The following vocabulary items appear in the reading. Circle the ones you know. Put a question mark next to the ones you do not know.

extinction	relevant	biodiversity	intense
uninhabitable	consequential	mammal	decline (n)

EXERCISE 3

A. Preview the excerpt from an article about climate change and species extinction. Notice the photo and title. Then discuss the questions with a partner.

1. How is climate change connected to species extinction?

2. Which species have been affected by climate change in the past? Which species are most affected now? Why?

Climate Change and Species Extinction

1 History teaches us that climate change on Earth is closely connected to the survival of plant and animal species. Evidence from paleoclimate studies shows that during periods of dramatic climate change, many of the world's plant and animal species became extinct. This connection is relevant, as the planet is steadily growing warmer, and the loss of biodiversity has begun to accelerate in recent years.

2 There have been five mass extinctions on Earth, the most recent of which occurred when the dinosaurs became extinct 65 million years ago. This extinction coincided with a global climatic change from a warm, mild climate to a cooler one in which many of Earth's plant and animal species could not survive. Most

scientists agree that this cooling was caused by a massive asteroid that crashed into Earth, creating clouds of dust and ash that blocked the sun. The extinction of the dinosaurs may be the most famous in history, but the largest extinction occurred 250 million years ago, when approximately 90 percent of marine life, 70 percent of land creatures, and nearly all of the trees disappeared. Because this extinction happened so long ago, it is difficult to determine the exact cause; however, there is strong evidence that "The Great Dying" was caused by intense volcanic activity from an expanse of volcanoes in what is now Siberia. Over the years, these volcanoes produced massive amounts of greenhouse gases, which created acid rain and severe global warming. This could have caused an increase in CO_2 and a decrease in oxygen levels in the oceans, making them uninhabitable for most life.

3 Today, climate change is once again contributing to biodiversity loss. According to a recent UN report, climate change is creating "widespread and consequential" harm to animals and plants. A 2015 review of 130 studies of the effects of climate change on plants and animals revealed that one in six species could face extinction due to warmer conditions. In one recent study, approximately 47 percent of 976 plant and animal species have gone extinct "locally," which means they were forced to move from historic habitats in order to survive. For example, the alpine chipmunk, a small mountain-dwelling mammal, is relocating to higher altitudes to seek cooler temperatures, making its survival uncertain. Similarly, the polar bear population is experiencing dramatic decline due to loss of its sea-ice habitat and access to food. The US Geological Survey predicts that two-thirds of polar bears will disappear by 2050. The recognizable harm to plant and animal species that global warming is already causing will likely worsen as temperatures rise.

B. Read the passage. Then read the statements and write *T* (True) or *F* (False). Correct the false statements.

.... 1. Extinction of plants and animals is correlated historically with climate change.

.... 2. The extinction of the dinosaurs occurred during a period of global warming.

.... 3. "The Great Dying" 250 million years ago was probably caused by a global cooling period.

.... 4. Excess CO_2 in the oceans may have resulted in the extinction of marine life 250 million years ago.

.... 5. Today, global warming is a factor in the loss of plant and animal species.

.... 6. Higher temperatures may cause some species such as the Alpine chipmunk to relocate to new habitats in the future.

.... 7. The Alpine chipmunk will become extinct due to global warming.

.... 8. Loss of sea ice and reduced access to food are causing a dramatic decline in polar bear populations.

C. Read the passage again. Check your answers to Part B. Then compare answers with a partner.

D. Read the excerpts from the reading. Choose *causation*, *possible causation*, or *correlation*. Then discuss your answers with a partner. What language signals the relationship between events?

1. History teaches us that climate change on Earth is closely connected to the survival of plant and animal species.

    a. causation
    b. possible causation
    c. correlation

2. This extinction coincided with a global climatic change from a warm, mild climate to a cooler one in which many of Earth's plant and animal species could not survive.

    a. causation
    b. possible causation
    c. correlation

3. Most scientists agree that this cooling was caused by a massive asteroid that crashed into Earth.

   a. causation
   b. possible causation
   c. correlation

4. There is strong evidence that "The Great Dying" was caused by intense volcanic activity from an expanse of volcanoes in what is now Siberia.

   a. causation
   b. possible causation
   c. correlation

5. Over the years, these volcanoes produced massive amounts of greenhouse gases, which created acid rain and severe global warming.

   a. causation
   b. possible causation
   c. correlation

6. Today, climate change is once again contributing to biodiversity loss.

   a. causation
   b. possible causation
   c. correlation

7. According to a recent UN report, climate change is creating "widespread and consequential" harm to animals and plants.

   a. causation
   b. possible causation
   c. correlation

8. Similarly, the polar bear population is experiencing dramatic declines due to loss of its sea ice habitat and access to food.

   a. causation
   b. possible causation
   c. correlation

E. **Work with a partner. Answer the questions about understanding causation and correlation.**

1. What types of relationships occur most often in the text: causation, possible causation, or correlation? Why do you think it was necessary for the writer to use hedging signals to limit the certainty of some of the causal relationships?

2. How easy or difficult was it for you to distinguish between causation and correlation? If you were confused, what caused the confusion? How did you resolve it?

3. In which type of texts are you most likely to find language for causation and correlation? Why?

> **TIP**
>
> Popular media often report about research findings. As you read them, be careful to ask questions that will help you to interpret the results critically. Who conducted the research? Where was it done? How large was the study? Have the results been repeated in other studies? Do the results indicate causal relationships, correlation, or just possible causation? How strong is the evidence?

VOCABULARY CHECK

A. **Review the vocabulary items in the Vocabulary Preview. Write the new items and add examples. Use a dictionary if necessary.**

B. **Complete each sentence using the correct vocabulary item from the box. Use the correct form.**

biodiversity	consequential	decline (n)	extinction
intense	mammal	relevant	uninhabitable

1. The Bramble Cay melomys had lived on a low-lying island of the Great Barrier Reef in Australia until rising sea levels made this region .... for the small mouse-like animal, and in 2009 it became extinct.

2. Learning about past periods of climate change is .... today, as history has much to teach us about current and future changes in climate.

3. .... is greatest in the Southern Hemisphere. Overall, tropical rainforests are thought to contain 50–90 percent of all species.

4. Many scientists believe that 250 million years ago, volcanic eruptions in Siberia were so .... that they produced as much as 2.7 million square miles (7 million square tons) of lava, destroying most life on Earth.

5. Climate change has had .... effects on the orange-spotted tilefish, which is highly sensitive to temperature change. For example, it died off in Japan during a period of warmer ocean temperatures in 1988.

6. Whales and dolphins are marine .... that give birth underwater.

7. Scientists are not certain what caused the .... of the dinosaurs, but they do know that a huge die-off took place 65 million years ago.

8. The black rhinoceros population has suffered a serious .... , decreasing by 96 percent between 1972 and 1996.

⬤ Go to MyEnglishLab to complete a vocabulary exercise and skill practice, and to join in collaborative activities.

INTEGRATED SKILLS
USING FLOWCHARTS TO NOTE CAUSES AND EFFECTS

WHY IT'S USEFUL Using flowcharts to note cause-and-effect relationships can help you to visualize the relationship between steps or stages in a chain of causes and effects. This helps you to improve your comprehension of a text. Noting causal chains also allows you to review the key information later.

A **flowchart** is a type of graphic organizer that allows you to represent the stages in a process or causal chain visually. Flowcharts can take different forms depending on the organization of the text, but a key element is to organize the information in the correct order of events and link them together using arrows that signify the sequence of events or actions.

Flowcharts to Show Block Organization of Causes and Effects

Sometimes writers will list multiple causes that lead to one effect, or one cause that leads to multiple effects. In this case, you may want to create a simple flowchart that allows you to note all of the causes in one box, followed by another box with the effect(s), or vice versa.

Example:

WHAT CAUSES CLIMATE CHANGE?

Natural Factors

* orbital patterns
* solar output
* volcanic activity

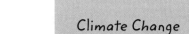

Climate Change

Anthropogenic Factors

* greenhouse gas emissions
* deforestation

Flowcharts to Show Order of Events in a Process or Causal Chain

Sometimes writers will explain cause-and-effect relationships as a process or series of events. In this case, you can represent the process or causal chain in a series of boxes connected by arrows. This type of flowchart allows you to see the detailed relationship between events or actions.

THE GREENHOUSE EFFECT

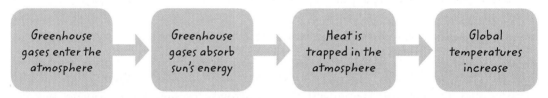

Greenhouse gases enter the atmosphere → Greenhouse gases absorb sun's energy → Heat is trapped in the atmosphere → Global temperatures increase

TIP

Flowcharts are also a useful tool for noting the steps in an assignment or procedure. A flowchart helps you to easily see and follow the required steps in the correct order.

VOCABULARY PREVIEW

The following vocabulary items appear in the reading. Circle the ones you know. Put a question mark next to the ones you do not know.

adverse	triggering	evaporation	capacity
vulnerable	exacerbated	saturated	

EXERCISE 4

A. Preview the excerpt from an article about global warming and extreme weather. Predict three cause-and-effect relationships you believe will be discussed.

1. ....

2. ....

3. ....

B. Read the first paragraph of the article. Complete the flowchart to represent the cause-and-effect relationships between global warming and extreme weather events. Then compare charts with a partner.

Global Warming and Extreme Weather Events

1 Global warming has a ripple effect on many of Earth's climatic processes and ecosystems. One impact of rising temperatures is a greater likelihood of "extreme" weather events such as heat waves, intense rainfall, droughts, flooding, hurricanes, snowstorms, and tornadoes. It is true that this kind of severe weather has always occurred, and it is difficult to attribute single weather events to climate change. In recent decades, however, global warming has almost certainly increased the likelihood of extreme weather events. In particular, heat waves and heavy rains have become more common, creating adverse effects on societies and the environment and triggering other natural disasters such as wildfires and landslides.

Temperature rises → Extreme weather events become more likely:

e.g., ...
....
....

→ • Adverse effects on .... are created

• ....
....
are triggered

C. Read the next section of the article. Create a flowchart that represents the causes and effects of heat waves. Compare flowcharts with a partner.

2 As the global climate has warmed, heat waves have become more frequent, intense, and long-lasting. In Australia, for example, the summer of 2012–2013 earned the nickname "the angry summer" because the season broke more than 100 weather records for heat. Since that summer, every summer has had unusually severe heat waves that have broken multiple records, leading experts to expect that every summer will be "angrier" and warmer than usual. And Australia is not alone. Record-setting heat waves have been occurring with greater frequency across the globe, and such events are expected to continue. A study published by the National Academy of Sciences concluded that anthropogenic global warming has significantly increased the likelihood of record heat events in more than 80 percent of the world.

3 Heat waves are of concern because of the immediate effects they have on human health and on the land. There are sharp increases in hospitalizations and heat-related deaths during heat waves. Further, higher-than-average temperatures lead to more water evaporation, which can result in drought and crop failure. Higher temperatures also create the perfect environment for wildfires. Studies show that extreme heat waves are likely to worsen as the planet grows warmer, with heat waves possibly increasing 30-fold by 2100 if global greenhouse emissions continue unabated.

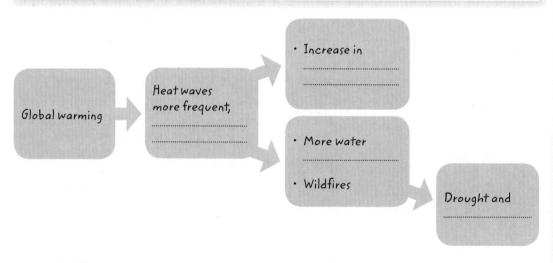

D. Work with a partner. Use your notes from Parts A, B, and C to discuss your answers to the questions.

1. Look at your predictions in Part A. Did you predict the cause-and-effect relationships in the text?

2. Did your use of flowcharts help you to understand and organize the causes and effects mentioned in the article?

3. What are the benefits of using a flowchart rather than taking notes or making an outline? Do you think you will use flowcharts to take notes in your courses? Why or why not?

VOCABULARY CHECK

A. Review the vocabulary items in the Vocabulary Preview. Write their definitions and add examples. Use a dictionary if necessary.

B. Complete each sentence using the correct vocabulary item from the box. Use the correct form.

adverse	capacity	evaporation	exacerbate
saturate	trigger	vulnerable	

1. A potential .... effect of global warming is the spread of infectious diseases. As temperatures increase, insects that carry diseases such as malaria could spread into new regions, infecting greater numbers of people.

2. Global warming can .... extreme weather of all kinds, including hurricanes and snowstorms.

3. The Arctic fox is another animal that is .... to extinction due to Arctic habitat loss.

4. Increased temperatures lead to increased .... of water and drier conditions.

5. Once clouds become .... and can hold no more water, they release the water as precipitation.

6. The world's oceans have a huge .... to absorb heat.

7. Hurricanes are expected to become stronger and more intense as global temperatures increase, which will only .... the damage done to coastal areas already affected by rising sea levels.

⬥ Go to MyEnglishLab to complete skill practices.

LANGUAGE SKILL

UNDERSTANDING PASSIVE AND ACTIVE VOICE

WHY IT'S USEFUL Understanding the difference between passive and active voice helps you to recognize the focus of a sentence or passage—whether it is on the person or thing performing an action, the object of the action, or the event or action itself.

⊙ Go to MyEnglishLab for the Language Skill presentation and practice.

VOCABULARY STRATEGY

UNDERSTANDING COLLOCATIONS

WHY IT'S USEFUL Recognizing collocations can help you to expand your vocabulary, make it easier to read more quickly, and make predictions as you read.

Collocations are pairs or sets of words that appear together. If words appear together frequently, they are said to have a *strong* collocation. Recognizing strong collocations and reading them as single vocabulary items instead of separate words can help you to read more quickly. Understanding the types of words that frequently go together can also help you to predict while you read.

Collocations appear in various combinations. Here are some common types:

Noun + Noun	greenhouse gas
Adjective + Noun	global warming
Phrasal Verbs	heat up
Verb + Object or Complement	solve problems
	connect to (+ object)

One way to learn collocations is to notice which words appear together as you read and to note examples of combinations in your notecards or vocabulary journal. Looking up words in a learner's dictionary can also provide you with examples of how words appear together in context. Often word combinations will be marked in bold.

Notice how collocations and examples are noted for the first meaning of the noun *climate* in the *Longman Advanced American Dictionary*.

cli·mate /'klaɪmɪt/ ●●○ *noun* [countable] ◄))

ETYMOLOGY COLLOCATIONS

1

a) EARTH SCIENCE the typical weather conditions in a particular area:

◄)) *Los Angeles **has** a warm, dry **climate**.*

climate in/of

◄)) *The **climate in** Canada is different depending on the region.*

◄)) *Many scientists are studying **climate change** (= a permanent change in weather conditions).*

b) an area with particular weather conditions:

◄)) *These flowers will not grow in **cold climates**.*

From this entry, you can see that the verb *has* often occurs before the word *climate*. You can also see that *climate* can be followed by *in* or *of*. Two other collocations are the noun + noun combination *climate change* and the adjective + noun combination *cold climates*.

Conducting an online search with sets of words in quotation marks can also reveal if and how words appear together.

EXERCISE 5

A. Read the sentences. Underline the adjective + noun, noun + noun, or verb + complement collocation in each sentence.

1. Glacial periods, or ice ages, have occurred approximately every 100,000 years.

2. At the heart of survival in early human settlements was access to fresh water.

3. Today, however, the main driver behind climate change on our planet is anthropogenic factors.

4. There is strong evidence that the extinction was caused by volcanic activity.

5. In climates where fresh water was plentiful enough to grow crops, successful civilizations developed.

6. Smog is a type of air pollution caused when fog mixes with smoke or other airborne pollutants.

7. Earth's orbital patterns influence temperature as the planet moves closer to or farther away from the sun.

8. Conservation efforts must focus individually on local species to try to curb extinction rates.

B. Read the pairs of words. Circle the correct collocation. Consult a dictionary or search engine if you need help.

1. endangered species   at-threat species

2. cause problems   cause solutions

3. adverse causes   adverse effects

4. adapt to   adapt out

5. food chain   food series

6. fluctuate between   fluctuate into

7. vital part   vital consequence

8. danger factors   risk factors

C. Work with a partner. Create collocations for each of the nouns, adjectives, or verbs. Check your combinations by consulting a dictionary or search engine. (**Note:** The items in the list can be the first or second part of the collocation.)

1. marine ....

2. habitat ....

3. heat ....

4. extreme ....

5. visible ....

6. alarming ....

7. block (v) ....

8. cultivate ....

APPLY YOUR SKILLS

WHY IT'S USEFUL By applying the skills you have learned in this unit, you can gain a better understanding of this challenging reading about critical thresholds and climate tipping points.

BEFORE YOU READ

A. Discuss these questions with a partner or group.

1. What do you think *critical thresholds* and *climate tipping points* refer to? Have you ever encountered the terms *threshold* or *tipping point* in other contexts?

2. Look at the visual. What is the albedo effect? How could it influence climate change and tipping points?

B. The passage you will read is about critical thresholds and climate tipping points. As you read, think about these questions.

1. What do the terms *critical threshold* and *tipping point* mean in the context of climate change?

2. What are the three main critical thresholds mentioned in the reading?

3. What is the critical threshold for atmospheric carbon dioxide? When did we cross it?

4. What is the albedo effect and how does it affect global warming?

5. How does the Amazon rainforest help to limit global warming? What is causing it to reduce the amount of CO_2 it can absorb?

C. Review the Unit Skills Summary. As you read the passage, apply the skills you learned in this unit.

UNIT SKILLS SUMMARY

Understand cause-and-effect relationships

• Understand the reasons behind events and actions and their outcomes.

Understand causation and correlation

• Understand the difference between an event that causes another and two events that occur together.

Use flowcharts to note causes and effects

• Use flowcharts to visualize and note key steps in cause-and-effect chains.

Understand passive and active voice

• Understand the difference between active and passive forms, how they are used in academic writing, and how each voice affects the focus in a sentence.

Understand collocations

• Understand how words are commonly used together.

READ

A. Read the article. Use flowcharts to take notes on the answers to the questions in Before You Read, Part B.

Critical Thresholds and Climate Tipping Points

1   The term *critical threshold* as it applies to global warming means a point at which the climate system takes a turn that will have major, and often negative, consequences in the future. This term is often used synonymously with the phrase *tipping point*, which simply means "a point of no return." "Tipping" the climate system by crossing multiple critical thresholds will cause irreversible changes to human civilizations and the planet we share. Many of these negative changes will play out in the coming decades and centuries, and they will result in damaged ecosystems, food scarcity, war, mass migrations, and severe economic loss. Climate tipping points include, but are not limited to, the rising level of atmospheric carbon dioxide, escalating sea and glacier ice melt, and a decrease in the amount of carbon dioxide the Amazon rainforest absorbs.

2   Scientists often point to a carbon dioxide atmospheric concentration of 400 parts per million as a major critical threshold. The world permanently crossed this threshold in 2016. The level of CO_2 prior to the Industrial Revolution in the 18th century was about 280 ppm, but that level has risen dramatically over the past century as a result of the burning of fossil fuels. This increase in CO_2 has led to a rise in global temperatures.

Temperatures today are about 1.1 degrees Celsius (2° Fahrenheit) warmer than they were at the turn of the 20th century, and the warming trend has escalated in the past 15 years. Because greenhouse gases can stay in the atmosphere for hundreds of years, the planet will continue to warm for centuries to come, no matter how much we limit our current emissions. If emission levels continue to rise, it will be impossible to avoid warming by several more degrees.

3 With warmer temperatures, icebergs and glaciers melt, and the melting of ice in the Arctic, Greenland, and Antarctica are also considered major tipping points in climate change because of the irreversible chain reaction that is triggered by the melting. Sea ice is bright white and reflective, so it has a high albedo, which means it does not absorb much solar energy. *Albedo* is Latin for "whiteness," and in climate science it is a measure of the

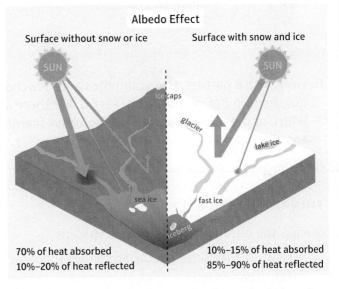

Albedo Effect

Surface without snow or ice

Surface with snow and ice

SUN

SUN

ice caps

glacier

lake ice

sea ice

fast ice

iceberg

70% of heat absorbed
10%–20% of heat reflected

10%–15% of heat absorbed
85%–90% of heat reflected

ratio of light reflected off a surface. As sea ice melts into sea water, it becomes dark and has a low albedo, meaning it absorbs a high amount of solar energy. The more solar energy sea water absorbs, the warmer it becomes, which further contributes to the melting of ice. In addition, as glaciers begin to melt, rising waters can cause flooding and melting of permafrost areas. When permafrost melts, it releases massive amounts of greenhouse gases that are stored in soil. As greenhouse gas levels increase and the planet warms further, this increase contributes to more sea ice and glacial ice melting, which will eventually cause sea level to rise and flood low-lying cities and nations.

4 Yet another critical ecological threshold in climate science is the point at which the Amazon rainforest slows in its absorption of CO_2. Scientists fear this is already beginning to happen. The Amazon rainforest acts like a sponge, absorbing large amounts of harmful CO_2 from the air. Recent studies show that the rainforest is absorbing and storing less carbon than it has in previous decades. The reasons for this phenomenon are complex. The Amazon is vulnerable to extreme weather—a side effect of global warming—and two severe droughts in 2005 and 2010 caused trees in the rainforest to die. Carbon, a natural fertilizer, encourages growth in the forest, which is a positive effect of increased CO_2. However, this increase in CO_2 may contribute to trees that grow fast but have less supportive root systems and, consequently, are more likely to die young. The death of these trees contributes to a reduced carbon absorption rate. If the Amazon experiences more droughts and tree death in the future, the rainforest will absorb less CO_2 than expected.

(Continued)

5　Crossing even one critical climate threshold increases the likelihood that other thresholds will also be crossed. For this reason, limiting emissions is the only way to stop or at least slow the damage to the ecosystem. Many of the consequences of passing a tipping point do not happen abruptly. Rather, they take many years, even decades or centuries. For this reason, carbon reduction policies have long-term effects but no immediate impact on the environment. The effects of global warming will occur, however, and future generations will continue to be impacted by decisions made today.

B. Work with a partner. Use your notes and flowcharts to discuss the answers to the questions in Before You Read, Part B. Are there any questions you cannot answer? Which of the other reading skills you have learned in this unit could help you answer them?

🔘 Go to MyEnglishLab to read the passage again and answer critical thinking questions.

THINKING CRITICALLY

Discuss the questions with another student.

1. How does the writer of the article feel about the severity of global warming? How can you tell?

2. What actions does the writer believe we need to take to curb global warming? Do you think that humans will take the steps needed to accomplish these actions?

3. What do you think is the most severe consequence of global warming? Use evidence from the reading to support your opinion.

THINKING VISUALLY

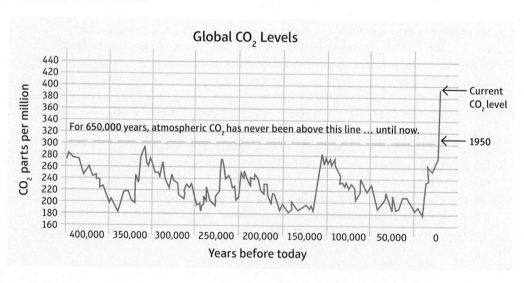

A. Study the graph and refer back to the reading as needed. Then answer the questions with a partner.

1. Based on what you have learned about past climate change, what do you think caused the rise and fall of CO_2 levels before 1950? What was the highest level CO_2 reached before 1950?

2. In what year did global CO_2 levels pass 280? At what level is global CO_2 today?

3. At what level do you predict CO_2 to be in 50 years? 100 years?

B. Choose a different greenhouse gas, such as methane, or choose another climate variable such as temperature. Do an Internet search of the changes in this variable over time. If you choose temperature, choose a specific place, such as your hometown. Create a graph like the one above and give a report about your findings to your partner or group. If possible, include the following in your report:

- The changes that occurred over time
- Explanations for the changes
- Your projections for the future

THINKING ABOUT LANGUAGE

Underline the passive verbs in each excerpt from "Critical Thresholds and Climate Tipping Points." With a partner, discuss why the passive is appropriate in each example.

1. The term *critical threshold* as it applies to global warming means a point at which the climate system takes a turn that will have major, and often negative, consequences in the future. The term *critical threshold* is often used synonymously with the phrase *tipping point*, which simply means "a point of no return."

2. With warmer temperatures, icebergs and glaciers melt, and the melting of ice in the Arctic, Greenland, and Antarctica are also considered major tipping points in climate change because of the irreversible chain reaction that is triggered by the melting.

3. The occurrence of crossing even one critical climate threshold increases the likelihood that other thresholds will also be crossed.

4. The effects of global warming will occur, however, and future generations will continue to be impacted by decisions being made today. (two answers)

⊙ Go to MyEnglishLab to watch Dr. Osborne's concluding video and to complete a self-assessment.

MEDIEVAL CULTURE

Author's Purpose and Tone

UNIT PROFILE

In this unit, you will read about various topics related to the art and literature of the Middle Ages. You will read about medieval women writers, architecture of the period, and examples of medieval art in various regions of the world.

Preview the reading "Appreciating Non-Western Art from the Middle Ages" on page 282. Quickly skim it to understand the main idea. Then try to answer the following set of questions: What is the author's attitude toward non-Western art from the Middle Ages? What is the author's purpose for writing this article? Who is the intended audience?

OUTCOMES

- Determine an author's purpose
- Recognize an author's tone
- Use descriptive imagery
- Recognize figurative language
- Differentiate between denotation and connotation

For more about MEDIEVAL CULTURE, see ❶❸.

See also W and |OC| MEDIEVAL CULTURE ❶❷❸.

GETTING STARTED

➤ Go to MyEnglishLab to watch Professor Galvez's introductory video and to complete a self-assessment.

Discuss these questions with a partner or group.

1. The Middle Ages lasted for approximately ten centuries, and from this period came countless important works of art, architecture, and literature. What do you already know about medieval artistic accomplishments? What do you know about the role of women in medieval literature?

2. There is a great deal of symbolism—the use of pictures, shapes, or colors to represent an idea—in medieval artwork. Think of some pieces of art that you are familiar with. Can you think of any examples of symbolism in those works?

3. In the introduction to this section, Professor Galvez mentions the difference between medieval poetry and poetry composed today. What do you think some of those differences might be?

CRITICAL THINKING SKILL

DETERMINING AN AUTHOR'S PURPOSE AND TONE

WHY IT'S USEFUL Learning to identify an author's purpose will assist you in recognizing the message an author is attempting to communicate to an intended audience. By identifying purpose, you will be better able to understand why an author conveys a particular attitude.

Purpose is an author's reason for writing a text. The three main purposes are to inform, to persuade, and to entertain. The two former purposes are staples of academic writing. Examples of other, more specific purposes an author may have include: to analyze a situation or data, to explain a concept, to argue against an idea, or to praise an action.

Authors must take into consideration what they hope their audience will feel or believe after reading their text. A purpose could also be to inspire action—to encourage readers to do something with the information imparted in a text.

Once authors have identified their purpose for writing, their next task is determining which tone will most effectively convey that purpose to their particular audience. **Tone** is the general feeling or attitude expressed in a piece of writing by means of word choice, facts and opinions, examples, and so on. Writers must be aware of who their readers are and take their assumed beliefs and feelings into consideration in order to best appeal to and engage them. Some examples of tone are *critical, supportive,* and *neutral,* but many more exist.

It is important to note that purpose is not the only factor involved in an author's choice of tone. Other factors such as genre, publication type, and an author's personal writing style also contribute to the tone that is ultimately expressed.

This unit breaks down determining an author's purpose and tone into two supporting skills:

- understanding purpose
- recognizing tone

VOCABULARY PREVIEW

The following vocabulary items appear in the reading. Circle the ones you know. Put a question mark next to the ones you do not know.

devotion	doctrine	bizarre	ordeals
quest	dictated	authenticity	

EXERCISE 1

A. Discuss the questions with a partner before you read.

1. Do you think there were many female writers during the Middle Ages? Why or why not?

2. What do you think society's attitude toward female writers might have been in medieval times? Why?

3. Are there any particular topics you think female medieval writers may have written about? Which ones?

B. Preview the passage. Read the title and study the image. Then skim the passage. What do you think the author's purpose may be? How would you describe the author's tone? Who might be the intended audience of the passage?

Purpose: ....

Tone: ....

Intended audience: ....

Margery Kempe: A Peculiar Medieval Writer

[1] Margery Kempe (1378–1438) is often cited as the author of one of the first autobiographies in English literature, *The Book of Margery Kempe*, but this claim is disputed by many. [2] Kempe, born in the town of Norfolk in England, wrote medieval Christian mystical literature, which focused primarily on personal religious experience, prayer, and devotion to God. [3] This genre often included highly personal accounts that did not always align directly with church doctrine. [4] *The Book of Margery Kempe* is the story of Margery's rather bizarre beliefs and her pilgrimages to holy sites such as Jerusalem, Rome, and Spain. [5] Kempe's story details the various ordeals she endured in her quest to devote her life to God, as well as the fact that she was mocked and regarded with suspicion for the peculiar ways in which she expressed her religious beliefs. [6] These behaviors were so outrageous that she was accused of heresy multiple times. [7] Among her many odd traits, Kempe frequently exhibited uncontrollable, loud weeping spells that left others unsure of how to react. [8] Yet despite the fact that Kempe is a rather unlikable main character, her story reveals interesting information about early 15th-century English society. [9] Kempe dictated her story to a number of different people decades after the incidents in the book occurred, and it is believed that those who recorded her story may have had some hand in altering it, putting the book's authenticity into question. [10] For this reason, though the work may be cited as an important source of medieval mystical writing by a female author, Kempe's reliability as an author is questionable.

> ## Glossary
>
> Pilgrimage: a trip to a holy place for religious reasons
>
> Heresy: a belief that disagrees with the official principles of a particular religion

C. Read the passage. Then read the statements and write *T* (True) or *F* (False). Correct the false statements. Compare answers with a partner.

.... 1. Some believe that Margery Kempe wrote one of the first English autobiographies, but others do not share that belief.

.... 2. Kempe's own religious experience and prayers were not given great emphasis in her writing.

.... 3. *The Book of Margery Kempe* describes Kempe's strange attitudes as well as the many problems she faced as she worked to dedicate herself to God.

.... 4. Kempe was initially ridiculed for the odd manner in which she exhibited her religious beliefs but was later cleared of such ridicule.

.... 5. People did not know how to respond to Kempe when she was found sobbing uncontrollably.

.... 6. Kempe was quite pleasant as both a person and as a writer.

.... 7. While it is known that some changes have been made to Kempe's story over time, this does not impact its authenticity.

.... 8. Many readers consider *The Book of Margery Kempe* to be a strong example of mystical writing composed by a medieval female author but the author of the article disagrees.

D. Read the passage again. Answer the questions.

1. Review your answers to Part B. Can you elaborate on the author's purpose after having reread the passage? Be as specific as possible.

2. Think about the elements of writing that may contribute to the development of tone. Identify language or ideas in the passage that led you to determining its tone.

3. Is there any type of information that is particularly emphasized or repeated in this passage? If so, what? How do you think this contributes to the development the passage's tone?

VOCABULARY CHECK

A. Review the vocabulary items in the Vocabulary Preview. Write their definitions and add examples. Use a dictionary if necessary.

B. Complete each sentence using the correct vocabulary item from the box. Use the correct form.

authenticity	bizarre	devotion	dictate
doctrine	ordeal	quest	

1. The young woman demonstrated great .... to her religious group, consistently volunteering to lead fundraisers.

2. As the old man was illiterate, he .... his poems to his son, who then wrote them down.

3. Convincing the author to revise the literary work was quite a(n) .... , but the editor was ultimately successful.

4. Critics called the theater production ".." due to its complicated plot. Audience members left not knowing what to think about what they had just seen.

5. The .... of the sculpture was disputed. Some historians stated that it was entirely characteristic of the medieval sculptor's style, while others pointed out small differences that suggested otherwise.

6. The historian was determined to pursue her .... to discover the truth about the events in *The Book of Margery Kempe* even if it meant spending time in distant European libraries.

7. Major religions have .... that their followers follow with utmost respect. Such beliefs often differ substantially from one religion to another.

⬥ Go to MyEnglishLab to complete a vocabulary exercise and skill practice, and to join in collaborative activities.

SUPPORTING SKILL 1

DETERMINING AN AUTHOR'S PURPOSE

WHY IT'S USEFUL By learning to recognize an author's purpose and intended audience, you can be a better judge of the importance or usefulness of a reading to your academic needs. This can help you to decide how quickly or slowly to read or whether to take notes, for example. Your comprehension of an author's purpose can then help you to understand the tone that an author uses.

The **purpose** of a reading is an author's primary reason behind writing a text. This is directly connected with the reaction the author hopes to elicit from readers. Does the author wish to convince readers of a certain point of view? Is the intention to advocate for a change? Or is the purpose merely to transmit information?

An author does not always have just one purpose in writing a given text. In fact, a text may have been composed with a number of objectives in mind, so purposes are often multiple and complex. For example, a writer may hope to first inform readers of something and then persuade them to take action related to the information they have just read. Or, an author may compare and contrast two options, then critique one and praise the other in hopes of persuading readers to adopt a certain point of view.

Regardless of the situation, strong writers consciously think about their intended goal before and while writing a piece, taking into consideration their readers' feelings, thoughts, background knowledge, and potential actions. Authors then work to develop a tone that best appeals to their particular audience(s) and aligns with the genre and publication type.

An author's purpose may be neutral, intended mainly to convey information, or biased—intended to persuade or convince. As previously stated, the three main purposes are to inform, to persuade, and to entertain. Some other common authorial purposes include:

Neutral Purpose	Biased Purpose
interpret	interpret
review	review
analyze	criticize / critique
classify	praise
compare	promote
contrast	
define	
describe	
discuss	
explain	

You will notice that two typical authorial purposes—*interpret* and *review*—are listed in both categories. Depending on the situation, these purposes can be either neutral or biased. For example, one author may interpret data objectively, while another author may use personal opinions to interpret the meaning of parts of a text. In the same vein, one author might objectively review published studies on a topic, while another might write a review of an invention incorporating personal biases.

TIP

In academic writing, the most common authorial purpose is **to inform**. A second common purpose is **to criticize**. This is often seen in research articles, where authors sometimes discuss the weaknesses of other authors' studies and then explain the strengths of the present study.

VOCABULARY PREVIEW

The following vocabulary items appear in the reading. Circle the ones you know. Put a question mark next to the ones you do not know.

floor plans	invaders	humbler	endured
fortified	evolved	stunning	wonder (n)

EXERCISE 2

A. Preview the passage. Note the title and images and skim the passage. What do you think the overall purpose of the text is: to inform, to persuade, or to entertain? Predict three things you believe will be discussed. Write two questions you have.

Predictions

1. ....

2. ....

3. ....

Questions

1. ....

2. ....

Periods of Medieval Architecture

1 ¹ In Europe, the Middle Ages refers to the roughly ten centuries between the fall of the Roman Empire and the cultural rebirth known as the Renaissance. ² A wide range of architectural styles developed over this lengthy period of time, but for the sake of convenience, medieval European architecture is divided into three main stages: early, middle, and late. ³ Despite the variety of styles and designs found in these periods, medieval architecture overall does share some similarities. ⁴ These include the building materials, which were primarily stone and wood, as well as the floor plans of cathedrals, which were often in the shape of the Latin cross with a long hall, or *nave*, and an area forming right angles to the nave called the *transept*. ⁵ Castles of the Middle Ages, like cathedrals, also had similar design plans, which included battlements, or low walls around the top of a castle from which arrows could be shot to defend against invaders.

2 ⁶ The earliest medieval architecture was characterized by structures much humbler in appearance than the grand and inspiring cathedrals of the later Middle Ages. Anglo-Saxon architecture, which began in 5th-century England and endured well into the 11th, was usually produced with only wood and thatch—tightly packed, plant-based materials such as straw or reeds. ⁷ Builders at the time were unskilled in masonry, and consequently, few Anglo-Saxon structures survive to this day.

House in recreated Anglo-Saxon village, West Stow, England

⁸ Those that remain reveal functional structures that were rather dull and small compared to the decorative cathedrals and heavily fortified castles of the later Middle Ages.

3 ⁹ The Romanesque style asserted itself in Europe around the year 1000 as the Anglo-Saxon style declined. ¹⁰ As the name implies, the Romanesque style imitates ancient Roman architecture, especially the rounded Roman arch. ¹¹ Many Romanesque designs have rounded arches, thick walls, and a low, stocky profile. ¹² Compared to early medieval architectural styles, however, Romanesque structures are usually quite large. ¹³ Eventually, the Romanesque style evolved into the Gothic, which featured steeper, pointed arches, vaulted ceilings, spectacular stained-glass windows, and the famed flying buttresses, external arches that help support a building. ¹⁴ One stunning example of Gothic architecture is the Chartres Cathedral, built between the late 12th and early 13th centuries on the ruins of a Romanesque church in Chartres, France. ¹⁵ One of the finest examples of Gothic architecture, it is alive with magnificent sculptures and

breathtaking stained-glass windows. [16] It is more than simply a beautiful building, however. It is also an engineering wonder of its time, with its elegant flying buttresses that support the remarkably large stained-glass windows housed within.

CULTURE NOTE

Besides the cathedral at Chartres, other well-known Gothic cathedrals include the Florence Cathedral in Italy, the Cologne Cathedral in Germany, and the Salisbury Cathedral in England.

Romanesque Rotunda of St. Martin at Vysehrad, Prague, Czech Republic

Flying buttresses of the Gothic Chartres Cathedral in Chartres, France

B. Read the passage. Then read the statements and write *T* (True) or *F* (False). Correct the false statements. Compare answers with a partner.

.... 1. The materials used in the construction of medieval buildings over the three main periods of medieval architecture differed significantly.

.... 2. The design plans of castles and cathedrals in early medieval architecture were similar to those of castles and cathedrals in late medieval architecture.

.... 3. Many Anglo-Saxon buildings are still in existence today.

.... 4. Structures from the early period of medieval architecture were richer in design than structures built later in the Middle Ages.

.... 5. The Gothic style evolved into the Romanesque style, with structures in the former style boasting features such as stained-glass windows and vaulted ceilings.

.... 6. The Chartres Cathedral used advanced engineering techniques to design the flying buttresses that support the cathedral's stained-glass windows.

C. Read the excerpts from the passage. Refer back to the chart of common authorial purposes on page 260. Determine the purpose(s) of each excerpt. Some items have more than one possible answer. Then compare answers with a partner.

1. … the Middle Ages refers to the roughly ten centuries between the fall of the Roman Empire and the cultural rebirth known as the Renaissance. ....

2. … for the sake of convenience, medieval European architecture is divided into three main stages: early, middle, and late. ....

3. … medieval architecture overall does share some similarities. These include the building materials, which were primarily stone and wood, as well as the floor plans of cathedrals, which were often in the shape of the Latin cross with a long hall, or *nave*, and an area forming right angles to the nave called the *transept*. (3 answers) ....

4. The earliest medieval architecture was characterized by structures much humbler in appearance than the grand and inspiring cathedrals of the later Middle Ages. (4 answers) ....

5. Those [Anglo-Saxon buildings] that remain reveal functional structures that were rather dull and small compared to the decorative cathedrals and heavily fortified castles of the later Middle Ages. (4 answers)

   ....

6. One of the finest examples of Gothic architecture, it is alive with magnificent sculptures and breathtaking stained-glass windows. (2 answers)

   ....

D. Work with a partner. Answer the questions about determining an author's purpose.

1. Think of two or three academic and nonacademic texts you have read recently. Describe them to your partner. What was the author's main purpose in writing each text? Who was the intended audience?

2. Think of an example of a piece of academic writing that you have done. Explain it to your partner. How would you describe your purpose(s)?

3. You read that authors must consider not only their audience but also their intended genre and publication type when deciding on their purpose for writing a text. Why are the latter two factors also important to consider?

VOCABULARY CHECK

A. Review the vocabulary items in the Vocabulary Preview. Write their definitions and add examples. Use a dictionary if necessary.

B. Complete each sentence using the correct vocabulary item from the box. Use the correct form.

endure	evolve	floor plan	fortified
humble	invader	stunning	wonder (n)

1. The tour guide explained the engineering features that had made it possible for the stained-glass windows of the Gothic cathedral to .... for centuries despite earthquakes, conquests, and bad weather.

2. The .... of the newly constructed European churches were nearly identical, with all of the rooms laid out in almost the same manner.

3. Engineering practices of the past have gradually .... into the methods of today.

4. The ancient city was .... by high walls and towers, protecting it from armies that sought to attack and take control.

5. The older, somewhat dated home in the suburbs was .... than the chic new apartment downtown.

6. As they were touring a medieval French castle, the students studied the battlements that were used to protect inhabitants from ....

7. The blogger's list of the Seven .... of the Medieval World included the 12th-century tower of Pisa in Italy, famous today because it leans at an angle of about 4 degrees.

8. The enormous, intricately designed windows in the front of the redesigned building downtown were especially .... in the afternoon light.

⬆ Go to MyEnglishLab to complete a vocabulary exercise and skill practice, and to join in collaborative activities.

SUPPORTING SKILL 2

RECOGNIZING AN AUTHOR'S TONE

WHY IT'S USEFUL Recognizing tone and understanding the techniques authors use to establish it will help you better understand authors' attitudes toward a topic. It will also make you a more engaged reader and help you to determine a source's reliability.

Tone is the general feeling or attitude expressed in a piece of writing by means of word choice, facts and opinions, examples, and so on. Academic writing is usually written in one of three tones: neutral (impartial, objective), positive (supportive), or critical (negative, disapproving). A neutral or impartial tone is more common in informative writing or genres, such as textbooks. In addition to the three types of overarching tone just mentioned, many other, more specific words can be used to describe the tone of a piece. A few examples include:

Neutral	Positive	Critical
factual	humorous	angry
formal	loving	apathetic
informal	optimistic	bitter
serious	sympathetic	depressed

A number of literary techniques can be used to set a certain tone. These include:

- word choice, including the connotations certain words carry
- syntax (the way words are arranged in order to form sentences or phrases)
- level of detail and imagery provided
- use of comparatives and superlatives (words like *younger*, *least important*, and *fastest*)
- repetition of ideas
- dismissing selected points as invalid or only mentioning them in passing
- formatting or graphic features that draw attention to certain points or ideas

It is important to note that, while a piece of writing can be supportive, critical, or neutral *overall*, that does not mean that every sentence of the piece will have that particular tone. An author could be critical of something at one point in a piece while setting a supportive tone overall. For example, an author could dislike one element of Romantic art yet find the genre inspiring as a whole. Good readers do not look at isolated chunks of text to determine an author's overarching tone. Rather, they look at the "big picture" while expecting that variations in tone can occur at any point in a text.

> **TIP**
>
> If an author sounds too supportive or critical, especially if not many facts are provided to support that attitude, then it is possible that the piece may be biased. In general, the more neutral a piece sounds, the more trustworthy a source it is.

VOCABULARY PREVIEW

The following vocabulary items appear in the reading. Circle the ones you know. Put a question mark next to the ones you don't know.

mastery	iconic	undoubtedly	phenomenal
extensively	exclusively	portrayed	

EXERCISE 3

A. Preview the article. Read the title and look at the images. Predict three things you believe will be discussed. Then read the passage. Were your predictions correct?

1. ....

2. ....

3. ....

Noteworthy Artwork of the Middle Ages

1   From elegant frescos—pictures painted onto wet plaster on a wall—to intricate mosaics to timeless architecture, the art of the Middle Ages showed a mastery of many different mediums and forms. Two of the most iconic and memorable styles dating back to the early and middle medieval periods are undoubtedly the Byzantine and Romanesque. The Byzantine Empire, with its heart in Constantinople (today's Istanbul) in the eastern Mediterranean, gave its name to an art genre famous for its mosaics and expertly stylized, or designed, figures. Romanesque art, in contrast, developed farther west and is known to this day for its phenomenal architecture, stained glass, and sculpture. Both Byzantine and Romanesque art use religious iconography extensively and almost exclusively, reflecting both the importance and the power of the Christian Church at the time.

Glossary

Medium: a means or way of communicating information (e.g., the Internet) or art (e.g., painting)

Religious iconography: the way that a religion is represented in pictures or imagery

Representational: a style of art that shows things as they appear in real life

Commission (v): to formally ask someone to do something for you, such as write an official report or produce a work of art

Brilliant Byzantines

2   Byzantine mosaics were created by setting tiny pieces of brilliantly colored precious materials close together to create a striking image (see Figure 1). These materials included mother-of-pearl, colored glass, and gold leaf, which gave the mosaics a luminescent, glittering quality. Most of the subjects portrayed in mosaic art were religious figures stylized in a way that is iconic to the period. Byzantine art was not representational (that is, realistic); the figures are simplified and painted or shaped with rigidly formal postures. Though Byzantine architecture and sculptures may seem like bland afterthoughts compared to the mosaics and paintings of the era, there are some stunning examples of these forms as well, including the Hagia Sofia, the so-called crown jewel of Byzantine architecture, which was first an Eastern Orthodox cathedral and later a mosque.

Figure 1: A Byzantine mosaic

Remarkable Romans

Figure 2: The Leaning Tower of Pisa, a famous example of Romanesque architecture

3   Romanesque art, which evolved to the west of the Byzantine Empire, is as fascinating as but distinctly different from its Byzantine counterpart. As in Byzantine art, many of the forms in Romanesque art were religious icons. Unlike Byzantine art, however, the Romanesque style is primarily remembered for its architecture, stained glass, and sculpture. Romanesque art reached its greatest height in the 11th century, when the church commissioned large, elaborate cathedrals that supported other forms of art within, including brilliant sculptures, bright fresco wall paintings, and stained-glass windows (Figure 2). Without question, the art of the Romanesque and the Byzantine periods paved the way for the types of art that evolved later into the works of the Renaissance.

B. Read the passage again. Then read the statements and write _T_ (True) or _F_ (False). Correct the false statements. Compare answers with a partner.

.... 1. Romanesque and Byzantine artwork were the only styles of art in the Middle Ages.

.... 2. Byzantine artwork originated in the eastern Mediterranean, and Romanesque artwork originated in the west.

.... 3. Byzantine artwork is best known for its architecture.

.... 4. The materials for Byzantine artwork were relatively cheap.

.... 5. The Hagia Sofia is an example of Byzantine architecture.

.... 6. Romanesque and Byzantine artwork had many different styles and characteristics.

.... 7. The Romanesque period was primarily in the 1000s.

.... 8. Romanesque cathedrals were usually rather simple and had little artwork inside.

C. Go back to the article "Noteworthy Artwork of the Middle Ages" and underline instances where the author uses techniques from page 267 to establish a certain tone. Then complete the chart. Write at least one example of each technique.

Author's Technique	Example from the Passage
1. Repeated use of positive or negative adjectives	
2. Repeated / emphasized ideas throughout the text	
3. Ideas dismissed, mentioned only in passing, or ignored	
4. Level of detail or imagery provided	

D. Reread the sentence in the second paragraph that begins *Though Byzantine architecture and sculptures may seem like bland afterthoughts.* **Then answer the questions about determining an author's tone.**

1. What is the author's attitude toward Byzantine architecture in the first part of the sentence?

2. Does it match the overall tone of the article?

3. How does this sentence affect the overall tone of the passage, in your opinion? Why?

4. What does this sentence tell you about tone at the sentence level versus the overall tone of a passage?

VOCABULARY CHECK

A. Review the vocabulary items in the Vocabulary Preview. Write their definitions and add examples. Use a dictionary if necessary.

B. Match the vocabulary items with their meanings.

.... 1. exclusively

.... 2. extensively

.... 3. iconic

.... 4. mastery

.... 5. phenomenal

.... 6. portray

.... 7. undoubtedly

a. definitely true

b. extremely impressive or surprising

c. to describe, show, or represent something or someone, especially in a book, movie, article, etc.

d. to a great degree or in a large amount

e. very famous or admired as a representative of an important idea, style, or group

f. made of, including, or involving only one thing or group

g. great knowledge or skill

◎ Go to MyEnglishLab to complete a vocabulary exercise and skill practice, and to join in collaborative activities.

INTEGRATED SKILLS
USING DESCRIPTIVE IMAGERY

WHY IT'S USEFUL Descriptive imagery helps readers to form a mental image of what a writer is describing or explaining. Especially when there is no visual available, such imagery can lead to more effective communication between a reader and writer.

Using descriptive imagery involves painting a picture with words. To do so involves the use of adjectives, prepositional phrases, adverbs of manner, relative clauses, and other linguistic devices to describe a given scene or object. In academic writing, descriptive imagery can be used to depict graphics, processes, and other concepts that the writer wants readers to visualize.

The following strategies can help you to use descriptive imagery to describe a scene:

- Start with the **focal point**, which is the main focus of a scene and is usually the largest or most central image that viewers' eyes will be drawn to.

- Describe what you see in a **clockwise pattern** or **left to right** direction because this is how people are typically used to looking at something or reading.

- Use **prepositional phrases**, **participial phrases**, **or adverbs of place** to describe how things are situated in relation to each other in the visual.

- Move from **general to more specific** details.

- Use **specific adjectives and adverbs** to modify nouns and verbs. For example, the sentence *Gothic architecture is characterized by its sharp spires, gigantic heights, pointed arches, and monstrous gargoyles* is far more descriptive than the bland statement *Gothic architecture has tall spires, arches, and gargoyles.*

- If possible, make **comparisons or contrasts** between the thing you are describing and something else that would be familiar to the reader.

- **Reread** what you have written to see if you can visualize it based on your own description. Make sure you haven't left out essential details.

- If you choose to **discuss an implication or interpretation** of the scene, do so only after giving at least a literal (basic and factual, without interpretation) description first.

TIP

If you have composed a good description, the reader or listener should be able to draw a picture that matches what you have described. Practice using descriptive imagery to describe one of your favorite pieces of art. Ask a friend to make a drawing based on your description.

EXERCISE 4

A. Preview the excerpt "Symbolism in *The Unicorn Is Found*" from a textbook chapter about medieval artwork. Note the title, art, and underlined descriptive language.

Symbolism in *The Unicorn Is Found*

1 The European medieval period is rich in many different types of art, including painting, sculpture, architecture, and other arts that receive less recognition, such as textiles. Tapestries, a form of textile art, were common in medieval times, and, like paintings, they were pictorial, meaning that they represented individuals, animals, and scenes from everyday life or from the Bible. Some tapestries were produced in series, and when these series were all displayed together, they told a larger story, much like a multipanel mural. *The Unicorn Is Found* is one such tapestry. Made in the late 1400s, it is the second in a series of seven large unicorn-themed tapestries. *The Unicorn is Found* is an intriguing example of medieval art because of its mystery, its lively composition, and its carefully selected details.

> **Glossary**
>
> Commemorate: to remember a person by having a special ceremony, or by making or building something special
>
> Negative space: the space around and between an object in an image, which helps to define the boundaries of the object

A. .... 2 The tapestry's focal point is a fountain, around which 12 people and many different types of natural animals and mystical beasts are gathered. Situated at the foreground of the painting is a unicorn lowering its horn into a stream of water. The stream pours from a gold lion's head spout.

B. .... Around the fountain, 12 men are engaged in conversations with one another and appear to be discussing the scene before them and the unicorn's actions.

C. ....

D. ....

The men are clearly paused in a hunt, spears held high. Their hand gestures and their lively placement around the fountain introduce a sense of flowing movement into the tapestry. In the top left-hand corner of the tapestry's background, the towers and crenellations of a castle are visible. An orange tree blossoms with bright fruit in the bottom right-hand corner, and other flowering plants fill the negative space behind and in front of the men.

E. ....

F. ....

3 The material from which the tapestry is made—silk, wool, gold, and silver—implies a sense of wealth and luxury and gives the tapestry a glossy appearance. The rich blue and red clothing of the men, too, conveys wealth. Yet the image in the tapestry symbolizes more than just a group of men on a hunt. The number of the hunters—12—was no coincidence. As in many medieval artworks, religious symbolism is inserted into pictures of everyday life, and major artworks were inherently also Christian artworks. In this case, the 12 hunters represent the 12 disciples, or followers, of Christ. Finally, the "star" of the tapestry, the unicorn itself, is a symbol of Christ and purity. Woven in silver and white thread, the unicorn willingly kneels and lowers its horn into the water of the fountain to purify it of poison, which is symbolic of Christ purifying humankind of sin.

4 Much is unknown about the tapestry. Its creator, its recipient, and parts of its message are a mystery. For example, a cipher, or an unknown code, with the letters "A" and a backwards "E," appears repeatedly in *The Unicorn Is Found*. The letters are woven into each of the tapestry's four corners and into its center, where the letters appear on either side of the fountain. The cipher's positioning indicates its importance, yet its meaning remains unclear. Scholars have hypothesized that the tapestry was meant to commemorate the wedding of Anne of Brittany and King Louis XII of France, but this is disputed by many. Even the unicorn symbol itself, when examined in all seven tapestries in the series, is somewhat puzzling. Unicorns in the Middle Ages meant many things—symbols of Christ but also immortality, wisdom, purity, and marriage. One fact that is definitively clear about the tapestry is that it was made around 1495.

(Continued)

G. .... 5 <u>For all its mystery, *The Unicorn Is Found* and the other unicorn tapestries are a rich source of information about the culture of the Middle Ages</u>. Each outfit worn by the hunters represents the stations of the men and allows modern scholars a clear view of the fashion of the time. Similarly, the different types of plants in the tapestry give us an idea of what type of herbs and trees were present in the Netherlands and elsewhere in Europe where the tapestries may have been created.

B. Reread the passage. Match each underlined section to a feature of descriptive imagery from the list. Write the numbers in the margins next to the text.

1. Describing details in a clockwise or left-to-right direction

2. Using prepositional phrases, participial phrases, or adverbs of place

3. Comparing or contrasting with another familiar work

4. Beginning with the most obvious part of an image

5. Using specific adjectives and adverbs to describe nouns and verbs

6. Discussing implications or interpretations

7. Moving from general to more specific details

C. Work with a partner. Scan the text and highlight additional examples of the descriptive features from the list in Part B.

D. Work with a partner. Answer the questions about using descriptive imagery.

1. How well does the description in the text match the image of the tapestry, in your view? Are there descriptive details that you would add to the text if you were the author?

2. Why is it important to describe the larger details of a scene before the smaller ones?

3. How does the presence of descriptive imagery help you as a reader?

4. Is it easy or difficult for you to include descriptive details in your own writing?

5. What are situations in which you would or would not include your opinion while using descriptive imagery?

VOCABULARY CHECK

A. Review the vocabulary items in the Vocabulary Preview. Write their definitions and add examples. Use a dictionary if necessary.

B. Complete each sentence using the correct vocabulary item from the box. Use the correct form.

coincidence	dispute	engage in	foreground
gesture (n)	imply	indicate	textile

1. The writer's tone clearly .... that she had little confidence in the proposed idea.

2. The art gallery did not want to .... direct discussions with the painter, preferring instead to deal with the artist's agent.

3. Beautiful .... copied from ancient Chinese tapestries are being manufactured and used to make popular clothing.

4. The authenticity of the tapestry is being .... A number of experts believe it may be fake.

5. The types of materials used in a piece of art may help to .... the time period it belongs to.

6. At the opening of his new show, the artist made a(n) .... toward his family in the crowd as he thanked them for their support and loyalty.

7. It is a(n) .... that the musician has the same name as a famous 17th-century painter. The singer's parents were not aware of the painter's existence or work.

8. With a field of horses in the background and a farmer in the .... , the painting depicted everyday life on a local farm.

● Go to MyEnglishLab to complete skill practices.

LANGUAGE SKILL
RECOGNIZING FIGURATIVE LANGUAGE

WHY IT'S USEFUL Figurative language can help readers form vivid mental pictures about the information in a text. Forming mental images in this way can help readers to understand and remember information efficiently and clearly.

◐ Go to MyEnglishLab for a Language Skill presentation and practice.

VOCABULARY STRATEGY
DIFFERENTIATING BETWEEN DENOTATION AND CONNOTATION

WHY IT'S USEFUL By recognizing the connotations of vocabulary items, you will be able to accurately interpret their meaning.

An important strategy related to vocabulary acquisition is learning to differentiate between denotations and connotations of a word. The **denotation** of a word is its direct or "dictionary" meaning, whereas the **connotation** is the feeling or idea associated with the word. It is important to understand this difference because there are many words that may appear to be synonyms or near-synonyms, yet they have different connotations. Compare these sentences using the apparent synonyms *youthful* and *childish*:

The employer was surprised at how youthful the interviewee was.

The employer was surprised at how childish the interviewee was.

While both words have meanings related to a young age, *youthful* carries the positive connotation of liveliness, while *childish* connotes immaturity, a negative characteristic.

As a second example, consider the words *talkative* and *verbose*. To describe a person as *talkative* is to say literally that the person talks quite a bit. This word is not typically used in an insulting manner. Describing someone as *verbose*, however, can imply that the person talks too much.

Good dictionaries have usage labels that indicate the connotation or connotations of a word. These labels can be extremely useful when you are trying to decide which word best fits your intended meaning in your own writing. Look at the dictionary entry for the word *verbose*. What is the usage label?

---

ver·bose /vɚˈboʊs/ *adjective formal disapproving* ◀))
talking too much, or using or containing too many words

→ **verbosity** /vɚˈbɑsət̬i/ *noun* [uncountable]

→ **verbal**

Dictionary entries can also provide other kinds of connotative information. For example, they can tell you if a word is generally applied to a specific population, such as men, women, children, or even animals; if it is literary, informal, slang, or obsolete (not used anymore); if it applies to living creatures or objects; and much more.

If the dictionary you are using does not provide usage labels, or if you are reading quickly and do not wish to stop and consult a dictionary, you might also try using the context surrounding a vocabulary item to determine its connotation. For example, if you notice that an unknown item is surrounded by others that you know have negative connotations, you may be able to make an educated guess that the unknown item also carries a negative connotation.

EXERCISE 5

A. The items in the following sets have similar denotations. However, their connotations are different. Use a good dictionary to look up the definitions, usage labels, and example contexts of the items in each set. Write this information on the lines. Then compare answers with a partner. Discuss: How do the connotations of the items differ from one another?

1. bizarre, wacky, strange (adj)

2. quest, investigation, hunt (n)

3. dictate, verbalize, twitter (v)

4. stunning, cute, good-looking (adj)

5. gigantic, big, massive (adj)

   ....

   ....

   ....

6. barbarous, mean, nasty (adj)

   ....

   ....

   ....

B. **The following items are excerpts from readings in this unit. Notice the boldfaced item in each sentence. Replace it with the near-synonym in parentheses. Is the connotation the same as or different from that of the original item? Discuss your answers with a partner.**

1. Kempe, born in the town of Norfolk in England, wrote medieval Christian mystical literature, which focused primarily on personal religious experience, prayer, and **devotion** to God. (allegiance)

2. Kempe's story details the various ordeals she endured in her quest to devote her life to God, as well as the fact that she was mocked and regarded with suspicion for the **peculiar** ways in which she expressed her religious beliefs. (atypical)

3. Though the paintings have faded and certain colors, such as green, have oxidized and blackened with time, when they were fresh, medieval paintings had **stunning**, vibrant hues. (superb)

4. Because the stone [lapis lazuli] was so rare and **valuable**, ultramarine was often used with extreme care on important figures in works of art. (expensive)

5. Castles of the Middle Ages, like cathedrals, also had similar design plans, which included battlements, or low walls around the top of a castle from which guns or arrows could be shot, to **defend** against invaders. (guard)

6. It was difficult for female writers to rise to popularity during the Middle Ages as they had to overcome the **burden** of social expectations in order to do so; nevertheless, a few managed to beat the odds and do just that. (issue)

C. Work with a partner or in a small group. Choose one set of words from Part A. Go online and find real uses of the words in the set. Copy one sentence for each word. Discuss the connotation of each word in the context of the sentences you wrote.

....

....

....

D. Write an original sentence for each word in the set you looked up in Part C. Make sure the contexts you write matches the connotations in Part C. Share your sentences with a partner or group.

....

....

....

APPLY YOUR SKILLS

WHY IT'S USEFUL By applying the skills you have learned in this unit, you can gain a better understanding of this challenging reading about medieval artwork that originated in regions outside of Europe.

BEFORE YOU READ

A. Discuss these questions with a partner or group.

1. In this unit, you have read primarily about the culture and history of the Middle Ages in Europe. What do you know about the history or culture of other regions of the world in the years between 500 and 1500?

2. Look at the genre and the title of the reading "Appreciating Non-Western Art from the Middle Ages." Can you tell what the purpose of the article is? What tone do you expect? Why?

B. You will read a passage about non-Western artwork that was created during the Middle Ages. As you read, think about these questions.

1. What four major regions of the world does the author focus on?

2. Which famous cultural landmark is described for each region? What is the author's overall tone when describing these landmarks?

3. What is the meaning of the term *post-classical period*?

4. Which artistic genre is the focus of the article?

C. Review the Unit Skills Summary. As you read the passage, apply the skills you learned in this unit.

UNIT SKILLS SUMMARY

Determine an author's purpose

• Consider an author's audience and reason—or reasons—for writing a text.

Recognize an author's tone

• Notice techniques the author uses to create a positive, negative, or neutral attitude in a sentence or text.

Use descriptive imagery

• Use techniques to help create a mental image of a scene in a listener or reader's mind.

Recognize figurative language

• Understand ways that authors use language to help readers develop a deeper understanding of a text.

Differentiate between denotation and connotation

• Use a dictionary or the context to understand not only the literal definition of a word (denotation) but also the feeling associated with it (connotation).

A. Read the passage. Annotate and take notes on the answers to the questions in Before You Read, Part B.

Appreciating Non-Western Art from the Middle Ages

1 In the West, there is a long and unfortunate tradition of sidelining the art of non-European nations. Historically, Westerners have tended to either look down on non-Western art or to ignore it completely. However, art history during the centuries that coincided with the European Middle Ages (known in world history as the "post-classical" period) reveals incomparable artistic accomplishments in societies wholly separate from European medieval traditions. Many large buildings of the post-classical period were designed and constructed for religious purposes and for defense. People built with natural materials and what was available locally and regionally, and style varied tremendously from nation to nation. In this article, we will go on a brief around-the-world tour of four important post-classical achievements in architecture from four different parts of the world: Africa, Asia, the Americas, and Muslim-ruled southern Spain.

The Great Mosque of Djenné in Mali

Angkor Wat Temple in Cambodia

Machu Picchu in Peru

The Alhambra Palace in Spain

2 Starting in Africa, the Great Mosque of Djenné in what is today Mali is one of the most famous landmarks in all of Africa. According to legend, the mosque was built in the 12th century when the city's ruler decided to use local materials and traditional building practices to construct the town's first Muslim place of worship. The mosque is the largest building in the world made from sun-dried mud bricks, a material also known as *adobe*. The terra-cotta color of the material gives the Djenné Mosque a deep orange glow in the sunlight. Timbers in the inner walls add support to the structure, and the wooden frames are visible at the top of the mosque's crenellations and along the face of the towers. In fact, the entire mosque has a somewhat formidable, spiky appearance, and it is easy to mistake the mosque for

a fortress at first glance. The mosque's layout closely imitates the architectural forms of other mosques, however, including an open courtyard with a covered prayer hall.

3 Thousands of miles to the east, one of the most impressive architectural feats of the post-classical period is Angkor Wat, which is located in present-day Cambodia. Originally built in the 12th century by architects of the Khmer Empire (802–1431 CE), Angkor Wat is the largest Hindu temple in the world. It covers almost 200 hectares and is constructed entirely of sandstone. Four towers crown the top level of the temple, with a fifth tower—the largest—in the center. The tops of the towers are sculpted in the shape of curved stone lotus flowers that pierce the sky. An almost endless number of decorative relief sculptures covers the temple's walls, towers, and roofs. Female religious figures carved into the stone feature detailed hairstyles, beaded headdresses, ornate necklaces, and other fine details. Other sculptures depict dancing spirits from Indian mythology, holy armies riding to battle, and roaring lions that stand guard over the temple.

4 Across the Pacific, the sprawling ruins of Machu Picchu stand out as an architectural wonder even to modern builders. Machu Picchu, located high in the Andes Mountains in modern-day Peru, was constructed in the mid-15th century just before conquerors from Europe came and destroyed the native Inca civilization. Most archaeologists think Machu Picchu may have been built as an estate for the Inca emperor Pachacuti and his family, but the complex also has buildings that were used for religious purposes. Sophisticated stone drainage systems provided water to terraces that look like bright green steps cut into the mountainside. These curved and layered levels provide clues to modern historians that Machu Picchu's builders were expert urban farmers.

5 A final example of non-European architectural achievement comes from southern Spain. Though technically part of Europe, this region was governed by the Moors, Muslims from North Africa, from 711 to 1492. The Moors built many mosques, but these were not their only notable architectural achievement. Spectacular fortresses and palaces were constructed as well. One of these was the Alhambra, completed in the 15th century toward the end of Muslim rule in Spain. The name *Alhambra* is derived from Arabic *Al-hamra*, or "the red one." The palace was constructed with iron-rich clay, which gives it a distinctly reddish appearance. Like the Djenné Mosque, it is luminous in the sun. The Alhambra has many Islamic stylistic features, including the use of repetitive geometric designs and delicate symmetrical arches, which are particularly elegant in the palace's courtyard reflecting pool.

6 The Djenné Mosque, Angkor Wat, Machu Picchu, and the Alhambra Palace are only a small sampling of architectural treasures from the post-classical period worldwide. Interestingly, all four of these structures fell into disrepair, were abandoned, or were destroyed outright in the centuries that followed their construction. All have since been restored and named as UNESCO World Heritage sites. Art and architectural studies programs in Western universities would be wise to place a greater importance on teaching about the art and design of these types of sites. The exaggerated focus on western Europe has deprived art students and the general public of the opportunity to appreciate the brilliance of non-Western art for too long.

B. Work with a partner. Discuss the answers to the questions in Before You Read, Part B. Are there any questions you cannot answer? Which of the other reading skills you have learned in this unit could help you answer them?

Go to MyEnglishLab to read the passage again and answer critical thinking questions.

THINKING CRITICALLY

Discuss the questions with another student.

1. The author says there is a long tradition of Westerners disregarding non-Western art. What could be the reason for this?

2. What are some examples of natural building materials used in non-Western architecture?

3. The author indicates that university programs are lacking in their teaching of non-Western art and architecture. Have you ever taken an art history class? If so, do you agree or disagree with the author?

THINKING VISUALLY

Analyze the map of UNESCO Cultural World Heritage sites in South America. Choose the site that interests you most and do some research on it. Then prepare a short presentation, describing the site and providing an explanation for why it is valued.

Venezuela: Ciudad Universitaria de Caracas

Suriname: Historic Inner City of Paramaribo

Colombia: National Archaeological Park of Tierradentro

Ecuador: Historic Centre of Santa Ana de los Ríos de Cuenca

Peru: Sacred City of Caral-Supe

Bolivia: Historic City of Sucre

Brazil: Historic Town of Ouro Preto

Paraguay: Jesuit Missions of La Santísima Trinidad de Paraná and Jesús de Tavarangue

Chile: Historic Quarter of the Seaport City of Valparaíso

Uruguay: Historic Quarter of the City of Colonia del Sacramento

Argentina: Cueva de las Manos

THINKING ABOUT LANGUAGE

Underline the figurative language in the excerpts from "Appreciating Non-Western Art from the Middle Ages" and identify which type of figurative language is used. There may be more than one example in each sentence.

1. In the West, there is a long and unfortunate tradition of sidelining the art of non-European nations.

2. However, art history during the centuries that coincided with the European Middle Ages (known in world history as the "post-classical" period) reveals incomparable artistic accomplishments in societies wholly separate from European medieval traditions.

3. In this article, we will go on a brief around-the-world tour of four important post-classical achievements in architecture from four different parts of the world: Africa, Asia, the Americas, and Muslim-ruled southern Spain.

4. The terra-cotta color of the material gives the Djenné Mosque a deep orange glow in the sunlight.

5. Four towers crown the top level of the temple, with a fifth tower—the largest—in the center.

6. An almost endless number of decorative relief sculptures covers the temple's walls, towers, and roofs.

7. The tops of the towers are sculpted in the shape of curved stone lotus flowers that pierce the sky.

8. Sophisticated stone drainage systems provided water to terraces that look like bright green steps cut into the mountainside.

▶ Go to MyEnglishLab to watch Professor Galvez's concluding video and to complete a self-assessment.

How the study of molecules relates to the real world

MATERIALS ENGINEERING

Visuals

UNIT PROFILE

In this unit, you will consider the subject of regenerative medicine. Some topics you will read about are the use of polymers in medical devices, the role of scaffolds and extracellular matrices in regenerative medicine, and bone and tissue engineering. You will also learn about the market for regenerative medicine as well as the role of nanotechnology in fighting cancer.

Preview the reading "How Nanotechnology Fights Cancer" on page 319. Read the title, look at all of the visuals, and note textual references to them. What is the article about? How can you determine this based on your preview of the text?

OUTCOMES

• Understand textual references to visuals

• Interpret information in visuals

• Explain information in visuals

• Understand the use of passive voice in research writing

• Recognize Greek, Latin, and Germanic word roots

For more about **MATERIALS ENGINEERING**, see ① ③.
See also W and OC **MATERIALS ENGINEERING** ① ② ③.

GETTING STARTED

🔊 Go to MyEnglishLab to watch Professor Heilshorn's introductory video and to complete a self-assessment.

Discuss these questions with a partner or group.

1. Polymers were the main subject of MATERIALS ENGINEERING, Part 1. What role do you think these materials might play in the field of medicine?

2. Stem cells are a topic that has been in the news quite a bit in recent decades. What do you know about them? What could be their importance in the treatment of disease?

3. In the introduction to this unit, Professor Heilshorn introduces the field of *regenerative medicine*. Have you heard this term before? If so, what do you know about it? If not, what do you think it might involve?

CRITICAL THINKING SKILL
UNDERSTANDING VISUALS

WHY IT'S USEFUL To extract key information from a text containing visuals, it is essential that you learn to recognize and effectively analyze the visuals.

In your university courses, you will read a variety of types of texts, including textbooks, academic journal articles, and discipline-specific publications such as scientific magazines. In such texts, key information is frequently expressed not only through text but also through visuals. Becoming familiar with different types of visuals, the information they express, and the way they express it will help you to comprehend sophisticated academic texts. Here are some of the most commonly used types of visuals in academic publications.

Diagram
A diagram—sometimes referred to as a **chart**—serves to represent processes or relationships between concepts or things. Diagrams have a variety of forms, including bubbles, boxes, or arrows containing text. Some examples of diagram types are block, tree, and Venn diagrams.

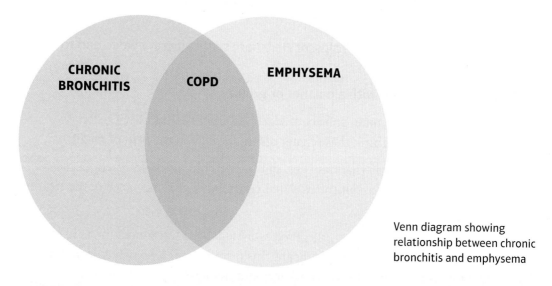

Venn diagram showing relationship between chronic bronchitis and emphysema

Graph

A graph is generally made up of a set of horizontal and vertical lines that depict information related to a category on the x (horizontal) and y (vertical) axis, demonstrating the relationship between these two sets of measurements. This type of visual can come in the form of a line, bar, or dot graph. Graphs are frequently found in research articles, as they offer an ideal format for demonstrating the relationship between two (or more) factors.

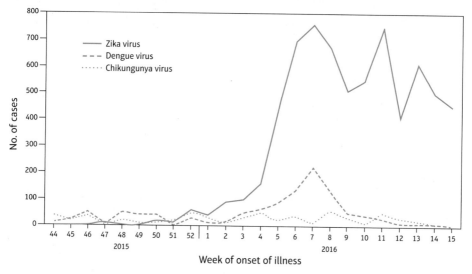

Line graph showing cases of Zika, dengue, and chikungunya viruses by week of onset of patient's illness. Puerto Rico, November 1, 2015–April 14, 2016. From the Centers for Disease Control and Prevention.

Illustration

An illustration is a photo or drawing of an object. It is typically designed using graphic design software. This type of visual is often chosen when an author is describing a small or very complex object with many parts or pieces. An illustration makes it possible to "zoom in" and label components.

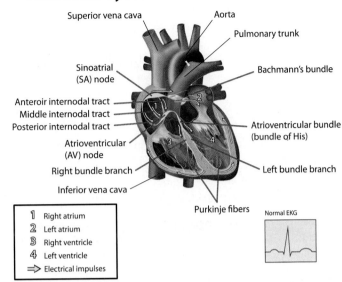

Electrical System of the Human Heart

Superior vena cava

Aorta

Pulmonary trunk

Sinoatrial (SA) node

Bachmann's bundle

Anteroir internodal tract
Middle internodal tract
Posterior internodal tract

Atrioventricular (AV) node

Atrioventricular bundle (bundle of His)

Right bundle branch

Left bundle branch

Inferior vena cava

Purkinje fibers

Normal EKG

1 Right atrium
2 Left atrium
3 Right ventricle
4 Left ventricle
⇒ Electrical impulses

Map

A map visually represents features of a space, most commonly geographical features. A geographical map is often employed when an author wants to convey information about a particular area while still showing the reader the so-called bigger picture. A map can depict an area as small as a building or campus or as large as the world. Other types of maps include topographic maps, climactic maps, and weather maps.

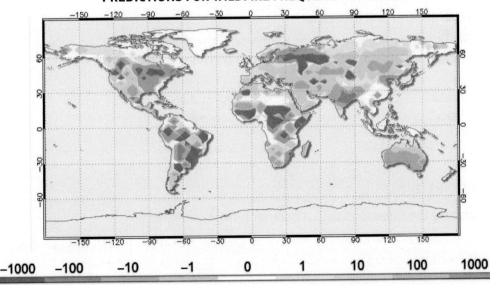

PREDICTIONS FOR WILDFIRE FREQUENCY BY 2100

−1000 −100 −10 −1 0 1 10 100 1000

Table

A table is made up of rows and columns and may be used to report data from a study. This type of visual is often found in academic journal articles.

	2014	2015	2016	2017
Study 1	$45.5 million	$62.3 million	$70.6 million	$101.2 million
Study 2	$23.3 million	$56.5 million	$62.3 million	$71.3 million
Study 3	$55.2 million	$83.7 million	$92.6 million	$109.9 million
Study 4	$112.2 million	$123.4 million	$158.9 million	$184.6 million

Investment in regenerative medicine. (For demonstration purposes only. Not real studies.)

TIP

Two terms—*chart* and *figure*—can refer to a number of different types of visuals. Some varieties of charts are flowcharts, and pie, line, and bar charts. The term *chart* is also sometimes used to refer to graphs, tables, or diagrams but not to illustrations. The term *figure* can refer to essentially any type of visual and is the term most commonly used to refer to visuals in an academic text. Almost any academic text will likely contain a number of different visual types referred to as figures. The abbreviation *Fig.* is often used in place of the entire word, especially in parentheses.

This unit breaks down understanding visuals into two supporting skills:

- understanding textual references to visuals
- interpreting information in visuals

VOCABULARY PREVIEW

The following vocabulary items appear in the reading. Circle the ones you know. Put a question mark next to the ones you do not know.

fleece	arteries	generation	woven
vessel	in the works	refined	

EXERCISE 1

A. Discuss the questions with a partner before you read.

1. What are some materials or devices that are implanted in (put into) people during surgeries?

2. Do you think these materials or devices have evolved over time? In what way(s)?

3. What kinds of concerns might patients and medical professionals have about materials and devices used in medical procedures?

B. Preview the passage, Read the title and study the images. Write two questions you think this reading might answer.

....

....

Bioresorbable Coronary Stents

1   Many useful products are made of polymers. In the auto industry, for example, lightweight automobile parts are made of different kinds of plastic. In the textile industry, popular materials like polyester fleece and spandex are made with polymers. In the healthcare industry, polymers are useful in a variety of applications, including in materials used inside the human body, such as coronary stents. Coronary stents, or heart stents, are expandable tubes that help open arteries in the heart. In a process called *angioplasty*, a stent is inserted into a narrowed artery in the heart and expanded with a balloon to open the artery (see Fig. 1). Once open, the stent helps blood flow to the heart.

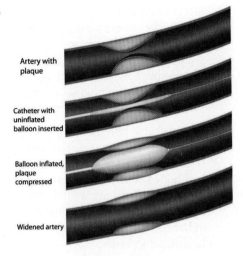

Artery with plaque

Catheter with uninflated balloon inserted

Balloon inflated, plaque compressed

Widened artery

Figure 1: Balloon angioplasty

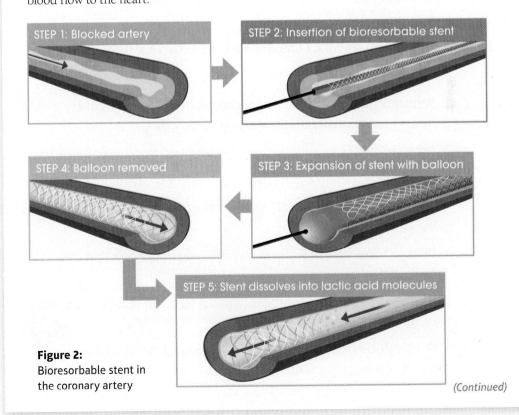

STEP 1: Blocked artery

STEP 2: Insertion of bioresorbable stent

STEP 4: Balloon removed

STEP 3: Expansion of stent with balloon

STEP 5: Stent dissolves into lactic acid molecules

Figure 2:
Bioresorbable stent in
the coronary artery

(Continued)

2 The first generation of heart stents was made solely of metal. Second-generation heart stents, which are still widely used today, are made with metal and coated with a thin, dissolvable polymer material that slowly releases medication as it breaks down. This medicine helps keep the artery open and prevent scar tissue. As can be seen in the close-up detail of a stent in Figure 2, the walls of the device are a woven mesh material. This mesh holds the polymer coating. In the newest stent devices, which are called "bioresorbable" stents, the metal mesh is replaced entirely with dissolvable polymer materials. The polymer completely disappears in approximately three years. By comparison, metal stents remain in the artery for the remainder of a patient's life, restricting natural movement of the vessel.

3 Bioresorbable polymer stents have been in the works for about a decade now, and in 2016 the first type was approved by the United States Food and Drug Administration (FDA) for use in patients. So far, results have not been as promising as researchers had hoped. There has been a higher rate of device thrombosis—a blood clot on the device—than occurs with the metal variety (Wykrzykowska 2017). It is likely that bioresorbable polymer stents, which are still relatively new, will continue to be refined in the coming years. Once they are improved, they may be more widely used in the healthcare industry.

C. Read the passage again. Then read each statement and write *T* (True) or *F* (False). Correct the false statements. Compare answers with a partner.

.... 1. Polymers are found in fleece and spandex clothing.

.... 2. Polymers have a number of applications in the textile industry, primarily in devices and materials inserted into the body.

.... 3. Coronary stents become narrower to facilitate blood flow to the heart.

.... 4. A balloon is used in conjunction with a stent in an angioplasty.

.... 5. Second-generation coronary stents differ from first-generation ones in that the latter contain medicine.

.... 6. Bioresorbable stents are made up of polymer materials that can completely dissolve.

.... 7. Bioresorbable stents are similar to metal stents in that the stent stays in the artery for as long as a person lives.

.... 8. Device thrombosis has occurred more frequently with bioresorbable polymer stents than with metal stents.

D. Answer the questions. Refer to the passage as needed. Then discuss your answers with a partner.

1. What types of visuals were included in the reading?

2. How many times did you look at each visual for information? When?

3. Highlight the language that the writer uses to refer to the visuals in the text. Does this language describe the type of visual in each case? Why do you think that may be?

4. What information did the visuals provide that the reading did not?

VOCABULARY CHECK

A. Review the vocabulary items in the Vocabulary Preview. Write their definitions and add examples. Use a dictionary if necessary.

B. Complete each sentence using the correct vocabulary item from the box. Use the correct form.

artery	fleece	generation	in the works
refine	vessel	woven	

1. After the young woman learned how warm polymer-based .... jackets are, she went to the store and bought one for the winter.

2. The threads of the polymeric material were .... together so tightly that it was impossible to distinguish one thread from another.

3. There are some new policies .... at the university that will make it more difficult for researchers to obtain funding for their studies.

4. The femoral .... is the second biggest in the human body. It is located in the thigh and is the primary supplier of blood to the leg.

5. The hospital was located in an extremely rural area, and therefore carried only first-............................ equipment. Patients who lived in the area often traveled great distances to hospitals that had more modern facilities.

6. The materials engineer who spoke at the medical conference stated that polymeric materials would undoubtedly be .... in the near future to ensure better results in procedures.

7. Arteries, veins, and capillaries are all types of blood ....

🔊 Go to MyEnglishLab to complete a vocabulary exercise and skill practice, and to join in collaborative activities.

SUPPORTING SKILL 1

UNDERSTANDING TEXTUAL REFERENCES TO VISUALS

WHY IT'S USEFUL It is important for you to learn phrases used to reference visuals in order to be able to recognize and understand such phrases when you encounter them in academic texts.

Academic texts—especially research articles and textbooks on topics related to STEM (science, technology, engineering, and mathematics)—tend to contain visuals to support and complement the information presented. In a text, authors use a variety of phrases to refer readers to a given visual. Some of these include:

Common Phrases Used to Reference Visuals
In Text
Figure 1 demonstrates / represents / shows ...
Notice that in Figures 2a and 2c, ...
Table 1 contains / shows ...
The results in Figure 2d indicate / reflect / show ...
As can be seen in Figure 3, ...
As demonstrated / displayed / shown in Figure 4, ...
As is evident in Figure 13, ...
In Figure 1b, ...
... as demonstrated by the diagram
... as depicted / illustrated / indicated / shown in the chart / map / illustration
... as seen in X of Figure 5d
X is depicted / illustrated / indicated / shown in the map / photo / illustration
X is given / presented / listed / provided in the illustration / in Table 3
X is represented by ...
In Parentheses
(Fig. 2b and 2c)
(Figure 11, top)
(see Fig. 1)
(Table 1)

VOCABULARY PREVIEW

The following vocabulary items appear in the reading. Circle the ones you know. Put a question mark next to the ones you do not know.

ambitious	rejuvenate	spontaneously	scab
platform	stimulus	transplanted (v)	malfunctioning (adj)

EXERCISE 2

A. Preview the passage. Note the title and visuals. Working with a partner, predict three things you believe will be discussed.

....

....

....

B. Now read the passage. Which of your predictions from Part A were discussed? Compare answers with a partner.

Scaffolds in Regenerative Medicine

1 Regenerative medicine has an ambitious goal, which is to help the body rejuvenate, or heal, its own cells. Unfortunately, humans cannot spontaneously regenerate parts of the body the way animals like frogs can—at least, not outside of superhero movies. The body does have some capacity to heal itself, however. Broken bones can repair themselves. Cuts will form a scab and then heal. As shown in Figure 1, in the normal wound-healing process, blood flows to the surface of a wound, where a blood clot then forms. Under the scab, a fluid called *exudate* is excreted from blood vessels, and then brand-new connective tissue—called *granulation tissue*—grows within the wound. In cases where this normal process does not occur, however, doctors can only attempt to manage or medicate damaged or sick body parts.

Glossary

Excrete: to get rid of waste material from your body through your bowels, your skin, etc.

Collagen: a protein substance in the bodies of people and animals

Biopsy: the removal of body tissue in order to examine it in a laboratory for disease

In vitro: in artificial conditions outside of the body

(Continued)

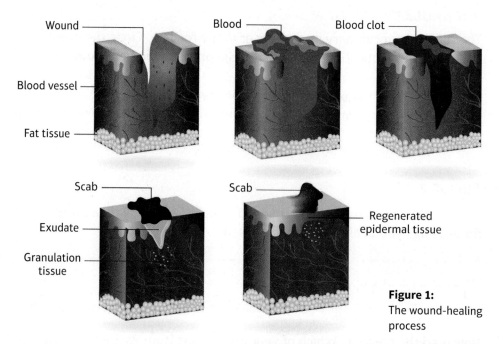

Wound

Blood

Blood clot

Blood vessel

Fat tissue

Scab

Scab

Exudate

Granulation tissue

Regenerated epidermal tissue

Figure 1:
The wound-healing process

2   The field of regenerative medicine—also known as tissue engineering—is helping to change this. Regenerative medicine aims to enhance the body's own cells, replace diseased cells, and use cell therapies to regenerate damaged tissue. Sometimes scientists use a patient's stem cells (see Fig. 2) for tissue engineering. Stem cells are self-renewing cells that can be made into any other type of cell in the body.

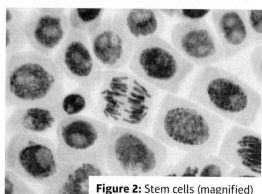

Figure 2: Stem cells (magnified)

3   To help cells grow before they are implanted into the body, scientists need to provide the cells with some support. This support comes in the form of medical scaffolds. The term *scaffold* is taken from construction scaffolding. A scaffold, as displayed in Figure 3, is a temporary structure built on the outside of buildings to support workers and materials during

Figure 3: Construction scaffold with workers

the building process. In the case of tissue engineering, scaffolds are like a platform to stand on, while cells on the scaffold are like the builders. Scaffolds are usually three-dimensional (for example, cube-shaped), and they are made of many different kinds of materials. These include collagen, which is a natural substance, and biodegradable plastic, which is a synthetic substance.

4 Figure 4 demonstrates the process of tissue engineering. First, cells are removed from a patient in a biopsy and multiplied in vitro. Then, as depicted in the flowchart, the scaffolds are "seeded," or layered, with cells, and some sort of stimulus is applied to the cell-infused scaffold. The stimulus can be mechanical or chemical, and it helps different kinds of cells to grow. Finally, the cell scaffold is surgically placed on the injured area of the patient's body, as can be seen in the third part of the image.

5 Tissue scaffolds have been used successfully to repair injuries related to the skin, such as burns. There have also been a few successful cases of entire organs being replaced with synthetic organs that are grown with tissue scaffolds. For example, new bladders grown in vitro with a synthetic polymer and cell scaffolds have been successfully transplanted into several patients who had malfunctioning bladders. In the future, researchers are hopeful that injured and diseased parts of the body will be able to be treated and healed with these types of cell therapies.

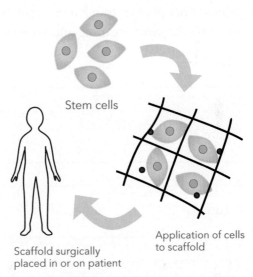

Stem cells

Application of cells to scaffold

Scaffold surgically placed in or on patient

Figure 4: The tissue engineering process

C. **Read the passage again. Then read each statement and write *T* (True) or *F* (False). Correct the false statements. Compare answers with a partner.**

.... 1. The ultimate objective of regenerative medicine is for the body to be capable of quickly regenerating parts.

.... 2. As a wound heals, exudate is eliminated from blood vessels following the formation of a blood clot.

.... 3. At times, regenerative medicine involves the use of a patient's stem cells.

.... 4. Construction scaffolds are similar to medical scaffolds in that they both serve as support structures.

.... 5. Collagen and biodegradable plastic materials are the two materials from which medical scaffolds are made.

.... 6. The purpose of affixing a mechanical or chemical stimuli to a scaffold infused with cells is to assist in the growth of cells.

.... 7. In some cases, tissue scaffolds have been used to create synthetic organs.

D. Answer the following questions for Figures 1–4. Then compare answers with a partner.

- What type of a visual is it?
- How was the visual referenced in the reading? (*Hint:* Some visuals may be referred to more than once.)
- Which other phrases to reference visuals could replace the original phrase while retaining the same meaning and sentence structure? Write three possibilities.

1. Figure 1

....

....

2. Figure 2

....

....

3. Figure 3

....

....

4. Figure 4

....

....

E. Work with a partner. Answer the questions about textual references to visuals.

1. Both Figure 1 and Figure 4 demonstrate processes. Why do you think the author used multiple textual references to visuals for Figure 4 but only one for Figure 1?

....

2. A textual reference to a visual is present in the following sentence from the passage: "A scaffold, as displayed in Figure 3, is a temporary structure built on the outside of buildings to support workers and materials during the building process." Rewrite the sentence, using a different phrase referencing Figure 3 and changing the sentence structure.

....

3. Think about your field of academic study. Which references to visuals have you come across in the readings for your courses? Do you think some references are more frequently used than others?

VOCABULARY CHECK

A. Review the vocabulary items in the Vocabulary Preview. Write their definitions and add examples. Use a dictionary if necessary.

B. Complete each sentence using the correct vocabulary item from the box. Use the correct form.

ambitious	malfunctioning (adj)	platform	rejuvenate
scab	spontaneously	stimuli	transplant (v)

1. The accident left the patient with a(n) .... nervous system, meaning that it could no longer send signals from some parts of the body to others.

2. The surgeon successfully .... a donated kidney into the body of a man who had been on dialysis for years.

3. The wound on the child's knee began to form a(n) .... a few days after she fell while biking.

4. There are certain viruses and injuries from which individuals sometimes recover .... without any form of treatment.

5. The .... medical student, having worked diligently to achieve her goals, was accepted into the residency program at a highly respected university hospital.

6. The workers stood on a(n) .... high above the ground in order to fix the broken equipment near the top of the building.

7. Pain is felt after exposure to .... such as injections or cuts.

8. In an effort to .... her skin, the woman bought a number of expensive lotions and spent a significant amount of money on various facial treatments.

⬥ Go to MyEnglishLab to complete a vocabulary exercise and skill practice, and to join in collaborative activities.

SUPPORTING SKILL 2
INTERPRETING INFORMATION IN VISUALS

WHY IT'S USEFUL Visuals associated with articles and other written pieces are intended to help explain a text or provide additional information. Being able to correctly interpret information found in visuals is important to better understand the content of a text and to gain information that may be represented more clearly in visual, graphic, or chart form, rather than in writing.

Many genres of writing, from magazine articles to research reports, include visuals as a means of enhancing what is written. Whether they are pictures, graphics, diagrams, or charts, visuals add additional detail or other information to a written piece. Just as importantly, however, visuals associated with a text should, ideally, be able to stand alone, meaning a reader should not have to rely on the text to interpret what is presented in the visuals.

Looking at a visual, a reader should be able to understand its main idea and recognize its purpose. This can be tricky, however, because visuals often contain a significant amount of information presented in a compact format. An author also expects readers to be able to examine a visual critically and make relevant interpretations of the information, without all information being explicitly explained.

Many of the reading skills you use when reading an article—such as skimming, scanning, and thinking critically about what you read—can be used when interpreting visuals. However, you should also pay attention to the unique features of visuals in order to gain the best understanding of the information presented.

Key Features to Notice in Visuals

- **Title:** This will prepare you to know what you are looking at or for in a visual.

- **Labels:** If there are key features you should notice, the author might have already pointed them out for you.

- **Captions:** For visuals such as charts and photographs, captions provide a brief summary of what to look for.

- **Icons or symbols:** Arrows, for example, show the direction or sequence of the process being illustrated.

- **Key:** If a lot of symbols or colors are used in a visual, a key is used to illustrate what they represent.

- **References back to the text:** As described in Supporting Skill 1, texts typically reference their visuals, but oftentimes visuals also make references back to the text. For example, the caption might reference data described in the text to help the visual make more sense.

> **TIP**
>
> After you understand the main idea of the visual, think about *why* the author included it and *how* it enhances your understanding of the text. Doing so will help you to better understand and recall the information.

- **Source:** Knowing where the information in the visual came from will help you to assess its reliability and give additional insight into the information.
- **Inset:** This is a section of a photograph or diagram that is enlarged because it contains especially important information or is too small or detailed to see as part of the larger photograph or diagram.

Consider the diagram of balloon angioplasty, on page 291. Look at the labeled parts of the visual, and compare them to the purposes of these parts as described above.

Visual-Specific Features

Because there are so many different types of visuals that accompany texts, the features previously described are quite general. Here are a few visual-specific features to consider for the following types of visuals:

- **Illustrations:** Labels and zoomed-in sections are common in illustrations.
- **Diagrams:** Arrows to illustrate processes, mentions of time, and other symbols to show relationships often appear in diagrams.
- **Graphs:** Pay especially close attention to labels on the x and y axes of graphs, as well as any captions that may be included.
- **Tables:** Some tables can be very dense and contain a lot of information in a small space. Noticing the headings and labels is helpful for managing all the information.
- **Maps:** A map key is often included to define key colors and symbols on the map. Other key labels include directions and distances.
- **Charts:** As a chart can come in many different forms, consider why an author chose to present the information in this specific shape or form. For example, a pie chart can be useful for demonstrating contrasts if one category, or "piece of the pie," is much larger than the others.

VOCABULARY PREVIEW
Read the vocabulary items below. Circle the ones you know. Put a question mark next to the ones you don't know.

fractures	heal	composite
customized	trigger (v)	marketable

EXERCISE 3

A. Preview the passage. Read the title and study the visuals. Predict three things you believe will be discussed.

1. ....

2. ....

3. ....

B. Now read the passage. Review your predictions from Part A. Were they correct?

Bone Tissue Engineering Materials

1 Natural bone tissue has considerable regenerative capacity compared to other parts of the body. If your arm breaks, for example, it will usually heal itself after being set in a cast. At the microlevel, bone tissue is made of circular units called *osteons*, which have nerves, veins, arteries, and lymphatic vessels in their central canals, or cores. Osteons contain concentric circles of membrane, or *lamellae*, which resemble tree rings (see Fig. 1). Osteocytes, or bone cells, lie within these rings. Osteoblasts lie on the surface of the osteon, and produce more bone cells. The osteoclasts, also located on the surface of an osteon, remove old bone, which allows for new growth. Scientists have found that these cells create a constant cycle of renewal within bones.

Glossary

Regenerative: growing again after having been damaged

Concentric: used to describe circles that have their center at the same point

Degenerative: (of an illness) becoming gradually worse until it cannot be stopped

Cadaver: a dead human body

Porosity: the amount of an object that is not solid in relation to its total size and weight

OSTEON

Figure 1: Osteon development and structure

2 While the renewal process usually works just fine in normal bone fractures, some bone injuries and diseases do not heal on their own. Injuries include bone infections and bone loss, which are more common among the elderly, who often suffer from weakened bones. When bone tissue is damaged beyond repair, the treatment is often a bone graft, a procedure in which healthy bone tissue is transplanted onto the damaged site to help stimulate new growth.

The most common place for bone grafting is in the mouth, for tooth replacements. Bone grafting is also done in the spine in a procedure known as *spinal fusion*, which joins two or more vertebrae (see Fig. 2). Spinal fusion treats issues that arise with old age or degenerative disease.

3   Traditionally, the bone tissue used in a bone graft comes from another place on the patient's own body. One of the most common places is from a small area on the iliac crest, which is the outer wing of the hip bone (Fig. 3). Another source of bone tissue is from a cadaver donor. Neither of these options is ideal, however. When bone tissue is taken from the patient's own body, there is pain and risk associated with the surgery. When donor tissue is used, there is a risk that the body will reject the material.

4   For these reasons, researchers are looking for alternative bone-grafting materials. Some synthetic materials are already in use, such as ceramic composite materials and polymers. As seen in Figure 4, these materials usually resemble bone in terms of porosity and hardness, and they are usually customized for the body in some way, such as by "seeding" them with cells and other agents that help trigger bone growth. In the future, scientists hope to use new technologies like bioprinting to make materials for bone grafts. Bioprinting uses biocompatible substances, such as the mineral hydroxyapatite, which is found naturally in bone tissue, to print—or produce— materials for use in bone grafts. While this technology is extremely promising, much more research and development needs to be conducted in the future before it becomes marketable for patients.

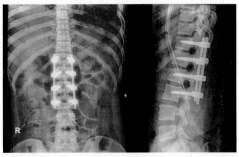

Figure 2: X-ray image showing spinal column with implant, screw placement, and fusion

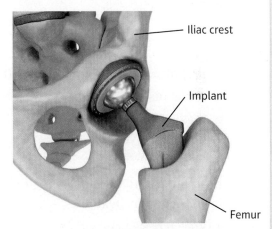

Iliac crest

Implant

Femur

Figure 3: Human pelvic bone with implant

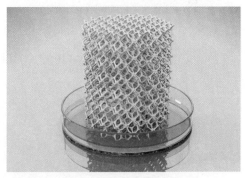

Figure 4: Model of bioprinting of human bone: petri dish with spongy structure in the medical laboratory (3D illustration)

C. Read the passage a second time. Then choose the correct answer to each question according to the reading.

1. In Figure 1, what term is used to name the concentric circles?

   a. nerve
   b. osteoblast
   c. lamellae
   d. central canal

2. According to the illustration in Figure 1, which of the following is NOT part of the central canal?

   a. veins
   b. lymphatic vessels
   c. arteries
   d. osteocytes

3. What procedure does Figure 2 illustrate?

   a. spinal fusion
   b. degenerative disease
   c. tooth replacement
   d. bone infection

4. In addition to that shown in Figure 2, what is another form of bone grafting referenced in the text?

   a. knee replacement
   b. tooth replacement
   c. bone loss
   d. nose reconstruction

5. Paragraph 3 mentions the hip bone. How is this body part referred to in one of the visuals?

   a. spinal column
   b. pelvic bone
   c. iliac crest
   d. cadaver donor

6. Which of the following is NOT a reason the iliac crest is labeled in Figure 3?

   a. to highlight a specific area of the hip bone mentioned in the text
   b. to provide a clearer explanation than what can be provided in the written text
   c. to demonstrate the most common area where the hip bone breaks
   d. to indicate a common source of bone tissue for bone grafts

7. What material is the object in Figure 4 made from?

    a. synthetic materials

    b. human bone

    c. animal bone

    d. metal

8. Which of the following is true of the item shown in Figure 4?

    a. It is the exact same material as human bone.

    b. It shows a real example of bioprinting that scientists have already used.

    c. It will be used in a human spine.

    d. It is not a picture of an actual bone graft.

D. Discuss your answers with another student. Use information and examples from the passage to explain and support your answers.

VOCABULARY CHECK

A. Review the vocabulary items in the Vocabulary Preview. Write their definitions and add examples. Use a dictionary if necessary.

B. Complete each sentence using the correct vocabulary item from the box. Use the correct form.

composite	customize	fracture	heal	marketable	trigger (v)

1. Thanks to recent medical advances, the recovery rate for major surgeries is dropping, and patients are .... faster and faster.

2. An adverse reaction to an organ implant surgery may .... an infection in a patient's body.

3. To make new medical procedures more .... , both the costs and the associated risks of the procedures need to be lowered.

4. People who lack calcium in their diet are at a higher risk for bone

....

5. The new .... materials used in spinal surgery are thought to be better than traditional metal rods because they can be constructed to meet individual patients' needs.

6. Researchers hope to develop implant material that is .... to each patient's specific body, bone, and blood type.

🔊 Go to MyEnglishLab to complete a vocabulary exercise and skill practice, and to join in collaborative activities.

INTEGRATED SKILLS

EXPLAINING INFORMATION IN VISUALS

WHY IT'S USEFUL Being able to explain information found in visuals is an important academic skill. Equally important, being able to articulate such information in your own words helps you to understand it better yourself.

Now that you have become familiar with interpreting different types of visuals and understanding their significance to an associated text, it is important to be able to demonstrate that understanding in your own words. During your university career, you will be expected to summarize visuals you have found in readings or have created on your own. This includes a visual itself as well as its caption and any description of it in the text.

There are many reasons why it is important to be able to explain the information found in visuals. For instance, if you include a visual in a classroom presentation or at an academic conference, you should be able to explain it well enough so that your audience is able to interpret it quickly and efficiently. If you include a visual with a research paper, you often need to reference it at least briefly in order to introduce it to the reader. And most importantly, being able to explain a visual helps you to understand it better yourself and to retain what the author hoped you would gain from it.

As with all summaries, your job when explaining information in visuals is to present the big picture and main ideas. You do not typically have unlimited time to describe a visual, so look for the key points, and do not include all the minor details. Here are some key language areas to consider:

- **Language to introduce the visual:** *As you can see* (more common with speaking), *… ; The visual / chart / graph / figure demonstrates / illustrates / describes / compares …*

- **Language for overall trends:** *Overall, … ; There has been a steady increase / decrease in … ; The majority …*

- **Language for comparison and contrast:** *While / Whereas X is … , Y is … ; both X and Y … ; neither X nor Y …*

- **Language for outliers:** *While the majority of … is … , X is …*

- **Language for numbers and statistics:** *XX percent of … is … ; there was a dramatic increase / decrease in X between the years … ; The graph peaks at … ; There was a sharp rise / fall in …*

- **Language to draw attention to something:** *In particular, … ; Please note …* (more common with speaking); *The most significant … is …*

Consider the following. Then read the summarized version under the chart to find examples of language for restating visuals.

Types of Mesh	Advantages	Disadvantages
Synthetic	Inexpensive, low recurrence rate, durable	Higher rates of infection, more discomfort, inflexible
Biologic	Less likely to cause infection, flexible	High recurrence rate, expensive
Hybrid	Durable, strong, flexible, less likely to cause infection, low recurrence rate	Limited test results

Table 2: Advantages and disadvantages of surgical meshes

Table 2 compares synthetic, biologic, and hybrid materials used in hernia repairs. **While both** synthetic and hybrid forms have a lower recurrence rate than biologic meshes, biologic and hybrid mesh are less likely to cause infection than synthetic meshes. **Overall**, all three forms have their respective pros and cons, but the results of tests on hybrid mesh are too limited for the disadvantages to be fully known.

VOCABULARY PREVIEW
The following vocabulary items appear in the reading. Circle the ones you know. Put a question mark next to the ones you do not know.

robust	chronic	altered
combating	innovative	to date (time phrase)

A. Read the passage and look at the visuals. Notice how the different types of visuals are used to present different types of information.

The Regenerative Medicine Market

1   Regenerative medicine is a medical field that aims to replace or regenerate human organs and tissue through gene therapy, stem cell technology, and tissue engineering. Many of the recent developments in the field are still in the research and development stage, and for this reason, regenerative medicine is often considered to be on the frontier of modern medicine. In fact it may be another 20 to 30 years before the full potential of regenerative medicine technologies can be utilized. However, the potential applications of regenerative treatments are so promising that the market is quite robust today. In 2016, for example, investors financed approximately $5.22 billion in regenerative medical research.

2   There are several reasons why public and private investment in this field is growing. Investors are looking for treatments that are more successful at treating chronic and degenerative diseases—including types of cancer. Gene therapy and other regenerative medical procedures are novel treatments compared to existing technology. For example, in the first-ever gene therapy that is close to being approved by the US Food and Drug Administration (FDA), leukemia is targeted with a patient's own cells, which are genetically altered to attack tumor cells. In addition to combating disease in innovative ways, regenerative medicine also offers a solution to the issue of organ-donor shortages by engineering synthetic organs. As demonstrated in Figure 1, other reasons why the regenerative medicine market is growing today include current advancements in tissue regeneration, nanotechnology, and stem-cell technology.

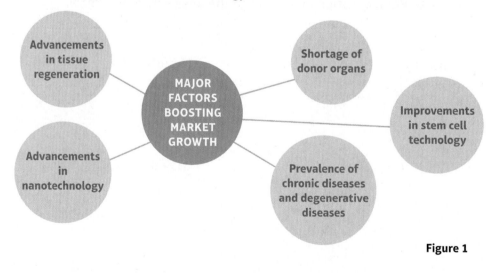

Figure 1

3 The major question about regenerative medicine therapies that many doctors and patients ask is when the treatments will be ready for use. First, the therapies must move out of the research stage and into clinical trials, which test treatments on humans. Notably, the number of clinical trials in regenerative medicine rose considerably from 2015 to 2016. Figure 2 shows that in 2015, there were 631 clinical trials underway. That number rose to 804 in 2016, meaning that researchers are moving closer to making certain regenerative treatments a viable option for patients. Phase I trials, which represent the early stages of a drug trial, rose from 192 in 2015 to 261 in 2016. Phase II trials rose from 376 in 2015 to 475 in 2016. Finally, Phase III trials, which are also called late-phase trials, rose slightly, from 63 in 2015 to 68 in 2016.

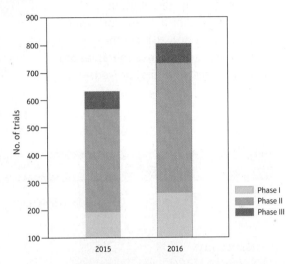

Figure 2: Clinical trials in regenerative medicine

4 Most of these trials involve cellular therapies and gene therapies. In 2016, worldwide there were approximately 425 gene-therapy trials and 533 cell-therapy trials. There were also 20 clinical trials in the field of tissue engineering in the same year (see Fig. 3). Some clinical trials had crossover between cell therapy and gene therapy, which is why the total number of clinical trials by type in Figure 3 exceeds the 804 total clinical trials for 2016. The United States is currently the nation with the largest number of clinical trials of all types. For example, researchers found that between 1989 and 2015, the United States was home to 66.81 percent of all gene-therapy clinical trials.

CULTURE NOTE

There are normally three phases in clinical trials for drugs or medical devices trying to get FDA approval. *Phase I* is the initial testing stage that looks for basic safety and possible side effects of the drugs, usually with a small number of volunteer patients. *Phase II* uses a larger number of patients and further tests the effectiveness of the drug or medical device. At this stage, researchers usually give the drug to one group of patients and a *placebo* to another group of patients to compare the results. A placebo is a fake drug that has no effect on a patient (it can be just sugar), but patients do not know whether they are receiving the real drug or not. *Phase III* tests the new product on an even larger group of people over a longer period of time. FDA approval is not possible until a product has successfully passed through the third phase.

(Continued)

5　The United Kingdom had the second highest number during the same period, with 9.45 percent of all gene-therapy trials. Figure 4 demonstrates the distribution of all gene-therapy clinical trials worldwide between 1989 and 2015. In the coming years, more regenerative therapies are likely to be tested and approved.

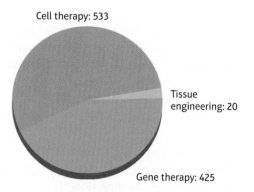

Cell therapy: 533

Tissue engineering: 20

Gene therapy: 425

Figure 3: Clinical trials in regenerative medicine by type, 2016

GENE-THERAPY **CLINICAL TRIALS** BY COUNTRY, 1989–2015

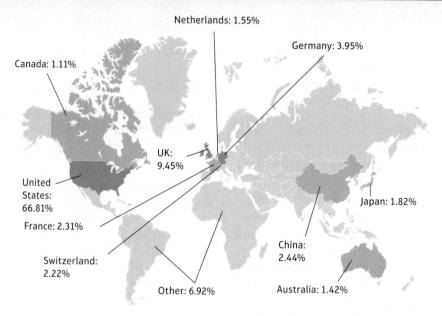

Netherlands: 1.55%

Germany: 3.95%

Canada: 1.11%

UK: 9.45%

United States: 66.81%

Japan: 1.82%

France: 2.31%

China: 2.44%

Switzerland: 2.22%

Other: 6.92%

Australia: 1.42%

Figure 4: Information retrieved from: https://www.ncbi.nlm.nih.gov/pmc/articles/PMC5328344/

B. **Use the visuals from "The Regenerative Medicine Market" to complete the following activities.**

1. Read Paragraph 2 and study Figure 1 again. Can you think of a different visual representation of the major reasons why the regenerative medicine market is growing? Sketch your diagram and compare it with a partner's.

2. Work with a partner. Partner A should look at and describe Figure 3. Partner B should try to draw exactly what Partner A describes. Compare your drawing to the actual chart in Figure 3.

3. Look at Figure 4. Make a list of the overall trends in the visual. That is, do not simply write down every percentage for every country—look only for the main ideas. Compare your summary with a partner's and make any necessary changes.

C. **Write a one-paragraph summary of Figure 4 on page 310 and use some of the suggested language for explaining visuals from page 306. Then read your summary aloud to a partner as he or she tries to recreate the graph. Check your partner's graph. Edit your summary if necessary. Then switch roles.**

D. **Work with a partner. Answer the questions about explaining information in visuals.**

1. In Parts B and C, how did your description of the visuals compare to your partner's? What types of edits did you have to make?

2. Go back to the passage and reread how the text refers to each of the four visuals. What information was included in the passage, and what information was only available in the visuals? Why do you think the author chose to present the information this way?

3. Compare your descriptions of the visuals to the references made to them in the passage. What was the same, and what was different? Are there any additional words or phrases from the passage that you could use to reference visuals that were not already presented in the list on page 306?

VOCABULARY CHECK

A. Review the vocabulary items in the Vocabulary Preview. Write their definitions and add examples. Use a dictionary if necessary.

B. Complete each sentence using the correct vocabulary item from the box. Use the correct form.

alter	chronic	combat (v)
innovate	robust	to date (time phrase)

1. _____ , the United States has been the country that has conducted the majority of gene-therapy clinical trials.

2. The most _____ clinical trials include three phases and follow all procedures required by the Food and Drug Administration.

3. Researchers feel confident that advancements in regenerative medicine could help to _____ many forms of serious illness in the future.

4. _____ diseases, such as asthma, can affect people's health for many years and cost many thousands of dollars to treat.

5. Some _____ nonsurgical treatments have replaced surgery and can now be performed in a doctor's office instead of in a hospital.

6. If a new drug does not prove effective, scientists must _____ it to improve its quality and effectiveness.

⬤ Go to MyEnglishLab to complete a skill practice.

LANGUAGE SKILL

UNDERSTANDING THE USE OF PASSIVE VOICE IN RESEARCH WRITING

WHY IT'S USEFUL Understanding how and why authors of research articles employ the passive voice, particularly in the methodology section, can help you to better interpret authors' research methods and learn to apply this genre-specific technique to your own research writing.

⬤ Go to MyEnglishLab for the Language Skill presentation and practice.

VOCABULARY STRATEGY
RECOGNIZING GREEK, LATIN, AND GERMANIC WORD ROOTS

WHY IT'S USEFUL By becoming familiar with word roots from Greek, Latin, and Germanic languages, you will be able to better decipher the meanings of unknown English words.

English has strong ties to a number of languages, including Greek, Latin, and many Germanic languages. Many words that you have encountered in your English studies have **roots**—the historical base form of a word that conveys its main meaning—that come from these languages. Roots are combined with prefixes and suffixes, which also have historical roots in the aforementioned languages, to form words. The term **prefix** refers to a group of letters that is added to the beginning of a word, changing its meaning. A **suffix** is a group of letters that is added to the end of a word, which results in the formation of a new word.

An example of a root is the Greek *bio*, meaning "life." When combined with the Greek suffix *-ology*—which means "the study of"—the word *biology* results. This new word literally means "the study of life."

Familiarizing yourself with common Greek, Latin, and Germanic word roots and their associated meanings is essential for your vocabulary development. A knowledge of roots can help you decipher the meaning of unknown words you encounter while reading. Mastering this strategy will increase your reading efficiency, as it will allow you to continue reading a text without frequently stopping to look up the meaning of words.

Another strategic reason to familiarize yourself with roots is that you will begin to recognize the relationship between words that you might not otherwise have considered similar. One example is the not-necessarily-obvious relationship between the time-related vocabulary items *chronic* and *chronology*.

CULTURE NOTE

While English has adopted words from many languages, approximately one-third of English vocabulary is derived from French, which in turn evolved from Latin.

GREEK ROOTS

Root	Meaning	Example from Unit
-auto-	self	automobile
-chrono-	time	chronic
-cycl-	circle	cycle
-hydro-	water	hydrogel
-mech-	machine	mechanical
-meter-	measure of	nanometer
-micro-	small	microlevel

GREEK ROOTS, *continued*

Root	Meaning	Example from Unit
-oste-	bone	osteon
-phys-	nature	physicians
-plasm-	development or formation	cytoplasm
-poly-	many	polymer
-techn-	science, art, skill	technologies
-tele-	distance	television
-therm-	heat	thermoplastic

LATIN ROOTS

Root	Meaning	Example from Unit
-cella-	small chamber	cells
-cent-	hundred	percent
-con-	together, with	connective
-duc-	lead, bring	products
-gen-	produce	generation
-inter-	between	interchangeably
-juv-	young	juvenile
-magn-	big	magnetic
-mal-	bad	malfunctioning
-man-	hand	manufacture
-multi-	many	multiplied
-nano-	one-billionth	nanosecond
-non-	not	non-fiber
-port-	carry	support
-sens-	feel	sensitive
-stim-	encourage, drive	stimuli
-struct-	build	structure
-sup-	above	superior
-syn-	together	synthesize
-tain-	hold	sustain
-temp-	time	temporary

LATIN ROOTS, *continued*

Root	Meaning	Example from Unit
-trans-	across, through	transfer
-uni-	one	United States
-vari-	different	various
-vis-	see	vision

GERMANIC ROOTS

Root	Meaning	Example from Unit
-bod-	body	body
-brec-	break	broken
-gro-	grow	growth
-heal- / -heal + th-	heal / health	healthcare
-hert-	heart	heart
-liht-	light	light-sensitive
-red-	ready	ready
-skap-	shape	cube-shaped
-stand-	stand	stand
-straht-	straight	straight
-streng-	strengthen	strengthens
-under + stand-	understand	understanding

EXERCISE 5

A. List one word you know for each root. Compare lists with a partner and discuss how the meaning of the root relates to the words you wrote down.

GREEK

Root	Word
-auto-	
-cycl-	
-micro-	
-phys-	

LATIN

Root	Word
-con-	
-gen-	
-multi-	
-uni-	

GERMANIC

Root	Word
-bod-	
-gro-	
-heal- / -heal + th-	
-skap-	

B. The following items are excerpted from readings in this unit. Circle the root in each underlined word. Use the meaning of the root to try to define the word. Then write the meaning on the lines. Discuss the meanings with a partner.

1. Second-<u>generation</u> heart stents, which are still widely used today, are made with metal and coated with a thin, dissolvable <u>polymer</u> material that slowly releases medication as it breaks down.

    ....

    ....

2. <u>Regenerative</u> medicine has an ambitious goal, which is to help the body <u>rejuvenate</u> … its own cells.

    ....

    ....

3. A scaffold, as displayed in Figure 3, is a <u>temporary</u> <u>structure</u> built on the outside of buildings to <u>support</u> workers and materials during the building process.

    ....

    ....

4. ... [N]ew bladders grown in vitro with a <u>synthetic</u> <u>polymer</u> and cell scaffolds have been successfully <u>transplanted</u> into several patients who had <u>malfunctioning</u> bladders.

....

....

5. ... [C]ertain drug-carrying <u>nanomedicines</u> are <u>sensitive</u> to light.

....

....

C. **Consider the meaning of the word roots to choose the word that best completes each sentence. Use the correct form. Consult a dictionary if needed.**

chronology	deduct	heartburn	intervene
malignant	thermometer	technical	understand

1. To respond to the question about developments in regenerative medicine over time, the scientist listed the most important events and discoveries in .... order.

2. The language Dr. Lee used to describe her work in chemistry was very .... It was unlikely that readers outside of her field would be familiar with many of the words that she used.

3. The cancer patient was thrilled to hear that his .... tumor had been reduced in size following just two sessions of chemotherapy.

4. The therapist .... when she recognized that the argument between the individuals would only intensify if allowed to continue.

5. While calculating her taxes, the recently-graduated PhD student learned that she could .... $2,500 of student loan interest from her total tax obligation.

6. I couldn't believe my eyes when I read the ....—it was over 30° Celsius in the middle of winter!

7. The receptionist began to experience .... as a result of indigestion, feeling a somewhat painful burning sensation in her stomach and chest.

8. It was .... that the patient had no recollection of the medical procedure; he had been under general anesthesia.

APPLY YOUR SKILLS

WHY IT'S USEFUL By applying the skills you have learned in this unit, you can gain a better understanding of this challenging text about ways that materials engineering and nanotechnology are being used to combat cancer.

BEFORE YOU READ

A. Discuss these questions with a partner or group.

1. What types of existing cancer treatments do you know about?

2. If you had a serious illness, would you be willing to try an experimental treatment method?

3. Why do you think new medicines take so long to be approved by the US Food and Drug Administration (FDA)?

B. You will read a passage about nanomaterials used in cancer treatment. As you read, think about these questions.

1. In your own words, what is nanotechnology?

2. According to the text, how can nanomaterials improve upon traditional cancer treatments?

3. How do nanomedicines attack cancer cells?

4. What are some different ways that nanomedicines can be activated?

C. Review the Unit Skills Summary. As you read the passage, apply the skills you learned in this unit.

UNIT SKILLS SUMMARY

Understand textual references to visuals

• Understand how a text directly refers to its accompanying visuals.

Interpret information in visuals

• Understand information that is presented in visual form.

Explain information in visuals

• Summarize or interpret information presented in visuals.

Understand the use of passive voice in research writing

• Recognize how passive voice is used in the research genre.

Recognize Greek, Latin, and Germanic word roots

• Learn common roots from other languages to determine the meanings of new words.

READ

A. Read the passage. Annotate and take notes on the answers to the questions in Before You Read, Part B.

How Nanotechnology Fights Cancer

1 Nanotechnology is often touted as the next big step in science, and nanomaterials are being developed for an increasingly wide assortment of products, from electronics to textiles to medicine. As the term implies, nanotechnology is the manufacturing of materials at the nanolevel. The unit of measurement used in nanomaterials is the minuscule nanometer, which is a mere one-billionth (10^{-9}) of a meter. For comparison, a nanomaterial such as a carbon nanotube—which resembles a mesh rod—is smaller than a virus in the human body. It is tens of thousands of times smaller than the width of a human hair (see Fig. 1 for a scale comparison).

COMPARATIVE MEASUREMENTS FOR NANODEVICES

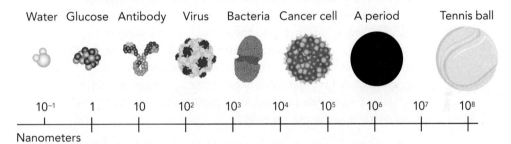

| Water | Glucose | Antibody | Virus | Bacteria | Cancer cell | A period | | Tennis ball |

| 10^{-1} | 1 | 10 | 10^2 | 10^3 | 10^4 | 10^5 | 10^6 | 10^7 | 10^8 |

Nanometers

Figure 1: Size of the nanoscale

2 Since the inception of nanotechnology nearly two decades ago, there has been immense interest and investment in developing nanomaterials to fight cancer in new ways, particularly in drug-delivery methods. Nanomaterials used in innovative drug-delivery products use nano-sized polymer materials that are combined with cancer-fighting medicines. These drug-delivery products are sometimes called *polymer therapeutics* or simply *nanomedicines*.

(Continued)

3   New drug-delivery products are very appealing because of the harshness of conventional treatments for cancer. Cancer is one of the leading causes of death in the United States, and more than a million new cases are diagnosed each year. Treatments, unfortunately, are limited. Traditional therapies like chemotherapy and radiation are toxic to cancer cells, but they are also toxic to regular cells in the body. Frequently, these therapies cause damaging side effects. In addition, cancer cells can become resistant to chemotherapy drugs.

4   Nanomedicines, on the other hand, deliver drugs straight to the tumor sites. This limits their toxicity, which is perhaps their most promising factor. In addition, they can be released in a controlled manner as needed.

5   There are a number of drug-delivery methods involving nanomaterials. For example, cancer-fighting drugs can be encapsulated (contained) within a nanomaterial or added to it, thus acting as a kind of "homing beacon" to cancer cells. In other words, the nanomaterial actually targets the tumors. Once these nanomedicines are injected into the body, the circulation system pushes them throughout the vascular system. When they reach a tumor, they encounter the equivalent of an open door. Tumors cells have "leaky" walls due to their structure, allowing the nanomedicines to pass through them easily. The nanomedicines usually linger in the tumor afterward because cancer cells have decreased lymphatic drainage. After a short time—days, usually—the nanomaterials begin to disintegrate, releasing their drugs and killing the cancer cells.

6   Some nanomedicines can be "activated" to release medicines by different stimuli. For example, certain drug-carrying nanomedicines are sensitive to light. Others are sensitive to temperature. Yet others respond to a magnetic field. These so-called "smart" nanomaterials transform under different conditions to release their drug payloads. For instance if a light-sensitive nanomedicine is injected into tumor cells, doctors can apply a near-infrared light where the tumor is located. This light creates heat that triggers the medicine to deploy. Once triggered, the medicine explodes into the tumor and kills the cancer cells. Gold nanoparticles, depicted in Figure 2, are an example of a light-sensitive nanomaterial.

Figure 2: Gold nanoparticles, 3D illustration (magnified)

7 Nanomedicines have all sorts of different architectures—that is, they come in different shapes and sizes. They can be square, spherical, star-shaped, and more. Liposomes, for example, are like tiny, spherical bubbles, as illustrated in Figure 3. In the rendering, the polyethylene glycol (PEG) coating can be seen on the shell of the liposome. This nontoxic polymer acts as a kind of shield or protection for the nanomedicine. The figure reveals the lipid membrane and internal aqueous—or liquid—space inside the liposome, along with the cancer-fighting drug.

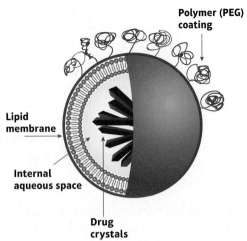

Polymer (PEG) coating

Lipid membrane

Internal aqueous space

Drug crystals

Figure 3: Diagram of liposome used for drug delivery

8 Another type of nanoparticle drug carrier is known as a *dendrimer*. Dendrimers are somewhat branchlike in appearance, as can be seen in Figure 4. Dendrimers are another example of nanomaterials found to perform well as drug carriers.

Figure 4: Microscopic view of dendrimer

9 Several nanomedicines have been approved by the FDA. Doxil®, for example, a liposome formulation, treats a number of different types of cancer. Abraxane®, another nanomedicine that is bound to a natural polymer called *albumin*, treats metastatic pancreatic cancer as well as lung and breast cancers.

10 Despite these successes, however, most nanomedicines remain firmly in the research and development stages. How soon they will move into use in clinical practice is a matter of speculation. Plenty of nanomedicines perform well in lab tests, but when they are put to the ultimate test and injected into a cancer patient, they have not always met expectations. Clearing particles from the body remains a concern in some cases. Figuring out how to get the nanomedicines to effectively target the tumor cells and not get caught in other parts of the body, such as the liver or spleen, is also a concern.

(Continued)

Ultimately, nanomaterials are incredibly complex, and they require tinkering and tuning for various features like precise size and surface characteristics.

11 If we take a step back, however, and remember that nanomaterials have only been around for about a decade and a half—a blink in the evolution of medical technology—the progress in the field is tremendous. Though they may not be ready for use yet, nanomedicines will very likely play a major role in cancer treatments in the future.

B. Work with a partner. Use your annotations to discuss the answers to the questions in Before You Read, Part B. Are there any questions you cannot answer? Which of the reading skills you have learned in this unit could help you answer them?

⬡ Go to MyEnglishLab to read the passage again and answer critical thinking questions.

THINKING CRITICALLY

Discuss the questions with another student.

1. You read about several types of "smart" nanomedicines—for example, medicines that are light- or temperature-sensitive or that respond to a magnetic field. What other ways can you imagine in which nanomedicines could be "smart"? In other words, what other stimuli can you think of that a nanomedicine might be able to respond to?

2. The author refers to chemotherapy and radiation as examples of harsh treatments for cancer and praises the benefits of nanomedicines over these traditional treatments. What downsides of nanomedicines can you think of, if any?

3. The author mentions two drugs, Doxil® and Abraxane®, that have received FDA approval. Do a bit of research on *one* of these two drugs. Try to answer the following questions:

   • How was it developed?

   • What kind(s) of testing did it go through?

   • How exactly is the drug delivered?

   • How successful is the drug in killing cancer cells?

THINKING VISUALLY

In this unit, you have read about the development of nanotechnology, specifically nanomedicines. Go online and find information about major milestones in the field of nanotechnology in the last few decades. The United States National Nanotechnology Initiative website is a strong resource, but information regarding advances in nanotechnology can also be found on many other sites. Then complete the timeline with what you consider to be the five most important developments in nanotechnology. Write the year that a development took place across the top of the timeline and a brief description of the event beneath it. Then compare timelines with a group of classmates.

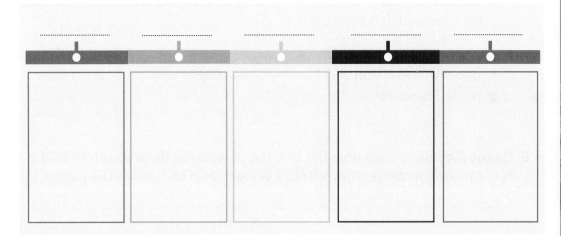

THINKING ABOUT LANGUAGE

A. Use the passive voice to reword and combine the pairs of sentences below. Underline the passive voice verbs. Then compare sentences with a partner. Each item has more than one correct answer.

1. a. Gold nanoparticles are an example of a light-sensitive nanomaterial.
   b. Figure 2 depicts this.

   Gold nanoparticles, which are an example of a light-sensitive nanomaterial, are depicted in Figure 2.

2. a. Liposomes, for example, are like tiny, spherical bubbles.
   b. Figure 3 illustrates this.

   ....

3. a. Dendrimers are somewhat branchlike in appearance.
   b. Figure 4 shows this.

   ....

4. a. Figure 2 shows this.

   b. The walls of a stent are a woven mesh material.

   _____

5. a. Figure 1 shows this.

   b. This material is semirigid and holds its shape well despite being flexible and permeable.

   _____

6. a. Figure 2 demonstrates this.

   b. The catheter is inserted into a blood vessel in the groin and threaded through the vessel until it reaches the heart.

   _____

7. a. You can see a close-up of a hip replacement implant.

   b. Figure 3 depicts this.

   _____

B. Choose five other visuals from this unit. Use phrases like those you underlined in Part A to write sentences that refer to a key feature in each visual. Use passive voice.

1. _____

2. _____

3. _____

4. _____

5. _____

◉ **Go to MyEnglishLab to watch Professor Heilshorn's concluding video and to complete a self-assessment.**

Extended Reading

Part 3 presents authentic academic content written and delivered by university professors. Academically rigorous application and assessment activities allow for a synthesis of the skills developed in Parts 1 and 2.

LINGUISTICS

Accent and Affect

UNIT PROFILE

In this unit, you will read an essay about the connection between accent and *affect*, or emotions. In particular, you will learn about the effects of smiling on vowel sounds, and how different regional accents can communicate positive and negative affect. In the online extended reading, you will learn about vocal fry, or *creaky voice*. As a capstone to the unit, you will research how other accents of English are produced and affect vowel production.

EXTENDED READING

BEFORE YOU READ

Think about these questions before you read "The Effects of Smiling on Your Accent." Discuss them with another student.

1. What factors determine people's accents? In other words, what can you tell about people by their accents?

2. How can our affect influence the sound of our voice? Give examples.

3. How might smiling affect the way we produce vowel sounds?

4. Can accents communicate affect? Do you know of any accents that might convey a positive or negative affect?

READ

Read the essay. Then answer the questions after each section.

The Effects of Smiling on Your Accent

TIP

Previewing a text before you read it can help you to make predictions about the information that might be in the passage. You can preview a text before you read it by noticing the title, looking at visuals, and reading the introduction, conclusion, and subheadings to help you form questions you would like the text to answer. To learn more or to review previewing a text, refer to LINGUISTICS, Part 1, page 7.

Glossary

Correlate: to closely relate to

Discern: to see or hear something, especially something that is not easy to see or hear

Acoustic: relating to sound and the way people hear things

Retract: to move back; withdraw

Resonate: to produce a frequency of vibration

Formant: a band of frequency that determines the phonetic quality of a vowel.

Manipulate: to make something move, turn, or change in the way that you want

Taboo: describes a subject, word, activity, etc., that people avoid because they think it is extremely offensive or embarrassing

1 We usually think about accents in terms of geography. In fact, we typically label accents according to the countries (British), regions (Southern), states (California), or cities (New York City) where they are spoken. But accents convey much more about their speakers than simply where they live or grew up. We can define an *accent* as "a recognizable set of speech sounds that distinguishes speakers on the basis of identity." The strength of our accents might communicate information about relatively stable aspects of identity, such as age, gender, social class, race, and even our political orientations.

(Continued)

Accent strength can also signal more ephemeral dimensions of our identities, such as expressions of affect. Of course, even though we use language to display affect, we also draw on other modalities, including how we configure our bodies, to express emotion. This essay focuses on one form of embodied affect—the act of smiling—and explores its connection to the predominant accent in California. I will show that speakers produce stronger California accents when they are smiling and suggest the value of thinking about regional accents in terms of their potential to signal affect.

2 Before discussing the connection between language and affect, we need to establish the more transparent connection between smiling and affect. Smiles can convey a variety of affective stances, and even though they vary in terms of their sincerity, foundational work in psychology has illustrated that they are conventionally used to communicate positive affect. For example, Ekman, Friesen, and Ancoli (1980) asked subjects to watch a video and then report on their emotional states, after which the subjects' facial expressions were measured. They found that people who smiled more were more likely to have reported being happy, and also that the magnitude of their smiles correlated with the intensity of their reported happiness.

3 It turns out that smiles are observable not just visually, but also auditorily—that is, smiles can be heard. Drahota, Costall, and Reddy (2008) report that subjects can discern whether speakers are smiling on the basis of audio alone. That smiles are hearable can be attributed, at least in part, to the fact that the physical act of smiling has acoustic consequences. As the lips spread and retract for a smile, the lips become thinner at the front of the mouth (Fagel 2010), which shortens the vocal tract. More specifically, it is the part of the vocal tract *in front of* the tongue that is shortening. Effectively, this part of the vocal tract forms a tube, which resonates at a frequency known as the second formant (or F2, for short). When the front tube shortens, like it does during a smile, the F2 is higher. Compare a piccolo to a flute; the former is higher (resonates at a higher frequency) because it is shorter. F2 works in the same way.

Piccolo   Flute

4 Speakers can manipulate F2 by smiling (which shortens the front tube of the vocal tract), but they can also do it by virtue of how they position their tongues during pronunciation of a vowel. Pushing the tongue forward also shortens the front tube, which can have a similar effect on F2 as smiling. A handful of linguists have argued that speakers manipulate their tongue position, and thus F2, to attain social goals.

Wong (2014), for instance, argues that Irene (a preadolescent New Yorker) produces the word *poop* with a high F2 to offset the social offense of discussing a taboo topic. Similarly, Eckert (2010) argues that Collette (a preadolescent from Northern California) produces low F2 in order to convey a stance of negative affect.

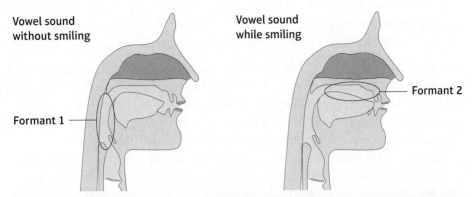

Figure 1: The effects of smiling on vowel production

5   Even though the size of the vocal tract's front cavity can signal information about affect, it also signals information about the speaker's regional accent. For example, vowel sounds that are usually pronounced with the tongue relatively far back in the mouth (as in words like *goose, foot,* and *goat*) are produced with fronter tongue positions in many regional accents, including the California accent. The fronting of the back vowels is an element of what linguists sometimes describe as the California vowel shift. Linguists characterize this as a *shift* because speakers' tongue positions for these vowels are not stable over time, but instead shift from backer to fronter. Each new generation of speakers produces a fronter tongue position different from that of the generation before. Another important element of the California vowel shift is the lowering (and to some extent, retraction) of the front lax vowels. The front vowels of English are typically divided into tense vowels and lax vowels. Tense vowels include those in words like *fleece* and *face*, while lax vowels include those in words like *kit, dress,* and *trap*. In California the lax vowels are lowering (and backing), to the point that *kit* sounds like "ket," *dress* sounds like "drass," and *trap* sounds like "trop."

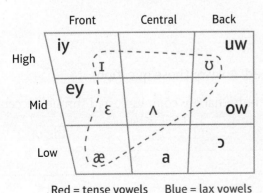

Red = tense vowels   Blue = lax vowels   **Figure 2**

(Continued)

6   Previous studies that have drawn a connection between vowel pronunciation and affect have been limited in two respects. First, they have focused on the behavior of single individuals, which constrains our ability to draw generalizations. Second, they have not considered whether speakers are smiling when they are producing vowels with higher $F2$ values. It is therefore unclear whether higher $F2$ values are simply automatic consequences of smiling, which speakers typically do when expressing positive affect, or whether the connection between affect and vowel production is more fundamental.

7   In order to address these two limitations, my colleagues and I conducted a larger-scale study that investigated not only vowel acoustics but also whether speakers were smiling when they produced particular vowels. A group of 42 speakers (26 female, 16 male), all native speakers of Western United States variety of English, came to the International Sociophonetics Laboratory at Stanford University and engaged in unscripted conversation with someone they already knew for about 30 minutes. The laboratory was staged like a living room (to encourage relatively unguarded conversation) but had the acoustical specifications of a sound-recording booth (so that high-quality audio recordings could be collected). The laboratory was further equipped with inconspicuous video cameras so that various forms of embodiment, such as smiling, could be analyzed. All participants nevertheless knew that they were being recorded in both the audio and video modalities. Acoustic measurements were obtained automatically by script, and all formant values were normalized to eliminate the effects of differently-sized vocal tracts. Whether speakers were smiling was determined by running each frame of video recordings through a smiling classifier trained on hand-annotated photographic data. In the end, the study analyzed all 23,311 tokens of stressed vowels produced by the 42 speakers.

TIP

Recognizing and understanding statements of opinion can help you get the full meaning of a reading and interpret the author's attitude toward a topic. One way to recognize opinions is to look for subjective (qualitative) adjectives and adverbs that signal the author's opinion.

To learn more or to review recognizing and understanding statements of opinion, refer to LINGUISTICS, Part 2, page 170.

CHECK WHAT YOU'VE LEARNED

PARAGRAPHS 1–7

A. Think about the section you just read. Answer these questions.

1. Name six aspects of a person's identity that are communicated through accent. Which one is the least stable?

....

....

2. How does smiling affect the sound of the voice?

....

....

3. What are two elements of the California vowel shift? How is it changing over time?

....

....

4. In Paragraph 4, the author states that speakers can manipulate their tongue position to achieve social goals. How does he support this idea?

....

....

5. In Paragraph 6, the author states that "previous studies that have drawn a connection between vowel pronunciation and affect have been limited in two respects." Is this a statement of fact or opinion? How do you know? What is the purpose of pointing out the limitations in previous studies?

....

....

B. Read the section again. Check your answers. Then continue to the next section.

The Effects of Smiling on Your Accent, *continued*

8 I will focus on both components of the vowel shift discussed above, the fronting of the back vowels and the lowering of the front lax vowels, beginning with the former. While a number of the back vowels are undergoing fronting in California, my discussion will center on the vowel in *goat* only. Other vowels, such as those in *goose* and *foot*, occur less frequently and therefore yield insufficient numbers for proper statistical representation. It is important to note that even though I will not discuss at length the effects of linguistic factors on the F2 of *goat* and other vowels, such factors were included in the statistical models. That is, any effects of smiling occur over and above the effects of other factors.

Glossary

Reflex: a sudden movement that the muscles make as a natural reaction to a physical effect

Arousal: excitement

Amplitude: the distance between the middle and the top or bottom of a wave such as a sound wave

Toughness: the quality of not being weak or easily defeated

Alluded to: mentioned in an indirect way

Decoding: translating a secret or complicated message or a signal into a form that can be easily understood

Covert: secret or hidden

(Continued)

The F2 of *goat* is higher (i.e., the vowel sounds as if it is produced with a fronter tongue position) for shorter vowels and after consonants that are produced with the tip of the tongue. There is no effect of speaker age, and male speakers tend to produce higher F2 than female speakers. Most importantly for the purposes of the question at hand, vowels that were produced while smiling exhibited a higher F2 than vowels that were not smiled.

9 The fact that smiled vowels are characterized by higher F2 is, on the one hand, an expected finding. On the other hand, we have to ask whether smiling is a confound here. Is a higher formant frequency an automatic consequence of smiling, or is there a deeper connection between affect and vowel quality? One way to address this question is to examine variation in some other dimension along which vowel pronunciation can vary. While F2 characterizes the length of the front cavity in the pronunciation of a vowel, the first formant (F1) characterizes the length of the back cavity (between the vocal folds and the place in the mouth where the tongue reaches its highest position). So high vowels have a relatively long back cavity, and thus a low F1, while low vowels have a relatively short back cavity, and thus a high F1. The F1 patterns for the front lax vowels in California would be especially illuminating, since—in contrast to F2—F1 is not directly influenced by the physical act of smiling. If there is a fundamental connection between affect and the vowel qualities characterizing the Western shift, we should still observe a correlation between smiling and F1.

10 Turning to the results for F1 on the front lax vowels (*kit, dress,* and *trap*), we see that F1 is influenced by duration (longer vowels have higher F1) and that there is no effect of speaker age or sex. But we see a strong effect of smiling, such that speakers produce higher F1 (i.e., the vowel is produced with a lower tongue position) in phrases when they are smiling. We can therefore conclude that movement in the F1 dimension—the shifting of the front lax vowels—is not an automatic reflex of smiling.

11 Patterns for an additional form of embodied affect—overall body movement—further support the claim that accent features like vowel production convey affect. Work in both psychology and kinesiology has shown that the extent to which speakers move their bodies overall directly correlates with emotional arousal, or the intensity of emotion (Pollick et al. 2001; Pollick et al. 2002; Camurri et al. 2003; Atkinson et al. 2007). Accordingly, the amount of movement in all the video data was quantified using the method advanced in Voigt et al. (2013), which dynamically sums the number of pixels that change value across frames, resulting in what they call a *movement amplitude measure*. Results reveal that movement amplitude correlates with F1, such that vowels exhibit higher F1 (or are more shifted) when speakers are moving their bodies more; the effect of movement amplitude is greater for *dress* and *trap* than it is for *kit*. The movement amplitude data provide additional evidence for the connection between vowel production and affect, and crucially (and in contrast to smiling), this form of embodied affect has no direct influence on vowel acoustics.

12 To sum up, we have seen evidence that California vowels are more shifted when speakers are smiling (and expressing positive affect). Importantly, these smiled vowels are more strongly shifted regardless of the direction in which vowels are shifting—the back vowel, *goat*, shows the same pattern as the front lax vowels, *kit, dress,* and *trap.*

13 What do these findings suggest? At a minimum, it appears that the range of meanings that accents can communicate must expand to include affect. I would also like to suggest the value of thinking about regional accents in terms of their affective valences. The geographical region that anchors each accent is emblematically represented by character types that embody particular kinds of affect. For example, I have argued that shifted vowels in the West, particularly in California, convey positive affect, affect that can be found in representations like surfers, Valley girls, and less specifically Californian types like slackers and stoners. The same pattern would not be expected in other varieties, especially ones associated with working-class toughness, as found in Eastern cities like Philadelphia and Pittsburgh. It is quite possible that the shifted vowels of these accents correlate with expressions of negative affect, exhibiting opposite patterns from those presented here for California. And of course, Southern English might pattern differently still, as a warm, friendly affect underlies many of this region's character types, including the Southern belle, and even more negative representations, such as the redneck. I do not mean to suggest that all components of a regional accent should necessarily pattern the same way in terms of affect. Eckert (2000) found that some components of the Northern Cities vowel shift, such as fronted variants of *lot*, were led by the more middle-class, corporate-oriented jocks of the high schools she studied in suburban Detroit. Yet other components of the shift, such as backed *dress*, were more prevalent in the speech of working-class, locally-oriented burnouts. Clearly, these two groups participate in very different kinds of affective display, with jocks generally valuing positive affect, while negative affect affords burnouts greater social currency.

14 In an influential paper on language and affect, Benier (1990: 428, emphasis added) explains that even though the expression of affect is important to human interaction, its linguistic rendering is indirect: "In probably all speech communities, emotions can be described (e.g., *I hate him*) although such overt avowals in the first person are likely to be associated with rather marked situations. More commonly, emotions are *alluded to*, and the decoding task is a process of 'reading off' complex *covert* messages." As language users, we always have access to a symbolic resource: our regional accents. So while our words are busy conveying one message, we recruit our accents to simultaneously convey another one.

CHECK WHAT YOU'VE LEARNED
PARAGRAPHS 8–14

A. Think about the section you just read. Answer these questions.

6. What connection did the researchers find between smiling and F2?

   ....

   ....

7. How is F1 different from F2? Why is that significant for this study?

   ....

   ....

8. How does body movement affect F1? How does that support a connection between affect and vowel production?

   ....

   ....

9. What conclusion does the author make about accents based on the results of this study?

   ....

   ....

10. In Paragraph 13, the author states that negative affect "affords burnouts greater social currency." What is the author suggesting about burnouts?

    ....

    ....

11. In Paragraph 14, the author quotes another researcher when he states, "More commonly, emotions are *alluded to*, and the decoding task is a process of 'reading off' complex *covert* messages." How does this quote support the author's ideas about accent and affect?

    ....

    ....

B. Read the section again. Check your answers.

C. Summarize in your own words the key points of the reading.

THINKING CRITICALLY

Think about the situation considering what you have read in "The Effects of Smiling on Your Accent." With a partner, apply what you know about accents and affect to respond to the situation.

According to the author, emotions are usually expressed indirectly. For example, speakers can manipulate their tongues to produce a positive affect. With your partner, discuss some other ways that speakers can manipulate their voice to produce a positive affect. For example, what are some ways speakers can sound happy, excited, or friendly? Provide examples.

◐ Go to MyEnglishLab to complete a critical thinking exercise.

THINKING VISUALLY

A. Work with a partner. Look back at Figure 1 (p. 329) from the reading. Discuss how the changes in the vocal tract that occur while smiling affect the way that vowel sounds are produced. Provide examples of words mentioned in the reading that demonstrate this effect.

B. Review what you read about the effect of body movement on vowel production. Using Figure 1 as a model, create a graphic that demonstrates this effect. Your graphic should show how vowels shift to affect F1.

THINKING ABOUT LANGUAGE

UNDERSTANDING PRO-FORMS

Underline pro-forms in the following excerpts from the essay. Then draw an arrow to the word or words they replace.

1. Smiles can convey a variety of affective stances, and even though they vary in terms of their sincerity, foundational work in psychology has illustrated that they are conventionally used to communicate positive affect.

2. When the front tube shortens, like it does during a smile, the F2 is higher. Compare a piccolo to a flute; the former is higher (resonates at a higher frequency) because it is shorter.

3. The fronting of the back vowels is an element of what linguists sometimes describe as the California vowel shift. Linguists characterize this as a *shift* because speakers' tongue positions for these vowels are not stable over time, but instead shift from backer to fronter.

4. Previous studies that have drawn a connection between vowel pronunciation and affect have been limited in two respects. First, they have focused on the behavior of single individuals, which constrains our ability to draw generalizations. Second, they have not considered whether speakers are smiling when they are producing vowels with higher F2 values.

5. It is therefore unclear whether higher F2 values are simply automatic consequences of smiling, which speakers typically do when expressing positive affect, or whether the connection between affect and vowel production is more fundamental.

6. The same pattern would not be expected in other varieties, especially ones associated with working-class toughness, as found in Eastern cities like Philadelphia and Pittsburgh.

UNDERSTANDING STRUCTURES USED FOR HEDGING

Read these excerpts from the essay. Underline the words and phrases used for hedging.

1. I will show that speakers produce stronger California accents when they are smiling and suggest the value of thinking about regional accents in terms of their potential to signal affect.

2. That smiles are hearable can be attributed, at least in part, to the fact that the physical act of smiling has acoustic consequences.

3. Another important element of the California vowel shift is the lowering (and to some extent, retraction) of the front lax vowels.

4. The front vowels of English are typically divided into tense vowels and lax vowels.

5. The laboratory was staged like a living room (to encourage relatively unguarded conversation), but had the acoustical specifications of a sound-recording booth (so that high-quality audio recordings could be collected).

6. At a minimum, it appears that the range of meanings that accents can communicate must expand to include affect. I would also like to suggest the value of thinking about regional accents in terms of their affective valences.

7. It is quite possible that the shifted vowels of these accents correlate with expressions of negative affect, exhibiting opposite patterns from those presented here for California. And of course, Southern English might pattern differently still, as a warm, friendly affect underlies many of this region's character types, including the Southern belle, and even more negative representations, such as the redneck.

8. In probably all speech communities, emotions can be described (e.g., *I hate him*) although such overt avowals in the first person are likely to be associated with rather marked situations.

🔊 Go to MyEnglishLab for more practice reading an extended text and using your reading skills.

RESEARCH PROJECT

The reading in this unit discusses qualities of the California accent and how the California shift affects vowel production. By doing additional research, you can learn how other accents of English are produced and affect vowel production.

A. The following is a list of English-speaking countries. **Choose one of these countries and then find a region within it to research.**

- England
- Scotland
- Wales
- Ireland

- the United States
- Canada
- Australia
- New Zealand

B. **Conduct your research. As you read about your subject, formulate a thesis. Gather information that supports your thesis. Use the following ideas to help guide you:**

- Interview a native speaker of the accent, and record your interaction or obtain a recording online.
- Explain how certain vowel or consonant sounds are produced that distinguish this accent from others.
- Identify any changes or shifts that have occurred in this accent.

C. **Create a list of discussion questions about interesting points related to your topic. Choose a presentation style from the box, or use your own idea, and present your research to the class. Then pose the questions to the class and have a group discussion.**

short audio documentary
short lecture with audio and visuals
short video documentary

Go to MyEnglishLab to complete a collaborative activity.

How cultural and ethical values define a successful business

BUSINESS ETHICS

Sustaining Values

UNIT PROFILE

In this unit, you will read an essay about the role played by Goldman Sachs in causing the Great Recession of 2007–2009 and the public mistrust that developed as a result. In the online extended reading, you will learn about frameworks for engaging in a global business context and explore the influence of religion in understanding business cultures in different areas of the world. As a capstone to the unit, you will research another organization that has experienced fraud or ethics violations.

338   BUSINESS ETHICS   PART 3

Goldman Sachs is a large multinational investment bank that is based in New York City. The Great Recession was a period of economic decline that caused severe reductions in economic production and investment and high levels of unemployment in many countries across the globe. It began with a collapse of the real estate market that caused many homeowners to lose their homes through foreclosure, meaning they were unable to pay banks back enough of the money they borrowed to buy their properties.

EXTENDED READING

BEFORE YOU READ

Think about these questions before you read "Sustaining Values: Goldman Sachs After 2008." Discuss them with another student.

1. Were you or anyone you know affected by the Great Recession? If so, what happened? Who or what do you think was to blame for the financial crisis?

2. What do investment banks do? How did they contribute to the Great Recession?

3. What should businesses consider in order to make ethical decisions?

4. What ethical challenges do you think investment bankers face? How can CEOs of investment banks such as Goldman Sachs create an ethical environment within their organizations?

READ

Read the essay. Then answer the questions after each section.

Sustaining Values: Goldman Sachs After 2008

1 How can a business create and maintain a positive ethical climate over time, especially after an economic crisis that it seems to have had an important role in causing? Public anger and mistrust focused on Wall Street investment bank Goldman Sachs during and after the Great Recession of 2007–2009.

Glossary

Compensation: money paid to employees in exchange for the services they provide, including salaries, cash rewards, and benefits

Subprime mortgages: home loans given to borrowers who are at high risk of being unable to repay the money they have borrowed

Bankrupt (v): to cause to be unable to pay debts

Federal Reserve System: the central bank of the United States that regulates the US monetary and financial system

Contained: controlled

Bailout money: money paid or lent by a government to a business to save it from failing

Securities and Exchange Commission (SEC): the US government regulatory agency that oversees financial markets

Disclose: to make information known publicly

(Continued)

This essay describes the background and then presents a practical framework for analysis that can be used in any situation of moral decision making in business.

2 In 2007, when more than 40 percent of total corporate profits in America came from the financial services sector, Goldman Sachs was the lead Wall Street firm. It accounted for $20 billion of the $53 billion in total compensation for those who worked in the financial industry that year. CEO Lloyd Blankfein took home $68 million, and Goldman compensation amounted to $661,000 per employee (Sorkin 2009). Wall Street firms were creating risky investments by fashioning and selling (and buying) financial products that packaged subprime mortgages that had been sold to low-income real estate buyers, often with little or no documentation. Meanwhile, these firms were highly leveraged with a debt to capital ratio of 32-to-1. That is, they had only $1 on hand to pay off every $32 in debt that they had incurred.

CULTURE NOTE

Wall Street is a street in the Financial District of Manhattan in New York City. Two of the world's largest stock exchanges are located there, and Wall Street is known as the leading financial center of the world. Many people refer to investment banks as "Wall Street." On the other hand, "Main Street" is often used to refer to individuals who invest their money but do not work for financial and investment companies. It can also be used to refer to the interests of working people and small businesses.

3 Although it was known that a collapse in the real estate market could bankrupt Wall Street firms and radically affect liquidity and credit availability, not only on Wall Street but also nationwide and even worldwide, somehow few people were able to foresee what was coming. Ben Bernanke, chairman of the Federal Reserve System from 2006 to 2014, testified before Congress's Joint Economic Committee in March 2007 that "The impact on the broader economy and the financial markets of the problems in the subprime markets seems likely to be contained." Before joining the Federal Reserve, Bernanke had been a tenured professor of economics at Princeton University and was an expert on the Great Depression. Less than a half-year after his testimony, the $2 trillion subprime market had collapsed.

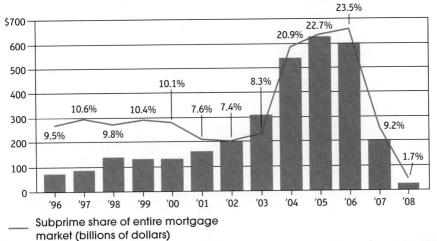

Figure 1: Subprime mortgage market, 1996–2008

Subprime share of entire mortgage market (billions of dollars)

4   Between March and October of 2008, three of the top five Wall Street firms had been bought out at huge discounts or gone bankrupt. The two remaining, Morgan Stanley and Goldman Sachs, had converted from investment banks to bank holding companies, regulated by the Federal Reserve, and had been provided taxpayer bailout money in the amount of $10 billion each. The government assistance was repaid with interest by June 2009, though. Goldman Sachs went on to report $3.4 billion in earnings for the second quarter of 2009. As 2.8 million properties received notices of foreclosure in the United States in 2009, and the US unemployment rate soared past 10 percent, Goldman Sachs received a lot of blame. As Lloyd Blankfein later explained, "We became symbols of Wall Street greed. People didn't like us, didn't trust us. Goodwill was reduced to a thimble."

5   In April of 2010 Goldman found itself in more trouble when the Securities and Exchange Commission (SEC) filed a civil fraud complaint against the firm "for making materially misleading statements and omissions in connection with a synthetic collateralized debt obligation [that Goldman Sachs] structured and marketed to investors." Essentially, the issue was not disclosing to its clients that the high-risk instruments it was selling to them were at the same time being bet against by Goldman itself taking a financial short position. As he was pressed on this in a US Senate hearing later in the month, Blankfein was told, "Goldman Sachs did well when its clients lost money. Its conduct brings into question the whole function of Wall Street." Internal emails were found where Goldman Sachs employees knew that the securities they were selling were "junk" or "a piece of crap" and were simultaneously taking a short position against them to benefit Goldman Sachs's own account. Two months later Goldman Sachs agreed to pay a record $550 million penalty to settle the SEC charges.

(Continued)

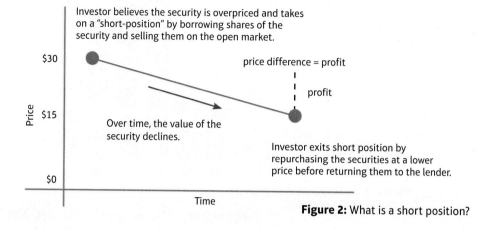

Short selling is an investment strategy that investors use to make a profit when they believe that a shares of a security are overpriced and the price will decline.

Investor believes the security is overpriced and takes on a "short-position" by borrowing shares of the security and selling them on the open market.

$30

price difference = profit

profit

Price

$15

Over time, the value of the security declines.

Investor exits short position by repurchasing the securities at a lower price before returning them to the lender.

$0

Time

Figure 2: What is a short position?

CHECK WHAT YOU'VE LEARNED
PARAGRAPHS 1–5

A. Think about the section you just read. Answer this question.

1. What caused public anger and mistrust of Goldman Sachs during and after the Great Recession of 2007–2009? ....

....

....

....

2. In Paragraph 3, the author describes the response of Ben Bernanke, the chairman of the Federal Reserve System from 2006 to 2014, to the potential problems in the economy in 2007. What type of support does the author provide to explain Ben Bernanke's response to the financial situation in 2007? What details does the author mention about Bernanke's qualifications? What might this imply about Bernanke's response to the financial situation in 2007?

....

....

B. Read the section again. Check your answers. Then continue to the next section.

Sustaining Values: Goldman Sachs After 2008, *continued*

6 So, what are the ethical issues at this point, and what should CEO Blankfein do about them? Harvard ethicist Ralph Potter some 50 years ago created what is now affectionately known as "Potter's Box" as a tool to facilitate ethical decision making. It has four quadrants: facts, values, principles, and loyalties. Let us work through each of them to analyze how Lloyd Blankfein might be helped in sorting out his thinking.

> ### Glossary
>
> Transparency: the quality of allowing people to see the way you do things so they can see that you are doing things honestly and fairly
>
> Stakeholders: people, groups, or organizations that have an interest in or are affected by a business
>
> Shareholders: people who own stock in a business

7 First, in relation to facts, Blankfein needs to know exactly what his employees did, and may be continuing to do, and who knew or knows about it at what point. Likewise, what kind of instruments are currently being created or sold by Goldman Sachs, and how much transparency is being provided to its clients about them, their pricing, and their market prospects? What is the reality of Goldman Sach's internal culture, and how are employees being trained and supervised?

FACTS	VALUES
PRINCIPLES	LOYALTIES

Figure 3: Potter's Box

8 Second, regarding loyalties, Blankfein needs to enumerate and prioritize all of the stakeholders or constituencies that are affected by the actions of Goldman Sachs. Certainly its clients are up near the top of the list, and traditionally the firm's stockholders or owners would have the highest priority. Then there are its own employees and the financial industry as a whole. What about the homeowner mortgagors or borrowers on "Main Street" who lie behind the real estate instruments Goldman has been selling? There are also government regulators and the taxpayers who could be asked to guarantee the risks that Goldman Sachs takes through providing bailout money if needed. How about the country as a whole, and the world beyond, if the actions of Wall Street firms could be contributing to creating a major recession or even depression? Of course, the CEO will doubtless be thinking about himself too: Could he face major losses (or gains) in his compensation, be fired, or find himself facing major civil or criminal liability that might land him in a state or federal penitentiary?

(Continued)

9   Third, Blankfein will be using a particular mode or modes of ethical reasoning in his decision making, whether he recognizes it explicitly or not. He may be using ends-based reasoning—like asking how to make the greatest profit (or avoid the greatest losses) or how to realize the greatest good for the greatest number of a particular stakeholder group or of all the stakeholders as a whole. Or, he may be using duty-based reasoning, thinking about what specific responsibilities are owed to particular stakeholders—say, full disclosure and transparency for its clients while avoiding conflicts of interest; benefitting shareholders; helping employees thrive; making sure the financial industry as a whole is not damaged and liquidity can continue to be provided to society as a whole; not contributing to mortgage default and loss of peoples' homes; being just and law-abiding in relationship to the government and its regulators; and not creating greater burdens on taxpayers or putting the national or world economy at risk. Or, Blankfein might be using virtue-based reasoning: furthering virtues like honesty, prudence, fairness, courage, trust, and respect, while avoiding vices like lying, recklessness, cheating, stealing, arrogance, greed, and envy.

10 Fourth, whether he knows it or not, Blankfein as CEO will be operating within a particular worldview, say, of "economic man," who pursues self-interest single mindedly in a free market, which then supposedly maximizes the distribution of goods and services through the "invisible hand" referenced by economist Adam Smith; or of an American citizen trying to uphold legal rights of life, liberty, and property for all; or of a nationalist trying to put America first and make the United States the most competitively successful country in the world; or of a religious person who thinks first about the plight of "widows and orphans" or operates with a "preferential option for the poor"; or a number of other possible worldviews.

TIP

Identifying main ideas and supporting details can help you to focus on the key points in a text and the evidence that supports those points. To determine the main idea of a text or paragraph, ask yourself the question "What is the writer's main point or main comment about the topic?" To identify types of supporting details, look for definitions, examples, facts, reasons, and quotations that support the writer's main idea.

To learn more or to review identifying main ideas and supporting details, see BUSINESS ETHICS, Part 1, page 33.

CHECK WHAT YOU'VE LEARNED
PARAGRAPHS 6–10

A. Think about what you just read. Answer these questions.

3. According to the author, what are the four areas that CEO Lloyd Blankfein should consider to address ethical issues at Goldman Sachs?

....

....

4. Who are the stakeholders that are affected by Goldman Sachs?

....

....

5. Which of the four quadrants of Potter's Box does the author consider to be most important for Blankfein to identify? Why?

....

....

6. In Paragraph 10, the author states that "whether he knows it or not, Blankfein will be operating within a particular worldview." What does the statement "whether he knows it or not" imply about a person's worldview?

....

....

B. Read Paragraphs 6–10 again. Check your answers. Then continue to the next section of the reading.

Sustaining Values: Goldman Sachs After 2008, *continued*

11 What has Blankfein actually done so far to repair the damage? Starting in 2010, he created a Business Standards Committee to "ensure that the firm's business standards and practices are of the highest quality; that they meet or exceed the expectations of … clients, other stakeholders,

(Continued)

Glossary

Fiduciary: someone who has legal control of the money belonging to others

Due diligence: careful research or analysis of a company or organization done before entering into a business transaction

Reputational: relating to what people think about a person or group based on what happened in the past

Conflict of interest: a situation in which someone cannot make a fair decision because they may be personally affected by the results

Robust: strong and not likely to have problems

Backstop: to prevent from getting worse

and regulators; and that they contribute to overall financial stability and economic opportunity." Eight months later a 63-page "Report of the Business Standards Committee" was released with 39 recommendations for change. There were three core themes that integrated the recommendations and shaped their implementation:

12 1) <u>A higher standard of client care</u>, including distinguishing duties to clients based on what role Goldman Sachs was playing: a) banking advisor (providing the best advice and disclosing conflicts); b) fiduciary or asset and private wealth manager (essentially same as (a), being sure to act in the sole interest of the client); c) underwriter (due diligence on the issuer and disclosing of conflicts; ensuring no material misstatements; making a secondary trading market); d) market maker (standing ready always to both buy and sell; setting pricing reflecting market conditions; but not advising, disclosing conflicts, or acting as a fiduciary).

13 2) <u>Reputational awareness, including classifying clients</u> into three segments based on their experience, capacity, and sophistication (professional investors, institutional accounts, and high net-worth individuals) and also classifying product complexity.

14 3) <u>Individual and collective responsibility, including employee training programs</u> and assessment on annual performance reviews.

15 So, it seems that an "economic man" worldview was used with a stated loyalty priority to clients' interests coming first, followed by government regulators'. Employees were expected to fulfill specific duties, with new training and performance reviews, which related to clients and to legality—in particular providing clarity and transparency about the type of client and product—and avoidance of conflict of interest. Hovering over all was the end or goal of providing superior returns to the firm's shareholders in a highly competitive business environment. Among the stated virtues for individual employees were good judgment, fidelity to the law, honesty, and trustworthiness.

16 What was seemingly missed in this process, though, that a robust use of Potter's Box might have revealed? First, it is unclear how much factual analysis was undertaken of past ethical violations by the firm. A number of important stakeholder loyalties seemed to have been disregarded, starting with the nation and the world and asking what the firm's overall social impact is and what positive benefits it provides to "Main Street" and to society at large. There was no examination of what kind of moral responsibilities were owed to the homeowners whose high-risk mortgages were packaged in complicated financial instruments. There was no consideration of playing a role in industry-wide reforms to help prevent systemic failures in the future, especially if some Wall Street firms continue to be considered "too big to fail" and have their risk-taking backstopped by taxpayers. The size of CEO and employee salaries and bonuses was not addressed, although it had, as a matter of fact, a considerable negative impact on firm reputation and goodwill. There may also have been a lost opportunity to examine the formal "Goldman Sachs Business Principles" that had been in effect for many years, challenging them and possibly rewriting them in relation to what was revealed during the financial crisis.

17 Creating and maintaining a positive corporate ethical climate over time is a difficult task, requiring constant vigilance, appraisal, and renewal. Using Potter's Box as a method of analysis, reflection and decision making can help to provide a wide-ranging and comprehensive view of the values that shape the life of a business enterprise.

TIP

Implications are ideas that a writer does not state directly. Inferences are logical conclusions that you reach based on your background knowledge and evidence that is presented in a text. To make strong inferences, look for clues in the text that indicate the author's intended meaning.

To learn more or to review these strategies, see BUSINESS ETHICS, Part 2, page 195.

CHECK WHAT YOU'VE LEARNED
PARAGRAPHS 11-17

A. Think about what you just read. Answer these questions.

7. In your own words, what is the main idea of this section of the passage?

....

....

8. What were the three core themes recommended by the "Report of the Business Standards Committee" for change at Goldman Sachs?

....

....

9. Which stakeholders' interests were considered most in the changes implemented at Goldman Sachs?

....

....

10. In Paragraph 16, the author asks, "What was seemingly missed in this process, though, that a robust use of Potter's Box might have revealed?" What is the author suggesting about the efforts to create a positive ethical culture at Goldman Sachs?

....

....

11. In Paragraph 16, the author states that "a number of stakeholder loyalties seem to have been disregarded." Which stakeholders does the author mention as having been disregarded by Goldman Sachs? What is the author implying about the ethical obligations of investment banks?

....

....

B. Read the section again. Check your answers.

C. Summarize in your own words the key points of the reading.

THINKING CRITICALLY

Think about the situation considering what you have read in "Sustaining Values: Goldman Sachs after 2008." With a partner, apply what you know about ethical decision making to discuss the situation.

In Paragraph 16, the author mentions several considerations that Goldman Sachs did not take into account in response to the organization's role in causing the financial crisis. Imagine you are the CEO of Goldman Sachs. What other changes would you implement in order to create a more positive ethical environment and prevent future crises from occurring?

▶ Go to MyEnglishLab to complete a critical thinking exercise.

THINKING VISUALLY

A. Work with a partner. Look back at Figure 1 (p. 342) from the reading. Discuss how investment banks took a short position in order to profit from the selling and buying of financial products that packaged subprime mortgages. Why do you think investment banks expected these securities to decline in value?

B. The following information represents the number of US properties that went into foreclosure between 2006 and 2010. Review these numbers and create a graph that best communicates the information.

Year	US Properties with Foreclosure Filings
2006	717,552
2007	1,285,873
2008	2,330,483
2009	2,824,674
2010	2,871,891

THINKING ABOUT LANGUAGE
SIMPLIFYING COMPLEX SENTENCES

Read these excerpts from the reading. Break down each complex sentence into smaller parts and write them on the lines. Compare answers with a partner.

1. Wall Street firms were creating risky investments by fashioning and selling (and buying) financial products that packaged subprime mortgages that had been sold to low-income real estate buyers, often with little or no documentation.

2. Fourth, whether he knows it or not, Blankfein as CEO will be operating within a particular worldview, say, of "economic man," who pursues self-interest single-mindedly in a free market, which then supposedly maximizes the distribution of goods and services through the "invisible hand" referenced by economist Adam Smith; or of an American citizen trying to uphold legal rights of life, liberty, and property for all; or of a nationalist trying to put America first and make the United States the most competitively successful country in the world; or of a religious person who thinks first about the plight of "widows and orphans" or operates with a "preferential option for the poor"; or a number of other possible worldviews.

3. So, it seems that an "economic man" worldview was used with a stated loyalty priority to clients' interests coming first, followed by government regulators'. Employees were expected to fulfill specific duties, with new training and performance reviews, which related to clients and to legality—in particular providing clarity and transparency about the type of client and product—and avoidance of conflict of interest.

UNDERSTANDING NOUN CLAUSES

Read these excerpts from the reading. Underline the noun clauses. Write *S* for subject, *O* for object, or *OP* for object of the preposition.

.... 1. Let us work through each of them to analyze how Lloyd Blankfein might be helped in sorting out his thinking.

.... 2. First, it is unclear how much factual analysis was undertaken of past ethical violations by the firm.

.... 3. Harvard ethicist Ralph Potter some 50 years ago created what is now affectionately known as "Potter's Box" as a tool to facilitate ethical decision making.

.... 4. First, in relation to facts, Blankfein needs to know exactly what his employees did, and may be continuing to do, and who knew or knows about it at what point.

.... 5. He created a Business Standards Committee to "ensure that the firm's business standards and practices are of the highest quality; that they meet or exceed the expectations of … clients, other stakeholders and regulators; and that they contribute to overall financial stability and economic opportunity."

⬥ Go to MyEnglishLab for more practice reading an extended text and using your reading skills.

RESEARCH PROJECT

The reading in this unit discusses how the CEO of Goldman Sachs could have used a framework for ethical decision making to create a positive ethical environment in his organization. By doing additional research, you can learn how other organizations could do the same.

A. The following is a list of companies that have experienced problems due to fraud or ethics violations. Choose one of these companies or another organization not in the list to research.

- Enron
- Worldcom
- Countrywide
- Takata

- Volkswagen
- Lehman Brothers
- Other: ....

B. Conduct your research. As you read about your subject, formulate a thesis. Gather information that supports your thesis. Use the following ideas to help you:

- Find out what type of fraud occurred at the company and what decisions were made that led to problems.

- Explain how using a framework of ethical decision making, such as Potter's Box, could help or could have helped the company's leaders make more ethical decisions.

- Identify changes that could be made or could have been made to create a positive ethical environment.

C. Create a list of discussion questions about interesting points related to your topic. Choose a presentation style from the box or use your own idea, and present your research to the class. Then pose the questions to the class and have a group discussion.

> a group presentation
> a short lecture with visuals
> a panel discussion

⬆ Go to MyEnglishLab to complete a collaborative activity.

Decisions we make today will shape our future

Climate and Environmentalism

UNIT PROFILE

In this unit, you will read an essay about the ways that paleoclimatology can contribute to our understanding of climate and inform our response to climate change. In the online extended reading, you will learn about environmentalism in the 21st century. As a capstone to the unit, you will research climate studies of different regions of the world.

EXTENDED READING

BEFORE YOU READ

Think about these questions before you read "An Introduction to Paleoclimate." Discuss them with another student.

1. Climate is the long-term measure of atmospheric patterns, such as temperature, air pressure, wind, precipitation (rain or snow), and humidity (the amount of water in the air). How does climate vary from one part of the world to another?

2. According to the author, "Paleoclimatology is the study of the natural patterns and trends in Earth's climate system." What are some climate patterns and trends that have occurred in Earth's history?

3. How have humans influenced climate? What are some current effects of climate change?

4. How could an understanding of climate in the past help us to better understand current climate change?

READ

Read the essay. Then answer the questions after each section.

An Introduction to Paleoclimate

1   Paleoclimatology is the study of the natural patterns and trends in Earth's climate system. Why do ice sheets expand and retreat? How do the ocean and atmosphere exchange energy, and carry heat from the tropics and the poles? How has the chemistry of the atmosphere changed through time? In general, what is the overall "baseline" of natural climate variability? These are just a few examples of the overarching questions we explore in this field of science.

Glossary

Hypothetical: based on a situation that is not real but might happen

Gloss over: to ignore something or treat it as if it is not important

Intricacy: a complicated detail

Fluctuate: to change between one level or thing and another

Diffuse: to spread over a large area or in many places

Oscillation: the regular movement between two limits

2   All of these questions are especially important in the context of climate change, so it is important to take a minute to talk about our basic understanding of the human influence on the global climate system. The majority of the energy we humans use—whether it is energy for electricity that powers our homes and businesses, or whether it is energy to power our cars and transportation systems—comes from burning coal, oil, and natural gas. Collectively, these sources of energy are known as fossil fuels, and when we ignite fossil fuels, we release carbon dioxide and other greenhouse gases into the atmosphere.

(Continued)

These gases essentially act like a blanket that traps heat. The more greenhouse gases we put in the atmosphere, the more heat is trapped at Earth's surface. Over the last 250 years or so we have been burning fossil fuels at an increasingly higher rate, and greenhouse gases are reaching

TIP

Understanding cause, effect, and correlation can help you to see how certain events are connected to one another. Understanding the language used to signal these relationships can also help you to make predictions as you read, organize your notes, and increase comprehension.

To learn more or to review the language that signals cause, effect, and correlation, see EARTH SCIENCE, Part 2, page 235.

levels in our atmosphere not seen in hundreds of thousands of years. As a result, the best available instrumental data shows that the global temperature has been on a steady march upward for several decades.

Some radition is reflected from the Earth and its atmosphere.

Some infared radiation is absorbed by greenhouse gases and re-emitted into the atmosphere. This warms the Earth's surface and low atmosphere. Some passes through the atmosphere.

Atmosphere

Earth's surface

Infared radiation is emitted by the Earth.

Some radiation is absorbed by the Earth to heat the surface.

Figure 1: The greenhouse effect

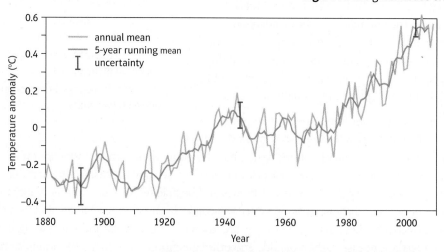

Figure 2: Global mean surface temperature, 1880–2000

3   Just to be clear, climate change is not some far-off threat or hypothetical concept. The temperature of the planet has already risen to some of the highest levels ever recorded, and if our society does not transition to low-carbon energy sources soon, the problem is going to become significantly worse in the coming decades.

4   So, at first pass all of this sounds very troubling, but nonetheless easy to understand. However, this explanation of climate change glosses over many important details. Earth's climate is a complex system, and understanding the intricacies, connections, and processes is important for both minimizing the harm of climate change and preparing for its impacts. There are natural cycles in the climate that may help explain more subtle patterns from year to year, decade to decade, and century to century. This is where paleoclimate comes into play. A more detailed understanding of the internal workings of the climate can help inform our decisions as a society as we face this enormous problem.

5   To put it another way, the fundamental connection between greenhouse gas emissions and climate change is well understood, but there are important scientific questions that scientists still hope to answer. Just how sensitive is Earth to changes in greenhouse gases? How do greenhouse gases fluctuate naturally, and how does that compare with the speed of greenhouse-gas accumulation in the atmosphere today? Are there unknown tipping points in the climate systems, or will Earth respond to warming in a uniform and predictable fashion?

6   From a scientific standpoint, there are a few ways to approach these questions. One strategy is to build models that represent fundamental processes in the climate system. Among other aims, these models seek to capture the physics and chemistry of the ocean, the land, the biosphere, the atmosphere, and, maybe most importantly, how the different parts of Earth interact with one another. It is also necessary to understand the overall energy budget for our planet, which means understanding how we receive energy from the sun and how that energy is distributed and circulated around Earth.

7   So before going any further, it is helpful to stop and explain some of the essential features of Earth's climate system. The oceans cover 70 percent of Earth's surface, and ocean circulation is a key part of how our planet redistributes energy around the globe. The ocean and the atmosphere are connected—you might even say they "communicate" with one another—so scientists often talk about the coupled ocean–atmosphere system. Ultimately all of the energy on Earth is derived from the sun, and scientists call this *incoming solar radiation*. The majority of incoming solar radiation is concentrated at the tropics, and incoming solar radiation becomes more diffuse as you move poleward from the equator. If there were no ocean–atmosphere circulation—that is, no mechanism for redistributing energy around our planet—the tropics would be significantly hotter, and the North and South Poles would be much colder. All of this is important because understanding the climate system in large part starts with developing an appreciation for the role ocean–atmosphere circulation on *all* time scales.

(Continued)

8   Direct measurements of Earth's climate are somewhat scarce, and this poses a challenge for climate scientists. There are a handful of instrumental measurements that date back a few centuries, but it really wasn't until the 20th century that we had true global coverage of weather stations and other climate monitoring systems. Beginning shortly after World War II, there was an international effort to have weather stations recording standard information. Global coverage of the climate system improved dramatically starting in the 1970s when the National Aeronautics and Space Administration (NASA) and other space agencies launched satellites to measure Earth. As you might imagine, the relatively short period of instrumental climate coverage makes it hard to understand climate change in the distant past. Once again, this is why paleoclimate is important.

9   So how exactly do we collect information about the past, about the time periods before humans were measuring variables like temperature, precipitation, wind, humidity, cloudiness, and everything else related to the climate? This question of time scale becomes very overwhelming when you consider the fact that Earth is about 4.6 billion years old. Fortunately, not all time scales are relevant to understanding the problem of global warming, but nevertheless it is helpful to begin with the big picture before zooming to time scales of years and decades.

10   When we look at the climate system on time scales of thousands to hundreds of thousands of years, glacial–interglacial cycles are partially explained by Milankovitch cycles. These cycles are named after the Serbian scientist Milutin Milankovitch, who first described these processes in the early 20th century. Milankovitch's contributions came to be the foundation of our understanding for why Earth periodically goes into and out of ice ages. Scientists refer to the advance and retreat of ice sheets as glacial–interglacial cycles.

11   Simply put, the Milankovitch theory describes small variations in the way Earth revolves around the sun. Collectively these are called *orbital variations*. For example, there are time periods when Earth travels around the sun in a pattern that looks more like an oval, and there are other phases where the pattern is more like a circle. The oscillation between the more oval pattern and the more circular pattern is referred to as the eccentricity cycle. Another orbital variation is the axial tilt, which refers to phases when the tilt of Earth's axis is more at an angle versus more straight up and down. The third and final orbital variation is the precessional cycle, which you can envision as Earth wobbling like a spinning top. It turns out that all three of these orbital variations are predictable because they are the result of gravitational pull acting on Earth from different celestial bodies in our solar system. Each of these orbital cycles is important because it changes the year-to-year timing of when Earth is exposed to energy from the sun. For example, if the Milankovitch cycles align in such a way so that Earth experiences especially cold winters in the Northern Hemisphere and these conditions persist for thousands of years, ice sheets can grow

and extend further each winter. Milankovitch modeled all of these processes using math and the equations he derived were a close match with the geologic record of glacial–interglacial cycles. In other words, his equations did a great job of predicting ice ages.

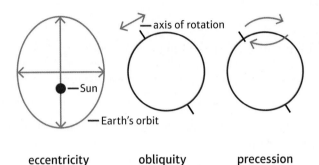

Figure 3:
Milankovitch cycles

eccentricity   obliquity   precession

12 However, it turns out that the advance and retreat of large ice sheets is not a uniform, linear process. There are periods where Earth undergoes climate transitions at rates much faster than what can be explained by the Milankovitch theory alone. That means feedbacks internal to the climate system must be operating during glacial–interglacial cycles. Put another way, the variations in the way Earth revolves around the sun are not sufficient to explain all observations of ice-sheet advance and retreat. Occasionally there are abrupt events that occur on time scales as short as years to decades, so something must be going on within the ocean–atmosphere system that kicks off a series of feedbacks. In fact, the potential for triggering an abrupt event is one of the more troublesome prospects of 21st-century climate change.

13 The existence of abrupt climate-change events also helps focus on an important question: Does an abrupt event unfold in just one specific region, or is it connected to other regions across the planet? This is a central problem of climate science because the goal is to understand internal mechanisms and what we call teleconnections. The term *teleconnections* refers to processes by which different parts of the ocean–atmosphere system communicate over vast distances. In order to understand all of the teleconnections acting across time, you need paleoclimate records from all over the globe.

CHECK WHAT YOU'VE LEARNED

PARAGRAPHS 1-13

A. Think about the section you just read. Answer these questions.

1. How can paleoclimate contribute to our understanding of climate change?

   ....

   ....

2. Why are direct measurements of Earth's climate so scarce?

   ....

   ....

3. How do Milankovitch cycles help to predict ice ages? What else contributes to periods of warming and cooling?

   ....

   ....

4. In Paragraph 3, the author states that climate change "is not some far-off threat or hypothetical concept." What does this suggest about climate change?

   ....

   ....

5. In Paragraph 13, the author defines *teleconnections*. What are teleconnections, and how does the study of paleoclimate help us to understand them?

   ....

   ....

B. Read the section again. Check your answers. Then continue to the next section.

An Introduction to Paleoclimate, *continued*

14 Think of this as a jigsaw puzzle problem, where the basic idea is to have different kinds of records for different regions. Scientists can then take all the regional records together and test hypotheses about the underlying physics. If successful, these studies can offer insights into lead–lag relationships. For example, if we observe large climate swings in the North Atlantic

Glossary

Deduce: to make a judgment about something based on the information you have

Locus: a place or position where something is particularly known to exist or happen

Convection: the circular movement in a gas or liquid caused by an outside force

Pandemic: an illness or disease that affects the population of a very large area

region, followed sometime later by variations in the strength of the East Asian monsoon, then we can explore the mechanisms by which these two geographically separated regions might be connected. The first step in all this, though, is to collect climate histories for each region.

15 There are several different geological records or archives that are helpful for assembling this jigsaw puzzle, each of which offers advantages and disadvantages. First, let us lay out a few general principles. One of the fundamental rules of geology is that the further back in time you go, the less you know. Earth's surface is constantly being worked over by the forces of deposition, erosion, and geologic cycling. In practice, this means that we know much more about what was going on 100 years ago than we do about what was going on 1,000 years ago, and we know more about what was going on 1,000 years ago than we do 10,000 years ago, and so on. A second general principle is that we do not have direct measurement of the past, so our understanding is entirely reliant on what we call *proxy records*. Essentially, a proxy is a substitute measurement for something you actually want to measure. For example, we might want to know the temperature of the ocean at some time in the past. Since we can't go back in a time machine and stick a thermometer in the ocean, we can instead look for rocks in the ocean that contain minerals which capture the temperature at the time of deposition. In other words, we can measure the chemical composition of certain minerals, and then from there deduce past temperatures.

16 So with all this in mind, let us talk about a few examples of different paleoclimate archives. One example you may be familiar with are tree rings. Trees grow a new ring every year, and the width of each ring is often related to the climate conditions of the year in which it grew. If you have a really wide ring, it indicates healthy growth. It depends on the region and the species, but wider rings may be associated with increased temperatures or increased rainfall. Narrower rings may indicate the opposite conditions. Some trees grow for hundreds or even thousands of years, so by measuring the width of different rings, we can put together a history that spans decades and maybe even centuries.

Tree trunk showing growth rings

17 Another type of paleoclimate archive that is hugely important is ice cores. Ice cores are especially useful when they are collected from large ice sheets like those that are found on Greenland or the Antarctic continent. One of the reasons these records are so important is because inside each layer of ice are tiny bubbles that contain little pockets of the ancient atmosphere. By carefully extracting and studying these little

Ice core

(Continued)

pockets of ancient air, scientists can know the composition of the atmosphere in the past, and, importantly, they can know the overall concentration of greenhouse gases like carbon dioxide. In addition, scientists can also measure subtle variations in the chemistry of certain molecules that indicate the annual temperature when the ice was deposited. However, one of the limitations to ice records is that they are only found in regions that are cold enough to maintain ice year round. If we want to understand warmer regions of the globe, we will have to look for another type of record.

18 Corals are especially useful for tracking climate change in the tropics, particularly on time scales spanning a few decades to a few centuries. Certain species of corals deposit calcium carbonate every year in a manner similar to tree rings. Small changes in the geochemistry of the coral skeletal minerals are correlated with fluctuations in the temperature of the surface ocean. Other geochemical indicators are correlated with the sea-surface salinity. Salinity is an important variable because the relative saltiness or freshness of the seawater is related to the balance of precipitation versus evaporation. Coral paleoclimate records have been especially useful for understanding the frequency and strength of changes associated with El Niño.

Coral reef

19 In recent years, scientists have also been studying records from cave deposits. Collectively, cave deposits such as stalagmites and stalactites are called *speleothems*, and these records offer important advantages. First, caves are sheltered environments, so they are protected from the forces of erosion acting on Earth's surface. Caves also have extremely stable temperatures, and the temperature of the cave is an average of annual surface temperatures. Finally, caves are distributed throughout the tropics and midlatitudes, so there is an opportunity for paleoclimate reconstructions in parts of the globe that don't have other types of records. Some of the most important work involving speleothem reconstructions comes from China, where these records document long-term variations in the strength of the Asian monsoon.

Stalagmite

Stalagtites

20 A final category of paleoclimate archives worth discussing is sediment cores. These are sequences of mud, silt, sand, and other geologic material that are collected in depositional basins. This may be freshwater lake systems, or they might come from the ocean. Depending on the depositional environment, there may be numerous geochemical indicators that serve as proxies for past climate conditions. Oftentimes these sediment cores contain ash layers from volcanic eruptions in the distant past. This is important because large volcanic eruptions in the past may have altered the chemistry of the atmosphere and the overall balance of incoming solar radiation.

21 The effort to fill in this jigsaw puzzle of paleoclimate archives is ongoing, but there are a few regions of the globe that seem especially important to understand. Let us discuss a few examples, but first a caveat: There are still large regions of the planet that are undersampled, and more paleoclimate work needs to happen in the future. In general, there are far fewer paleoclimate archives from the Southern Hemisphere. However, the research that has been done globally offers insight into fundamental processes, and the hope is that offering these examples will stir your imagination.

CULTURE NOTE

The trade winds are winds that blow from the east in the tropics near the equator. There are two bands of trade winds that encircle Earth: one in the Northern Hemisphere, which blows from the northeast to the southwest, and the other in the Southern Hemisphere, which blows from the southeast to the northwest. The westerlies are winds that blow from the west toward the east in the middle latitudes.

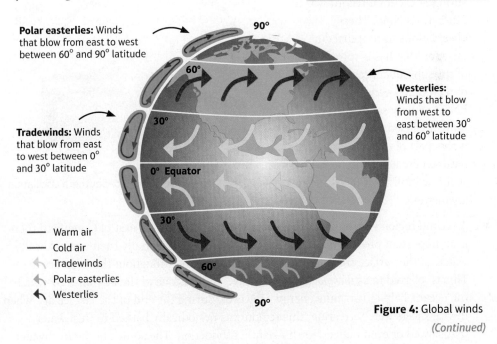

Polar easterlies: Winds that blow from east to west between 60° and 90° latitude

Tradewinds: Winds that blow from east to west between 0° and 30° latitude

Westerlies: Winds that blow from west to east between 30° and 60° latitude

— Warm air
— Cold air
↖ Tradewinds
↖ Polar easterlies
↖ Westerlies

Figure 4: Global winds

(Continued)

22　The first region worth exploring is the tropical Pacific. In the modern climate, global teleconnections are closely associated with the El Niño–Southern Oscillation (ENSO). ENSO emerges in the tropical Pacific, which is sometimes referred to as Earth's heat engine. Essentially ENSO is a measurement of the distribution of sea surface temperatures across the tropical Pacific. The expanse of warm waters in the tropics determines the locus of atmospheric convection. Stated another way, the warm ocean waters in the tropics help arrange the major atmosphere high-pressure cells, which then act to export heat out of the tropics and toward the midlatitudes. The importance of ENSO on year-to-year climate variability can hardly be overstated. ENSO is correlated with such phenomena as hurricane activity, pandemics, monsoon strength, crop yields, fish catch, forest fires, and a range of regional climate extremes. Changes in the ENSO system could potentially lead to abrupt climate events in the mid- to high latitudes by way of atmospheric teleconnections. This idea first surfaced in the late 20th century after we witnessed strong El Niño events in 1982–83 and again in 1997–98. The strongest event on record was the 2015–16 El Niño. These observations have spurred a question that has inspired much of the subsequent research: Is the observed 20th-century increase in ENSO activity somehow linked to human-caused climate change, or is this part of the baseline of natural climate variability? At this point, we still don't have an answer.

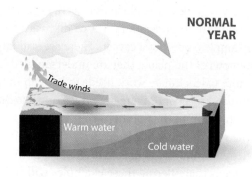

NORMAL YEAR

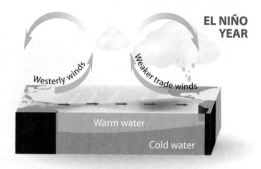

EL NIÑO YEAR

Figure 5: El Niño–Southern Oscillation

23　A second region worth discussing is the North Atlantic. Just east of Greenland there is an important process involving ocean circulation. Essentially there are cold salty waters at the surface that subduct and drive currents throughout the deep ocean. This is referred to as *thermohaline circulation*, and it is one of the key ways by which the oceans help redistribute energy. However, during the end of the last ice age when the ice sheets were retreating, this region was periodically bathed in freshwater that slowed or even halted North Atlantic subduction. The source of the freshwater remains a mystery, but it was likely due to rapid deglaciation and high runoff.

In any case, the result of the freshwater hosing of the North Atlantic was that Earth was temporarily plunged back into ice age conditions for a period of time. While this originated in the North Atlantic, the effects were felt all over the globe. This is one of the most striking examples of an abrupt climate event, and the exact series of processes is still a matter of some investigation.

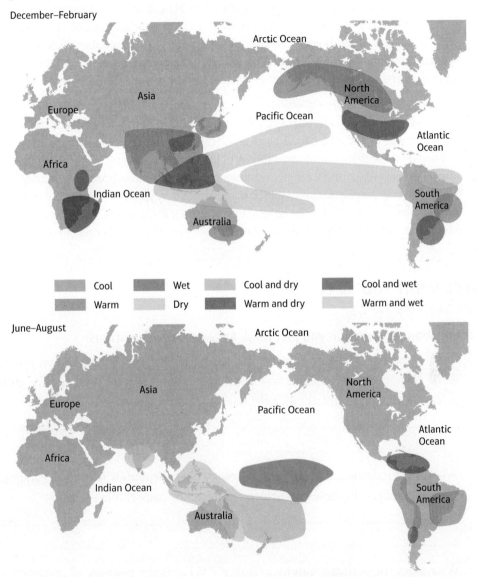

Figure 6: Effects of El Niño on climate

24 The third region worth discussing is the Southern Ocean. If you were to hold a globe of Earth in your hand and look downward on Antarctica, you would see that the entire continent is surrounded by the Southern Ocean. Since Earth is spinning,

(Continued)

this stretch of ocean is rotating around and around with incredible intensity, essentially stirring and mixing the Atlantic, Pacific, and Indian Ocean waters. The highest waves on Earth are found here, and the Southern Hemisphere westerly winds lie over the Southern Ocean and circulate over a wide stretch of latitudes. There is evidence that the westerlies may have shifted north and south during glacial–interglacial cycles, which would alter the strength of ocean mixing. The Southern Ocean holds enormous quantities of dissolved carbon, and ocean mixing there is tied to carbon-dioxide concentrations in the atmosphere. Many paleoclimate scientists are interested in collecting records from Patagonia, as this region of South America is the only land mass that protrudes into the westerly wind belt.

25   Overall, paleoclimate scientists still have much to learn about the intricacies of the climate system. While the fundamental link between greenhouse-gas emissions and climate change is well understood, there is still much we do not know about year-to-year and decade-to-decade climate variability. A richer understanding of teleconnections, abrupt climate events, and the inner workings of the ocean–atmosphere system may help our society prepare for inevitable changes wrought by global warming. The priority for the global community should be to reduce greenhouse emissions, but while we work toward that goal, paleoclimate investigations will be critical for furthering our knowledge.

CHECK WHAT YOU'VE LEARNED
PARAGRAPHS 14–25

A. Think about the section you just read. Answer these questions.

6. In Paragraph 14, the author mentions a "jigsaw puzzle problem." What problem is the author referring to and how is it like a jigsaw puzzle? What are the different pieces of information that can help scientists solve this puzzle?

....

....

7. What two fundamental principles of geology does the author refer to in Paragraph 15? What challenges do these two principles create for paleoclimate scientists?

....

....

8. What does the author mean by a "proxy"? What is the purpose of proxies? What examples of proxies are mentioned in the text?

....

....

9. In Paragraph 21, the author first mentions that much more paleoclimate work needs to be done in the future. Why, then, does the author go on to describe research that has already been done?

   ....

   ....

10. In Paragraph 22, the author describes the El Niño–Southern Oscillation (ENSO), What is the author's opinion about the importance of ENSO? What examples does the author provide to support this idea?

   ....

   ....

B. Read the section again. Check your answers.

C. Summarize in your own words the key points of the reading.

THINKING CRITICALLY

Think about the situation considering what you have read in "An Introduction to Paleoclimate." With a partner, apply what you know about examining proxy records to determine climate change in the past to respond to the situation.

You are a climate scientist. You want to determine if volcanic activity occurred in a region in the past, and if so, how it may have affected the climate. What type of paleoclimate archive, or proxy, could you use to determine if a region experienced volcanic activity in the past? How could other types of paleoclimate archives reveal information about temperature or precipitation changes at the time?

🔾 **Go to MyEnglishLab to complete a critical thinking exercise.**

THINKING VISUALLY

A. Look at the map with the reading passage that shows the El Niño–Southern Oscillation (ENSO). In your own words, summarize how this phenomenon causes climate variability. What types of abrupt climate events might occur in the different areas affected by ENSO that are pictured in the map?

> **TIP**
>
> Using graphic organizers, such as charts and diagrams, is an effective way to write information and see the relationships between the key ideas in a reading.
>
> To learn more or to review graphic organizers, see EARTH SCIENCE, Part 1, page 77.

B. Review what you read about paleoclimate archives (proxy records). Then create a graphic organizer that compares and contrasts the paleoclimate archives mentioned in the essay. You may want to organize your graphic organizer to include such categories as the location, method for gathering and examining the information, the information provided, and the advantages and / or disadvantages of each paleoclimate archive.

THINKING ABOUT LANGUAGE

RECOGNIZING RELATIVE CLAUSES FOR DEFINITION

Read the following definitions of terms from "An Introduction to Paleoclimate." Underline the relative clauses or appositives in each sentence. Circle the term being defined.

1. The majority of incoming solar radiation, which is all of the energy on Earth that is derived from the sun, is concentrated at the tropics and becomes more diffuse as you move poleward from the equator.

2. Milankovitch cycles, named after the Serbian scientist Milutin Milankovitch, describe small variations in the way Earth revolves around the sun.

3. The advance and retreat of ice sheets, which scientists refer to as *glacial–interglacial cycles*, are only partially explained by the Milankovitch cycles.

4. The goal of climate science is to understand internal mechanisms and teleconnections, which are processes by which different parts of the ocean-atmosphere system communicate over vast distances.

5. Proxy records are measurements that substitute for things you actually want to measure.

6. Speleothems, which are cave deposits such as stalagmites and stalactites, offer important advantages.

UNDERSTANDING PASSIVE AND ACTIVE VOICE

Work with a partner. Circle the subjects and underline the verbs in each excerpt from "An Introduction to Paleoclimate." Then decide if each verb is in active or passive voice. Discuss why you think the author decided to use passive or active voice in each case.

1. Collectively these sources of energy are known as fossil fuels, and when we ignite fossil fuels, we release carbon dioxide and other greenhouse gases into the atmosphere.

2. Simply put, the Milankovitch theory describes small variations in the way Earth revolves around the sun. Collectively these are called *orbital variations*.

3. When we look at the climate system on time scales of thousands to hundreds of thousands of years, glacial-interglacial cycles are partially explained by Milankovitch cycles.

4. There are periods where Earth undergoes climate transitions at rates much faster than what can be explained by Milankovitch theory alone.

5. Ice cores are especially useful when they are collected from large ice sheets like those that are found on Greenland or the Antarctic continent.

6. However, the research that has been done globally offers insight into fundamental processes, …

Go to MyEnglishLab for more practice reading an extended text and using your reading skills.

RESEARCH PROJECT

The reading in this unit discusses the ways that paleoclimatology can contribute to our understanding of climate and inform our response to climate change. By doing additional research, you can learn what paleoclimate has taught us about climate change in different regions of the world.

A. The following is a list of regions that are mentioned in the passage as areas that are of interest when studying paleoclimate and climate change. Choose one of the regions listed below to study or another region that interests you.

- the Tropical Pacific
- the North Atlantic
- the Southern Ocean
- Other: ....

B. Conduct your research. As you read about your subject, formulate a thesis. Gather information that supports your thesis. Use the following questions to help you:

- What type of research are scientists currently doing in this region? How are they conducting their research? What findings have been made?
- What type of proxies are scientists examining as part of their research?
- What climate changes have occurred in this region in the past? What changes are currently being experienced in this region?

C. Create a list of discussion questions about interesting points related to your topic. Choose a presentation style from the box, or use your own idea, and present your research to the class. Then pose the questions to the class and have a group discussion.

> a group presentation
> a short lecture with visuals
> a short video documentary

Go to MyEnglishLab to complete a collaborative activity.

MEDIEVAL CULTURE

Medieval Feasting

UNIT PROFILE

In this unit, you will read about the role of music in feasts in western Europe in the 13th and 14th centuries. In the online extended reading, you will learn how medieval feasts involved interactive artistic performances. As a capstone to the unit, you will research feasting in another culture.

EXTENDED READING

BEFORE YOU READ

Think about these questions before you read "Songs About Medieval Feasting." Discuss them with another student.

1. Feasts are large meals to celebrate special occasions. What special occasions do you think people in western Europe celebrated in the Middle Ages? Who hosted feasts? Who attended?

2. Besides eating, what other activities took place at feasts?

3. What kind of music do you think was performed at feasts? What kinds of instruments did musicians play?

4. What do you think musicians sang about?

READ

Read the essay. Then answer the questions after each section.

Songs About Medieval Feasting

1 During the Middle Ages, feasts in elite households were sumptuous affairs. In European courts of the 13th and 14th centuries, such banquets included special multicourse meals, as well as various forms of entertainment: music, theater, and ritualized activities. Participants at the table were often nobility of the region, and the banquet was a way to celebrate their shared values of feudal culture. Through the rituals of the feast, participants showed their loyalty to a certain ruler while he demonstrated his generosity and temperance at the table. This host also affirmed his authority over his assembled guests. Finally, feasts were also a way to negotiate social relations through various shared activities and cultivated art forms such as love song, chivalry, and demonstrations of religious piety. Medieval feasting really was an art form that played a crucial social role for those who participated in these ceremonial occasions.

> **Glossary**
>
> **Sumptuous:** very impressive and expensive
>
> **Temperance:** sensible control of the things you say and do, especially the amount of alcohol you drink
>
> **Piety:** respect for God and religion, often shown in the way you behave
>
> **Chronicles:** written records of events, especially historical events
>
> **Culinary:** relating to cooking
>
> **Ostensible:** a reason which appears to be true or is said to be true, but which may hide the real reason
>
> **Spectacle:** an impressive or exciting public show or event
>
> **Motet:** a piece of music on a religious subject
>
> **Siege:** a situation in which an army, police, or a group of people surround a place to get control of it
>
> **Statesmanship:** the activities of a political leader

(Continued)

2 The tradition of dining and music making is an old one in the Western tradition. Greek epics such as Homer's *Iliad* and philosophical texts such as Plato's *Symposium* relate the idea of the banquet as one that combines the pleasures of food and conversation as a social event in the highest sense: one that cultivates the spirit and the body, and creates civic harmony among people around the table. Music and dining are time-bound in nature, and just as the joys of feasting happen in "real time," we also have to remember that the live performance provided with the meal also unfolded in real time.

3 We can find out about what kind of songs were played and the nature of performances at feasts from medieval chronicles and romances during the 13th and 14th centuries. For example, the 13th-century Occitan romance *Flamenca* (Occitan was the language spoken in southern France between the 12th and 14th centuries) includes a lavish description of a wedding banquet.

TIP

Paying attention to the way that an author structures a reading and emphasizes certain ideas can help you to understand the **purpose** and **tone** of a reading. Other clues include examining the author's word choice, syntax, and level of detail and imagery provided about a subject.

To learn more or to review these strategies, refer to MEDIEVAL CULTURE, Part 2, page 255.

TIP

Remember that it is common to encounter ambiguous parts of academic texts, but you can **manage ambiguity** in a number of ways. For example, it is helpful to accept that discipline-specific readings will have challenging vocabulary and terminology. Use strategies for dealing with unfamiliar vocabulary, such as looking up only those vocabulary items that are essential for understanding the text. It is also useful to use a website such as *Wikipedia* to do some quick background reading on topics that contain unfamiliar cultural or historical references.

To learn more or to review managing ambiguity, refer to MEDIEVAL CULTURE, Part 1, page 101.

Although the romance might exaggerate for effect, it gives us a good idea of the range of music and performers at such events and what kinds of songs they performed. We are told that 3,000 knights with ladies arrive at a palace that could hold 10,000 knights with "room to spare." In addition to knights, ladies, squires, and their pages who accompany them, there are 1,500 minstrels. "A great variety of food is served" as the guests sit on silk cushions and all admire the new bride of Lord Archambaud, Flamenca. After the guests have eaten, they stay to drink wine and listen to the minstrels or "joglars":

> Then the minstrels stood up;
> each one wanted to be heard.
> Then you would have heard resound
> strings of various pitches.
> Whoever knew a new piece for the viol,
> a song, a descort, or lay,
> he pressed forward as much as he could.

One played the lay of the Honeysuckle,
another the one of Tintagel;
one sang of the Noble Lovers,
and another which Yvain composed.
One played the harp; another the viol;
another, the flute; another, a fife;
one played a rebeck, another, a rote;
one sang the words; another played notes;

[…]
some did gymnastics and tumbling tricks;
another danced with his cup;
one held the hoop; another leapt through it;
everyone performed his art perfectly.
(*Flamenca* 33–35)

In this passage, minstrels play the favorite tales of the time. Songs were musical performances, most likely improvised for the audience with theatrical elements. The minstrels perform a "lay," a short musical poem composed by Marie of France, a celebrated female composer of the time, and other love stories. The minstrels sing with the musical accompaniment of various instruments such as a medieval fiddle or viol, and a fife, a high-pitched flute. Some of the minstrels sing, others play, and some entertain by doing physical tumbling and tricks.

Viol

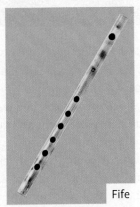
Fife

Lute

4 In these descriptions of aristocratic feasts, ceremony, appearance, and performances called *entremets* are the focus over the visual description and taste of the food. These performances were "between" (*entre*) "dishes" (*mets*) and could be all sorts of entertainment including song, dancing, and culinary inventions such as birds flying out of breadbaskets. A famous banquet attended by Philip the Good of Burgundy and his son Charles the Bold was held so that an order of knights, called the Knights of the Golden Fleece, could assemble and pledge vows of pious service as holy warriors.

(Continued)

This so-called Feast of the Pheasant held at Lille in 1454 featured among many other dramatic and musical presentations the composition "I Have Never Seen Her Like." This composition is an entremet and involved a young 12-year old boy who circled the hall and sang while mounted on a stag. For those attending the feast it appeared as if both the young boy and the white stag were singing the song together. When the boy and stag finished and left the hall, singers from the church took the stage to sing. In the tradition of the pageantry of the feast, the accompanist pulled his lute from one of the pastries prepared for the feast.

Feast of the Pheasant

5 The Feast of the Pheasant was the culmination of 18 days of other events and jousts. While the ostensible purpose for the feast was so that Philip and other courtiers could take crusading vows to rescue Constantinople, which had fallen to the Turks the previous year, a more practical reason was that the feast allowed Philip to assert his control over the nobility of his territories and create a unified community over shared values of the Burgundian state. The feast was supposed to display the largesse, or generosity, of the state's ruler, and the grandeur of the spectacle was meant to encourage the nobleman of his lands and subjects to serve God and embark for the Holy Land without constraint. As if to temper the pleasurable concoction of music and pageantry taking place in the banquet hall, the motet emerging from the church after the singing of the stag reminds its audience about the moral and spiritual intentions for the assemblage.

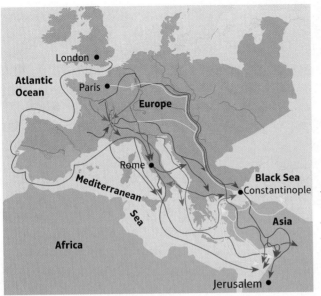

London •

Atlantic Ocean

Paris •

Europe

Rome •

Mediterranean

Sea

Black Sea
• Constantinople

Asia

Africa

Jerusalem •

→ First Crusade, 1096–1099

    Second Crusade, 1147–1149

→ Third Crusade, 1189–1192

→ Fourth Crusade, 1202–1204

▓ Roman Catholic, about 1096

▓ Eastern Orthodox, about 1096

▓ Islam, about 1096

6 Textual and visual descriptions of royal banquets convey similar elements of feasts that appealed to multiple senses (see, for example, Figure 1). One banquet image from the Grandes chroniques de France owned by Charles V (Grandes Chroniques de France de Charles V, Paris, BnF, MS fr. 2813, fol. 473v) is featured in a part of the manuscript dedicated to the visit of the Holy Roman Emperor Charles I to the French court. Charles V is seated in the center with other important noblemen. The image gives visual prominence to three men who are seated in front of a cloth of gold bordered with fleur-de-lys and with three table boats (nefs) before them. Like textual descriptions in the image, less description is paid to the food served although we do see a plate of meat being carried by a young male server in the middle of the miniature. A prominent feature of this image is the entremet or between-course entertainment, happening during the feast: The crusaders' capture of Jerusalem in the 11th century is restaged ostensibly to engage the guests to think about their duties as military leaders. From this feasting scene one sees the importance of rank and the diplomatic or political function of royal banquets.

7 Theatrical presentations also blur the boundary between fantasy and reality. A culinary or theatrical entremet could also play with the boundary between the realms of the Church and the courtly hall with their respective spiritual versus earthly values (see, for example, Figure 2).

(Continued)

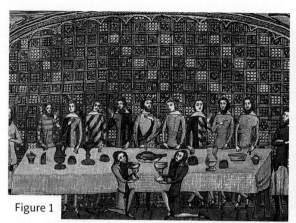
Figure 1

Figure 2

8 What can we learn about the nature of feasting songs from images such as the one of King Charles and accounts such as that of the Feast of the Pheasant? Let us take the Feast of the Pheasant and the description of the entremet. First, many people were involved in these entremets: Painters, artisans, and cooks created an elaborate set of a child in a costume of costly, luxurious materials on a stag, as well as culinary inventions such as instruments being plucked out of pastries. Secondly, these performances moved among the audience, creating a moving theater within the banquet hall and probably interacting with various audience members in different ways. While "I Have Never Seen Her Like" might have had a more precise setting by a composer, other songs may have been improvised compositions based on a soloist in the earlier medieval tradition we see in *Flamenca*.

CULTURE NOTE

Feudalism is a social system that existed in western Europe during the Middle Ages. In feudal society, people received land and protection from those of a higher rank when they worked and fought for them. High-ranking people in feudal society, or *nobility*, were given titles depending on their position. Feudal society in western Europe was also heavily influenced by the Roman Catholic Church, which held a great deal of power and played an important role in people's lives.

NOBEL RANKS

Emperor	Empress
King	Queen
Grand Duke	Grand Duchess
Grand Prince	Grand Princess
Archduke	Archduchess
Duke	Duchess
Prince	Princess
Marquess	Marchioness
Count/Earl	Countess
Viscount	Viscountess
Baron	Baroness
Knight	Dame
Lord	Lady

CHECK WHAT YOU'VE LEARNED
PARAGRAPHS 1–8

A. Think about the section you just read. Answer these questions.

1. According to the author, what was the purpose of feasting?

   ....

   ....

2. What are some ways that historians can learn about feasting in the Middle Ages? Which examples of these accounts are mentioned in the passage?

   ....

   ....

3. Who were minstrels? What did they do?

   ....

   ....

4. In Paragraph 5, the author explains the purpose of the Feast of the Pheasant. What was the stated reason for this feast? What does the author suggest was the real reason? Why might this true purpose of the feast not have been stated publicly?

   ....

   ....

5. In Paragraph 1, the author describes feasts as "sumptuous affairs" that involve "various forms of entertainment" including "shared activities." How does the description of an entremet (performance) at the Feast of the Pheasant in Paragraph 7 demonstrate these qualities? Provide examples from the text.

   ....

   ....

Songs About Medieval Feasting, *continued*

9 Just as the ritual activities of this elite audience such as jousting and feasting required the active involvement of participants in order to ensure and affirm communal values, so the entertainment such as the singing stag involved the active participation of the viewer. Olivier de La Marche, a member of the organizing committee of the Feast and official chronicler, describes how such entertainment triggered wonder in their viewers by playing with appearances—the artifice of the singing stag, for example. Sharing in this splendor by interacting with the media—often the participants played roles in the theatrical entertainment, for example—created a community of ideals cultivated by the shared experience of such multisensorial delights.

> **Glossary**
>
> Virtuous: behaving in a very honest and moral way
>
> Civilize: to influence someone's behavior, by teaching him or her to act in ways acceptable to society
>
> Prowess: great skill at doing something
>
> Aural: relating to the sense of hearing
>
> Jovial: friendly and cheerful
>
> Camaraderie: a feeling of friendship that a group of people have, especially when they work together

Here is the song "I Have Never Seen Her Like" in translation:

> Never did I see your equal,
> my gracious Lady;
> for your beauty, upon my soul
> surpasses any other.
>
> On seeing you I marvel
> and say: is this our Lady?
> Never did I see your equal,
> my gracious Lady.
>
> Your very great sweetness awakens
> my spirit and touches my eye,
> my heart, and that I can rightly say,
> since it disposes me to serve you.
>
> Never did I see your equal,
> my gracious Lady;
> for your beauty, upon my soul,
> surpasses any other.
>
> (Gilles Binchois, "Je ne vis oncques la pareille," Cummings 363)

This song appears in manuscripts of the period attributed to the 15th-century composers Gilles Binchois or Guillaume du Fay and is a polyphonic song for three voices. Such entertainment alternated with dining, dancing, masked processions, and the wonder of watching inventions such as mechanical machines that moved. We need to understand song making and listening to music as part of a continuous sequence of events of the feast.

10 "I Have Never Seen Her Like" belongs to a tradition of medieval love songs in which a male singer dedicates himself to a beautiful, high-born, virtuous inaccessible lady. Poet-performers in southern France during the 12th and 13th centuries called *troubadours* are known for inventing this tradition, which is a refined form of love song combining words and sound in complex rhyme and meters. In this song tradition, the "lover" follows a convention in which he performs loyalty and service to his beloved through song, thus proving his worthiness. This kind of courtly service "civilizes" the lover in that he dedicates himself to a worthy ideal in the form of a lady, and aspires to better himself morally through artistic prowess. Following this love song tradition, in "I Have Never Seen Her Like" the singer describes his choice to serve an unsurpassed beauty because her "sweetness awakens" his "spirit."

11 While many songs performed at feasts were for a solo singer most likely with musical accompaniment—as troubadour songs would have been performed—during the time period of the Feast of the Pheasant, this song tradition expanded into an art form with multiple voices (polyphonic song) and instruments. As "I Have Never Seen Her Like" is a love song that celebrates love as a visual and spiritual experience, beauty having effects on the soul, so another layer of the aural and visual would have been added in this song's aspect as a polyphonic song featured in a dramatic entremet: The song would have a dazzling and amazing effect on the ears and eyes as viewers watched a boy on top of a singing stag. The other voices emerging from the stag would have solicited wonder for the artifice of the hidden voices in the animal. By the time of such feasts, people believed that the diverse polyphonic sound of multiple voices recalled the classical tradition of the banquet that celebrated music making and dining as a multisensory celebration of the senses, one that cultivated knowledge, intellectual community, and morals coming together at the feasting table.

12 Thus in these two banquet scenes, one sees the medieval tradition of ritualized feasts in which participants subscribed to and celebrated a common courtly tradition of dining and music making, offering songs that celebrated courtly love service to a noble lady. This tradition affirmed the values of nobility through multisensorial, multimedia events. Music, eating, and spectacle were pleasures that complemented each other, and those at the feast participated in all these activities as part of the feast. The activities involved the nobility but also minstrels, artisans, and other servants of the court, such as an official court chronicler like Olivier de la Marche— it was he who wrote about the Feast of the Pheasant.

(Continued)

Through the feast, both sensual pleasures of the mouth, eye, and ear could encourage moral improvement and communal action: From a wedding banquet in *Flamenca* to a ceremony such as Feast of the Pheasant, feasts were an occasion for a ruler to demonstrate his authority and to garner the loyalty of regional associates, or to firm up political alliance. They were an occasion for a ruler to demonstrate his authority. By seeing how "I Have Never Seen Her Like" was performed as part of an entremet in the Feast of the Pheasant, we see how feasts recruited all the senses so that corporeal pleasures could be rightly directed to intellectual or spiritual pursuits (courtly service in the love song) and virtuous civility (the entremet framed within an occasion affirming the spiritual and political mission of the Burgundian state).

13   Finally, one has to remember other kinds of feasting songs existed in the Middle Ages, and one cannot rule out the possibility that more popular songs might have been performed at events such as the wedding in *Flamenca* and the Feast of the Pheasant. Even in a literary account such as *Flamenca*, for instance, we can guess that popular songs for dancing and drinking might have been performed at courtly gatherings in the 12th and 13th centuries. While this drinking song attributed to Guillaume du Fay is from the same period as the Feast of the Pheasant, it comes from a long tradition in many cultures of festive popular song making that takes up the theme of drinking and revelry during feasts:

> Since you are a fighter,
> willingly I would fight with you
> to see if I could, if I could,
> I would compete with you, to be a good
> drinker;
>
> And if you were a sapper
> I would also compete to dig with you.
> Since you are a fighter,
> willingly I would fight with you.
>
> You think me a poor drinker,
> but I would easily down three jars,
> truly, or I would go off and hide, and hide
> as the worst in the world.
>
> Since you are a fighter,
> willingly I would fight with you
> to see if I could, if I could,
> I would compete with you, to be a good
> drinker (Fallows)

14   This song shows another side of the feast, the competitive, humorous spirit of drinking songs that brings people convivially together. Such songs usually involve making fun of the other person in a jovial manner. Another group of songs dated to

around 1280 appears in a songbook and depicts the life of Paris as one of eating and being with friends:

> One speaks of threshing and winnowing, of digging and cultivating; but these pleasures quite displease me, for the only good life is to take one's ease with good, clear wine and capon, and to be with good friends, happy and joyful, singing and joking and loving, and to have for comfort, when in need, one's fill of beautiful ladies: and all this you can find in Paris.

15 Unlike the refined courtly songs and entremets that we saw earlier, this song catalogues the labor that goes into the cultivation of food, and the urban pleasures of camaraderie, ladies, drinking, and food that one can find in Paris. The song continues with more civic descriptions of food and the markets of the street. We even have echoes of people selling their produce, with a separate voice who sells berries:

> In Paris, morning and evening, you can find good bread and good, clear wine, good meat and good fish, every sort of friend, clever wits, great merriment, beautiful, joyous noblewomen; and, in the middle of it all, you can find it all at the lowest price for the man short of funds.
>
> New strawberry, noble mulberry, mulberry, noble mulberry!
> New strawberry, noble mulberry, mulberry, noble mulberry!
>
> (Montpellier Codex, fols. 368^{v}–369^{v}; Dillon 86–87)

16 In thinking about this urban "soundscape" (Dillon 88) in relation to the feasting songs, it is important to note that like the courtly representations of *Flamenca* and Feast of the Pheasant, such songs drew from their environments and are echoes of live, improvised performances in particular court or urban settings, with various actors and artificial inventions.

17 In conclusion, from court to the street, feasting songs celebrated the art of conviviality through pleasures that engaged all the senses. Feasts cultivated bodily senses to affirm the values of an elite class, to encourage political or religious causes, and in general were a social celebration towards communal intellectual and moral pursuits. During the medieval period it is clear that celebratory meals considered song and music as a necessary component to the camaraderie that happens around the table.

CHECK WHAT YOU'VE LEARNED
PARAGRAPHS 9–17

A. Think about the section you just read. Answer these questions.

6. According to the author, feasts such as the Feast of the Pheasant "recruited all the senses." In what ways did feasts accomplish this? What was the purpose of doing this?

....

....

7. What convention is followed in love songs such as "I Have Never Seen Her Like"? How does this "civilize" the singer, or "lover"?

....

....

8. What were polyphonic songs? How did they contribute to the dramatic effect of the performance of "I Have Never Seen Her Like"?

....

....

9. In Paragraph 13, the author discusses the performance of popular songs for dancing and drinking. Does the author know that these types of songs were performed at feasts, or is this an inference? How do you know? Provide examples from the text.

....

....

10. In Paragraph 14, the author states that the drinking song by Guillaume du Fay shows "the competitive, humorous spirit of drinking songs." What kinds of competition does this song mention? Provide evidence from the song.

....

....

B. Read the section again. Check your answers.

C. Summarize in your own words the key points of the reading.

THINKING CRITICALLY

Think about what you have read in "Songs About Medieval Feasting." With a partner, apply what you know about medieval feasting to discuss your answers to the questions.

According to the passage, medieval feasts served specific purposes. What were they? What are some examples of celebrations that serve similar social, political, or religious purposes today? How are they similar to or different from medieval feasts? Provide examples.

🔘 Go to MyEnglishLab to complete a critical thinking exercise.

THINKING VISUALLY

A. Work with a partner. Look back at the image showing how a culinary or theatrical entremet could play with the boundary between the realms of the Church and the courtly hall with their respective spiritual versus earthly values (Image 2) on page 374. Describe the image based on what you have read in the passage.

- Who is pictured? What are they doing?
- Which aspects of feasting that you read about are pictured in this image?
- Which are not pictured?

B. Review what you read about Image 2. Create an organizational chart that describes the people and objects pictured, their roles, and their purposes or goals at the feast.

People / Objects	Roles	Purposes or Goals at the Feast

THINKING ABOUT LANGUAGE

UNDERSTANDING LANGUAGE ASSOCIATED WITH CHRONOLOGY

Complete each sentence with an appropriate word or phrase from the box.

at the turn of the	by the close of the century	era
lead-up (n)	over the course of time	simultaneously

1. The Middle Ages is the middle .... of three main periods of Western history: the classical period, the medieval period, and the modern period.

2. The First Crusade occurred .... 11th century when Pope Urban II called for a crusade to the Holy Land in 1095.

3. The .... to this first crusade occurred when the Byzantine emperor Alexius Comnenus requested help in reconquering territory from the Turks.

4. In 1096, a People's Crusade was led by about 20,000 lesser nobles and peasants from northern France and Germany to recapture the Holy Land. .... , the Princes' Crusade was led by dukes and counts.

5. _____ the First Crusade concluded with the capture of Jerusalem in 1099.

6. _____ , tens of thousands of people were killed in the Crusades, and as few as one in 20 Crusaders survived to reach the Holy Land.

RECOGNIZING FIGURATIVE LANGUAGE

Underline at least one form of figurative language in each excerpt from "Songs About Medieval Feasting" and indicate what type of figurative language it is an example of.

Text from Reading	Type of Figurative Language
1. As if to temper the pleasurable concoction of music and pageantry taking place in the banquet hall, the motet emerging from the church after the singing of the stag reminds its audience about the moral and spiritual intentions for the assemblage.	
2. Your very great sweetness awakens my spirit and touches my eye, my heart, and that I can rightly say, since it disposes me to serve you.	
3. This kind of courtly service "civilizes" the lover in that he dedicates himself to a worthy ideal in the form of a lady, and aspires to better himself morally through artistic prowess.	
4. During the time of such feasts, people believed that the diverse polyphonic sound of multiple voices recalled the classical tradition of the banquet that celebrated music making and dining as a multisensory celebration of the senses, one that cultivated knowledge, intellectual community, and morals coming together at the feasting table.	
5. In thinking about this urban "soundscape" (Dillon 88) in relation to the feasting songs, it is important to note that like the courtly representations of *Flamenca* and Feast of the Pheasant, such songs drew from their environments and are echoes of live, improvised performances in particular court or urban settings, with various actors and artificial inventions.	

🔘 Go to MyEnglishLab for more practice reading an extended text and using your reading skills.

RESEARCH PROJECT

In the reading in this unit, you learned that feasts were important social occasions in Western Europe in medieval times. By doing additional research, you can learn how important social occasions were celebrated in other cultures during this period.

A. Choose a medieval kingdom or empire in Africa, the Americas, Asia, or the Middle East to research, such as the Byzantine Empire, the Ottoman Empire, the Ming Dynasty, or the Inca Empire.

B. Conduct your research. As you read about your subject, formulate a thesis. Gather information that supports your thesis. Use the following ideas to help you:

- Search online or at a library for various sources of information about celebrations in the culture during the medieval period: historical accounts, artwork and music, literary works, and so on.

- Describe the following:
  - the types of events that were celebrated
  - the social, political, and / or religious significance of the events
  - who hosted and participated in the events
  - food and drink that was served
  - the music, entertainment, and activities that took place

C. Create a list of discussion questions about interesting points related to your topic. Choose a presentation style from the box, or use your own idea, and present your research to the class. Then pose the questions to the class and have a group discussion.

> a group presentation with visuals
> a short lecture with audio and / or visuals
> a short video documentary

⟐ Go to MyEnglishLab to complete a collaborative activity.

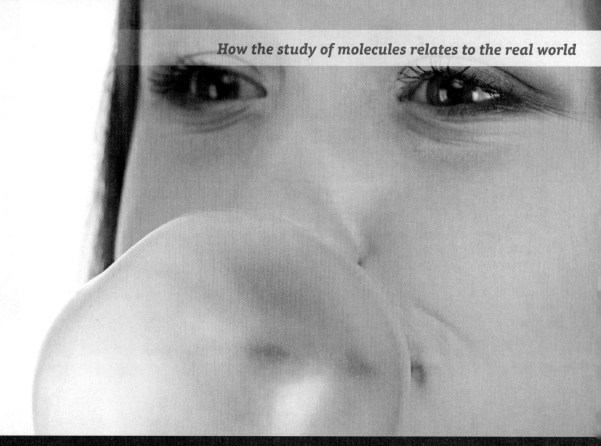

How the study of molecules relates to the real world

MATERIALS ENGINEERING

Polymers: Regenerative Medicine

UNIT PROFILE

In this unit, you will read about the effects of time and temperature on polymer mechanics and objects made from polymeric materials. In the online extended reading, you will learn about designing materials for regenerative medicine. As a capstone to the unit, you will research common uses of polymers.

EXTENDED READING

BEFORE YOU READ

Think about these questions before you read "Why Do Polymers Behave Differently Depending on Their Conditions?" Discuss them with another student.

1. Chewing gum is an example of a polymer. How is chewing gum different before you put it into your mouth compared with after you put it in your mouth and chew it? What might cause it to change?

2. Imagine you remove some chewing gum from your mouth and then use your hands to pull it apart slowly. What happens? What happens when you pull on it quickly?

3. When developing new polymeric materials (materials made with polymers), scientists need to consider the conditions under which the materials will be used. Think about the materials needed to build a rocket being sent into space. What conditions would these materials need to withstand in order to make the journey into space?

4. Think about the materials needed to create artificial joints, such as artificial hips and knees. What properties would these materials need to have in order to function as bones and joints in a human body?

READ

Read the essay. Then answer the questions after each section.

Why Do Polymers Behave Differently Depending on Their Conditions?

The Effect of Time on Polymer Mechanics

1 Imagine that you are chewing a great big piece of bubble gum. You take it out of your mouth, pinch it using the thumb and forefinger of each hand, and then very slowly pull your hands apart. What does the gum do? Now imagine that you put the gum back in your mouth and chew it some more. Next, you take the gum out of your mouth, you pinch it just like before using both hands, except this time you pull your hands apart as quickly as you can. How does the gum behave now? To answer this question, it might help to remember that chewing gum is made from a type of rubber.

(Continued)

Glossary

Abruptly: suddenly and unexpectedly

Compliant: flexible, or adaptable

Stiff: hard and difficult to bend

Covalent bonds: chemical bonds formed between atoms that share electrons

Wiggle: to move with small movements from side to side or up and down

Tangled up / entangled: twisted together in a messy way

Deform: to change the natural form or shape of something

Goopy: thick and sticky

Suspended: kept from falling or sinking

2   In the first case, the gum stretches out as you pull your hands apart slowly. It changes its geometric shape and becomes longer and thinner. As you continue to pull on the gum it becomes thinner and thinner in the middle until it eventually breaks. In materials science and engineering, we call this *ductile* behavior.

3   In the second case, the gum abruptly snaps into two pieces as you pull your hands apart quickly. The gum doesn't stretch out or change its shape very much before it breaks. In materials science and engineering, we call this *brittle* behavior.

4   In both instances, the chewing gum is made of the exact same molecules, yet those molecules are behaving very differently depending on their conditions. The gum appears to have different mechanical properties depending on how quickly you pull on it. In the ductile case, the gum is behaving as a more "compliant" object. In the brittle case, the gum is behaving as a "stiff" object. How can the same material, chewing gum, behave so differently depending on its conditions?

5   The answer lies in the structure of the molecules that make up chewing gum. These molecules are an example of the class of materials called *polymers*. Polymers are long, chain-like molecules. The links of these chains are held together by strong covalent bonds that can rotate. As the links rotate, the entire chain can wiggle around; thus, polymers can be thought of as long, flexible molecules that are constantly in motion. Now picture thousands of these long, wiggly molecules all tangled up together. Each of the molecular chains is constantly moving around, and it is easy to imagine how two or more chains could become tangled up, essentially forming a molecular knot in the chewing gum. If you slowly pull on the chewing gum, the chains have sufficient time to slide past one another and become disentangled. The chains keep sliding until you eventually pull them completely apart in a ductile manner. In contrast, if you quickly pull on the chewing gum, the molecular chains do not have time to slide past one another and they remain knotted. The tension on the individual chains causes them to snap and break apart in a brittle manner.

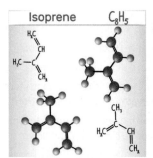

Isoprene C_8H_5

Figure 1: Polymer chain structure of rubber (polyisoprene)

TIP

Interpreting information in visuals associated with articles can help you to better understand what you have read and to gain information that is represented more clearly in a visual format than in writing. Noticing important features of visuals such as the title, labels, symbols, captions, and references back to the text can help you to better understand visuals and how they support or add to the reading.

To learn more or to review Interpreting information in visuals, refer to MATERIALS ENGINEERING, Part 2, page 300.

6 All objects made from polymeric materials will display changes in their mechanical behavior depending on how quickly you try to deform the object. As discussed above, this is because polymers require a discrete amount of time to move around and slide past each other. Thus, if you deform a polymeric object slowly, it acts compliantly; but if you deform the same polymeric object quickly, it acts stiffly. This is even true for liquids made from polymeric materials. Have you ever made a mixture of cornstarch and water? Cornstarch (also sometimes called *corn flour*) is a naturally occurring polymer that makes up part of the kernel of corn. A little bit of cornstarch is commonly used in cooking to thicken sauces and soups. However, if you add a lot of cornstarch to water (achieved by slowly mixing two parts cornstarch into one part water), you will make a goopy substance. (Note, this is not edible, so don't eat it!) If you stir the mixture slowly, it behaves like a liquid. The cornstarch polymers have sufficient time to slide past each other and disentangle; the spoon moves through the mixture easily. If you stir the mixture quickly, it behaves more like a solid. The cornstarch polymers do not have enough time to slide past each other, and they get knotted up; the spoon gets stuck in the mixture.

7 This high concentration mixture of cornstarch and water is sometimes referred to as *oobleck* in the United States. Oobleck is a strange substance that appears in a children's story written by the beloved American author Theodore Seuss Geisel, under the pen name Dr. Seuss. Cornstarch and water mixed together in this way is also a strange substance. If you make enough of the cornstarch and water mixture to fill up an entire swimming pool, then people can take turns running across the surface of the mixture. The cornstarch polymers are tangled up with each other, and when someone deforms the top surface of the mixture with their foot, the polymer chains do not have time to slide past each other. They stay entangled together and act like a net to keep the person suspended on top of the mixture. What would happen if someone stopped running when they were halfway across the pool? You can try this experiment for yourself, or you can do an Internet search to find many entertaining videos that show you the answer.

CULTURE NOTE

Bartholemew and the Oobleck is a children's book written in 1949 by Dr. Seuss (Theodor Geisel). It tells the story of a boy named Bartholomew who rescues his kingdom from a sticky, green substance called Oobleck, which is raining from the sky.

A. Think about the section you just read. Answer these questions.

1. What are polymers?

   ....

   ....

2. Why does gum stretch out as you pull it apart slowly? Why does it break when you pull it apart quickly?

   ....

   ....

3. What causes a concentrated mixture of cornstarch and water to act compliantly? What causes it to act stiffly?

   ....

   ....

4. Why is a concentrated mixture of cornstarch and water called *oobleck*?

   ....

   ....

5. In Paragraph 7, the author asks what would happen if someone stopped running halfway across a pool filled with oobleck. What do you predict would happen? Why?

   ....

   ....

B. Read the section again. Check your answers. Then continue to the next section.

Why Do Polymers Behave Differently Depending on Their Conditions? *continued*

The Effect of Temperature on Polymer Mechanics

8 Now let us imagine our piece of chewing gum again. This time you have two cups in front of you: one with ice water and another with boiling water. You take the chewing gum out of your mouth, divide it in half, and put one-half of the gum into each cup. You wait one minute and then you try to stretch out both pieces of gum.

Glossary

Vibrate: to shake continuously with small fast movements

Knot: a tangled mass or lump in something

Propelled: moved or pushed forward

Combustion: the process of burning

Hierarchical: organized into levels according to importance

Elevated: higher than normal

You pull on each piece of gum with the exact same speed. Will the ice-cold chewing gum appear more compliant or stiffer than the boiling-hot chewing gum?

9   The ice-cold chewing gum will appear stiffer and is more likely to be brittle. In contrast, the boiling-hot chewing gum will appear more compliant and is more likely to be ductile. To understand how the temperature is affecting the mechanical properties of the chewing gum, we again need to consider the movement of the polymer molecules. As molecules heat up, they are able to move more quickly. Their chemical bonds can vibrate and rotate faster, resulting in more molecular motion. Materials scientists and engineers often refer to this as *thermal energy*. For polymeric materials, this means that their chain-like molecules can wiggle around more quickly when they are hotter. On the other hand, the chains wiggle more slowly when they are cooler.

10 When a piece of chewing gum is placed into ice-cold water, the polymer chains that make up the chewing gum begin to move more slowly. The colder chains require more time to move a specific distance. In contrast, when a piece of chewing gum is placed into boiling-hot water, the polymer chains begin to move more quickly. The hotter chains require less time to move a specific distance. Therefore, when you pull on a piece of chewing gum that is cold, the slow-moving chains do not have sufficient time to slide past one another and instead remain tangled up in a knot. This molecular knot prevents the chewing gum from being easily stretched, and the gum appears stiff and brittle. On the other hand, when you pull on a piece of chewing gum that is warm, the fast-moving chains can quickly slide past one another to become disentangled. This rapid sliding of chains makes it easy to stretch out the chewing gum, and the gum appears compliant and ductile.

11 All objects made from polymeric materials will display changes in their mechanical behavior depending on their temperature. For this reason, most objects made from polymeric materials will have a suggested temperature range over which they should be used. If the temperature is too hot, the polymer may become too ductile; however, if the temperature is too cold, then the polymer may become too brittle. This materials science fact was one of the main contributing factors to the space shuttle *Challenger* disaster. On January 28, 1986, the American space shuttle *Challenger* exploded a little over one minute into its flight, killing the entire crew of seven astronauts. This space shuttle had already completed nine other successful trips into orbit, so what caused the disaster on this particular flight?

CULTURE NOTE

The space shuttle was a manned spaceflight vehicle that was operated by the US National Aeronautics and Space Administration (NASA) from 1981 to 2011. The space shuttle was designed to orbit Earth and was fueled by liquid hydrogen and liquid oxygen tanks, with reusable solid rocket boosters. The space shuttle was used to launch satellites and probes, conduct experiments, and construct and maintain space stations. Five orbiters were built as part of the space shuttle program, two of which were destroyed in accidents.

(Continued)

12 Part of the answer lies in the temperature at the time of the launch, which was about −1°C (30°F). Previously, the lowest temperature on record for a space shuttle launch had been 12°C (54°F). The *Challenger* space shuttle was propelled by two solid rocket boosters. Each solid rocket booster used several flexible, polymeric O-rings as seals. Whether on a space shuttle or for your kitchen sink, to function properly, an O-ring must be made of a polymeric material that is compliant and ductile. However, because of the unusually low temperature on the day of the *Challenger* launch, the space shuttle O-rings had stiffened and become brittle. The O-rings were unable to seal the hot combustion gases, eventually leading to the structural breakup of the space shuttle. After the disaster, the space shuttle program was grounded for nearly three years while an investigation took place to determine the root causes of the accident. While the final report clearly cited the obvious failure of the O-ring due to low temperature, it is also worth noting that the report also cited several other engineering and managerial issues that directly contributed to the space shuttle failure. Other causes responsible for the accident include the original, faulty design of the O-ring sealing system and a hierarchical, managerial system that prevented efficient communication about safety concerns.

Putting It All Together: Comparing Time and Temperature Effects

13 In the previous sections of this essay, the mechanical behavior of the polymeric material depended on how quickly (or slowly) the chain-like molecules could move relative to how quickly (or slowly) the material was being stretched or deformed. When the molecular chains have sufficient time to wiggle and move around, they can easily slide past one another, and the polymer behaves as a compliant, ductile material. When the molecular chains have insufficient time to wiggle and move around, they remain entangled, and the polymer behaves as a stiff, brittle material. Thus, the effects of time and temperature on a polymeric material are similar, both in terms of their underlying physical causes and their resulting mechanical behavior.

14 This similarity between the effects of time and temperature can be very useful to materials scientists and engineers. This concept is known as *time-temperature superposition*. If you want to know how a polymeric object will behave over very long time periods, you can simply test it at a warmer temperature for shorter time periods.

This is very convenient when designing polymeric materials for objects that are meant to be in use for a great amount of time. For example, many orthopedic implants such as artificial hip joints or knee joints contain one or more polymeric materials. In addition, these artificial joints are often surgically placed into the patient with the use of a polymeric bone cement to help fix the implant into its proper position. Ideally these polymeric materials would be designed to display the appropriate mechanical behavior for the full lifetime of the patient, which is often several more decades. However, it would be impractical to subject each of these polymeric materials to mechanical tests that last over ten years when trying to design a new artificial joint. Instead, the materials scientists and engineers can test the mechanical behavior of the polymeric

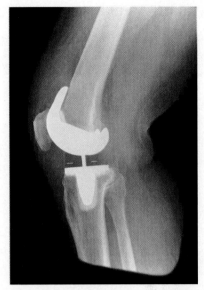

Figure 2: Artificial knee

materials for shorter amounts of time at elevated temperatures. Mathematical relationships then allow the engineers to accurately predict what the mechanical behavior would be over much longer periods of time. This allows engineers to quickly try out several different polymeric designs to identify those materials with the desired long-term mechanical properties.

15 The underlying molecular motion of polymeric chains dictates the mechanical properties of polymeric materials. Anything that causes the polymeric chains to be more entangled (for example, stretching them quickly with insufficient time to wiggle around or cooling them down to slow down the molecular motion) causes the material to behave in a stiffer and more brittle manner. Anything that allows the polymeric chains to be more disentangled (for example, stretching them slowly with adequate time to slide past each other or heating them up to speed up the molecular motion) causes the material to behave in a more compliant and ductile manner. Many interesting mechanical behaviors of polymeric objects can be explained with this simple concept.

CHECK WHAT YOU'VE LEARNED
PARAGRAPHS 8–15

A. Think about the section you just read. Answer these questions.

6. What creates thermal energy? How does it affect the behavior of polymers?

_____

_____

7. Why does cooling a piece of gum cause it to become more stiff and brittle? Why does warming gum cause it to become more ductile?

_____

_____

8. What is the concept of *time-temperature superposition*? How is this concept useful to materials scientists?

_____

_____

9. Why does the author mention the temperature at the time of the launch of the space shuttle *Challenger*?

_____

_____

10. In Paragraph 12, the author states that one of the causes revealed by an investigation of the space shuttle *Challenger* disaster was a "hierarchical, managerial system that prevented efficient communication about safety concerns." What does this statement imply about the role of those working on the *Challenger* in causing the disaster? How might this disaster have been prevented?

_____

_____

B. Read the section again. Check your answers.

C. Summarize in your own words the key points of the reading.

THINKING CRITICALLY

Think about the situation considering what you have read in "Why Do Polymers Behave Differently Depending on Their Conditions?" With a partner, apply what you know about polymers to discuss to the situation.

In the essay, the author explains how time and temperature affect the mechanical properties of polymeric materials, such as the O-rings used in the space shuttle *Challenger*. It also explains that materials scientists and engineers can test the mechanical behavior of polymeric materials to identify materials with the desired

mechanical properties, such as materials that are used in orthopedic implants. Many automobile parts are also made of polymeric materials. Imagine you are designing parts for an automobile. Consider two or three different parts, such as the seat covers, door seals, exterior panels, bumpers, and engine parts.

- What would be the desired mechanical properties of materials used to make each of these parts? For example, consider how ductile or brittle the material would need to be.
- What time and temperature conditions would the material need to be designed for?
- What problems could arise if the materials became very cold or very hot?
- How could scientists or engineers test the materials? What could tests reveal?

⊙ Go to MyEnglishLab to complete a critical thinking exercise.

THINKING VISUALLY

A. Work with a partner. Look back at Figure 1 on page 386. Describe the structure of the polymer chain in Figure 1 based on what you learned in the reading. Then consider the entangled polymer chains discussed in the reading. Describe what would happen if you were to heat these polymer chains. What if you were to cool them?

B. Review what you read about the properties of chewing gum. Then create two drawings of some chewing gum that has been chewed and then taken out of the mouth. In the first drawing, show the gum being stretched slowly. In the second drawing, show the chewing gum being pulled apart quickly. Explain how and why the gum behaves differently in each case. Describe what is happening in the molecular chains to cause this behavior.

THINKING ABOUT LANGUAGE
UNDERSTANDING MODIFIERS

Work with a partner. Underline the modifiers in these excerpts from the reading. For each modifier, write the type it is (adjective, adjective clause, adverb, adverb clause, prepositional phrase, or infinitive phrase) and discuss how it impacts the sentence it is in.

1. In the second case, the gum abruptly snaps into two pieces as you pull your hands apart quickly.

2. In both instances, the chewing gum is made of the exact same molecules, yet those molecules are behaving very differently depending on their conditions.

3. If you slowly pull on the chewing gum, the chains have sufficient time to slide past one another and become disentangled.

4. The tension on the individual chains causes them to snap and break apart in a brittle manner.

5. Their chemical bonds can vibrate and rotate faster, resulting in more molecular motion.

6. For this reason, most objects made from polymeric materials will have a suggested temperature range over which they should be used.

UNDERSTANDING THE USE OF PASSIVE VOICE IN RESEARCH WRITING

Underline the passive structure in each excerpt from the reading.

1. The links of these chains are held together by strong covalent bonds that can rotate around.

2. Polymers can be thought of as long, flexible molecules that are constantly in motion.

3. This high concentration mixture of cornstarch and water is sometimes referred to as *oobleck* in the United States.

4. When a piece of chewing gum is placed into ice-cold water, the polymer chains that make up the chewing gum begin to move more slowly.

5. The *Challenger* space shuttle was propelled by two solid rocket boosters.

6. … an O-ring must be made of a material that is compliant and ductile.

7. After the disaster, the space shuttle program was grounded for nearly three years …

8. Ideally, these polymeric materials would be designed to display the appropriate mechanical behavior for the full lifetime of the patient …

◗ Go to MyEnglishLab for more practice reading an extended text and using your reading skills.

RESEARCH PROJECT

The reading in this unit discusses how polymeric materials have different uses, such as in seals for rocket boosters and orthopedic implants. By doing additional research, you can learn about other uses of polymeric materials.

A. The following is a list of types of objects that commonly use materials made of polymers. Choose one type of object to research.

- packaging and containers
- clothing or fabric
- building materials, such as pipes
- electrical insulation
- toys
- cookware

B. Conduct your research. As you read about your subject, formulate a thesis. Gather information that supports your thesis. Use the following ideas to help guide you:

- Find specific examples of objects made from polymers.
- Learn about:
  - the type of polymeric material that is commonly used to make the object
  - the mechanical properties of the material
  - the conditions under which this material can be used (such as temperature, mechanical stress, repeated use)
  - the benefits of using this polymeric material over other materials
  - the downsides of using polymeric materials for this object
  - recent developments in polymeric materials for this object

C. Create a list of discussion questions about interesting points related to your topic. Choose a presentation style from the box, or use your own idea, and present your research to the class. Then pose the questions to the class and have a group discussion.

> a presentation with visuals
> a short lecture with visuals
> a short video documentary

⊙ Go to MyEnglishLab to complete a collaborative activity.

gases, greenhouse. *see* greenhouse gases

Geisel, Theodore. *see* Seuss, Dr.

general-to-specific organization, in descriptive imagery, 271

gene therapy, 308–310, 310f

geographical maps, 289, 289f. *see also* maps

geography
vs. geology, 85
in regional dialects, 9, 9f, 24

geology
vs. geography, 85
principles of, 359

Germanic languages, word roots in, 313–317, 315t, 316t

Germany, medieval architecture in, 263

ghazal poems, 103

glacial–interglacial cycles, 86–88, 356–357, 364

glaciers
on Mars vs. Earth, 87
melting of, 87, 232–234, 250–251

glides, 181

globalization, medieval spice trade in, 119–125

global warming. *see* climate change

global warming potential (GWP), 69, 81

glossaries, 67

gloss over, 353

gold, in dentistry, 144

Goldman Sachs, 338–351
Business Standards Committee of, 345
ethical decision making at, 342–344, 346

in Great Recession, 56, 338–351
penalties paid by, 56, 341
post-recession changes at, 345–347

gold nanoparticles, 320, 320f

Google, Inc., 39, 40

goopy, 385

GoQBot robot, 153–156, 155t

Gothic architecture, 262–264

governance. *see* corporate governance

gradations, 19

Grandes chroniques de France, 373

granulation tissue, 295, 296f

graph(s)
definition of, 288
example of, 288f
key features of, 301
types of, 288

graphic organizers. *see also* *specific types*
definition of, 77
notetaking with, 77–81
using, 365

Great Depression, 35

"The Great Dying," 237–239

Great Mosque of Djenné, 282–283

Great Recession
bailouts in, 56, 341, 343
definition of, 35, 339
effects of, 35
Goldman Sachs in, 56, 338–351
investment banks' role in, 54–57, 59
subprime mortgages in, 56, 341f, 348, 348t

Greece
debt crisis in, 207
uncertainty avoidance in, 207–209

Greek language, word roots in, 313–317, 313t–314t, 315t

greenhouse effect, 227, 354, 354f

greenhouse gases. *see also* carbon dioxide
in climate change, 68–70, 69f, 80–81, 227, 232, 353–355
definition of, 68
in ice cores, 360
from volcanoes, 227–228, 237

gross domestic product (GDP)
definition of, 57
US, growth rates in, 57–58, 58f

Gunarsson, Bjarni, 189, 193

gut, 98

GWP. *see* global warming potential

Hagia Sofia, 268

Hall, Edward, 220

headings
main ideas and supporting details in, 33, 37
in organizational structures, 62

heart stents, bioresorbable, 291–293, 291f

heat waves, and climate change, 243–244, 244f

hedging
in cause-and-effect relationships, 231
definition of, 184, 184⊙(LS)
understanding structures used for, 184, 184⊙(LS), 336

Herder, Johann von, 19, 21

heresy, 257

location of, 37
in outlining, 46–50
in paraphrasing, 211–213
in previewing, 33
signal words for, 37
Main Street, 340, 343
major supporting details
definition of, 46
in outlines, 46–47
Mali, medieval architecture in, 282–283
Malick, Terrence, 191
mallets, 152
management, in high- vs. low-context cultures, 220–221
manipulate, 327
manner, adverbs of, 271
manner of articulation, 180
Maori language, 13
maps
definition of, 289
of endangered languages, 30f
example of, 289f
key features of, 301
types of, 289
of US dialects, 9f
margin notes, annotation with, 16–17, 107
Marie of France, 371
market, for regenerative medicine, 308–311, 308f, 309f, 310f
marketing, in high- vs. low-context cultures, 220
Mars, climate change on, 85–89, 88t–89t
Mars Reconnaissance Orbiter, 86
The Martian (movie), 172
masculine cultures, 202–206, 211–212, 217
Masnavi (Rumi), 103

masonry, 262
mass extinctions, 237
meaning, relationship of sound and, 166–169
meat, in medieval period, 93, 98, 121, 373
media coverage, critical reading of, 240
medicine. *see* regenerative medicine
medieval architecture, 262–264
Gothic, 262–264
non-Western, 282–285
Romanesque, 262, 267–268
medieval art
Byzantine and Romanesque, 267–270
non-Western, 281–285
religion in, 267–268, 273, 283
symbolism in, 272–275
medieval feasts, 368–383
entremets at, 98, 371–375, 377–379
food at, 98–99, 373
images of, 92f, 98f, 368f, 372f, 373, 374f
literature describing, 370–371, 373
minstrels at, 98, 370–371
music at, 369–382
purposes of, 98, 369–370, 372, 378
medieval food
at feasts, 98–99, 373
social class and, 92–93
spice trade and, 119–125, 123f
medieval literature
autobiographies in, 257–258
feasts in, 370–371, 373
Persian poetry, 103–104, 106–107

religion in, 108–111, 257–258
symbolism in, 108–111
by women, 256–258
medieval period, 90–125, 254–285
definition of, 262
timeline of key events in, 123f
mediums, 267
mesh, 292, 307, 307t
Meshworm robot, 153–156, 155t
metals
in coronary stents, 292
in dentistry, 144–145
in robotics, 153–154
metaphors, 277⊙(LS)
methane
vs. carbon dioxide, 80–81
in climate change, 69f, 80–81
methodology sections, of research articles
passive voice in, 312, 312⊙(LS)
understanding, 127, 128t
writing summaries of, 142
microalgae collection systems, 138–141
microbes, 80
Middle Ages. *see* medieval period
Milankovitch, Milutin, 356–357
Milankovitch cycles, 87, 87f, 356–358, 357f
mindset
in cultural ethos, 197
definition of, 197
minor supporting details
definition of, 46
in outlines, 46–47

VA. *see* Virginia Algonquian
values, in ethical decision
making, 48–49, 48f, 342,
343f
vaulted ceilings, 262
veneers, 144
Venice, spice trade in,
121–122
Venn diagrams, 287
for comparison and
contrast, 79, 79f
definition of, 79
examples of, 79f, 288f
verbs
in collocations, 246t,
247–248
neutral, in statements of
fact, 164
phrasal, 148t, 185, 246t
reporting, in quotations,
177, 177t
as signals for correlation,
236t
subjective, in opinions,
171t
vibrate, 388
Villeneuve, Denis, 190, 193
viols, 371
Virginia Algonquian (VA)
language, 191
virtue-based reasoning, 53,
344
virtuous, 376
visuals, 286–324. *see also*
specific types
active voice in references to,
312⊙(LS)
explaining information in,
306–311
interpreting information in,
300–305, 386
key features of, 300–301
in previewing of texts, 7

summary of skills related to,
318
textual references to,
294–299, 294t
in tone, 266
types of, 287–290
vocabulary journals, 24, 24f
vocabulary learning strategies
choosing and writing words
in, 23–25
collocations in, 185–187,
246–248
connotations in, 277–280
dictionaries in, 184–187
guessing meanings from
context in, 216–218
multiword units in,
148–150
prefixes in, 51–53, 51t–52t
suffixes in, 51–53, 52t,
83–85, 83t
word roots in, 313–317,
313t–316t
for words with multiple
meanings, 113–119
vocabulary profilers, 23–24
vocal cues, 160, 161
vocal tract, 179–182, 179f,
328–330
voice (grammatical)
active, 246, 246⊙(LS), 312⊙(LS),
366–367
passive (*see* passive voice)
voice (human), emotion
conveyed through, 161
vulcanize, 144
volcanoes
in climate change,
227–228, 237
in sediment cores, 361
vowel sounds
definition of, 180
production of, 179–182,
179f, 180f, 328–336,
329f

Wall Street. *see also*
investment banks
definition of, 55, 57, 340
in Great Recession, 55–57,
340–341
weak inferences
definition of, 205
identifying, 205–210, 206t
weather
changes in, 63, 63f
vs. climate, 63–65, 65t, 72
definition of, 63, 72
extreme, and climate
change, 243–244, 243f,
244f
weather maps, 289
weather stations, 356
websites, in high- vs. low-
context cultures, 220
Weinreich, Max, 8–9
westerlies, 361, 361f, 364
white-collar crime, 46
Whorf, Benjamin Lee, 18–21
wiggle, 385
Wikipedia, 102, 370
windows, stained-glass,
262–263
winds, trade, 361, 361f
wobble, 86
Wolfram, Walt, 25, 28, 29
women, medieval literature
by, 256–258
wood, in medieval
architecture, 262
word(s)
connotations of, 277–280
with multiple meanings,
113–119, 114f–118f,
184–186, 184f, 185f
relationship between sound
and meaning of, 166–169

Credits

Page viii (top): Prasit Rodphan/Shutterstock; viii (bottom): Archimage/Alamy Stock Photo; x (top, left): Trevor Kittelty/Shutterstock; x (top, right): Luciano Mortula/Shutterstock; x (bottom): ART Collection/Alamy Stock Photo; xi: Pearson Education, Inc; Page 1: (multiple uses): Budai Romeo Gabor/Fotolia (gold coins); Nik_ Merkulov/Fotolia (green leaf with drops of water); Scisetti Alfio/Fotolia (old letter); Vichly4thai/Fotolia (red molecule/DNA cell); Tobkatrina/123RF (hands holding Earth); orelphoto/Fotolia (honeycomb background); Page 2: Carolyn Jenkins/Alamy Stock Photo; 5: Dinodia Photos/Alamy Stock Photo; 28: Monica Schipper/ FilmMagic/Getty Images; 32: Kentoh/Shutterstock; 34: Nestor Rizhniak/Shutterstock; 38: Dpa picture alliance/ Alamy Stock Photo; 55: Luckyphotographer/Shutterstock; 60: Visdia/123RF; 88: Stephen Girimont/Shutterstock; 90: Mikadun/Shutterstock; 92: Nejron Photo/Shutterstock; 98: NejroN/123RF; 103: Art Collection 3/Alamy Stock Photo; 109: North Wind Picture Archives/Alamy Stock Photo; 120: Belchonock/123RF; 126: StockAsso/ Shutterstock; 129: Auremar/123RF; 133: Wing Lun Leung/Alamy Stock Photo; 139: Ashley Cooper/Alamy Stock Photo; 156 (left): Flowgraph/Shutterstock; 156 (right): Josh McCann/Shutterstock; 158: Ibreakstock/Shutterstock; 190: Paramount Pictures/Everett Collection; 194: Rawpixel.com/Shutterstock; 197: Niyazz/Shutterstock; 202: Wavebreakmedia/Shutterstock; 214: Rolf_52/Shutterstock; 224: Volodymyr Goinyk/Shutterstock; 233: Don Bartletti/Los Angeles Times/Getty Images; 237: Freezingpic/123RF; 254: Prasit Rodphan/Shutterstock; 262: Archimage/Alamy Stock Photo; 263 (left): Bondz/Shutterstock; 263 (right): Lightworks Media/Alamy Stock Photo; 268 (top): Antony McAulay/123RF; 268 (bottom): Shutterstock; 274: Metropolitan Museum of Art / Gift of John D. Rockefeller Jr., 1937; 282 (top, left): Trevor Kittelty/Shutterstock; 282 (top, right): Luciano Mortula/Shutterstock; 282 (bottom, left): Mike Von Bergen/Shutterstock; 282 (bottom, right): Botond Horvath/Shutterstock; 286: Philippe Garo/Science Source; 289 (top): Peter Junaidy/123RF; 289 (bottom): Science History Images/Alamy Stock Photo; 291 (top): Alila Medical Media/Shutterstock; 296 (top): Tefi/Shutterstock; 296 (middle): Dimarion/ Shutterstock; 296 (bottom): Lisa S./Shutterstock; 302: Designua/123RF; 303 (top): Plepraisaeng/123RF; 303 (bottom): Sergii Iaremenko/123RF; 303 (middle): Alexmit/123RF; 320: Kateryna Kon/Shutterstock; 321 (top): Clusterx/Shutterstock; 321 (bottom): Victor Habbick Visions/Science Photo Library/Getty Images; 326: Tyler Olson/Shutterstock; 328 (left): Chris Stock/Lebrecht Music & Arts/Alamy Stock Photo; 328 (right): Bombaert Patrick/Shutterstock; 338: Andy Dean/Shutterstock; 340: Antonprado/123RF; 352: Songsak Paname/123RF; 359 (top): Jim Barber/Shutterstock; 359 (bottom): Ragnar Th Sigurdsson/Arctic Images/Alamy Stock Photo; 360 (top): Vlad61/Shutterstock; 360 (bottom, left): lapis2380/123RF; 360 (bottom, right): Kiraly Zoltan/123RF; 362: Designua/123RF; 368: ART Collection/Alamy Stock Photo; 371 (left): Niels Poulsen Mus/Alamy Stock Photo; 371 (center): Dario Lo Presti/123RF; 371 (right): Cenap Refik Ongan/Shutterstock; 372: Artokoloro Quint Lox Limited/Alamy Stock Photo; 374 (left): Lebrecht Music and Arts Photo Library/Alamy Stock Photo; 374 (right): MusicImages/Alamy Stock Photo; 377: Interfoto/Alamy Stock Photo; 384: Chris Tefme/Shutterstock; 386: Bacsica/Shutterstock; 390: Universal Images Group North America LLC/Alamy Stock Photo; 391: Skyhawk x/ Shutterstock; 393: Oleksiy Maksymenko/Alamy Stock Photo.